An African World
the Basongye Village
of Lupupa Ngye

An African World

the Basongye Village

of Lupupa Ngye

ALAN P. MERRIAM

Indiana University Press
Bloomington & London

Publication of this book was assisted by the
American Council of Learned Societies under
a grant from the Andrew W. Mellon Foundation

Published in Canada by Fitzhenry & Whiteside Limited,
Don Mills, Ontario
Manufactured in the United States of America

Library of Congress Cataloging in Publication Data

Merriam, Alan P   1923–
    An African world: the Basongye village of Lupupa
Ngye.

    Bibliography
    1. Bassonge.   2. Lupupa Ngye, Zaïre.   I. Title.
DT650.B367M47   916.75′12′06   74-377
ISBN 0-253-30280-3

To William R. Bascom . . . teacher
. . . advisor . . . colleague . . .
friend

Contents

Maps

Figures

List of Illustrations

Preface

The Basongye people occupy that portion of the present Eastern Kasai Region of the Republic of Zaïre which lies roughly between the fifth and sixth parallels south and about 24° to 27° east. Their territory is roughly bordered by the Lualaba River on the east and the Sankuru River on the west, and it is cut approximately in the middle by the Lomami River (Map 1). The Basongye have been in this general location possibly since the fifteenth century, when they were the founders of the first Baluba Empire. Dispersed by Arab intrusions, as well as by European exploration and settlement, they endured a thirty-year period, beginning about 1870, in which their society appears to have been almost totally disrupted. By approximately 1900, however, they had begun to regroup themselves into the several divisions which have remained essentially intact to the present.

Spelling of the tribal name varies considerably. Maes and Boone (1935:170) include the following in their survey of the peoples of what was then the Belgian Congo: "Basonge, Ba-Songwe, Bassonga, Bassonge, Bassongo, Bassonie, Wasonga," as well as "Baluba, Baluba ba Nkole, Bayembe." In a later work, Boone concludes that "Bayembe" is the true name of the Basongye; she writes: "Le vrai nom des Songye serait donc Bayembe; toutefois on ne le rencontre presque plus jamais, à l'encontre du nom de Basonge, introduit par les Européens et qui est connu et employé partout à l'heure actuelle" (1961:219). The evidence for this conclusion is not clear, although various statements are cited such as that of Verhulpen (1936:65): "Les Basonge étaient appelés Bayembe par les Baluba. Ils furent appelés Basonge par les Européens." This, of course, tells us nothing of what the people call themselves, and the Basongye known to me vigorously deny any knowledge of the term "Bayembe," although they do say that the Baluba term for them is "Basonge," while the Batetela term is

Map 1

Location of the Basongye

"Alembe." Boone has noted that "L'orthographe Songye est celle qui correspond le mieux à la prononciation locale" (1961:219), and indeed it is, save that the Basongye never refer to themselves as "Songye," using instead the full term. The word employed throughout this work as corresponding most precisely to local usage is "Basongye," though "Basonge" is most frequently found in the older literature, and "Songye" in recent writing.

The population of the Basongye has been the subject of a wide variety of estimates through the years (see, for example, Overbergh 1908:79–84), and accurate numbers are still impossible to obtain, though most writers suggest a contemporary figure of about 150,000. The most precise estimates available for the time period of this research are those presented by Boone (1961), but interpretation of her statistics is somewhat difficult. Under the formal heading, "Songye," she writes: "Le nombre total de Songye non compris les sous-tribus peut être estimé de 100.000 à 110.000 individus" (p. 217). Presumably "les sous-tribus" noted are those "Songye" whom she treats separately from the "Songye" proper; her figures for these groups indicate an additional 106,000 persons, for a total Basongye population, then, of approximately 206,000– 217,000. If the precision of these figures remains somewhat in doubt, it is simply because there is no way it can be checked.

Map 2

(After Boone 1961)

Neighbors of the Basongye

A glance at Map 2 will show the reader that the Basongye share a common border with a number of different neighbors; of these, by far the most important are the Baluba. Indeed, the Basongye are most often regarded as having a common origin and affinity with the Baluba, and thus early writers such as Schmitz, for example, spoke of the Basongye as "affinités avec les Baluba," Le Marinel wrote that "à mon avis, les Basonge sont des Baluba venus de l'Est," and Gilain added, "Je crois que les Basonge sont, en définitive, une grande peuplade de race Baluba" (Overbergh 1908:92–93). These early interpretations are apparently borne out by what is known of Basongye history, as well as evidence adduced from linguistic, anthropometric, and sociocultural data.

Samain, for example, apparently based his understanding of the origin and affiliation of the Basongye upon linguistic evidence. He wrote:

> They are a branch of the great Baluba people; they come from the environs of Lake Samba. Their language lies between Kiluba-Hemba and the Tshiluba of the Kasai. One finds many Kisonge words which are identical to those in one or the other of these dialects. Reflexive and reciprocal forms are the same as in Kiluba-Hemba. (1923:6) [Author's translation]

Other writers have also stressed Kisongye's relationship to Chiluba, and the two are most often placed in the same language grouping (see, for example, Bulck 1948; Guthrie 1948; Stappers 1953a, 1953c).

Basongye physical type has never been studied adequately, though some anthropometric measurements have been taken. Comments of the early explorers stressed physical characteristics which seemed admirable to Europeans of the time. Gilain, for example, commented as follows:

> The Basonge and the Batetela are of an incontestably superior physique.
> Taller than usual, the Basonge are strongly muscled and highly resistant to fatigue. Malingerers are rare.
> The women are taller than the average European woman; they are well proportioned; they have a proud bearing; when young, they are graceful. (Overbergh 1908:103) [Author's translation]

In 1894, Victor Jacques took anthropomorphic measurements of 108 Congolese who had been brought to the Universal Exposition in Anvers, and in his sample he included six male and two female "Sappo-Sap," representatives of a Basongye group which had split off from the main unit in 1887 (V. Jacques 1894–95). At the Universal Exposition of Brussels–Tervuren in 1896, Jacques continued his work, this time with a total sample of 335 persons, among whom were ten "Malela," who may have been Basongye, and eight more Sappo-Sap (V. Jacques 1897). The samples, of course, were extremely small and the results inconclusive, but it is of some interest to note that Jacques was emphatic in pointing out that the Sappo-Sap could in no way be confused physically with the Baluba he had also measured or with those Baluba previously measured by Wolff. He wrote:

> The Sappo are darker of skin, their forehead is straighter, their nose is straight or depressed and is far from showing the flattening that one observes in general among the Negroes; finally, the lips are rather thin—even very thin and not at all everted among some of them. We judge that the Sappo are removed from both the Baluba and the Baluba of Wolff. (1894–95:313) [Author's translation]

A number of years later, Friedrich Hautmann carried out what seem to have been some early genetic studies among the Basongye, as well as among other groups, but the published results are meager. For the Basongye, he reported that the incidence of albinism is 1:4,000, that six-fingeredness is present, and that a twin birth occurred in each 40 deliveries (Hautmann 1949–50:5).

The most extensive study of Basongye physical anthropology was carried out by Hiernaux, who took anthropometric measurements of 41 individuals living in Elisabethville (now Lubumbashi), and compared them with measurements taken from samples of Luba Katanga and Luba Kasai. His conclusion was that the three groups do not differ significantly in physical characteristics, and that this "reflète une similitude des patrimoines génétique des trois populations: celles-ci, à en juger d'après la proximité de leurs langues, ont une origine commune pas très lointaine . . ." (1964:338–39).

Thus the historical, linguistic, and anthropometric evidence at our disposal all seems to point to a close relationship between the

Basongye and the Baluba, and the sociocultural evidence indicates the same conclusion. While no point by point comparisons have been made, many authors have called attention to the similarities, and some, like Verhulpen (1936), regard the two groups as identical on sociocultural as well as other kinds of evidence.

A considerable number of works has been published concerning various aspects of Basongye society and culture, but this literature is heavily skewed in favor of discussions of visual art, primarily of woodcarving. Basongye masks and figurines are considered by experts to represent a distinct African art style, or sometimes a substyle (see Olbrechts 1959), and descriptions of many pieces and groups of pieces have been made. While two general ethnographic monographs exist, both are fragmentary and now of considerable age. The first of these, *Les Basonge* (Overbergh 1908), is a compilation of factual material and personal opinion derived from a thorough combing of the published literature to that time, and from direct correspondence between Overbergh and a number of individuals who had had personal experience with the Basongye. Included among the latter were military men like Baron Dhanis, and civilians like Robert Schmitz, among many others. The information was arranged under 202 specific headings which corresponded to those in the ethnographic questionnaire adopted, probably in 1905, by the *Société belge de sociologie*. Given this essentially mechanical format, as well as the fact that most of the contributors wrote as no more than interested observers, the result is a potpourri of scattered, though interesting, bits of information.

The second general ethnographic monograph is "Les Basonge," a 28-page chapter in *Notes ethnographiques sur des populations habitant les bassins du Kasai et du Kwango Oriental,* by E. Torday and T. A. Joyce (1922). Though brief, it presents a more cohesive picture of a way of life than does the Overbergh work, and it is illustrated. The material was apparently gathered among the Batempa, a Basongye subgroup located in the far northwestern corner of Basongye territory. Torday arrived in the village of Batempa probably no earlier than mid-December of 1907, and left on December 27 of the same year. He describes the information obtained during this short stay as applicable to the western Basongye, and not to the eastern, but he includes no maps nor does he describe specific areas (Torday 1910). His data match reasonably with those which I collected among a different Basongye subgroup, but dissimilarities in detail, and sometimes in major interpretation, occur frequently. While many other articles, and a few books, have been published, some of them of high caliber, the Overbergh and the Torday and Joyce publications remain the only two general ethnographic works.

Division of the Basongye into subgroups is a difficult matter, both because relatively little is known of the specific groups and because the history of the past 100 years indicates considerable change in their constitution and distribution. Long lists of subgroups can be found (see, for example, Verhulpen 1936; Moeller 1936), but we are uncertain of what such lists tell us. In her standard reference work, Boone (1961) refers to what might be considered "typical" or "classic" Basongye; it is this group to which she assigns a population of 100,000–110,000. She also includes entirely separate, though cross-referenced, entries to various subgroups, and these are listed below with the name assigned by Boone, the name much more frequently encountered in the literature in parentheses, and the estimated population figures as of 1959.

Ekiye (Beneki)	33,452
Ikalebwe (Bekalebwe)	43,986
Ilande (Belande)	27,000 (est.)
Milembwe (Bamilembwe)	5,763
Nsapo (Sappo-Sap)	No information

These do seem to be the major Basongye subgroups, on the criteria both of population size and, with the exception of the Belande and Bamilembwe, of historic importance. Boone's most recent ethnographic distributional map, however (1961:214), shows a substantial number of additional groups for which even less information is available. It is also instructive to compare Boone's map with Overbergh's (1908), for it is readily apparent that: 1) different subgroups are given different emphases; 2) either Overbergh's information was too imprecise to locate the various subgroups accurately, or demographic shifts have since occurred. Both suggestions are probably correct.

Two further points are of importance in connection with Boone's map. First, some subgroups are omitted, and this is true of the people with whom the present study is concerned; these are the Bala, who are located on Overbergh's map in roughly the northeast corner of the sector marked by 24°–25° east, and 5°–6° south. Second, the Boone map indicates that the people found in that specific area are Bekalebwe. From the standpoint of the people involved, however, the Bekalebwe distribution extends too far to the north.

It is the Bala, then, with whom we are concerned; they are found in the area from approximately 24° 35'–25° 15' E, and 5° 5'–5° 30' S, which places them somewhat farther north and east than the location assigned them by Overbergh. Map 3 shows their geographic relationship to the neighboring Basongye subgroups. The official population figure carried on the books of the Territoire de Sentery as of 1958 was 7,149 Bala, making it the largest group of those shown on the map, with the exception, of course, of the Bekalebwe. The origin of the Bala can be reconstructed only with difficulty, but their own origin legends confirm what has apparently been a general east-to-west Basongye movement over the period of their known history.

The Bala are in turn broken into subgroups, the precise number of which is a matter for dispute; officially, however, the Secteur de Tshofa in 1958 listed nine subdivisions. One of these subgroups is made up of the Bena Bapupa, or "Bapupa people," all of whom consider themselves to be closely related to each other; their three major villages are Makola, Lupupa Kampata, and Lupupa Ngye. It is the last of these three villages in which the field work on which this book is based was carried out.

Research in what was then the Belgian Congo and is now the Republic of Zaïre began early in July, 1959, and ended early in July, 1960, a few days after the Congo had celebrated its independence. Residence in Lupupa Ngye extended from mid-August, 1959, to late June, 1960. The focus of the research was ethnographic and ethnomusicological; the limited ethnographic research carried out to that time made the former important, and no work had ever been done with Basongye music. Information gleaned from a variety of sources in the United States had indicated that the Basongye were supporting an ongoing traditional life, and

Map 3

Neighbors of the Bala

that the various arts were flourishing. This turned out to be true, though the Basongye were in fact less active in the areas we call the arts than had been anticipated.

The specific problems under study were several in number. It was my contention then, and is now, that in order to be fully understood, music must be viewed not solely as sound, but equally, and in fact more importantly, as human behavior (see Merriam 1964). It is further my contention that music can only be understood when society and culture are understood, and thus that understanding can only be achieved along with general ethnographic competence. Finally, I carried to the field a general interest in all the arts and a special interest in attempting to comprehend interrelationships, if any, among them. A number of results of the research have been published, including specific materials concerning the Basongye, and general materials of broader application to ethnomusicology published in *The Anthropology of Music* (1964).

It was my original intention to spend fifteen months in the field, although the research grants covered only a twelve-month period. The first ten months were to be spent in a single village

concentrating upon general ethnography, but with constant attention given to music. The three following months were to be devoted
to intensive study of the music alone, based upon the ethnographic
information gathered by that time. Although I intended to make
recordings throughout the stay, the most intensive recording would
take place during this period. The last two months were scheduled
for spot-checking the data from the village against the situation in
neighboring villages in order to obtain an idea of the degree to
which my information could be generalized for wider-than-village
circles. My general emphasis was less upon music sound than upon
music viewed as an integral part of society and culture.

As is so often the case in anthropological research, outside
considerations forced modification of these plans. The original
grant had been for work in the Mayombe area at the mouth of the
Congo River, but early in 1959, political difficulties began to
emerge there, and since my wife and two small daughters were to
accompany me, it seemed expedient to change the research to the
Basongye. I have never regretted that decision. As time went on,
however, the political pressures began pointing clearly toward
independence, and Belgian administration and control began to
crumble; it was apparent that my family should leave early and
that I should not remain in a remote area of the country at the time
of independence. This, of course, cut the field time from fifteen to
less than twelve months' duration. It also produced a difficult year
both for the villagers and for ourselves; while Lupupa Ngye was not
immediately involved, word came into the village, long discussions
were held, and tension and unease arose, resulting in some sharp
changes in the traditional way of life (see Merriam 1961a: 173–94).
While all notes and tapes were sent or carried out of the country
successfully, some shipments were lost in the tragedy of the armed
conflicts which followed after independence, and this included some
music instruments which, for study purposes, were irreplaceable.

Since my aims were both general—to know Basongye society
and culture—and specific—to understand music as a part of that
society and culture—considerable quantities of data were gathered.
It is my hope to present this data in three separate volumes, of
which this is the first. Subsequent volumes will be devoted to music,
and to the other arts.

The purpose of this book, then, is to discuss the ethnography of a single Bala (Basongye) village, Lupupa Ngye, giving some special attention to music and to the other "arts," but holding as a general purpose the exposition of the system in which music works as a contributing part. I am thus not interested in making comparisons between the society and culture of Lupupa Ngye and of other Basongye villages as represented in the published literature; only occasional reference is made to that literature in the following pages. Further, since almost no literature exists concerning the Bala, and none whatsoever concerning the Bapupa, no close comparisons are possible in any case. What follows is an essentially descriptive sketch of the way of life of the people of Lupupa Ngye; no single aspect receives detailed or in-depth analytic attention, and thus the impact of the work is deliberately broad. It is a general ethnography that is sought here, and the "ethnographic present" in which it is cast refers to 1959–60. Since I am a man, my data undeniably reflects the male viewpoint; to whatever extent possible, this bias has been corrected by my own efforts, but primarily by the active collaboration of my wife. It will be noted that a number of species of flora and fauna remain unidentified; while various agricultural officers assisted us where they could, their knowledge was incomplete, and specimens simply could not be collected and shipped out of the region.

No research is ever the work of a single person, and it is my deep pleasure, as always, to give thanks for the assistance offered by my many direct and indirect collaborators. Yet in this case, I hardly know where to begin, for I should like to include the names of 240 Lupupans, and I have drawn up a minimal list of over 100 others who assisted in one way or another. It is simplest, in the face of that, to begin by saying that the research was underwritten by grants from the National Science Foundation and the Belgian American Educational Foundation; in addition, my wife, Barbara W. Merriam, received a grant from the Program of African Studies of Northwestern University to do photographic and ethnographic work. We received the support and cooperation in the Congo of what was then l'Université Lovanium (now l'Université Nationale du Zaïre, Campus de Kinshasa), and from l'Institut pour la Recherche Scientifique en Afrique Centrale, whose director, Louis van den Berghe, has been a valued friend and staunch supporter for more than twenty years. A sabbatical leave from Indiana Univer-

sity during the first semester of the 1969–70 academic year, coupled
with a John Simon Guggenheim Memorial Foundation Fellowship,
afforded me free time to index my notes for the third time, to
prepare a four-way, 1,500-word "dictionary" of Kisongye, to carry
out extensive library research, and to write the first four chapters of
this book.

Friends in Brussels, particularly those at the Musée Royal de
l'Afrique Centrale, were most generous of their time, assistance,
advice, and collections, and other friends, both European and
Congolese, were equally unstinting in Léopoldville (now Kinshasa).
All along the way, people helped, and I cannot fail to name M.
Marcel Dupont and his wife, Simone, whose kindnesses in Kabinda, a small town in Basongye territory which functioned as our
supply base, were unfailing; various Belgian administrators, among
them the wise and generous Fernand Pierre; Dr. Robert Vanden-
plas and his wife, who provided medical assistance and personal
hospitality on our many visits to Tshofa; M. Lallemand, who
struggled valiantly with Kisongye floral and faunal terms; M. van
der Beeken, in Kabinda, and M. Maviel in Léopoldville, who
struggled equally valiantly and with extraordinary good cheer to
keep my truck running—by no means an easy task; and literally
scores of others whose names I am truly sad to have to omit. Could I
fail to remember with thanks a visit with Henri Morlighem outside
Luluabourg, or the loans of tools from Father Mercenier and his
cohorts at the Mission Catholique de Tshofa, the hospitality of our
old friends, Victor and Yvette Robinson, and the help and
friendship of many persons at IRSAC bases in Lwiro, Astrida, and
Elisabethville? It is impossible to mention them all, utterly impossible, and I trust those omitted who may see this book will
understand that.

And then, of course, there is my own family. My wife,
Barbara, did her utmost in ethnographic research while running a
mud-and-thatch household and while carrying on with her splendid
photography; examples of her latter work have formed the basis of
a traveling exhibit, "Faces of the Congo," which showed at a
number of universities in 1960–61, and have been published in
numerous places, including this book. Virginia and Paige, our two
oldest daughters, were only 5 and almost 3 when we arrived in
Lupupa Ngye, and they will never be quite certain of what they

remember, but I can vouch for the fact that they were there and that their presence was cheering and reassuring. When they and Barbara left, almost two months before I was to leave, our house was instantly and immeasurably darkened. Our youngest daughter, Cynthia, missed the whole thing, because she was not yet on the scene—and she regrets it bitterly.

It is the people of Lupupa Ngye, of course, who deserve the thanks of all of us. They were patient in the face of our persistent questioning, firm in defense of the secrets they did not wish to divulge, and cordial in their efforts to make us feel welcome. Indeed, most of them became staunch friends, and again while I cannot name them all, I cannot omit special notice of Mankonde, an extraordinary man of great charm, wisdom, and learning; kind and patient Mayila; thoughtful Efile; and Kasambwe, who was here, there, and everywhere trying to lead his village in difficult hours. Kingkumba, the town crier, and Kingkumba, the farmer, were fascinating friends, and Yakyuka was a graceful dancer and of much assistance in many ways. My wife joins me in insisting upon special note of Kipa, her good friend, whose patience and wisdom marked her as a remarkable woman, indeed. All these, and many others, helped us in many ways, but one man in particular was the technical key to everything. Mulenda Kiabu (then Mulenda Arthur) was our interpreter, language teacher, general factotum, guide, and sensitive young friend. At the age of 21 he had had four years of primary schooling, and could communicate to varying degrees in six languages. Caught between our sometimes awkward and impatient interpretation of a new and strange society and culture on the one hand, and the sometimes visible resentment and impatience with us on the part of the villagers, he managed to soothe all, to lead us along the road to understanding each other, and to escape the wrath of both sides relatively unscathed, an agile feat, indeed. We hope we gave him, in return, a sense of his own worth, of his skill, his dignity, and his substantial capabilities as a human being. We know he learned much about his own society and culture, and that is something we both regarded as precious. This book is as much his as it is that of the people of his village, Lupupa Ngye, and as it is mine. We were all collaborators, in the best sense of the word.   A.P.M.

An African World

the Basongye Village

of Lupupa Ngye

Ebanda and child

1. Origin and History

The origin of the Basongye, as is so often the case with African peoples, has been the subject of a considerable number of speculations, no one of them apparently much more subject to empiric proof than any of the others. Verhulpen reports that theorists have suggested the Basongye are related to the Zulu, the Bechuana, the ancient Yaga, the Fang, and the Wanyamwezi (1936:44–45). Their origin has been said to be Lake Chad, Lake Samba (Samain 1923:6), and the Lunda kingdom (Barthel 1893:63–65). Frobenius in one publication explains the Basongye as migrants to their present area from the east (1893:328), in another as an offshoot of the Baluba coming from the south (1906:737), and in still another as part of a major cluster of peoples called the Ba Tshonga (1894). The south-to-north movement is espoused by M. E. De Jonghe

(1935:112), and an eastern origin in Southern Rhodesia by Bulck (1948:400–01) and Moeller (1936:8), among others. Vansina finds the earliest evidence of the Basongye-Baluba in thirteenth century sites at the southern tip of the Lakes Kisale-Upemba area of the Katanga near Bukama (n. d.:161), while Kerken stoutly denies any Basongye-Baluba relationship and locates the Basongye origin to the north and east near Kabambare in the Maniema (1919:29).

One of the most detailed studies of the problem has been made by Verhulpen (1936), who bases his work upon the myths and legends of the various people he regards as "Baluba et Balubaisés." This group includes the Basongye as well as the Bena Lulua, Bena Nkoshi, Kanioka, Kalundwe, Hemba, Sanga, and others who belong, in his view, to a single linguistic group. Verhulpen postulates a number of very early pre-human and human inhabitants of the Katanga area, the latter including Bushmen, Pygmies, and Hottentots; these peoples were succeeded by unspecified Negro groups who came in a series of migration waves from the north, northeast, and northwest. Later, but at an unknown time, the Basongye arrived in a general Bantu migration from the north, establishing themselves in the Maniema area, somewhere near the present location of Kabambare (Map 4). Thence, they spread out slowly to occupy the Lomami area, the northeastern Kasai, and the southern Maniema, before beginning a major southward migration.

Sometime "au cours du XVe siècle et peut-être même au cours du XIVe siècle," one Kongolo who, Verhulpen insists, was a Musongye, came out of the north, crossed the Lualaba near the present site of Kongolo, and installed himself in Mutombo-Mukulu on the middle Lubilashi. Under unknown circumstances, he became king of the various populations already established there, and his successors, apparently also named Kongolo, kept the kingdom intact and perhaps expanded it slightly. At a somewhat later date, another kingdom was founded by Bombwe Mbili somewhere to the east of Lake Kisale, and his brother, Mbili Kiluhe, led a gradual movement of these people into the lightly occupied areas of the Lualaba-Lovoi-Lomami-Lubishi-Lubilashi-Bushimae rivers region of the southern Lomami. Through a complex series of comparisons with other areas of the Congo, as well as a study of events in the histories of the Lunda, Babemba of Kazembe, and Cheti Mukulu of old Northern Rhodesia, Verhul-

Map 4

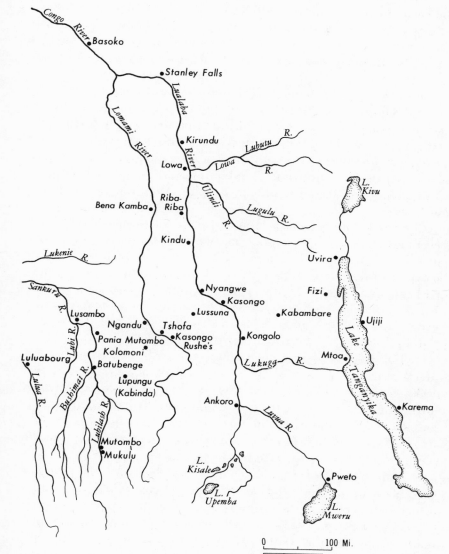

The Eastern Congo, 1870–1900

pen establishes the births of Bombwe Mbili and Mbili Kiluhe at about 1525.

In his travels, Mbili Kiluhe left hunters and friends behind him, and they founded families and groups in the area; eventually he reached Mutombo-Mukulu where he met the current Musongye king, Kongolo Mwana, who offered him his two sisters in marriage. From these unions were born Kalala Ilunga (also known as Ilunga Mbili), the son of Bulanda, and Kisulu Mabele, the son of Mabela. Mbili Kiluhe then returned to his home, possibly after a dispute with Kongolo Mwana, leaving the area between the two kingdoms colonized but unorganized; it is apparently at this time that Kongolo Mwana moved into the void, conquered the region between the Luembe and Lualaba rivers, and founded what Verhulpen calls the First Baluba Empire (Verhulpen 1936:88–96, and passim).

Kalala Ilunga, born about 1555, was named Kongolo's eventual successor, but his personal popularity among the people offended Kongolo, who threatened to kill him. Kalala Ilunga escaped to the land of his father in the east, returned eventually with an army, killed Kongolo Mwana and his own half-brother, Kisulu Mabele, and became king, reigning for perhaps twenty years, from 1585 to 1605. This was the beginning of the Second Baluba Empire (Verhulpen 1936:97–105, and passim).

This basic account of the Baluba empires has been discussed in many versions by a substantial number of authors (Verhulpen 1936; Vansina 1966; Studstill 1969, among many others), but its importance here lies in the suggestion that the first empire was founded by the Basongye, in the close relationship these historic traditions suggest between the Basongye and the Baluba, and in the parallels which exist between it and the Bala origin myth.

Vansina suggests that expansion of the Second Empire did not take place until after 1700; at this time Mwine Kadilo, who had directly succeeded Kalala Ilunga (note the discrepancy between this chronology and Verhulpen's), turned to the north and "fought many Songye groups, especially the Been' Ekiiye and the Beeka-lebwe, and defeated all of them with the exception of the Beekalebwe; but he did not incorporate any of them into his kingdom" (Vansina 1966:156). Vansina later adds that for this period (1700–1870), "little is known about the history of the . . .

6

Songye chiefdoms to the north . . . They resisted Luba encroach-
ment and seem rather to have themselves encroached on the Luba"
(ibid., p. 159). The Second Empire, however, did expand, and
Verhulpen states that the fourteenth direct descendant of Kalala
Ilunga, named Kasongo Kalombo, was the leader who fought with,
conquered, and incorporated into his kingdom "les *Bena Bala* ou
Bakoshi" during his reign from 1865 to 1885 (Verhulpen 1936:102,
137). Since this seems at first glance to be a rather late date for such
an event, it must be noted that the Basongye themselves were not
pulled together in the northern Lomami area until about 1884,
when ". . . Lumpungu, chef des Beekalebwe de Kabinda . . . mit
tous les autres groupes songye sous sa domination, non sans grandes
destructions d'ailleurs" (Vansina n. d.:162).

It is difficult to know how much of this historic accounting can
be accepted. It does at least seem probable, however, that the
Basongye arrived in the southward Bantu migration, that they
settled first in the Maniema (possibly in the Kabambare area), that
they moved both west and south in various migrations, that they
fought with the Baluba, and that late Baluba incursions caused
population movements until quite recent times, although these
latter movements are so little known that no very reasonable
conclusions can be drawn about them at present.

The first-known Basongye contacts with the nonblack African
world took place in approximately 1870, and these contacts
signaled the beginning of a series of momentous events which
developed one after the other over the next thirty years.[1] The result
was a shattering of Basongye society and culture: some populations
were wiped out and others dispersed; lineage groups, and even
families, sought refuge in the bush where they lived as isolated
social segments; whatever the prior nature of social and cultural
life, it was surely deeply disrupted and changed.

The initial agents of these stunning events were Arab traders
who penetrated Basongye country from the east and south, but they
were followed almost immediately by European explorers who
came from the same direction and, slightly later, from the west and
north as well. Each group brought its own seeds of destruction with

[1] These events and their consequences are discussed at considerably greater length
in Merriam (1974b), from which the present chapter is condensed.

7

it, but more importantly, the two penetrations inevitably came into conflict with each other.

Arab establishment on the East Coast of Africa, and particularly in Zanzibar, reaches far back in time, but it was not until Sayyid Sa'id bin Sultan transferred his capital from Musqat to Zanzibar about 1832, that the Arab era of commerce and exploration in central Africa began. Through gradual westward movement, caravan routes were established into the interior in response to the growing world markets for slaves and ivory (Alpers 1967, 1968). By 1830, a strong Arab outpost had been established at Tabora, Tanganyika, and in 1858, Burton and Speke, the first European explorers to reach Lake Tanganyika, found an Arab post at Ujiji on the eastern shore. From here, two principal Arab trade routes were established, of which the most important for the Basongye began with a lake voyage to Mtoa on the western shore of Lake Tanganyika and continued west and north through Fizi, Kabambare, Kasongo, and Nyangwe.

The earliest suggested date for the establishment of Nyangwe is 1856 (Wauters 1886b), but the first Arab trader to settle there was Dugumbi who has been variously cited as having arrived in 1860, 1863, 1868, and 1869. Whatever the date, Nyangwe almost immediately became a central point in Arab operations, functioning as the terminus of the long trade route from Zanzibar, and furnishing a permanent supply base for further Arab caravans which fanned out to the west, searching, as always, for slaves and ivory. Indeed, Hinde remarked some years later that "it used to be a common saying, in this part of Africa, that all roads lead to Nyangwe" (1895:442).

While Dugumbi was the first to establish himself in the area, the Arab whose influence most stringently affected the Basongye was the most famous trader of them all, Hamid bin Muhammed bin Jum's al-Murjibi, known more familiarly as Tippu Tip (see Brode 1907; Whitely 1966). Born in Zanzibar, probably in the 1830's, Tippu Tip was the grandson of an immigrant from Musqat and the son of a pioneer of the caravan routes who was often based at Tabora. Before he was eighteen, he had traveled into the eastern Congo in charge of one of his father's caravans, and sometime in 1869 or 1870, he set off toward the west with his own major caravan of four thousand persons. In this initial thrust, he speaks clearly of contact with the Basongye (Whitely 1966:61, 69, 71, 72–73, passim), and for the next three or four years, he traveled through the Lomami area, taking slaves and ivory and establishing personal control.

In the meantime, European exploration had begun in the eastern Congo, and Nyangwe was visited by David Livingstone in 1871 (Livingstone 1874:II, 116), by Verney Lovett Cameron in 1874 (Cameron 1877:263 ff.), and by Henry Morton Stanley in 1876 (Stanley 1899), the last arriving in the company of Tippu Tip himself. None of these early explorers traveled directly through Basongye territory, though Cameron skirted it to the east, and it was not until 1881 that the Pogge-Wissmann expedition, organized by the Deutsche Afrikanische Gesellschaft, left Loanda in Angola, moved north to the Kasai, traveled up the Sankuru River, cut straight across Basongye country along the Lukassi River, reached the Lomami, turned north and arrived in Nyangwe on April 15, 1882 (Wissmann 1883, 1902). Thus Basongye territory was shown to be accessible either from the east or the west, and it was not long before Stanley had traveled up the Congo River and established a station at Stanley Falls, which immediately became the base for European travel to Nyangwe from the north.

The European explorers soon drew the interest of major European states and their political leaders, and the Arab domains controlled by Tippu Tip in the eastern Congo began to be squeezed from all directions. The major forces were King Léopold II of Belgium and his personal Congo Free State, established in 1885; and Prince Bismarck of Germany and his German East Africa established in 1886. Both states—the Belgians from the west and the Germans from the east—put pressure on the Arabs whose control began to disintegrate.

The eventual result was the series of battles known as the Arab Slave Wars, fought out mostly in Basongye territory between the Arabs and the Belgians in 1892–94. Earlier events which helped to create the conflict included an Arab attack on the Stanley Falls station (Ward 1890:196–214); Belgian establishment of various stations deeper and deeper into the eastern Congo; the activities of Cardinal Lavigerie and his Société Antiesclavagiste de Belgique (Lavigerie 1888); the imposition of Congo Free State taxes on all ivory exported across Lake Tanganyika (A. Jacques 1907a&b); the

Vankerckhoven expedition which fought its way through the Uele area to the Nile, breaking up Arab strongholds and confiscating quantities of ivory (Deuxième Section 1952:125–40; Ceulemans 1959:326–31); and the annihilation of the Hodister expedition by Arab forces in 1892 (R. Cornet 1952:138–48).

Ceulemans (1966:192) has summarized the basic causes of the conflict under five general points: (1) The Congo Free State claimed sovereignty over the Arab-controlled areas because of the treaties it had made with other European powers; (2) While Tippu Tip had agreed to cede his territories to the Free State, and had implemented the cession, he could not speak for other Arabs in the area; (3) Since the Free State was unable at first to control these territories, it left them temporarily to the Arabs, and when it did begin to assert itself, the Arabs felt compelled to defend those areas they had settled; (4) Western imperialism was perceived by the Arabs as a direct threat; (5) The Arab methods of control and the nature of their commerce in slaves placed them in direct conflict with Western ideals. It may be added that the Free State was constantly moving toward control over the ivory trade, which further reduced Arab power and potential holdings in the eastern Congo (see also Ceulemans 1959).

Thus the two outside powers came into direct conflict in a two-year war which added further destruction to that already caused by Arab slaving in the Lomami area, and in which Basongye military forces and auxiliaries played a major part. When it ended, the struggle for power had been resolved in favor of the Belgians, who thenceforth moved as rapidly as possible to assert their control over the remaining African populations (for resumés of the Arab-Belgian campaign, see, among others, Ceulemans 1959; R. Cornet 1952; Comeliau 1943:61–143; Deuxième Section 1952:195–295; Hinde 1897; Wauters 1894).

The end of the war in 1894 might also have marked the end of the period of intense disruption for the Basongye had not the so-called Batetela Revolt erupted in Luluabourg (now Kananga) on July 4, 1895, and spun out its course in Basongye territory through the end of the following year. Prominent among the soldiers who mutinied from the ranks of the Free State military forces were a group of Batetela who had originally formed the personal forces of Ngongo Lutete, one of the leading African figures

10

of the Arab era. These soldiers, upset over the fate of their leader, and discontent with incompetent Belgian leadership, killed their commanding officer and marched through the countryside toward Ngandu, fighting, pillaging, killing, taking slaves, and causing new agonies for the local populations. By late 1896, the conflict had moved out of Basongye territory, although the end of the affair did not come until 1908, but of course much further damage had been done.

These thirty years of conflict had a deep effect upon the Basongye, and indeed, the consequences were temporarily disastrous. In the period from approximately 1870 to 1900, their society and culture were shattered and fragmented; from 1900 to perhaps as late as 1920, they were regrouping; and from 1920 to the present, they were solidifying a "new" organization. Thus, Basongye society as we know it today is probably neither of substantial antiquity nor as it was in precontact times, although the extent of the differences will probably never be known. At this point we must turn to an examination of the evidence upon which these conclusions are based.

It will be recalled that the first Arab trader in Nyangwe was Dugumbi, who arrived there sometime between 1860 and 1869. Although it is not known when, or even whether, he began slave and ivory operations to the west into Basongye territory, it is at least probable that it was not long after his arrival, and it is certain that Tippu Tip began traveling in the area in 1869 or 1870.

Historians are almost unanimous in their condemnation of early Arab activity in Africa, both because it was so strongly centered on the acquisition of slaves, and because slave raiding left such widespread devastation in its wake. Two notable exceptions to this general view were held at the time, however, by Alphonse Burdo and Arthur Hodister. Burdo's argument (1885) was essentially general and theoretical, based upon the assumptions that the Africans were savage, lazy, and unintelligent, while the Arabs, quite the opposite, brought order, suppression of local wars, and the establishment of agriculture. Burdo argued further that Arab slavery was not repressive in the same sense as was African slavery, and that, indeed, Arab slaves were well treated.

Hodister did not go quite so far as Burdo, and his arguments tended to be specific to his experience. While he recognized Arab

11

brutality in the eastern Congo, he laid the blame not on the Arab leaders, whom he regarded as generally enlightened, but upon their followers and lieutenants, who could not always be controlled. It is Hodister who left behind one of the best firsthand accounts of the organization of Arab operations in an interview given probably to A.-J. Wauters, and published in Wauters' journal, *Le mouvement géographique* (Anon. 1891a). Hodister answered the question *"How are their caravans organized?"* as follows:

> Generally, they are under the overall direction of an Arab, who represents a group of associates. This leader is seconded by a number of Nyamparas [subleaders] who have under their command sections of 20 to 30 men each. These latter are usually natives who have rallied to the Arabs and have come with them from the coast, be it Tabara [*sic*] or from the hinterlands.

The interview continued with *"What plan do the Arabs follow in the occupation of the country?"* and Hodister replied:

> Having arrived at the frontiers of the country the caravan is going to visit and exploit, the leader divides his men into small groups, each charged with exploring a part of the country; he indicates a general direction to be followed . . . as well as some landmarks and means of communication with his headquarters, where he is kept in touch and whence he directs everything. He advances himself only to the extent that the country is occupied and that his rear lines are assured.

> *When these flying columns arrive at a native village, how do they proceed?*

> A flying column which has arrived in a village tries to open trade, to make a pact of friendship, to become the protector of the village or the tribe against its enemies,—the Arab always presents himself as a *protector*, because the native is always at war against someone,—then, amicable relations established, the native chief turns over one of his kinsmen to the Arab as a hostage—often his son. The Arab, in his turn, leaves two men in the village to represent him. From this point forward, the native chief and the Arab's man are supposed to govern together, but the Arab's man, raised in a good diplomatic school, more flexible, more insinuating than the chief, and firmer, does not wait long before taking over much of the power. Soon he is the true chief. The men representing the Arabs are lodged, fed, and supported at the natives' cost.

After discussing the imposition of law and order, the construction of new houses, and the establishment of agriculture, Hodister turned to the problem of the evident excesses of the caravaneers.

You speak of the civilizing role of the Arabs. But is this role always worthy of praise? Excessive atrocities have been noted.

Certainly they do commit them, but this is not the fault of the Arab chiefs. Those who conduct themselves like brigands are only the subalterns. The cause of their abuses lies in the dispersion of the small groups they command, in their distance from superior authority, in the lack of control on the part of their chiefs, in the natural ferocity of the black who often takes the upper hand and abuses it by the superiority of his arms. Let us not forget that these auxiliaries, these subordinates, are natives themselves, sent by the Arab chiefs on a commercial expedition, and they abuse the authority that has been conferred upon them. [Author's translations]

While this type of organization in which authority was delegated outward on a decreasing scale kept overall control in Arab hands, it is evident that some of the subleaders attained considerable authority and power in their own right. The four major Africans of primary concern to the Basongye were Ngongo Lutete, who figured prominently as Tippu Tip's chief lieutenant and who, in turn, controlled Lupungu (Lumpungu), chief of the Bekalebwe, and later, of the Basongye, Zappo Zap, chief of the Beneki, and Pania Mutombo, chief of the Basanga, all major subtribes of the Basongye.

Ngongo Lutete was either a Musongye or a Mutetela, whom Tippu Tip first mentions in his journals late in 1883, as "my young slave, Ngunguru Tita," adding that "all the locals feared him" (Whitely 1966:114). According to Zandijcke, as a young man Ngongo and some others were delegated by their own chief to contact and make peace with the Arabs, who were beginning to penetrate westward from Nyangwe. His promise was noticed by the latter who made him a sentinel in the village of Lukule, and gradually he built up a band of comrades, went into the slave and ivory business for himself as a supplier to the Arabs, was given guns, and thus extended his sway along the right bank of the Lomami River. Zandijcke also suggests that Ngongo established himself at Ngandu as early as 1880, moving out from there to conquer the

Batetela and Basongye (Zandijcke 1953:126–27), though it is often averred that his rise came five years or so later (Comeliau 1943:77). Tippu Tip speaks of supplying Ngongo with "as many as 10,000 guns, notwithstanding the fact that they were the first they'd had" (Whitely 1966:117); this occurred early in 1884, and it must have been at this time that Ngongo Lutete became a true power in the area.

Ngongo and his village were described by a number of persons who were on the scene (for example, Hinde 1897:86–88, 90–91), and others have written of the constant supply of tribute and plunder which flowed in to him (Briart 1891:124). It is clear that he was the most powerful non-Arab force in the Lomami area, and that his influence extended to the south and west of Basongye territory proper (see Zandijcke 1953:130–44). It is equally clear that he was an astute politician, and that his defection from the Arab to the Belgian cause in 1892 was couched in highly pragmatic terms. He and his forces fought in the Arab Slave Wars, but he was soon thereafter accused of theft and of plotting a revolt against the Belgians, arrested, and shot as a traitor on or about September 15, 1893 (Hinde 1897:207–12).

The other major African figures in the Arab operations were far less powerful than Ngongo Lutete, and indeed, were more or less under his control, but each contributed heavily to the death and destruction characteristic of the period. According to some historians, Tippu Tip had been called into the Lomami area by Kalamba Kangoi, the father of Lupungu, who asked for assistance in putting down a revolt among his subjects (Gilain 1897:91–92; Vansina 1966:239); if this is so, Lupungu's early ties to the Arabs may well have been inherited from his father. Vansina indicates further that the alliance with Tippu Tip made it possible for Lupungu to put all the Basongye groups under his own control (n. d.:162). From at least this point forward, Lupungu acted both with the Arabs and with Ngongo Lutete, fighting, raiding, and operating as a slaving agent. His fellow marauder, Pania Mutombo, whose village (De Deken 1897c) was established in a location which put him into direct contact with almost all Europeans who traveled from Lusambo into the Lomami area proper, had been a slave of Lupungu's father but had risen, through machinations which remain in dispute, to be chief of the Basanga (Gilain 1897:91; De

14

Deken 1897a; Vansina 1966:240). Together, the two men apparently engineered the death of Zappo Zap, who himself had been a slaver for the Arabs, and in the late 1880's they turned against his son, then chief of the Beneki, a Basongye subgroup. The latter, already hard pressed by the Arabs, were driven westward and their population decimated, and in 1887, Zappo Zap and the tattered remains of the group appealed to Paul Le Marinel, who gathered them together and escorted them to the vicinity of Luluaburg, along with some Bena Koto and other scattered Basongye groups. The so-called Zappo Zap were well established in the new location by 1888 (Anon. 1892e), and still retain their identity there (Timmermans 1962).

By 1890, various Europeans were reporting that Lupungu had begun to change his ways (Anon. 1891b:39); in 1891, he signed a treaty with a representative of the Free State (Delcommune 1922:II,95), and a year later, made a final submission as did Pania Mutombo (Ceulemans 1959:346–47). From this point forward, both men remained reasonably faithful allies of the Free State, fought briefly in the Arab campaign, but were apparently involved in slaving operations against the Baluba at least until 1894 (Zandijcke 1953:146–53). While Pania Mutombo then seems to have slipped into obscurity, Lupungu continued as chief of the Basongye; he died in 1919, and was buried in the old capital named after his father, some four miles from Kabinda (Norden 1924:133).

Thus the Arab pattern of control described by Hodister was well formulated in the Lomami area. In overall control was Tippu Tip, later replaced by his son, Sefu, and to a certain extent, his colleague, Rāshid, but local control was placed in the hands of lieutenants in the field. Ngongo Lutete, Lupungu, Pania Mutombo, and Zappo Zap were the major forces, slaving, destroying, and paying tribute to the Arabs in exchange for weapons and ammunition and, undoubtedly, for power. Some of them were losers in the end, but the real losers were the Basongye.

We have no accurate means of obtaining population figures for the Basongye in these early days, but those suggested by contemporary Europeans showed consistently high and dense agglomerations. An anonymous report of Wissmann's first expedition in 1881 and 1882 says, "they had been previously struck by the great numbers of the wild Tushilange flocking around them by the thousands, but Lieutenant Wissmann states that the Basonge were even more numerous" (Anon. 1883:164). In 1886, the population of the upper Sankuru region was of ". . . une densité extraordinaire. Le Dr. Wolf a visité des villes de 10, 12 et jusqu'à 15,000 habitants" (Anon. 1886a:75). Wauters reported in 1886 that

> All the country which extends eastward to the Lomami and which is inhabited by the Bassonge tribes has an extraordinary population density. The villages are extremely numerous. A great number appear to be true cities, extending sometimes for 15 to 17 kilometers. Wissmann cites the case of one of the Basonge cities which took five hours to pass through. "It is very chancy, adds the traveler, to estimate the number of inhabitants of a country that one can only travel through. However, I do not think I err too much in estimating the population of the irrigated provinces along the Loubilach and the Lomami at 1,500 or 2,000 persons per square league, a figure which is near the population of the least peopled provinces of Germany." (Anon. 1886b:49) [Author's translation]

At various times in its history, Pania Mutombo's population was estimated at 10,000 and 12,000 (Wauters 1898:105; R. Cornet 1944:158; Gilain 1897:92; Laurent 1897:41; De Deken 1897c:94), Kolomoni's at 10,000 (Great Britain Naval Staff 1920:119), and Nyangwe's at as much as 40,000–45,000 (Mohun 1894–95:592). Gilain (1897:92) estimated the population of the "Bena-Kalibue à 27,000 âmes et le total des autres populations à 75 ou 80,000 hommes." In short, the population of the Basongye was considered astonishingly high by the early explorers and military men, but slave-raiding and other depredations soon cut the figures sharply.

While a number of descriptions of Arab slave-raiding attacks are found in the literature (see, for example, Wack 1905:87–88), Chaltin's seems to be as evenhanded an account as may be expected from one who was clearly anti-Arab. He wrote:

> He [the Arab] arrives near a village at night with his band of plunderers, and encircles it in the greatest silence.
> At an agreed-upon signal, generally at daybreak, the plunderers rush toward the huts, fire their guns haphazardly, shout, howl, beat the gong, sound the elephant horn trumpet, make an infernal uproar; in a word, work everything up to terrify the poor blacks. Wakened with a start, alarmed, aghast, the blacks sometimes put up resistance, but most often take flight.

At the start of the action, human life is not respected. But when it becomes clear that the natives have ceased to defend themselves, all efforts are made to capture slaves. The Arabs prefer young women and adolescents. Old people and very young children are massacred and handed over to armed cannibals who follow and assist the slave expeditions.

If there is no reason to conserve the village, it is pillaged and burned; the farms are destroyed. But often conquered villages become the center and the base of new operations because of their location or their importance. (Chaltin 1894:177–78) [Author's translation]

At this point, Chaltin's description of the situation of the captured village parallels that of Hodister, noted earlier. He says:

In this case, they are not destroyed, and the Arabs try in every way possible to bring back the people who have taken flight. They permit them to ransom prisoners. But in order to do that, the natives must give up all their ivory and make a complete and absolute act of submission. From that time forward, they are under the control of their conquerers: a more or less important Arab post will be established among them. Nothing belongs to them any more; the chiefs lose their authority, the people must submit to a thousand annoyances, and they are plundered of their harvests, their tools, the products of their hunting or fishing, and, in a word, of everything they possess. Even their women will not be respected. (Ibid., p. 178) [Author's translation]

Those who remained in the village, however, might well count themselves more fortunate than those taken as slaves. Chaltin continues:

When an expedition is ended, the prisoners are taken away in slavery and moved toward the large centers. For these unhappy people a period of horrible suffering begins. Hands tied behind the back, the yoke or fork at the neck, they are chained by groups of ten to twenty. Little or hardly nourished, often beaten, walking all the time under a sky of fire or in infected swamps, their flesh contused in the forests, they soon become feeble. Those who fall along the road from fatigue or hunger are pitilessly finished off with blows of the "fimbu." Any attempt to escape is punished by death.

When the chain of unfortunates arrives at its destination, the

17

number of slaves has diminished by three quarters. (Ibid., p. 179)
[Author's translation]

Thus slave raiding must in itself have accounted for much of the
population drop remarked upon in the writing of those who were
firsthand witnesses (see also Anon. 1907b:160–77).

As early as August, 1874, Cameron, who was then on the
eastern edge of Basongye country, reported that "after a time we
moved on, passing many deserted villages, with their crops destroyed by the late marauders from Nyangwé . . ." (1877:272).
Chaltin later wrote that "des bandes d'Arabes envahirent la zone
comprise entre le Lualaba, le Lomami et la Sankuru" between 1868
and 1879:

> They ravage and destroy everything as they pass. The country-
> side, formerly rich, prosperous and very populous, resembled a vast
> emptiness in 1886–1887. . . . The entire region had been ruined
> and become deserted. Many natives existed by seeking refuge in the
> depths of the forest, living in a nomadic state, and giving them-
> selves up to acts of brigandage in order not to succumb to hunger.
> (Chaltin 1930:25–26) [Author's translation]

Le Marinel noted that in the Sankuru area raided by Zappo Zap
". . . nous traversions d'abord une contrée déserte et aride . . . ;
on n'y voit guère de végétation qu'aux ruisseaux . . . et sur les
plateaux où s'alignent des milliers de palmiers sur cinq ou six
rangées, seuls vestiges des populations de Bena-Nkoto qui habi-
taient autrefois le pays" (Wauters 1891a:32).

It was also Le Marinel who noted similar conditions as he
traveled west along the Lukassi River in 1886: "Chez Milamba, les
plantations avaient été tellement ravagées par la bande de Saïdi,
que nous avons pas pu acheter autant de vivres que nous
l'espérions" (Le Marinel 1888). Twenty years later, he looked back
upon this expedition, and wrote:

> In effect, from the Lomami to the environs of the Sankuru, one
> could find during these times only burned ruins of interminable
> native villages, devastated by the raids.
> The survivors of these superb populations, still numerous,
> wandered in the bush like savage beasts at bay, dying everywhere,
> in the thickets and the high grasses, of the terrible illness that is

smallpox, or of the implacable famine which had already reduced them to skeletons.

It is impossible to have an idea, without having been there, of the frightful calamities that these bands of man-hunters left in their wake; it was not only by their direct criminal acts—by murder, theft, and fire—that these pillagers had an effect, but they opened up in their passage the sores of infectious and shameful maladies and, even more dreadful, the agonies of hunger which pushed their miserable victims to the final human disgrace: to cannibalizing cadavers covered with pustules and even in full putrefaction. (Le Marinel 1907:51) [Author's translation]

Briart's charts (1898) of the region from Ngandu to Lupungu in 1891 show frequent notations of burned or abandoned villages, and many explorers remarked on the country traversed in the five days' march south of Pania Mutombo, among them Hinde (1895:430) who wrote: "Crossing the Sankuru, we marched for five days southeastwards to Mona Kialo's, finding practically no food on the road. The vacancy of this district, devoid alike of men and food, had been created by slave-raiders in Tippoo Tib's employ." Later, on a trip in late 1892 between Ngandu and Kabinda, which must have taken him directly through Bala territory, Hinde reported:

We . . . resumed our march towards Katanga, following the ridge of the watershed between the Lomami and the Lubefu. During this march we came across hundreds of human skeletons—according to our Batetela guides, the victims of a smallpox epidemic. But there were bullet holes in some of the skulls, and the epidemic had probably been a Batetela slave-raid. (1897:93)

As late as 1895–96, Laurent (1896b:182) described some of the Basongye area through which he traveled in the following terms:

It is savanna almost everywhere. In several places I walked for more than an hour in groves of oil palms; they are regularly placed and of a nearly uniform height. Without doubt these are the old native plantations whose owners were chased out by the incursions of the Arabs. Some of these groves contained 40,000 to 50,000 trees. [Author's translation]

While no clear means exists of estimating the numbers of

Basongye who were killed or were taken from the area as slaves, Alpers (1967) gives general figures for slave shipments out of East Africa, and R. Cornet (1952:73) has suggested statistics for the Nyangwe trade. He writes:

> It has been calculated that in this period more than 20,000 ivory tusks were moved to Zanzibar in an average year. As to the number of slaves who were torn away from their homes, and of whom the greatest part came from the Maniema and neighboring regions, the average is more than 70,000 per year. If one considers the numbers of men, women and children killed in the course of the raids, as well as those who died along the interminable paths, it can be affirmed that a population loss of 300,000 individuals took place each year, and this only for the regions tapped by the traders from the east coast. [Author's translation]

This estimate applies most directly to the Maniema, but Dhanis attempted to assemble figures specifically for the Basongye area as of 1894 (Overbergh 1908:80–81). Basing his judgments on Lippens' calculation that 200 tons of ivory was moved each year toward the east coast of Africa, and calculating that each porter could carry ten kilograms, he deduced an annual exodus of 20,000 men. In addition, however, another 20,000 men and women were required as supplementary porters to carry food and other goods and supplies, making a total of 40,000 persons. "Pour un esclave pris, on peut admettre que trois ou quatre personnes ont été tuées pendant la capture, soit . . . 80,000 personnes," for a grand total annually of 120,000 individuals required simply to transport ivory. Dhanis also points out the ravages of smallpox and famine, but gives no estimates for these additional losses of human life.

It is Dhanis as well who points out the sharp drop, not only in total population, but in population density: "D'apres cette estimation, il n'y avait en 1894, après la guerre arabe, que *sept* habitants par kilomètre carré. Admettons que l'observateur ait été pessimiste et supposons qu'il y en avait le double, soit 14 habitants par kilomètre carré. En 1887, Wolf comptait 60 à 80 habitants par kilomètre carré" (Overbergh 1908:80). Finally, the figures given by Dhanis show sharp population drops from the estimates to which previous reference has been made.

This population devastation is nowhere better illustrated than in the case of the Beneki, first attacked by the Arabs and then harassed by Lupungu and Pania Mutombo, until in desperation they fled the countryside to take up new residence near Luluaburg. It is Wissmann who left the best account of the ravaging of the Beneki, for he traveled through their territory on his first expedition in 1881–82, and then followed almost exactly the same route on his third African journey in 1886–87. In 1881, Wissmann had found large population agglomerations organized in huge villages: "Eine solche Ortschaft der Benecki hatte einmal eine Ausdehnung von 17 km. der Marsch durch dieselbe nahm 5 Stunden in Anspruch" (Wichmann 1883:229). And, "from half-past six in the morning until eleven o'clock we passed without a break through this street of the town; and when we left it in an easterly direction it still extended, adapting itself to the features of the ground towards the south east. . . . this town of Bagna Pesihi must measure nearly ten miles in length" (Wissmann 1888:528).

Early in 1886, however, the scene had changed drastically.

In low spirits, therefore, we continued our journey to the east-south-east, as far as Kafungoi, where we found Pogge's and my route. But how much altered! Where formerly thousands of Benecki, the inhabitants of the strikingly beautiful and rich town, had joyfully welcomed us; where we had revelled in enjoyments such as an African country, inhabited by industrious natives, has to offer; where in peace and amity we had been conducted from village to village—we now found a waste, depopulated by murder and conflagration. The same huge groves of palm trees, which formerly had marked the town of the happy Benecki, welcomed us to their shadow. Only dismal silence, here and there interrupted by the chirping of the ploceidae, had given way to the welcoming sounds of the former harmless inhabitants. The niches in the palm thicket on both sides of the straight roads, which three years ago had been filled with the tidy farms of the Benecki, were now overgrown with grass of a man's height, whilst here and there a burnt pole, a bleached skull, and broken crockery were reminiscences of the existence of our former friends. (Wissmann 1891:181–82)

After discussing the causes of the displacement, that is, the early Arab raids, Wissmann continued:

The Benecki, not wishing to abandon their rich villages and fields, returned every time the rapacious troop turned their backs, and

21

began to cultivate the ground again, but as soon as the fields were ready for harvest the vagabonds reappeared, their expedition being greatly dependent on the food they found.

In this manner the pacific tribe of the Benecki was attacked several times in succession; many of the bravest, who defended themselves, were killed, many women and children were transported, while the greater number took refuge in the forest. The necessary consequence of the repeated devastation of the fields was a dreadful famine, with small-pox, brought in by the Arabs, following on its heels. War, slave-robbery, famine, and pestilence had actually been able completely to depopulate this densely populated territory, with its towns extending through many days' journeys; and we learned that only a dwindling remnant had taken refuge with Zappu Zapp on the Sankurru. (Wissmann 1891:185–86)

Other accounts, while not so dramatic or so detailed, indicate something of the life of those people who remained. In the summer of 1890, for example, Le Marinel noted the fear aroused by any passing caravan.

. . . the natives, hidden in the grass, gave savage cries in rising up as we passed, but in seeing us quietly pursue our route, their astonishment was so great that they imitated our silence to such an extent that one might have believed a miracle had occurred in which they had been struck not only immobile but also mute.

What an existence these natives have! Those who recognized Gongo-Lutete, an Arab, as master, were in constant fear of attacks by Dibree, with whom Boina-Solo represents the authority of the same Arab chief. They pillage each other; it is incessant anxiety, an eternal qui-vive! (Anon. 1891b:39) [Author's translation]

Schrader reports the same reaction during the first Wissmann expedition (1883–84:287–288), and fifteen years later, Cauteren (1904) noted the evident fear, as well as attacks on his caravan. Le Marinel, again, describes something of life among the Bakusu in 1890.

In passing everywhere like a hurricane, the war has left misery behind it. At each step we see the fearful native rise up and, like the hunted before the hunter, flee in great haste through the grasses and rushes, leaping over the ditches and ponds to hide himself in the thickness of a copse.

22

Debris of an exterminated nation, the Bakussu live here hidden under the thickets which border their old ruined villages; when the path leads to a wooded place, it is blocked by trees felled from all sides, and we must cut a new passage with axes. (Anon. 1891b:39) [Author's translation]

A further consequence was the relocation of villages, as described by Beak as late as 1907; at the time, he was apparently traveling in Basongye territory between Sentery and Tshofa. "Sickened by theft and pillage, the latter [natives of the area] have naturally withdrawn their villages from the transport routes, which are now deserted. I have marched as much as five days (100 miles) at a time without coming across a village" (Beak 1908:23).

Although each of these accounts is fragmentary, taken together they provide a bleak picture of the situation of the Basongye people vis-à-vis the late nineteenth century slave raiders. Entire populations disappeared and the remainder sought refuge in the bush; tens, if not hundreds, of thousands of people were carried off as slaves or killed as the consequence of slaving; and local warfare, stimulated by supplies of guns, powder, and ammunition from the Arab overlords, contributed heavily to the devastation. Yet the Arabs were not the only problem in these troubled times.

While we have no means of knowing the precontact situation, it seems apparent that both the Arabs and the Europeans brought new diseases into the area. Lenz's expedition fell prey to smallpox on the voyage between Stanley Falls and Nyangwe in the spring of 1886, and Wissmann's caravan suffered similar difficulty in December, 1886 and January, 1887 (Hassenstein 1891:60). Wissmann mentioned the disease among the Beneki sometime between 1882 and 1886, the Batetela used it as an excuse for the skeletons seen by Hinde between Ngandu and Lupungu in 1892, and Chaltin's troops suffered heavily from smallpox in the spring of 1893 (Chaltin 1930:40). Le Marinel's return from Nyangwe in 1886 took him straight through the Basongye area, and it was reported that "durant la plus grande partie du voyage, la variole a régné et a fait de nombreuses victimes parmi les serviteurs indigènes. Dix chefs Bachilangés qui accompagnaient l'expedition sont restés en route, et environs deux cents de leurs sujets. . . . Le pire est que la caravane a rapporté avec elle l'epidémie au pays," which it probably did (Anon. 1888:31; see also Le Marinel 1888). How widespread the disease became, we cannot know, but it struck both low and high, for Beak described Lupungu in 1907 as "pitted with small-pox, and blind in one eye" (Beak 1908:21).

While authorities agree that Portuguese traders did not penetrate the Basongye area proper, they were certainly known. Tippu Tip reported fighting Portuguese in Utetera, and Ngongo Lutete pressed his depredations to the west in the hope of obtaining arms from Portuguese traders through the Batshioko. Although south of the Basongye at the time, Cameron reported in 1874 that "the actual reason for our being attacked was, that a party from a Portuguese caravan had been within five miles of Kamwawi, destroying villages, murdering men, and carrying off women and children as slaves" (Cameron 1877:292). While these slavers did not reach the Basongye, they clearly caused indirect disruption by their near presence.

From 1874 on, and most specifically after Wissmann first crossed the area in 1881–82, the Basongye were continually disturbed by European caravans. While these caravans were essentially pacific in nature, and while their porters were brought from other areas, their leaders had to find both food and other supplies, as well as replacements for carriers who deserted or fell ill. Further, a considerable share of the Free State military campaign against the Arabs took place in Basongye country, including the opening battle at Chige; armed forces also require provisioning and men to serve both as porters and auxiliaries. And finally, both Lupungu's and Pania Mutombo's legions took direct part in the war, and part of Ngongo Lutete's forces were Basongye in origin.

It will be recalled that the end of the Arab campaign brought only a short period of relative peace to the Lomami area, for the Batetela Revolt swirled through it for another year and a half, beginning in July, 1895. Again slaves were taken, men were impounded as auxiliaries, and raids were carried out for food, other supplies, and loot; that the countryside was once again ravished is attested to by the fact that as late as 1896 it is reported that Michaux, then attempting to quell the revolt, had ". . . de grandes difficultés a nourrir tout ce monde dans un pays dévasté par les révoltés" (Deuxième Section 1952:377).

Even with the end of the revolt, however, the troubles of the

Basongye were not over, for as late as 1900, Commandant Borms (1901) indicates clearly that the countryside was still in turmoil. Petty chiefs, some of Arab origin, ruled despotically in small enclaves; former army auxiliaries, well armed, engaged in banditry. Borms found portions of the general population in a state of apathy, unwilling to rebuild villages or even houses, and producing a bare subsistence from the soil, presumably because of the many bitter lessons learned over the previous thirty years. Belgian authorities were still engaged in breaking the power of local rulers, and one of the consequences was the release of thousands of slaves who had to be reintegrated into society.

According to Beak (1908:33), the first case of sleeping sickness appeared in Kabinda at precisely this same time, the year 1900, and the insect pest carrying it was spreading from south to north. By March, 1905, says Beak, "Dr. Todd . . . found Kabinda and its vicinity heavily infected," and other reports indicate that the disease had spread to Tshofa, and thus presumably among the Bala, where it was endemic by 1905 (Polidori 1908; Anon. 1904). From this point forward, sleeping sickness became a major problem and the subject of considerable anxiety and debate within the Free State administration (see, for example, Wangermee 1908).

The final disruption, of course, was European acculturation, which must have begun with the first expeditions to cross the area, intensified with the establishment of the posts at Lusambo in 1890 and at Ngandu in 1892, and reached a sustained peak as peace slowly settled over the countryside and the Free State asserted civil control. While it is not our purpose to discuss European accultura-tion, but rather to indicate the disruptions of earlier times which profoundly affected Basongye society and culture, one specific example of the difficulties engendered by European control deserves to be noted.

In 1907, an acting British Vice-Consul, Mr. Beak, traveled through the Basongye area on a mission for his government, and he reported that the Free State was taxing the people by means of a monthly rubber quota. In the Bala area, the central collection point was apparently Tshofa, and it is probable that even at this early date, the village of Lupupa Ngye was supplying its quota to that center, only 25 miles away.

Beak also reported that "the whole of the material and

supplies for the Katanga" was at that time "conveyed in State steamers up the Kasai and Sankuru to Lusambo, where it is transhipped to a smaller steamer, which continues to Pania Mutombo" (Beak 1908:20). At Pania Mutombo, the steamers were unloaded once again, and the goods carried by porters to their final destinations. Two major caravan routes were followed, the first to Kabinda and thence via Kisengwa and Katombe to Ankoro, and the second, apparently the more important of the two, via Lubefu, Tshofa, and Buli to Ankoro. The latter route must have led directly through Bala territory, and more specifically, very close to Lupupa Ngye. Beak estimated that 10,000 loads left Pania annually, requiring 800 carriers per month except in the rainy season when the people were planting. While Lupungu apparently held a monopoly on supplying carriers, it is not unlikely that the Bala participated, and in any event, caravans must be supplied and sheltered. Beak also indicated that Lupungu was probably using, and misusing, slaves as porters, and it seems reasonable to assume that the caravaneers were not averse to picking up individuals along the route.

How can these generalized troubles of the Basongye be made specific to the Bala, and particularly to the village of Lupupa Ngye? Unfortunately, those who wrote in this period almost never mention the Bala by name; given the evident extent of population movements and dislocations in the entire Basongye area, it is at least hypothetically possible that the Bala moved into their present area at a very late date, though this, of course, does not entirely explain the fact that they are so seldom mentioned in the literature. The Bala are noted specifically on only three maps, of which the second was published in 1901 (Wauters 1901); this map shows the "BALAA" slightly south of their present location. Overbergh's map of 1908 shows the Bala centered on the Lumba River, which is also south and slightly east of their current location—the Lumba now forms the southern boundary of their area. The Bala are not mentioned separately from the Basongye in either of Boone's ethnographic compilations (1961; Maes et Boone 1935).

Of greatest interest, however, is that the earliest map, published in 1891 (Wauters 1891b), shows the "BALAA" in precisely the position they occupy today, thus throwing some doubt on the later maps and indicating that the Bala are probably not latecomers to the area, though admittedly the evidence for either position is scanty.

If the Bala have been in their present location, or approximately so, for the past 100 years, they must have been markedly affected by the events we have been describing. Lupupa Ngye is located approximately halfway between Tshofa and Ngandu though not on a precisely straight line; it could thus hardly have failed to be affected by the Arab campaign, particularly since Chige, where the first battle was fought, is only a few miles to the east. Any expeditionary force marching from Lusambo to Ngandu would pass just to the north of Bala territory, and travel of any kind from Lusambo to Tshofa would go directly through it. The Bala are on a direct route between Ngandu and Kabinda (Lupungu), a route traveled by explorers, armed forces in the Arab campaign, and the "Batetela" mutineers. The later supply caravans between Pania Mutombo and Tshofa must have traveled directly through the area.

While no special effort was made in my field study to deal with oral history, Ngongo Lutete was often mentioned by the people of Lupupa Ngye. Two older men claimed to have seen him, and a third, Yakalala of the sister village of Lupupa Kampata, claimed to have served with him; as evidence, Yakalala showed a hole in the lobe of his right ear which Ngongo's men cut when impressing him into service. One informant reported that Ngongo himself once came to Lupupa Ngye, but left when gifts were offered him; he was also said to have been afraid of a certain local poison used to coat arrow and lance points.

However accurate these recollections may be, the overriding impression carried of Ngongo Lutete is his cruelty. "Ngongo Lutete was the worst man in the world. He took everything; he took women; he used to cut pregnant women open to see whether there was really a baby inside them." "Ngongo Lutete used to put holes in the ears of people he captured, tie them together through the holes, and then jerk the string to see them cry." For a general slave, Ngongo pierced holes in both ears as a marking; a sentinel slave was marked by a hole in the deep center of the ear, either left or right; a soldier slave, whose principal task was to take more slaves, was marked by having both ears cut off. Followers of Ngongo often marked themselves voluntarily, women by making holes in the

27

nostrils and inserting a plug or a sliver of wood, men by piercing the septum and inserting a piece of chicken or human shin bone. A clear distinction between Ngongo's slaves and slaves of Lupupa Ngye was made, say the Lupupans, on the basis of markings, for slaves in Lupupa were never marked. Perhaps the most pointed comment made on Ngongo's cruelty was contained in an offhand remark of a xylophone maker as he burned a hole in a xylophone key: "This is what Ngongo Lutete used to do to people's eyes."

In addition to his reputation for cruelty, Ngongo left his mark on Lupupa Ngye in other ways. The time of his death, for example, was occasionally used to establish other dates of importance in the village. A particular route out of the village to Makola, was known as the route Ngongo used when he traveled to Kibombo, and probably, to Nyangwe. A female informant reported that the custom of selling women, as strictly opposed among Lupupans to the practice of marriage sanctioned by bridewealth, began with Ngongo: "The Batetela didn't have many chickens or much manioc, so they would come among the Basongye with women to exchange for food." And finally, it is said that Ngongo once ordered one of his soldiers to get a particular machete which he kept in a case in his house. The man did not listen well to his instructions, but simply said, "Yes, yes, I know where it is." Ngongo said, "If you don't find it, I'll kill you." The soldier did not find it, Ngongo killed him, and the words he said afterward became the truism: *Mbiya kwiupusa,* "One must listen well."

In addition to this historic presence of Ngongo Lutete, enough in itself to indicate a period of disruption, certain pieces of ethnographic information lead to the same conclusion. While the Lupupans speak of their relationship to other villagers, thence outward to the Bala as a whole, and finally to the Basongye, these relationships can never be traced except in the most general way. The necessary genealogies are lacking, as are the legendary or mythological connections; both break down at crucial points, apparently for lack of knowledge.

Similarly, while the villagers speak of a relationship to a chief and *chite* of the Bala, and perhaps to the Basongye as a whole, the political relationship is unclear to them and little attention is paid to it. In their internal organization, vestiges of former systems, such as an apparent age-grade structure, are evident, but they are not really functional and the people are confused as to their meaning. The historical evidence for disruption is intensified by what can be discerned of the history of the introduction of music instruments.

It seems clear that Lupupa Ngye and the Bala as a whole suffered the disruptions to their society and culture which were suffered by the Basongye as a whole. Plagued by slave raids and pillaging by the Arabs and their lieutenants; the population shredded, dispersed, and shifted; attacked by new diseases to which they had no immunity; pierced by European expeditions; their lands the battleground for the Arab campaign; pillaged again by the mutineers of the "Batetela" revolt; paying taxes in rubber to the Free State; and probably assisting in the portage of goods from Pania Mutombo to the Katanga, the Basongye, the Bala, and the Bapupa were indeed sorely tried. Yet their society lived to rise again from the ashes, and it is this reestablishment which will next occupy our attention.

For the people of Lupupa Ngye, the world is organized around the existence and activities of four central figures, chief among whom is Efile Mukulu, the creator of the world and everything in it, and the ultimate explanatory agency for all things and actions. Having created the world but never having been seen by man, Efile Mukulu is now more or less content to let the world and men run themselves, although at the time of their births he predestines men's lives down to the most minute detail, and although he has a hand in the control of men's affairs through regulation of the ancestral spirits. Even death is left primarily to men (Merriam 1961b), but Efile Mukulu is always watchful and may intervene as he sees fit.

In constant opposition to Efile Mukulu is Kafilefile, the essence of all that is bad. Kafilefile originated death, which was not in Efile Mukulu's scheme for man; he created accidents; he consorts with witches and is the creator of their special songs. Kafilefile taught men how to kill, and the struggle in men's hearts between good and evil is the struggle between Efile Mukulu and Kafilefile—some Lupupans say that all human beings have two hearts, one good, representing Efile Mukulu, and one bad, representing Kafilefile. Kafilefile talks with the ancestral spirits who come to see Efile Mukulu, tells them he is really God, and gives them bad advice. Efile Mukulu knows that Kafilefile does all these things, but he does not punish him because he says that if men want to follow

29

Kafilefile, then that is their affair, and he will punish the most flagrant by killing them.

Kalombo was a child who created himself long before the people on earth were created by Efile Mukulu. When he was born, he said, "Here I am. I wasn't born of woman. I wasn't born of Efile Mukulu. I was born of myself. Now I am going to show my power." Kalombo knew almost everything and he could do almost everything that Efile Mukulu could do; while some say that Efile Mukulu really created Kalombo, Kalombo denied this. "He was against Efile Mukulu." Kalombo was a trickster, not a creator or a helpful being.

> Once Kalombo told the people to make a house in a special spot and when they had made it he told them to go inside. But he had dug a big pit there and concealed it, and when the people went inside, they all fell into the pit. Another time he climbed a very tall tree, and when he came down he told the people that he had touched the sky. So they all climbed up to touch the sky, too, and they all fell off the tree.
>
> Kalombo had a wife. She was pregnant, but he said she was just sick and that he would operate on her. He did and she died. He had great magic, but he would not teach it to the people; it was only for him.

And so Kalombo was "against the people." He died "a long, long, long time ago."

Mulopwe Kamusenge assisted Efile Mukulu in his acts of creation; he brought fire and domesticated animals to the Bala, and he probably brought music as well. He was a human being, but no one knows where he is now.

The people of Lupupa Ngye do not engage in extensive speculation on these beings; rather, they accept what they know of them and use them and their actions as both broad and specific explanatory principles for the way things are. Thus it is not particularly surprising to find that elaborate creation or explanatory myths and legends are not found among them, and that those which do exist are poorly known and of small concern per se. The most elaborate version, told by Yakalala, who was about 80 years of age at the time, is as follows:

> It was Efile Mukulu who created the world and all that is in it. Then he created Mulopwe Kamusenge; everyone is descended from

Mulopwe Kamusenge, for he created all the people in the world. Mulopwe Kamusenge was married, but I do not know the name of his wife.

Mulopwe Kamusenge had a big stone; he stood on it with his wife, and both of them left their footprints in the stone. And not only are their footprints on the stone, but there is also blood on it; this is the blood that comes from a woman just before a child is born—it is her blood.[2]

Mulopwe Kamusenge and his wife stood on the stone, and at midnight he created many people. He created them instantaneously. He would point to a place and say, "Fifty people here; fifty people there." And they appeared. After he had created a lot of people, he began to divide and distribute them; he stood on the stone, saying, "I name this people the Batetela; I name this people the Bagonge; I name this people the Bakongo; I name this people the Baluba; I name this people the Kanioka; I name this people the Lulua; I name this people the Belande; I name this people the Bala; I name this people the Bekalebwe"; and so on.

Mulopwe Kamusenge then gave counsel to the people. "You must go and stay in your villages, and you must remain peaceful. You can dance and play and do your work. I have named all the tribes of people." He had made both men and women, and he had made the man first and then the woman. He made children, too.

At midnight that night he took a small signaling drum (*kiyondo*, pl. *biyondo*) and he sent out this message: "I have created the people. I have created the people. I have created everything." He waited. And suddenly someone signaled back to him with a *kiyondo:* "You have created many things, but there is something you have forgotten." Mulopwe Kamusenge thought, "What could this be that I have forgotten?" and he went home.

---

[2] Yakalala insists that this stone can still be found in the village of Kisonde, near Kabongo, which is outside present Basongye territory in the country of the Baluba-Katanga; he has "seen it with my own eyes." The stone is "forty kilometers" long on each side, and square. The footprints are still to be seen in it, as is the blood which came from the wife of Mulopwe Kamusenge. As indicated by the footprints in the stone, Mulopwe's wife stood on his right side when he was creating the people.

While it is not suggested that they are the same, Soors has noted the presence of large, flat humanly placed stones in the territory of Kasongo, and it is not without reason to suppose that similar phenomena may be found elsewhere in the eastern Congo. Soors wrote: "January 31st, 1936, found me camped in the village of the notable Twite of the chefferie of the Basonge of Kasongo territory . . . on the right bank of the Lualaba. . . . The elders informed me of the presence, in full bush, of a group of large flat stones erected like menhirs. . . . No doubt exists that these stones have been set in the ground by the hand of man" (Soors 1950). [Author's translation]

31

The second night he took his *kiyondo* again and sent the same message; the same response came back to him.

The third night it was all exactly the same.

The fourth night he took his policemen with him, and he said to them, "When I signal, you must be near me. When I send the message, 'I have created the world, I have created the world, I have created everything,' someone always sends back the message, 'You have created many things, but there is something you have forgotten'." And so he sent his message again: "I have created the people. I have created the people. I have created everything." And back came the message: "No, you have forgotten something."

So Mulopwe Kamusenge sent his police off, saying, "Go catch that man." The police found him and they asked him, "Are you the one who has been answering Mulopwe Kamusenge and saying that he forgot something?" And the man answered, "Yes, it was I."

"Come to Mulopwe," and they took him to Mulopwe. When he arrived he was frightened and began to cry. Then Mulopwe Kamusenge said,

"Are you the person who has been answering me and saying that I forgot something?"

"Yes."

"What did I forget?"

"You forgot to explain to us why we die."

"Yes, you must die, because if you do not die, then you cannot have children. When you die, then you can return as children." [3]

Now Mulopwe Kamusenge and his wife had a child; his name was Kalala Lunga. It was Kalala Lunga who showed the people Mulopwe Kamusenge had created how to make children with their wives.

One day Kalala Lunga arrived in a village where there was a river; all the women and children were there washing, swimming, getting water, and they were afraid of Kalala Lunga and fled from him. This happened four times. Kalala Lunga had two dogs with him, and also a man who carried his baggage.

The fourth time, he went to the village and said, "Where is the chief?" The people gave him food to eat, but they were eating their food without preparing it in any way. Kalala took two stones, struck them together, and produced fire; then he showed the villagers how

[3] The Bala believe that the human spirit (*kikudi*, pl. *bikudi*) is reincarnated, most often in children of the lineage. Reincarnation is usually thought to occur three times, after which the *kikudi* returns permanently to Efile Mukulu; a number of variant beliefs are held concerning these details.

32

to do it. He said, "You cannot eat food without preparing it. You must cook your food. Here is the means to have fire. Make it like this. Cha! Cha! Cha! Cha!" He struck the stones together four times. "When you strike the stones together, have lots of dry thatch close by. And if you do that, you will have fire." Then he showed them how to cook.

Afterward, he asked, "Is there a woman for me?" Someone gave him a woman, and then he showed the people how to marry with a woman; up to this time the men had remained separate from the women. He matched up all the people into couples. He stayed two days with his wife; on the third day he called all the people together, and he said, "I am going to leave to continue my work in other villages. My wife is going to stay here and she will show you a child. The child will stay with you a long time. If you are good to him, he will always stay, but if you are bad to him, he will follow me." The village was that of Kongolo Mwamba, who was the first old man and the first chief.

When Kalala Lunga left, he came to a river, and he said to the man who worked there,

"If you see a black child [Kalala] who wants to cross the river after me, show him the way. If you see a red [white] child, don't help him."

The name of the child was Kalala, and after he was born, he was almost like a god. Everyone liked him; all the children stayed and played with him, and as he grew older, everyone liked him and came to be with him. After some years, someone said to his mother, "Look at your child; he is getting too powerful; he is like a chief. We must look for a way to kill him."

So his mother called all the people of the region to search for a way to kill Kalala. They made a big hole in the ground (four meters deep), and covered it with a mat, and covered the mat with grass. Then they were singing and dancing and playing the drums and the xylophones, and they called to Kalala to come by a way that would make him walk across the mat that covered the pit. But there was one singer who was his friend, and this person called to him in an unknown language, "Stop! Stop! There is a hole in there." He stopped.

Kalala had a lance with him that someone had given to him. He threw the lance into the center of the mat, and the mat and all the grass fell into the hole. He said,

"Ah, you wish to kill me. I am going to rejoin my father."

Then he left, but no one could see how he left; he just disappeared.

After this he left to search for his father. He came to the river, and at the ford found a man who worked there. He crossed the river, and he found the path his father had taken. When he found his father, he explained everything to him, and to Mulopwe Kamusenge.

Mulopwe Kamusenge said,

"Now it is finished. I will make people afraid. You will be invisible in the villages, but everyone will know you are there." Now everyone fears God and no one can see him.

Mulopwe Kamusenge left after he had done his work, and no one knows where he went. He has never returned, but he still exists. He was a man like us. The same is true of Kalala Lunga and his son, Kalala; they were men; they disappeared, and they never returned.

Far more complex origin myths have been cited for the Basongye (for example, Moeller 1936:143–53), but this is the most detailed version found in Lupupa Ngye.

As is so often the case with the Lupupans, direct connections between two events—in this case the general creation of man and the following legend concerning the origin of the Bala—are tenuous. While Mulopwe Kamusenge appears as the central representative of Efile Mukulu in both, he is credited with one child, Kalala Lunga, in the myth above, while in the legend below, Kalala Lunga is not mentioned and Mulopwe Kamusenge's child is Lubembele. In any case, the account of the origin of the Bala is as follows:

> All of us, the Bala, came along one route with the Bekalebwe who are on the other side of the Ludimbi River. And those of us who are here are of one family. The Bekalebwe are the children of a woman, Kitoto, but we Bala are the children of a man, Lubembele. It is thus that we came from Mulopwe Kamusenge. We crossed the Lomami just south of Epongola south of Tshofa at Chief Ngoyi Lunkamba's. We were all on the other side of the Lomami, and Efile Mukulu distributed people there. He took the Bekalebwe and gave them land on the other side of the Ludimbi. The Bekalebwe are the children of a woman, Kitoto.
>
> Mwimbi was the child of Lubembele, who was the child created of Mulopwe. Lubembele also had Nundu, Kabemba, and Nkeba as his children. Lubembele looked up and down the river Lomami for a place for his children, but he could find no place and so they crossed the Lomami and came to the epata of the Bena Lutobo at the

junction of the Lombo and Lubwe rivers. From here we went to
Bambwa where the Bapina are now, but we could not cross the river
there, and so we turned back. We passed by Lutobo again and
crossed the river there. When we passed by Nkombe, some people
stayed there. We stayed on this side of the Lomami, and our father
Lubembele began to create villages. Mwimbi, Nundu, Kabemba,
Nkeba are all of our family, the same family. Nundu was the founder
of Lupupa. Kabemba was the founder of Bakankala. Nkeba was the
founder of the Bangungi (Sankia, Kitenge, Basanga, Kaa).[4] We are
all of one family; we all came from Mulopwe via Lubembele.

This is the way our fathers explained it to us. We came by one
route. We did not come separated, but by one route. After the people
had been divided, Efile Mukulu said,

"All is correct; now you are right. You people, don't forget your
brother who is your father."

Thus Mwimbi remained as the first Bala child; he is our brother
and our father. We are descended from him, from Mwimbi. We are
all one family. We are descended from Mulopwe Kamusenge. It is
like that.

The accompanying map (Map 5) is as close a representation
of this legend as it is possible to reconstruct, but the reader will
notice some omissions as well as obvious difficulties of interpretation. Among the former, it is impossible to locate Bambwa in the
Bapina area, or Bakankala, founded by Kyabemba; these may
represent areas instead of actual villages, or villages whose names
are changed on the official maps. The most difficult matter of
interpretation concerns the founding of the Bangungi by Nkeba, for
while the raconteur included Sankia, Kitenge, Basanga, and Kaa
as a part of this group, in contemporary fact Sankia is considered to
belong to a subdivision of the Bala, the Basembe, while the other
three villages do, indeed, fall among the Bangungi. Why the
narrator included Sankia in this group is not known, and in fact, it
seems probable that it was a slip of the tongue. Thus the route to
Basanga, Kitenge and Kaa, shown on the map as via Sankia, is
suspect. Neither is it certain at what point the groups broke into the
various separate divisions under their particular founders; Nkombe

---

[4] While it is not mentioned specifically in the legend, Mwimbi is considered to have
been the founder of the central Bala at Mitombe. The raconteur simply forgot to
include this piece of information, but added it on subsequent questioning.

Map 5

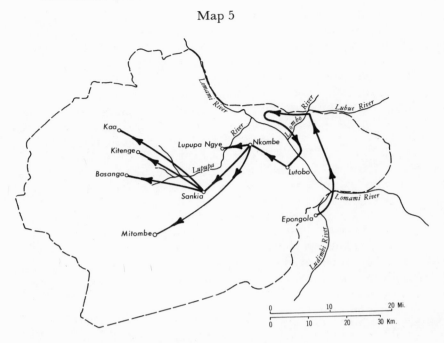

Origin Routes of the Bala

has been so chosen on the map simply because it is the last place mentioned before the division occurs.

In this version of the origin of the Bala, all begins with Efile Mukulu, who created Mulopwe Kamusenge; Mulopwe, in turn is the father of Lubembele, who is the father of Mwimbi, founder of the central Bala at Mitombe; Nundu, founder of Lupupa Ngye; Kabemba, founder of Bakankala; and Nkeba, founder of the Bangungi.

While this represents the most detailed version of the origin of the Bala, it is by no means the only one. Some Lupupans, for example, hold that Nundu was the first man of the Bala, with Lubembele as his wife and Mwimbi as their son; others say that Nundu had many wives, among them Lubembele; still others insist that Mwimbi, son of Nundu (male) and Lubembele (female) was the founder of the Bala.

The common core of assumption, however, is based on the genealogy noted above which begins with Efile Mukulu, and always includes Lubembele, Nundu, and Mwimbi, whatever the relationship attributed among them. It is also held by those who are knowledgeable that "la" means "river," and that therefore the Bala are "people of the river" (the usual word for "river" is *mwela*, pl. *miyela*). Finally, it is agreed that the people of three villages—Lupupa Ngye, Lupupa Kampata, and Makola—together constitute a subgrouping of the Bala called the "Bapupa." While some would add the inhabitants of Lumba Lupata and Lumba Bwembe to this group, the idea seems to be a recent one and is not accepted by the majority.

The division of the Bala into subgroups is a recognized principle of organization among the Lupupans, but the variety and number of espoused groupings is bewildering because of the lack of agreement from individual to individual. Mwembo, for example, reeled off twenty-eight such groups almost without pausing for breath, and followed the recital with the statement that a number of others existed for which he did not know the names. Mulenda, on the other hand, named fourteen groups, of which only eight appear on Mwembo's list. On the official lists at the offices of the Secteur de Tshofa in 1959, however, nine such groups were noted, as indicated on the stylized accompanying map (Map 6). The divisions are as follows:

	Name	Villages Included
1.	Bena Bapupa	Lupupa Kampata, Lupupa Ngye, Makola
2.	Bena Basembe	Sankia, Bakile, Imeno
3.	Bena Kenge	Basumba, Balungu
4.	Bena Babondo	Lumba, Ebondo, Kifuku
5.	Bena Baunga	Pania Mpinga, Kongolo, Kyambe, Kalanga Namwe
6.	Bena Bamilobo	Lumba Lupata, Ebondo
7.	Bena Babulwi	Ebulwilumba, Eshadika, Bala Lupata, Mitombe
8.	Bena Kaiyilwamba	Baluba, Kyunda I, Kyunda II, Mushimba
9.	Bena Kabwe	Makonde, Kabwe Matonondo, Kabwe Kakyele, Kabwe Mashiba, Kabwe Kamani, Kabwe Dyeno, Kongolo, Kapengapenga, Sankuru

Thus officially the Bala are subdivided into these nine groups, but in the minds of the Lupupans, the groupings are far more numerous.

Map 6

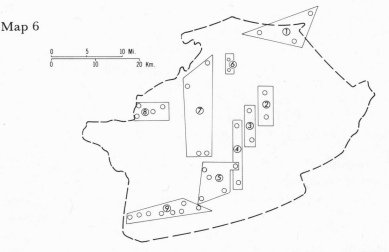

Subgroups of the Bala

At this point we move into the realm of personal memory, or at least, of memories removed one generation; this is also, of course, the realm of human claims, counterclaims, and uncertainty. The people of Lupupa Ngye are unanimous in their assertion that the first place at which the Bapupa were gathered together was called Kadiyala, but they do not agree on its location because of lack of information. Kadiyala clearly represents the first step in the regrouping of the people of this local area after the disasters of the late nineteenth century.

Yakalala said that when Ngongo Lutete was defeated (1892), he fled from his forced servitude in Ngongo's army and arrived in the present Bapupa area. After some searching, he came across people he knew at a spot about five kilometers north of the present Lupupa Ngye; gathered here were people who had fled from their own villages, and the location in which Yakalala found them may well have been Kadiyala.

Each recollection of the times is couched in its own terms, but all hold in common one central assumption: at Kadiyala, the people were not living together, for the location was a general one, and the Bapupa were scattered about within it. Among the elders living in 1959–60, Mukume, for example, said that the first place he remembered living was Kapongo (another name for Kadiyala). "The people were all scattered around at Kadiyala," and Mukume added that the idea of having a single village "was borrowed from the Europeans. The *bakulu* (s. *mukulu*, leaders, usually elders, of the lineages) decided the question, and it was the idea of Mulenda of Bena Yewusha. Mpumba was the first village built this way." Mayila, on the other hand, said that it was his father, Yankamba, who was the real organizer. At that time, Yankamba was living at Kadiyala, but "there were only a few people there; the households were scattered through the bush, separated from each other." Because there were "lots of leopards about, Yankamba gathered the people together into a village for their self-protection. This first grouping was at Kadiyala."

It is agreed that the breakup of the Bapupa into three subsequent villages occurred at Kadiyala when the people of the present Lupupa Ngye and of the present Lupupa Kampata fell into a dispute over women. The people of Lupupa Kampata left, presumably for their present location, and the people who subsequently settled in Makola went with them. However, at Lupupa Kampata the latter became dissatisfied with the rule of Chief Yamukoshi and left to settle at Makola.

These events left the founders of the present Lupupa Ngye alone at Kadiyala, and it is clear that a number of moves occurred before their 1960 location was reached. How many moves it took, and over what period of time are a matter of difference of opinion among the older men. The simplest version, advanced by Mankonde, is listed below in the left-hand column; the most complex, advanced by Senga, in the right-hand column.

Near the Lupupa River to the west	Near the Lupupa River to the west
	Near the Mpumba River
	Shidika
	South of the present location
Just north of the present location (50) yards)	Just north of the present location
1960 location	1960 location

Almost all versions of the moves include four major displacements, and we can accept them at least as a generalized outline of the wanderings of these Lupupans; the locations, after Kadiyala, are Mpumba, Shidika, Mukikulu, and the 1960 location.

While it is impossible to reconstruct precise dates in a society which is not much concerned with time, some reasonable approximations can be adduced. Time in years is reckoned by the Lupupans in a number of ways: simple memory, of course, is central, but local events are also often related to outside events of major significance. Thus among older men, World War I provides a handy reference point, particularly since some of them served in the armed forces at that time; for younger men, World War II is an equally convenient milestone. As horticulturalists, the Lupupans remember with considerable positiveness the number of times they have planted and harvested in comparison to a fixed reference point in time such as a world war. Similarly, major events of the life cycle provide fixed time points; if one does not speak in terms of a year, such as "1923," he does recall the number of times he has planted and harvested since a child was born or a father died. For older men, the death of Ngongo Lutete (1893) is still a standard dating point, and the succession of chiefs provides possibilities for some. Thus, while it is impossible to be completely certain of any date, it is almost sure that general time periods are quite accurate.

What, then, is the time of Kadiyala? It will be recalled that Yakalala, upon his escape from Ngongo Lutete's forces, found gathered together a group of people he knew, some five kilometers north of the present site of Lupupa Ngye. This may have been Kadiyala, and the date would most probably have been sometime in 1892, a time when the people would surely have been scattered in the bush. If we take this as a working figure, Kadiyala was probably inhabited approximately eight more years, since it is possible to date Yankamba's efforts toward creating a village at 1900—his son's establishment of this date depends on his own memory of the facts that he was approximately seven years of age at the time, and that Ngongo Lutete had been dead for six years; both reckonings point toward 1900.

It is impossible to say when the move to Mpumba was made, though it must have been shortly after 1900, nor are the reasons for the move clear. Mayila said, however, that Kadiyala was too much in the forest, that too many tsetse flies were present there, and that when it rained, the main street ran like a river. Mankonde also spoke of sleeping sickness, and the time with which we are here dealing correlates well with the known dates of the spread of sleeping sickness to the general Tshofa area. On the other hand, Senga said that the original location was too wet and too cold. Mpumba, however, can at least be located with reasonable precision; it lies to the west and slightly to the south of the 1960 village location at a distance of no more than a kilometer or two. It derives its name from the stretch of the Lupupa River on which it was located.

The move to Shidika is impossible to date and no reasons are given for it; since Shidika was located along the river, however, the reasons for leaving it may well have been the same as those for leaving Mpumba. The tsetse fly was blamed by Senga for the subsequent move to Mukikulu, and this could well have a basis in fact, since the new location is several hundred yards off the river and thus out of the heavy forest which borders the waterway, and into the open savannah. Some question exists as to whether "Mukikulu" is in fact a proper designation for this area, since strictly speaking, it is a land tenure term meaning "a former village site now grown to bush." The particular location, then, was not named before the village was located there, while Mpumba, at least, and probably Shidika, were both previously named stretches of the Lupupa River.

The same applies to the name "Lupupa Ngye"; the 1960 site was not previously named, and people are not quite sure of the derivation. The most commonly accepted explanation is that "Lupupa" comes from the name of the river, but some persons suggest that "Lupupa, Nundu, and Lubembele may have been the three children of someone." *Ngye* means "leopard," and it is said that the people took this name because they were so fierce, because "they had the mentality of the leopard." Some hold that the real name of the village should be Lupupa-Nundu-Lubembele, and others feel that this triple name in fact applies to the three villages of the Bapupa taken as a whole. In short, as is so often the case with history, no one version of anything is final, although the general outline noted above is as close as we can presently come to the truth.

41

Our final problem is the date of establishment of the village of Lupupa Ngye in its 1960 location; the most likely choice is late in the first decade of this century. Thus Kadiya, a slave, said he planted and harvested in the present location eight times before World War I, placing the move at 1906, while Mayila said he planted and harvested seven times before the same event, giving a date of 1907. Only Senga dissented strongly, saying that the move took place in 1919, though he did not venture any specific reasons for his conviction.

In January, 1960, the people of Lupupa Ngye became openly enthusiastic about moving the village site once again, and various plans were made. The initial reason for the suggestion stemmed from the death, in late September, 1959, of a much-respected, middle-aged man, who fell dead early one morning of no visible cause. That same evening some of the village elders noted in public discussion that the general fortunes of the village seemed to be running at a low ebb, and that with the shocking death of Kamanda, perhaps it was time to move. Other reasons were later added: the Lupupans felt that the women were not having the normal number of children; too many people were dying; too many people were having bad dreams. Still later, it was said that it was "cold" in the village, that because of the heavy surrounding vegetation, planted in years past and now grown up, the location was "too much like living in the forest."

By mid-May, great enthusiasm had been generated for bringing all the Bapupa together; discussions were held with the sister villages of Lupupa Kampata and Makola, and a tentative decision was reached to expand the then-existing site of Lupupa Ngye. This new scheme, while it grew out of the old, was directly triggered by the specter of the coming of independence to what was then the Belgian Congo. Consolidation would provide protection for the Bapupa who, expecting the worst, had become convinced that the most immediate consequence of independence might well be an attack against them carried out by the Baluba (see Merriam 1961a:173–82).

Such an attack never came, but the idea of consolidation did not die, and in 1964, the people of Lupupa Ngye and Lupupa Kampata together constructed new houses and outbuildings and moved "on the same day" into the new Lupupa Ngye, which was located about 400 yards north of the 1960 location. This arrangement lasted about four years, until a new series of events occurred: the chief of the village, a Kampatan, was deposed, the government dispensary was removed and nothing substituted, and "people began to fall ill" and "many died." In 1968, the Kampatans returned to their original ridgetop location about a kilometer and a half to the west, and thus Lupupa Ngye is once again back to the basic population descended from the ancestors who were its founders some sixty-five years ago.

Reconstruction of the roster of Lupupa Ngye's political leaders since the days of Kadiyala is as difficult to achieve as are village locations, but by piecing together many kinds of evidence, a tentative chronology of chiefs can be suggested. These chiefs, with the exception noted below, were considered to be the chiefs simultaneously of Lupupa Ngye and Lupupa Kampata, thus stressing the close relationship between the two villages. All the lineages represented on this chart (Fig. 1) are a part of the social organization of the indicated villages today, thus emphasizing social continuity.

Fig. 1
Chiefs of Lupupa Ngye and Lupupa Kampata

Name	Lineage	Village	Dates	Remarks
Yankamba	Bena Yankamba	Ngye	? –1911	
Muchipule	Bena Muchipule	Ngye	1911–12	Was chief of Ngye only
Kilomboshi	Bena Kyambwe	Ngye	1912–19	
Yamukoshi	Bena Yamukoshi	Kampata	1919–21	
Lumbila	Bena Lumbila	Kampata	1921–23	
Yampumba (Loshi)	Bena Yewusha	Ngye	1923–54	
Nkolomoni	Bena Yewusha	Ngye	1954–58	
Mankonde	Bena Muchipule	Ngye	1958–59	Deposed
Muwa	?	Kampata	April, 1960– July, 1965	Deposed
Efile	Bena Ekunyi	Ngye	Dec., 1965– date	

The same kind of continuity appears in lists of names given by elders when attempting to recall those who were leaders at

Kadiyala or in the subsequent early political history of Lupupa Ngye. In the following chart (Fig. 2), four such sets of recollections are compared. Yakalala (col. 1) is speaking of the year 1892 when he escaped from Ngongo Lutete's army and returned to find familiar faces in a location which was possibly Kadiyala. Senga (col. 2) is speaking of the *banunu* (s. *mununu*, old people) at the time of his childhood, that is, the period roughly between 1890 and 1900. Mayila (col. 3) is recalling those who formed the first village at Kadiyala, which he dates at 1900. Kadiya (col. 4) speaks of the "real founders" of Lupupa Ngye, but more specifically those who were in the village when it moved to its present site, according to him in 1906.

Almost all of these are familiar names in the village today, but it is especially significant that several persons were recalled by all four informants, for with some exceptions, these tend to be those remembered as having been important to Lupupa Ngye. Of equal interest is the fact that nine of the fourteen lineage names presently extant in the village are represented in the chart. Lineages are named, theoretically, for their founders, but since genealogies are remembered for a maximum of four generations back in time, actual founders are sometimes forgotten and other "founders" substituted. It is also frequently the case that while the founder is remembered, the lineage name has been transferred to some other illustrious person in the genealogy; thus some genealogies contain both names. Our thesis of the disruption of Bala culture and society suggests that events and persons occurring or in existence during or after the 1890's would tend to take strong precedence over anything occurring or existing during or before the disruption. Thus the existence of a number of lineage genealogies which contain both the names of the founders and the names of persons who lived later but after whom the lineages are presently named is not surprising. While remote founders are recognized, men like Yankamba and Chite Kamamba are the true founders of the present lineages, for it was they who brought the Bapupa together and who are thus historically relevant. Further, the crude computation of time from lineage genealogies indicates that all nine of those whose names are now the names of lineages could have been young to middle-aged men in 1900. Thus the genealogical information seems to be a further confirmation of the disruption interpretation.

Fig. 2
Founders of Lupupa Ngye

Yakalala	*Senga*	*Mayila*	*Kadiya*
Chite Kamamba	Chite Kamamba	Chite Kamamba	Chite Kamamba
Muchipule	Muchipule	Muchipule	Muchipule
Yabasanga		Yabasanga	Basanga
Kingombe	Kingombe	Kingombe	Kingombe
Chite Kadiya	Kadiya	Chite Kadiya	Chite Kadiya
Lukale			Lukale
Sambi			
Sefu			
Ngongo Sefu		Ngongo Sefu	Ngongo Sefu
Mukumadi			Mukumadi
Chite Makumbo		Chite Makumbo	
Yankamba	Yankamba	Yankamba	
	Kasongo		
	Mulenda		
	Chite Kambila	Chite Kambila	
	Yewusha		Yewusha
	Malemba		
	Dyangadyanga		
	Lufwala		
	Suku		
	Kyoluso		
			Fwamba Lukulu
			Piyani Kalonda
			Yamakumba
		Chite Fimpanga	
		Kadima	

In any case, the fourteen lineages in Lupupa Ngye in 1960 are as follows; those names marked with an asterisk are also to be found listed in Figure 2.

* Bena Chite Kamamba
* Bena Muchipule
* Bena Yewusha
* Bena Bwende (Kambila)
  Bena Mwepu Lombe
  Bena Bakwamwesha
  Bena Ekunyi

  Bena Kadiya
* Bena Ngongo Sefu
  Bena Kyambwe
* Bena Lukale
* Bena Chite Kadiya
* Bena Yankamba
* Bena Chite Makumbo

In the view of some Lupupans, these lineages are the direct result of the actions of Nundu (seen as male in this connection), who is said to have had several wives, by each of whom he had children. When the children grew up and were themselves married, social life became too complicated, and Nundu decided that the children of a single mother should build their houses together, and separately from the children of other mothers. This they did, and thus the lineage system was begun. Since it is presumed that the event took place long before the birth of Chite Kamamba or Muchipule, per se, the lineage system may well be much older than the times of which we have been speaking.

Thus the history of Lupupa Ngye, as explained by the villagers, accords well with the broader history of the Bala and Basongye. While genealogies extend far back in time, their reality begins at approximately 1890. The earliest personal recollections, of Yakalala, show him returning to the original area in approximately 1892, only to find the district deserted; when he did locate his former friends and relatives, they were in a new location. Subsequent knowledge indicates that the people at Kadiyala were scattered throughout the bush, exactly as we would expect, and that the regrouping process probably went on initially until approximately 1900. There follows a period of consolidation as the reorganized group moves restlessly from one place to another, possibly seeking an "ideal" location; this occurs through roughly the first decade of the present century. From that point forward, the village has been a stable entity, but its heroes, its leaders, its lineages, indeed, its history, are in the greatest part from the period postdating 1900. The catastrophe of the Basongye was equally the catastrophe of the Bala, the Bapupa, and Lupupa Ngye.

Lumami

Mulenda Kiabu

Mulenda

Mukume

Kipa

Eshiba

Kingkumba

Yakalala   Mayila

Kipa

Mankondẹ

2. Physical Surroundings

The village of Lupupa Ngye lies in the savannah region of the Congo (Zaïre) and thus escapes the extremes of temperature and rainfall found elsewhere in the country. Keay (1959:7) includes the Bala and, indeed, most of the Basongye area, in his Forest-Savanna Mosaic, of which he writes: "In this mosaic, patches of moist forest (not confined to streamsides) are surrounded by savanna of tall grasses. Moist forest (evergreen or practically evergreen) occurs along streams and on other moist ground . . . [and] moist forest patches . . . [are] also found on hills and plateau sites. The flora of the forest patches is relatively rich. . . . By contrast the savanna is usually poor floristically . . ." This description applies reasonably well to Lupupa Ngye, although in the specific environs of the village the moist forest patches are confined to streamsides, and the savannah is perhaps slightly more moist than Keay's words suggest.

Since the village was not a central point of Belgian administration, very few statistics apply specifically to it. The closest altitude figure found on the official map ("Territoire de Sentery," 1959) is a triangulation point at Kole—known to the villagers as Kaole—which marks the southernmost boundary of the lands claimed by Lupupa Ngye. The official altitude here is 707 meters, or 2,319.55 feet, a figure which is probably almost identical to what measurements taken in the village would show.

At this altitude, temperature, humidity, and rainfall are relatively benign, but again no figures exist for the village. At Tshofa, 40 kilometers southeast of Lupupa Ngye, official measurements for 1953 showed an average maximum temperature Fahrenheit of approximately 88°, an average minimum temperature of 65°, and an average temperature of 77°. The absolute maximum was 96° and the absolute minimum 59° (Institut National 1954). The accuracy of these figures for the region is revealed by comparison with those from nearby locations in 1959; Tshofa was not included in the official figures for that year (Institut National 1960). In the following chart, Sentery is probably closest in temperature to Lupupa Ngye, followed by Kabinda.

Fig. 3

Temperatures in the Basongye Area, 1959

	Kabinda	Kasongo	Lusambo	Sentery
Average maximum temperature	85.8	87.6	87.8	86.2
Average minimum temperature	66.4	67.6	68.4	66.7
Average temperature	76.1	77.5	78.1	76.8
Absolute maximum temperature	93.0	95.2	96.1	93.0
Absolute minimum temperature	60.3	60.4	60.8	62.1

No location closer to Lupupa Ngye than Luluaburg (Kananga) is represented in the official humidity figures, and thus all that are available are those taken in the close vicinity by Paul Briart in 1890. At the time, Briart was traveling from Ngandu to Lupungu with the Delcommune expedition and must have passed very close to the present site of Lupupa Ngye; his figures, taken daily in the month of May, show a humidity of about 25 percent (Briart 1898). Since the month of May is the beginning of the dry season, it is not surprising that the humidity figures are low.

The normal dry season in the Congo south of the equator runs from April through October 31, and the wet season from November 1 through March 30; local variations change this rough approximation markedly. No rainfall figures are available for Lupupa Ngye, but an official weather station was operated at the Westcott Mission in Mitombe, some thirty-five miles west and slightly south of it. While rainfall in Mitombe is somewhat heavier than in Lupupa Ngye, the figures show that the wet season begins in September and peaks usually in December, with the heaviest period from December through March. A fairly substantial decline takes place in April, and by May the dry season has begun. June and July are extremely dry months in Lupupa Ngye, but rainfall begins to increase once again in August. Figure 4 uses the official measurements taken in Mitombe (M. Nixon, personal communication; and Institut National 1960). Whatever their accuracy insofar as Lupupa

Fig. 4
Rainfall at Mitombe, 1957–60

	1957		1958		1959		1960	
Month	Quantity	Days						
January	230.9 mm.	12	135.2	12	179.0	18	175	16
February	289.6	16	145.9	11	163.2	12	249	14
March	262.4	12	132.0	14	198.0	15	121	15
April	155.3	16	114.6	13	121.0	5	248	15
May	27.5	3	52.4	4	45.3	7	5.5	2
June	6.0	1	7.8	2	6.9	2		
July	8.9	3	0	0	27.1	1		
August	69.3	5	93.1	8	20.5	4		
September	29.2	7	101.4	9	161.3	9		
October	176.6	10	192.2	16	215.0	12		
November	110.7	12	175.9	15	213.6	15		
December	365.2	23	234.0	19	117.6	15		
	1731.6	120	1384.5	123	1468.5	115		
	(68.1″)		(54.5″)		(57.8″)			

Ngye is concerned, rainfall figures make more sense from the point of view of the villagers if the year is considered to begin in September, for this is the start of the agricultural cycle; on this basis, the rainfall figures are fairly uniform from year to year.

September, 1957– August, 1958		September, 1958– August, 1959	September, 1959– May, 1960	
Quantity	*Days*			
1362.7mm.	116	1464.5 123	1500.5	113
(53.6″)		(57.4″)	(59.1″)	

During its year, then, Lupupa Ngye enjoys an average rainfall comparable to that of Jacksonville, Florida, and an average annual temperature approximately that of Honolulu, Hawaii; it is safe to say that the humidity in Lupupa Ngye is considerably lower than in either of these two United States cities.

The agricultural officer stationed at Tshofa knew of no soil studies made in the area, and none have come to light subsequently. However, the soil is described in his official reports as "sandy," to which it may be added that the laterite content appears to be somewhat lower than is usual in much of Africa.

While Lupupa Ngye actually lies in a valley, the surrounding hills are so low (at most, 200 feet) that the visitor has the impression of a fairly level savannah. The distance from the Kamikunga Hills on the west to the Newulu Hills on the east is no more than three miles, while from Muntula Hills on the north to the Bifulu Hills on the south the distance is less than a mile (Map 7). The overwhelming impression of the terrain is the north to south slope of the land toward the Lupupa River, as well as the west to east slope toward the Muntula River.

A stranger to the village would formerly have been able to enter it only from the east or west, via the major trails running from Lupupa Kampata to the west, or from Makola or Nkombe to the east. Today, a motor vehicle dirt road runs north and south very near the west end of the village, providing the only access for Westerners and the major access for most nonlocals. Walking to the village from the road, the traveler first passes two or three small stores owned by Westerners but staffed by Africans who are not native to the village; goods sold include small items such as matches, soap, and Western beer, and some larger items such as cloth and clothing, particularly trousers and shirts. To the left is the storage warehouse of the Cotonco and some other small structures built to serve Western agents. After passing through a small grove of trees, the visitor emerges at the west end of the single street of

50

Map 7

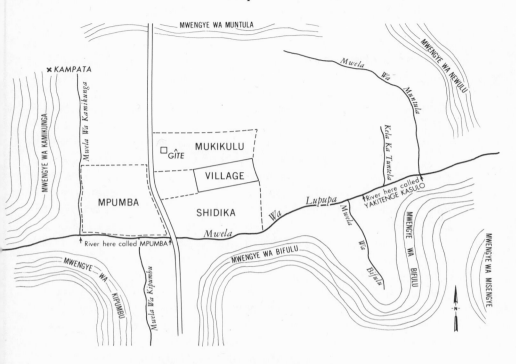

Sketch Map of the Lupupa Ngye Area

Lupupa Ngye. This avenue is about 40 feet wide, broken occasionally by a palm tree and, at certain times of the year, carpeted with red and pink wildflowers. The stranger's first impression is one of neatness and orderliness; the street is clean, and the houses are set back at an even distance from it; the only usual exception involves a few houses which are being allowed to fall into complete decay, and one or two others which were begun some time ago, but never finished.

Some of the older villagers think that the idea of a single main street with houses on both sides was introduced shortly after the Kadiyala period. If this is true, it once again indicates knowledge lost during the period of disruption and then regained from some other source, for the earliest accounts of European travelers indicate the same single-street organization (for example, Wissmann 1888:526–28).

51

At the far west end of the street is a large open space which once contained the schoolhouse in which the first three grades were taught; this structure collapsed late in 1959, and the school was moved to the verandah of the COTONCO warehouse. Beyond this space to the north is a large open field in which the young men play "futball" or soccer, and slightly west and north of this field is the Lupupa Ngye *gîte d'étape,* or resthouse.

Structures in the village include houses, cookhouses, or "kitchens" as they are called by the villagers, chickenhouses, goathouses, pigeonhouses, cotton storehouses, general storehouses, drying racks, and toilets. The main houses, which are the property and living quarters of men, are placed along the street with the other structures behind them. While the buildings belonging to each male household head are grouped together, the land on which they stand is divided not by households, but by lineages. Thus in the accompanying sketch (Map 8) which shows the arrangement of structures in part of the lineage Bena Chite Kamamba, the three main houses on the one side of the street belong to three brothers (Ngongo, Kiabu, Kamanda); a fourth brother's house and related structures are directly opposite on the other side of the main street.

Behind the main houses are the combined living quarters and cookhouses of the brothers' wives: Kamanda's wife, Ngolo; Kiabu's wives, Kitenge and Kama; Ngongo's wives, Lumami and Bwilu, and his mother, Ebambi. Scattered through each general household area are the small structures for livestock, as well as various trees owned by the individual brothers; the outdoor toilet is at the back of the property. Although not indicated on this map, many of the lineage areas include small glades, perhaps 20 feet square, which are cleared areas shaded by trees. It is here that the women pound manioc, and a wooden mortar and pestle are a permanent fixture in these spaces. No doorway faces east, the direction from whence come the prevailing winds, and this arrangement is a conscious one. The indicated lineage boundary lines are sometimes marked by hedgerows or trees, but usually they are simply imaginary, but well-remembered, lines across the earth.

Almost without exception the main living houses are built upon raised platforms of dirt which extend out to the eaves; these platforms are from six inches to a foot in height. Cookhouses, storehouses, and other smaller structures do not usually include this

Map 8

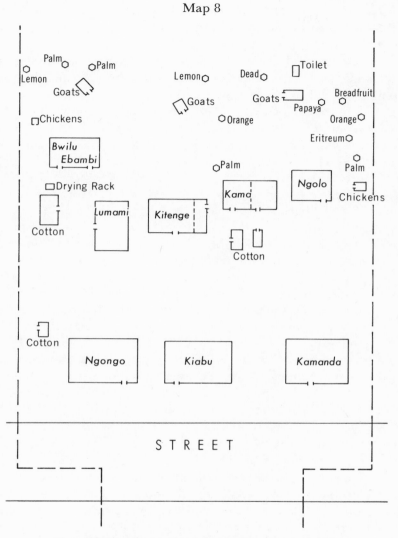

Bena Chite Kamamba (north side of street only)

construction feature. The main houses are built up from a framework of wooden poles with lathing on both sides of the wall studs. Ceiling joists and crosspoles form the basis for the ridgepole which is also supported by attachments from it to the four cornerposts of the house, and this provides the basis, in turn, for a

53

roofing framework covered with bundles of dried thatching grass. All of this construction is the work of men, but it is the women who prepare and apply the mud daubed between the lath to form the walls. After the walls have dried thoroughly, the women smooth on a finishing layer one to two inches thick, and since the mud is made from earth taken from termite hills, the final coating has a red-orange color. Finally, the thatching is cut off evenly about four inches below the eaves proper, and the house is finished. Inside floors are laid in mud and allowed to harden before use; they are re-mudded when necessary.

Every house has a porch, almost always on all four sides. This is achieved by placing forked posts at the four corners and at intervals along each side of the house, laying crossbeams on them, and lashing the roof overhang to the crossbeams. The amount of overhang, of course, is taken into consideration when building and thatching the roof, and the porch area is usually three to four feet wide; it is also above the level of the surrounding ground because of the platform base on which the house is constructed.

Porches are sometimes enclosed with a loosely woven screen of bamboo strips intertwined on a set of vertical sticks fastened to eaves and ground; this space is used for general storage. More tightly woven enclosures are found on a few porches, and these are used to store manioc, maize, peanuts, stovewood, and sometimes livestock. Another form of porch storage takes the shape of tubes made from stiff palm fronds. These tubes are about six feet tall and three and one half feet in diameter; they are stood up on the porches under the eaves and used exclusively to store peanuts.

Of the forty-five main houses in the village, all but seven have at least one window, and one house has five windows; eight houses have two doors, and one has three. On the other hand, only three of thirty-nine cookhouses have any window at all; two have one window, and one cookhouse has two. Door and window frames are carpentered by one of the two specialists in the village; the window openings are provided neither with glass nor screen, but rather with wooden shutters which are carefully and securely fastened at night, more against animals and malignant witchcraft than against theft.

House decoration is minimal. Twelve of the forty-five main houses have indentations in the outside walls about three feet off the ground; these are rectangular or square in shape and of various sizes. They are considered to be decoration. Doors are sometimes painted with European paints, and shutters are similarly treated very occasionally. Cookhouses are never decorated in any way.

Inside rooms are made by erecting studs to a ceiling joist, double lathing, and filling with daub and the finishing coat. A few houses in Lupupa Ngye have been left as a single room, and about equal numbers have two or three rooms. In houses with two rooms, the areas function as living and bedrooms or as a living and a storage room; in three-room houses, the rooms are usually a living room and two bedrooms, or living room, bedroom, and storage.

Although sixteen different exterior shapes are found in the various structures in the village, approximately 60 percent of them are plain rectangles, and 80 percent are either plain rectangles or squares. The other types are all variations on one of these two basic forms, and only one house of the 125 structures included has utilized any sort of curve. The village and its houses are essentially right-angled and straight-lined, although a few exceptions occur, particularly in the placement of small outbuildings.

The state of repair of the various village structures is not particularly good; indeed, some 66 houses and cookhouses are in a relatively poor state of repair or were never finished in the original construction. Far more cookhouses than main houses are in such shape; thus 37 cookhouses and only 26 main houses are in some state of disrepair, and five cookhouses are in imminent danger of collapse. It will be recalled that the main houses are primarily for men, and the cookhouses are used by women both for cooking and for sleeping. While these figures might seem to indicate a tumble-down village, the impression of general neatness noted above is accurate.

Household furnishings are either of Western origin or are locally made to Western models. Thus the main house contains such articles as Western chairs and tables, ashtrays, floormats, pictures on the walls (often framed), beds, mattresses, pillows and blankets, kerosene lamps and occasionally a Coleman lamp or stove, wash basins, and so on. Included also in the main houses are items of male personal property such as suitcases and clothing. Men own all houses and outbuildings, and they are theoretically theirs to sell or dispose of in any way they see fit, with the proceeds accruing to them. Men also own the property kept in the main houses.

Women, on the other hand, own their clothing, everything that concerns the preparation of food, and items of personal adornment. Children do not own property "until they are about eleven years old"; before that time, their toys and clothing are considered to be the property of their fathers. All livestock is male property, except for poultry (and eggs), considered either to be joint property or the property of women. Men and women together plant, care for, and harvest the crops, but it is held that such crops as cotton, rice, bananas, pineapple, and sugar cane are male property, while corn, manioc, sweet potatoes, beans, and similar crops are female property. Men own the various bearing trees planted on household property and also own trees in the fields. When asked for a list of male and female property, a typical male response is as follows: "A man owns traps, hook and line, house, axe, machete, hoe, clothing, goats, pigeons, ducks, all music instruments (save those noted below), locks, palm trees, house furnishings, knives, spoons, suitcases, bicycles. Possessions of a woman include pots, rattle (music instrument), mats, palm oil (palm nuts are the man's until he gives them to the woman), plates, tin cans." Held jointly are "chickens and the iron gong." Held by either are "slaves, maize, and peanuts. Manioc was formerly for men but is now for women." While the property of a woman is theoretically hers to dispose of in any way she sees fit, including sale for profit with the proceeds retained by her, it would in fact be considered a poor marriage if she did not consult her husband first in such matters. However, women do carry on a good many small transactions without consulting their husbands. On the other hand, a man has the right to dispose of any of his salable or transferable property without consulting his wife. Both sexes, however, are strongly enjoined from wanton destruction of any property.

In addition to the property held by men and by women, a few goods are communal property held for the village by a person either traditionally delegated or instructed through dreams. Such property includes the village protector figure, a wooden statue about three feet tall covered with magic amulets and preparations, certain paraphernalia connected with the figure, and several music instruments, including drums, rattle, double iron gong, and wooden gong; some of the last are also used in conjunction with the figure while others may be used by anyone at any time.

Land, in the broadest sense, is a communal asset with rights to its use based upon claims of occupancy and the inheritance of these claims; ultimate control of the land is vested in the chief who represents the corporate body and apportions land rights. In theory, land can neither be borrowed nor rented, though in fact, a plot may be used upon consent of the "owner." Land is obtained by requesting it from the chief, who apportions a plot from whatever free land is available at the time. The chief formerly had the power to retract his permission, and in such a case, the affected land reverted to the public domain. Another means of obtaining land is through simple occupancy, although this would technically be unsuccessful if opposed by the chief. Thus, Mukume lives apart from the rest of the village and outside the village limits because of the birth of an epileptic child in his lineage; this necessitated moving the mother and child, since epilepsy is believed to be contagious. Since a woman cannot live alone outside the village, a male must move with her, and since Mukume was the oldest man in the family, it was he who came. Mukume moved to this free land outside the village about nine years prior to the time of this research; he now considers it to be part of the land of his lineage, Bena Chite Kamamba. His occupancy made it so, and he states that even if he had no descendants and this plot were to be vacated, it would remain Bena Chite Kamamba land "forever." Thus a third means of obtaining land is through membership in a lineage, an automatic fact of life in Lupupa Ngye; in this case, of course, the land is held by the corporate lineage group. Finally, free land was formerly set aside for the use of strangers who requested permission to use it from the chief. When such strangers departed, the land reverted to the public domain and any crops that remained on it became the property of the chief; this land was conserved for use by other strangers.

Rights to the land are vested in men; such rights are never held by women. When a man dies, his interest passes to his son, his older brother, his younger brother, someone else in the family, in the order noted; if no one is available, the land reverts to the public domain. Rights, however, can be held for extended periods of time without use, and this is presumably possible because a great deal of free land is available and thus no pressure exists to obtain "owned" land which is not being used. Some Lupupans say that in former

57

times rights to crop land were held for four years before reversion to public domain; in present circumstances, letters would be written and, if no responses were forthcoming, the land would revert after four years. This, however, is more theoretical than real. Further, mere physical presence is enough to insure retention of rights; if a person falls ill, remains ill and unable to work his land for years, and has no relatives to work it for him, his rights remain unimpaired. Thus rights do not necessarily depend upon use.

The land is inalienable; it is not a commodity to be bought and sold. "If I sold my land then my children wouldn't have a place to stay." "If you sold your land, where would you stay?" "This is my home and I must keep land here." All such statements are responses to what is essentially an unanswerable question for a Lupupan; rights to land are part of being a member of the group, and it is the group itself which has the ultimate proprietorship.

The people of Lupupa Ngye are horticulturalists and thus the land has special meaning for them; this is reflected in many ways, among them the proliferation of terminology concerning land. Terms used include the following:

ebala, pl. *mabala* — fields in the bush where people are currently cultivating.

elungu, pl. *malungu* — land set aside for the ancestors; literally, "lands where insects are." A close connection exists in Lupupan thought between the ancestors and the insects, their representatives. This land is set aside by the village, not by individuals or lineages, and nothing is done with it; although it may be burned off when other land is burned, it is not planted, nor is it used in any other way except for paths which may go through it. "Our fathers told us to set aside this land." When wild pigs are seen on the land, the people know that the ancestors are using it, for the pigs are representatives of Efile Mukulu sent to indicate this fact to men. Ancestral land is always land near water.

eyanda, pl. *mayanda* — a place where many people cultivate together, either in the forest or in the bush. The main agricultural lands of Lupupa Ngye are *mayanda.*

kibunji, pl. *bibunji* — land on which a village currently stands.

kikulu, pl. *bikulu* — a place in the bush where a village formerly stood and which has now grown over into bush; it is considered an excellent place to cultivate.

kikuwa, pl. *mbikuwa* — land which has been cultivated several times, but which is not at present under cultivation. It is bush land, and it is distinguished by the fact that while no one is working it, various crops which have seeded themselves or which have been overlooked are still growing there. A different term, *mukipupu,* pl. *bikipupu,* is used for the same kind of land in the forest.

kumashama, s. & pl. — cemetery land.

kutema — land in the forest presently under cultivation.

lutunkyi, s. & pl. — swampland, marshland, or simply land on which water always stands under the vegetation covering it.

mapia, s. & pl. — free bush land. *Mwando,* pl. *miyando* is the comparable term for the forest, i.e., free forest land, while the forest itself is *mutamba,* s. & pl.

matekye, s. & pl. — land near the river which floods in high water. It is not considered good for cultivation, except possibly for rice. *Misegyeya* is land on the river bottom.

The general term, *kitololwa,* pl. *bitololwa,* means unowned and unwanted property; any use of the term, in regard either to land or to anything else, is rare in Lupupa Ngye, since all things are accounted for in terms of ownership or proprietorship.

The Lupupans also distinguish different types of soil, including among others, *kabalala,* pl. *tubalala* — poor soil; *kafinda* — black soil used in constructing the interior parts of house walls and not considered good for cultivation; *lusengyeya* — sandy soil; and *ntoshi* — white dirt and its derivatives of white coloring of all types, used as a sign of mourning and as protection for twins.

Although fishing provides part of the food supply, no specific water rights are applicable in Lupupa Ngye and its immediate surroundings. People control fishing rights to certain sections of the Lomami River, but this practice, while known, is not carried on in Lupupa Ngye. In 1957, the Belgian agricultural agent introduced artificial ponds into the economy of the village. These ponds, each about 20 feet square and from 6 inches to 18 inches in depth, were dug by the Lupupans under the supervision of the agricultural assistant; the water is obtained via short ditches dug from Tuntela Creek. The ponds were originally stocked with about a dozen telapia for which the owner paid two or three francs per fish, and the idea, of course, was to provide a ready source of animal protein which is in very short supply in the village.

In sharp contrast to land, the ponds are considered to be private property and a salable resource. While the villagers do not seem to be particularly enthusiastic about the ponds, their asking price is 1,000 francs,[1] but a reasonable offer from the point of view of a potential buyer is 100 francs if the pond has been in existence for one year, 200 for two years, and 300 for three years.

The people of Lupupa Ngye, then, are horticulturalists, interested primarily in the land and what it can be made to produce. Almost all men can be regarded as specialists in horticulture, and only a few other economic possibilities are open to a male Lupupan. In the traditional culture he can be a musician which offers a means of avoiding the normal male role in the village. He can be a *kitesha* (pl. *bitesha*), a male transvestite, but this is a role chosen by very few even though it, too, offers a means of avoiding the traditional masculine role. If he is a young man, he may avoid being a horticulturalist by taking up the specialized profession of raffia basketry making; this is a new economic role, introduced into the village about 1928. In addition to these major skills, almost every male has some special skills which both set him off as an individual and make his role in the economy more useful and important. Traditional special skills, as seen by the Lupupans, include trapmaker, musician (divided into singer, gong player, etc.), fisherman, blacksmith, hunter, palm nut cutter (with stress on the ability to climb trees), trader, cutter of dead bodies (important in certain funerals), maker of alcoholic beverages, finder of grubs in palm trees (a special delicacy), raffia gatherer, woodworker (including the subspecialties of making the mortar and pestle, and sculpting), dyer, tailor, weaver, magic worker, storyteller. Newly introduced skills include cabinet maker, mason, bicycle repairman, carpenter, night watchman, and tailor. At least one male in the village represents each of these specialties, both traditional and modern; many specialties are covered by two or more men; and every man has more than one special skill.

A number of further skills are included in the lists given by the Lupupans; while we would call these personal attributes, it is stressed that they are equally special skills so far as the villagers are concerned. They include sleeper, wrestler, hemp smoker, insulter, successful adulterer, drinker, teller of lies, debtor, one who cannot

---

[1] At the time of research, the Congo franc had a value of approximately 2 U. S. cents; 1,000 francs was therefore the equivalent of 20 U. S. dollars.

keep a secret, one who angers quickly, and one who can ride very fast on his bicycle. These, of course, are not productive skills in the economic sense; rather, they are either consumptive or are personal abilities or attributes.

None of the skills noted above enables an individual to be a complete economic specialist; one cannot make his living as a palm nut cutter or magic worker, mason or bicycle repairman. A musician, raffia worker, or male transvestite can come much closer to self-support, the two former through their special skills, the last because he is supported economically in his role by others and by his own assumption of odd jobs; but even in these cases, ties to the land are strongly kept, and the specialist himself, or members of his family, work the fields. Even the traveling professional musician, the *ngomba* (pl. *bangomba*), keeps a home base and fields, the latter worked by his family. Some Lupupans have stepped out of the traditional village life and economy to take jobs as soldiers, policemen, heavy equipment operators, clerks, and so forth, but they no longer live in Lupupa Ngye (nor does their family of procreation), and thus they have become economic strangers to it.

The usual male Lupupan, then, is a horticulturalist with two or more special and additional skills at his fingertips; this being the case, it is evident that the village is oriented toward an agricultural time schedule and agricultural labor patterns.

For the horticulturalist the day begins about 5:30 in the morning when he arises, washes, and about the time of *masasa* (s. & pl.), which is "sunrise" and the conceptual beginning of the day for the Lupupan, leaves for his fields. Almost all fields attached to Lupupa Ngye are on the other (south) side of the Lupupa River, away from the village, necessitating a walk of several kilometers which can take as much as an hour. The reason for this location is that the fields must be kept at some distance from the domesticated animals of the village, particularly the goats which wander more or less freely throughout the day. Labor in the fields continues until *ekotoka* (s. & pl.), which is the period from roughly 11:30 A.M. to 1:00 P.M., "when people leave their fields." After a short rest, the first meal of the day is taken in the fields or at home about 1:00 P.M., followed by any one of a variety of pursuits. The afternoon may be spent in rest, in a specialized pursuit such as fishing, in further labor in the fields, or in gathering some special product in the forest.

61

People return to the village about 4:00 in the afternoon, most of them having stopped at the river in order to enjoy a leisurely bath. This is followed by a period of rest in that portion of the day called *kyolwa* (s. & pl.), "sunset" (until approximately 6:00 P.M.). During this time, people visit with their families and with each other, and often engage simultaneously in small tasks that can be done with the hands, such as rolling raffia on the thigh to make string or fashioning a fishhook. The heavy meal of the day is taken about 7:00 or 8:00 in the evening, and sometimes as late as 9:00; older people go to bed soon thereafter and young adults perhaps an hour later. In the meantime, night (*bufuku*, s. & pl.) has fallen with the 6:30 P.M. end of *kyolwa*, but it, too, is divided into several periods. *Kamwilwabashobe* ("you see someone coming but you can't see who it is") is twilight; the period from approximately 10:30 to 11:30 P.M. is *kilo kya kumpala* ("waking" "first"), considered to be a time when one is wakened by night sounds; from 11:30 P.M. to 5:00 A.M. is *kilo kya kabidi* ("waking" "second"); cock's crow is *kilo kya kasetu* ("waking" "third"); and *namashika* ("cold") is dawn.

As the organization of the day is both specific and appropriate to the needs of the villagers, so are the broader divisions of time. While some evidence indicates a former four-day week, the Lupupans have adopted the Western seven-day week beginning, however, with Monday which is "first day" and followed by "second day," "third day," and so forth. Where formerly the months were lunar, each month beginning with the advent of the new moon, the Western calendar has also been adopted; the names of the months, however, remain traditional, as does the beginning of the year which is set at September to coincide with the beginning of the agricultural cycle. Finally, the year is divided into two parts: *eshipo* (pl. *mashipo*) meaning "windy, dry," and standing for the dry season from May to July inclusive, and *mpeshi* (s. & pl.) meaning "rain," and standing for the wet season from August to April inclusive.

The agricultural cycle begins with a flurry of heavy labor in late August and early September when the fields must be cleared and planted. The planting season continues more or less unabated through October, when weeding begins to occupy the time. In December, certain crops are harvested, and late in that month and early in January the cotton crop is planted. At approximately the

62

Fig. 5
The Months of the Year

ka/swa/mitunda few ant anthill	September	the time of starting to cultivate
ka/swa/ngoloso few ant termite	October	the time of termites
tu/swaswa many "big black bugs" or "termites" (?)	November	it is time to plant again when these come out
ma/swa/akata many ant many	December	time of many ants
mbwibwimaswa	January	the time of weeding
pashi/lukyena type of sunrise (?) insect	February	the month of peanuts
kapopwe lots of rain	March	the time to plant millet; also implied is that it is the time the bush grows up and closes paths because of heavy rains
kasika/kyenda close rain	April	time of the maturation of plants; the end of planting; the end of rain
eshika/bifunko ending thunder	May	end of the rain; no more planting
lwanga/mulume cultivate man without rain	June	harvest time—"a man who has force, who is well known"— the correlation is that this month is marked by great heat and strong winds
lwanga/mukashi cultivate woman without rain	July	the time of letting up of heat— the correlation is that women are not so strong as men
kafulumi/lemba sky covered hail with	August	the time of hail

beginning or sometimes the middle of February, the work rhythm begins to slacken, but it picks up again in mid to late April when the cotton must be weeded. The harvest of cotton and some other crops begins early in June, and this month and part of July are an extremely busy season. From approximately mid-July until the end of August, little agricultural work has to be done, and then the cycle begins again. The Lupupans divide the year more simply, saying that September to February (from the clearing of the fields through the peanut harvest) is a period of hard and continual work; March, or mid-February through March, or perhaps mid-April (from peanut harvest until the cotton begins to grow), is a period of light work and relaxation; April through mid-July (from the time the cotton must be weeded until it is harvested), is a period of hard work again; and mid-July through August is a period of rest and relaxation.

The land area claimed by Lupupa Ngye covers approximately twenty square kilometers, bounded on the east by the Tshofa-Lupupa road. The western boundary, some four kilometers to the west, is formed by the Minonga River, which flows north and empties into the Lupupa River; land on the western side of the Minonga belongs to the people of Sankia. The northern boundary is formed by the Lupupa River, and the land north of it belongs to the people of Lupupa Kampata. The southern limit, formed by natural geographic features and including the triangulation point, Kaole, is about five kilometers south of the Lupupa River; the border is shared with the people of Kombe. This area contains some rather hilly land, heavily vegetated areas along the creek bottoms, some swamp or marshland, and river bottom land. The best land is considered to be a northern slope leading down to the Lupupa River; it is a good hour's walk at a fast pace from the village (Map 9).

The area along the road, marked on Map 9 as A, rises steadily to the south and is covered with fields, some planted and some lying fallow; the north-south distance is approximately 700 yards. Toward the west, the land slopes down to Kipumbu Creek, and then climbs rather steeply up Kipumbu Hill; the fields in this area are widely scattered, though all the land is accounted for. Some portions have apparently never been cultivated, others are clearly lying fallow, some are old fields of manioc now choked with weeds, and still others are under cultivation. The farther one goes from the village, the less land is under cultivation: Lupupa Ngye does not suffer from land shortage, and sufficient land can and does lie fallow at any given point in time.

The fields of different members of the same lineage may or

Map 9

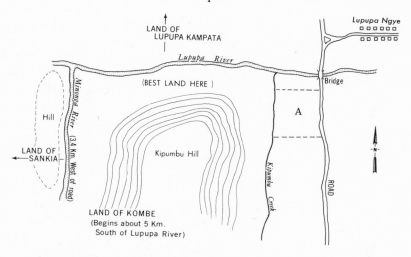

Sketch Map of the Agricultural Lands of Lupupa Ngye

may not be contiguous; this is considered to have been a matter of individual preference in the past when land use claims were first established. The fields are separated from one another by paths lined on both sides by manioc; most fields are also marked by a border of manioc no matter what their major crop. Fields also contain trees, usually fruit-bearing trees such as palm or banana, or single or small groups of pineapple plants. Those fields far from the village are marked with one-room structures made of bamboo and thatch which are used as resthouses and as overnight shelters when the work is particularly pressing; it is said that people sometimes stay out in the fields as long as a month, coming back to the village once a week to take care of their affairs. In rice fields, which are located near the river and most often on its north side, six-foot sticks are set in the ground and connected with a rope to which are tied bundles of brush. The rope leads to the owner's field house, and when birds come, he jerks the string, thus setting up a chain reaction through the connected sticks which shakes the brush bundles. No scarecrows per se are used, and no means are known for protecting the fields from birds when the owner is absent.

Since the crop land is not timbered, the work of clearing new fields, which is done by men, is not particularly arduous. Neither is

65

this a slash-and-burn technique in the strict sense, since a finite but ample area is involved, and since a steady rotation is practiced: the fields never really fall back into brush. When an old field is to be cleared, it may be burned, or the owner may simply cut the weeds and the stalks of the previous crop and burn the collected waste materials in piles. The ground is cleared by both men and women; once cleared it is turned over with short- and long-handled hoes wielded by both sexes. No rhythmic labor is used in the fields, nor is there coordinated cooperative labor such as that common in West Africa. While relatives, neighbors, and friends can be called upon for short-term assistance, each man and his wife or wives, along with older children on occasion, does the agricultural labor as a distinct work unit.

The three major food crops planted by the Lupupans are maize, manioc, and peanuts, and these are supported by a host of minor crops including beans, gourds, leeks, millet, onions, peppers, pimientos, sweet potatoes, rice, sugar cane, tomatoes, yams, and cucumbers, not to mention at least another score of vegetable crops. Tree crops include palm nuts, bananas, *coeur de boeuf,* guava, lemon, mango, orange, papaya, pineapple, citron, pistachio and other nuts. Cotton is grown as a cash crop, and tobacco is cultivated in small plots for personal use, as is hemp.

It has frequently been suggested that many of the crops grown by the Basongye were introduced to them by the Arabs. Most often cited in this connection is rice (Anon. 1891a:83; Anon. 1894a:47; Chaltin 1894:175; Stanley 1899:II,96; Wauters 1886b:73), and other food crops attributed to the same source include beans, millet, peas, sorghum, coffee (Laurent 1896a:350), citron, orange, guava, mango, papaya, lemon, avocado, pineapple, pawpaw, and pomegranate. Early accounts (Anon. 1890;Anon. 1891c) also indicate that Westerners began cultivating for their own purposes almost as soon as they were stationed in the area; frequently mentioned are Western vegetables, as well as rice, maize, and manioc.

While crops are theoretically planted at specific times each year, it is evident that much variation occurs. The minor vegetables are usually planted in October, but may be planted "whenever one has time." Maize, peanuts, and tobacco are usually planted in October, while manioc, yams, and cotton are planted in December. In many instances, however, two plantings are made of the same crop; peanuts, for example, are often planted in December as well as in October, manioc is planted in March and October, as well as December, and other crops may be planted at similarly varied times.

Peanuts (*Arachis hypogaea L.*) are planted in holes 4–5 inches deep, usually by the woman who holds a short-handled hoe in her right hand and a handful of peanuts in her left. With each chop of the hoe, a single peanut is dropped; the planter counts on the dirt turned over for the next hole to cover the seed. Peanuts may also be planted with manioc, and in this case two peanuts are dropped to the side of the prepared hole and covered with earth. When ready for harvest, the plants are pulled from the ground by women who allow them to dry about a week, either lying in the fields or stripped from the plants, taken to the village, and spread out on mats.

Maize (*Zea mays L.*) is planted in the same fashion as peanuts. The short-handled hoe is held in the right hand and the seed in the left; a swift chop is made into the already loosened ground, and with the same motion a seed is dropped into the hole. The hole in this case is covered with a twist of the hoe, and a small quantity of brush is raked over it to protect the seed from the birds.

Manioc (*Manihot esculenta crantz; manihot utilissima pohl.*) is planted in mounds about 18 inches apart, 4–5 inches high, and in rows about two feet apart. Branches from old plants are used; these are cut into 6–8 inch lengths and are put into the ground to a depth of approximately 3 inches with the nodules where new branches have begun to form pointing up. If the nodules point down, the manioc will not grow well. The sticks are planted, one to a mound, at an angle of about 45 degrees; if planted straight up and down, it is thought that the plant will go to useless root without producing tubers. Two species of manioc are planted, one slightly poisonous without preparation, and the other immediately edible.

The roster of known plant illnesses is neither extensive nor complex. The Lupupans hold that crop blight or failure may be caused by insects, magic, or poor soil. One of the remedies for poor soil is the use of goat manure, but such fertilizing is seldom practiced except occasionally around the bases of trees, although the villagers claim that the use of manure was known before the arrival of Westerners. Crop failure is exceedingly rare, and famine is virtually unknown. Indeed, the only instance of conditions

67

approaching a famine occurred sometime between 1914 and 1918 when a plague of locusts descended for approximately twenty-four hours; the result is now spoken of as a lean season when "nearly everyone went hungry," but it is also remembered as a unique event.

Agricultural practices were modified in the colonial era by the presence of Belgian agricultural officers, who attempted to enforce certain laws of the Belgian Congo and to introduce new methods of farming. The agent in Tshofa in 1959–60, for example, constantly argued the merits of fertilizer to the Lupupans, though his efforts were mostly unsuccessful.

Under the laws of the Belgian Congo, each male in the Secteur de Tshofa classified as "homme adult valid" and "cultivateur" was obliged to plant thirty *ares* (a plot 10 meters by 10 meters) of cotton; although he was further required to cultivate the plant, gather it, and prepare it for selling, he was not obliged to sell it, having the option of burning it instead. He was also required to clear his field of old cotton stalks before September 1 of each year. The second obligation of a farmer was to plant 20 *ares* of beans or peanuts, and to plant manioc in the same field at the same time. If peanuts were chosen, twenty-six kilos (57.2 lbs.) were to be saved for next year's seed, with the remainder of the crop to be disposed of at the choice of the farmer; if beans were chosen, no further regulations were in effect.

Thus, in theory, the farmer was only obliged to plant and to harvest; the disposition of the crop was his to decide. In fact, however, these plantings, and the subsequent sale of the crop to representatives of COTONCO and other firms, were absolutely necessary since the farmer was liable for annual taxes which had to be paid in cash. Chief among these was an "income tax" which the local administrator assessed by estimating the total income for the secteur, based primarily on cotton and peanut production, and dividing the total by the number of horticulturalists. For 1960, the average income for the Secteur de Tshofa was set at 5,500 francs, and computations were made on a sliding scale which resulted in a tax of from 20 to 1,020 francs. In addition, a polygynist paid a tax of 105 francs per wife for each wife over one; the *rachat de tribut*, 20 francs, went to the Chef de Secteur; the *taxe routier*, 50 francs, went for road upkeep and replaced former forced labor on the roads; the *impôt de capitation,* 100 francs, a head tax; and taxes of 42 francs on each bicycle and 70 francs on each gun. It was primarily from the sale of cotton and peanut crops that the money for these taxes was obtained.

Figure 6 shows the cotton production in Lupupa Ngye in 1959. Based on these figures, the "average" cotton farmer received an income of approximately 1,000 francs, or twenty dollars, which might or might not be sufficient to pay his taxes. Assuming that cotton production alone would not result in enough income for taxes, the following figures indicate other sources in 1959, including peanuts which are the second cash crop. In this case, however, no figures apply to yields in Lupupa Ngye specifically, and in the table, yields are based on averages for the secteur as a whole.

Fig. 6

Cotton Production in Lupupa Ngye, 1959

Planters	Number of Planters	Area		Production		
		Total Hectares	Average Area	Average by Planter	Average by Hectare	Total
Forced	34	20.57	60	232 kg.	383 kg.	7894 kg.
Free	20	6.11	30	114 kg.	377 kg.	2291 kg.
Total	54	26.68			381 kg.	10185 kg.

Production		Revenue			
First Quality	Second Quality	First Quality	Second Quality	Total	Per Person
5236 kg.	2658 kg.	30,629.60	10,632	41,261.60	1,213.5
1613 kg.	678 kg.	9,436.05	2,712	12,148.05	607.4
6849 kg.	3336 kg.	40,065.65	13,344	53,409.65	989.7

In 1959, the sale price of peanuts was 5 francs per kilo unshelled, and 18 francs shelled. If the average farmer produced an average adjusted yield of 231.46 kilos of peanuts, recalling that 26 kilos were held out for seed by law, making a marketable total of 205.46 kilos, assuming that none of the crop was kept for home consumption (highly unlikely), and counting upon the custom of the Lupupans of selling peanuts unshelled, the average income per farmer was 1,027.50 francs. Cotton and peanuts, then, produce the largest single share of the Lupupans' cash income, while the other

69

Fig. 7
Agricultural Production in the Secteur de Tshofa, 1959

Product	Planters	Area Total Hectares	Average Area	Average Yield/Hectare in Secteur de Tshofa	Total Yield: Lupupa Ngye	Average Yield/Planter: Lupupa Ngye	Adjusted Yield/Planter: Lupupa Ngye*
maize	42	18.66	44	1,600 kg.	29,856 kg.	710.85 kg.	473.9 kg.
millet	5	.82	16	1,430 kg.	14,929.20 kg.	347.19 kg.	231.46 kg.
peanuts	43	10.44	24				
beans	34	8.65	25				
manioc	40	25.62	64	14,850 kg.	380,457 kg.	9,511.42 kg.	3,170.47 kg.
rice	6	1.51	25				

* Average yield per planter: Lupupa Ngye, refers to the actual weight of fresh produce; the agricultural officer suggests that in order to obtain actual weights (which would apply for sale weights, for example), the total for manioc must be reduced to one third of the gross, and that for peanuts, beans, millet, maize, and rice must be reduced to two thirds of the gross. Thus the adjusted yield per planter: Lupupa Ngye.

crops (and to a considerable extent peanuts as well) are used for personal consumption.

In addition to horticulture, the people of Lupupa Ngye practice hunting, an activity which is looked upon favorably even though it yields little result. During the period from approximately September, 1959, through the middle of June, 1960, hunting from the village produced no more than four or five antelope of medium size, a bush pig or two, several pythons, a rather large number of bush rodents, and some guinea fowl. Despite the small yield, several 'men regard themselves as hunters and devote considerable time to it; they receive the general approval and plaudits of the community.

The master hunter, of which the village boasts of one, is called *fundi*; this is a title of respect which the individual himself uses initially and which is then adopted (or not adopted) by the villagers as a matter of consent and acknowledgment. A *fundi* cannot lose his title; once granted social recognition for his skill, he retains it even if he ceases to hunt. In addition to this general respect, the hunter who has killed a leopard receives special recognition; he ties a square of raffia cloth around his head and attaches the bright red feather of the *nduba* (s. & pl.) bird to it. He also may tie a square of the same cloth around his right wrist and left ankle, and wear all three pieces for a month.

Hunters list the following game in the area; those followed by (x) are represented by two or more types: antelope (x), wild pig (x), monkey (x), leopard (x), rat, python, lion, hippopotamus, crocodile (x), pheasant, and grouse (x). The type of animal hunted is the basis for nine "classes" of hunting, again as visualized, though not specifically named, by the hunters themselves. These classes are as follows: (1) leopards, lions, and water animals are not specifically hunted but are killed when encountered; they may also be trapped; (2) antelope of all types are hunted by net, gun, dog, and bow and arrow; (3) pigs are hunted with gun and with bow and arrow, but not with nets because pigs can destroy nets and escape; (4) monkeys are hunted with bow and arrow or with guns, but not with nets; (5) elephants can only be hunted with the gun and must be shot just above the eye; they are virtually nonexistent in the area; (6) rats are caught in snares and traps and may be taken with bow and arrow; (7) pythons are hunted with the machete; (8) hippopotami are hunted with the gun only; (9) birds are taken with gun, bow and arrow, and snares. With few exceptions, hunters take only antelope, pig, monkey, rat, python, and birds; the larger animals are extremely rare.

Hunters stress that their activities make it necessary that they be allowed to move everywhere, no matter who owns the land, and they do so. In theory, however, a hunter must obtain advance permission from the notables in order to hunt on the land of another village; this does not apply to the lands of Lupupa Kampata or Makola because "we are the same people they are." If permission is granted, the hunter gives the notables a chicken and they, in turn, make *kwela mukishi* for his success: this is a request to the spirits of the dead, accompanied by the sacrifice of a chicken which is decapitated and its blood allowed to drip upon the ground. In return for the hunting rights, the hunter must give the first animal and half of each subsequent animal killed to the *chite* (the second-highest political dignitary in the hierarchy) who in turn distributes the meat among the other notables. The same permission must be sought by strangers who wish to place animal traps on the land of another village, or who wish to fish in its streams or gather palm nuts from its trees.

Permission is normally granted, but it may be refused if a hunter asks permission a second time after not having met his obligations previously, or if he is known to be a disreputable or dishonest person. If someone hunts despite denial of permission, his kill may be taken from him by force or, in extreme cases, he may be captured and taken before the chief of the Bala for judgment—this is one of the few instances in which the Lupupans acknowledge a direct connection between their own affairs and the Bala authorities. If the judgment goes against the trespasser, he must pay a fine to the people of Lupupa Ngye and must also work a stated length of time for the chief of the Bala.

It seems virtually certain that hunting was more important in the past than at present, both because game was formerly more plentiful, and because of the considerable amount of magic practice which surrounds hunting today. Thus the *mwabi* tree on Bena Yewusha land was planted by the former chief, Nkolomoni; its existence assures the villagers of good fortune in hunting. When a lion or leopard has killed someone in the village, a hunter who is also versed in magic practice takes sand from the tracks of the animal, places it in the bark of the *mwabi* tree, ties the bundle in leaves of the *mbata* (s. & pl.) tree, and buries the entire package in one of the tracks. He then removes his own belt, since it is made of animal skin, and pursues the marauder; the magic ensures that it will be easy to find and, once found, easy to kill. Two houseyards in the village contain structures which stand on four legs with tails at either end. These are *milopwe a batwa* (s. & pl.), magic apparatuses which enable the owner to "be like a pygmy and do the things a pygmy does"; it is believed that the pygmies, who inhabit the area in scattered groups, have special knowledge of the forest and the animals within it, and that they are particularly sensitive and successful hunters. *Kwimonena* gives the hunter power to sight game before others. A special magic to prevent snakebite when hunting requires the head of a poison serpent and a wood chip from a place where someone else has been chopping (the type of tree does not matter); these are burned together. The hunter-magician then makes a cut in the top of his left wrist and rubs the charcoal into it; the magic is effective only for the individual, not for a group of hunters.

Hunters are also protected by special songs, *ngono ya bampibwe* (s. *lono lwa mpibwe*), sung both before and after the hunt. A small group of singers—no more than eight in number—is considered optimum, and the song may be accompanied by the *pandala* (s. & pl.), a side-blown antelope horn, or the *epudi* (pl. *mapudi*), an ocarina; a miming dance is part of the performance. The purpose of the song-dance before the hunt is to ask the ancestral spirits for success in the hunt. The participants may also perform a magic ceremony in which a small shelter is made, a chicken killed and its blood dropped on the hunters' guns, and a piece of chicken as well as maize-manioc bread thrown on the ground for the *mikishi* (s. *mukishi*, vengeful spirits of dead humans). The song-dance performed after the hunt is to thank the spirits of the dead for success and to obtain their cooperation and assistance for the next foray.

Hunting techniques recognized by the master hunter include tracking, *kubembela*, "he follows"; stalking, *kubinga*, "he hunts"; ambush, *kutengela*, "he waits"; running down, *kulonda*, "he pursues"; and surprising (to the hunter who happens to meet an animal without warning), *kufumankana,* "he meets." In ambush, hunters hide at water holes and wait for game, but the master hunter says that he does not stay very long in one place "because there are lots of water holes" and the animals may be elsewhere. Animals are said to drink in the morning from 5:45 to 7:00 A.M., and in the afternoon from 5:00 to 6:00 P.M.; the hunter arrives a little before these hours in order to be in good position. Natural salt licks are known, but the closest one is near Tshofa and hunters from Lupupa Ngye do not go that far to hunt. In running down an animal, the hunter may follow for as much as a day or a night, but if the quarry is not taken within that time, he feels it is no use to continue. Hunters do not disguise themselves by wrapping themselves in animal skins, nor do they use portable screens, blinds, or model decoys. Certain antelope may be attracted by wrapping one's head (with eyeholes cut) in white Americani cloth. The *mbudi* (s. & pl.) antelope is called by holding the nose, cupping the other hand before the mouth, and making a particular sound, while the *kasha* (s. & pl.) antelope is called by blowing across the edge of a leaf. No birds or animals, other than dogs, are trained for the chase.

The village *fundi* feels that the best way of hunting is with a group of people divided into two parts, one consisting of about ten men with guns, and the other of about five men with dogs. Dogs are used to drive game toward the hunters. No special training is provided young dogs; but a promising animal is given meat to eat, and if he continues well, he is finally taken over as a hunting dog. This involves special magic in which the hunter-magician takes a piece of the intestine of any animal, a piece of the brain of any animal, some dirt from the track of any animal, and a piece of the wood of the *kalonda mishi* tree, mixes them together with water, and puts a bit of the mixture into each nostril of the dog; this keeps the dog aware of the scent of animals and may be repeated before every hunt. If the hunter wishes to pursue a specific animal, he cooks a quantity of maize with the intestines of a monkey; at the time of preparation he names the animal he wishes to capture and gives the mixture to the dog to eat, so that it will pursue only the animal named. Besides driving game, the dog's work is to corner animals for the hunter to kill. Since dogs are not trained as retrievers (considered impossible because "dogs want to eat the meat"), it is up to the hunter to be on the spot when a small animal is cornered.

74

Dogs are belled so that the hunter will know where they are; the special wooden bells, which are stuffed with leaves to prevent noise when stealth is needed, are called *kidibu* (pl. *bidibu*). The side-blown antelope horn is used both to encourage the dogs into attacking an animal and to call them home. In spite of the availability and established practice of using dogs, the master hunter says he does not often use them because "they make too much noise and they always want to chase the game." He does take a dog, however, when he knows an animal with young is about, for it will search out the young.

Group hunting always involves drives of one sort or another. In a simple drive, a group of beaters flails the bush with long sticks and keeps up sustained noise as it moves in an arc toward those who are waiting with guns. No fences or other enclosures are built to guide game in a drive, nor are they built to hold animals at the end of a drive, but fire is sometimes used in driving. If game is known to be in a certain patch of land, fire is set on three sides of the area with the armed person or persons stationed on the fourth; this can only be done where cleared or cultivated land is located on the fourth side, or the hunter would be in too much danger. Game is not driven over cliffs or into pits.

Net hunting is also practiced with groups of people. In the forest an area can be completely encircled with nets (*bukoncha*, s. & pl.) and the dogs sent in to flush out the game. In more open country, a combination of the drive and nets is used. The master hunter often selects a small valley for the drive, and once his group has gathered he gives a number of instructions and reminders. He may tell his fellows not to let *anything* go by, for if they hope always to take something bigger they will almost surely be disappointed; he gives directions for placing the nets and for placing all members of the party; he tells all to be serious and not to giggle and laugh, saying that they are present to hunt, not to have a good time; he reminds them how to aim their guns; and he encourages them by pointing out the advantages of the spot chosen and assuring them that game will be taken.

If the area is a valley in which a stream is running, the nets are placed on both sides of the stream, along the edge of a path if one is present. The tips of the bush grass are bunched together and tied into a simple knot at the top in order to provide support for the nets

75

which are attached by draping a mesh over the knot. This support is strong enough to hold the net but also weak enough so that it will not collapse when even small animals hurtle into it. Some care is taken to see that the net is resting on the ground along its bottom edge, but the bottom is not fastened down in any way. The nets are eighty to ninety feet long and four feet high; they are made by, and bought from, neighboring pygmies at a cost of 150 to 300 frs., depending upon their length.

Once the nets are in place, the master hunter lays out his strategy and sends his fellows to their stations; equipment present usually includes two nets, several guns, and some bows and arrows, as well as the dogs. The beaters begin from as much as half a mile away and work toward the nets, shouting, blowing horns, singing, beating with sticks, and accompanied by the dogs with their bells unsilenced. The drive may last as long as forty minutes, and the game obtained varies from nothing to a small antelope or a bush pig.

One further net strategy has apparently been borrowed from the pygmies; in this case, the netting is placed as in the diagram below and arranged on sticks placed so that it will collapse on the animal that runs into it. The animals are driven from the indicated direction.

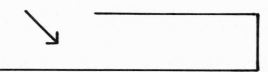

Poison is used on arrow and lance points; it is made from the vine, *lengo*. Some say that a portion of the vine alone is used; others say that a number of other ingredients must be added, including a knife, snake's teeth, leopard teeth, lion teeth, the tip of *mabamba* (s. *ebamba*, a bush grass), and a small piece of lance point. Whatever the case, the *lengo* is crushed in a mortar, combined with water, and left to soak for a day. On the second day, the brew is boiled, the undissolved pieces of vine removed, and the water reheated until the mixture thickens, when it is put in a covered pot. Before dipping weapons, the poison may be tried out on a small domesticated animal, and "if it can run more than ten meters without falling dead, the *lengo* is no good" and must be strengthened. *Lengo* is kept in liquid form, hung over the head of the owner's bed. Menstruating women must not touch the mixture, although they may see it, because it would become weak "like a woman." "When you shoot a poisoned arrow at someone, it will kill him within an hour, even if it only goes close to him." If the wrong man is wounded, he can be saved by bathing him for an hour in water only. When a hunter kills an animal by this means, he cuts out a chunk of meat around the wound in order to avoid poisoning those who will eat the flesh; hunters believe that the mixture works by circulating through the animal's bloodstream.

Small loop snares are placed over field mouse and field rat holes, and snares are also used to capture birds. Glue is sometimes smeared on tree branches, and a nearby termite hill opened to attract birds; when they alight, their feet stick, and when they try to peck them loose, their beaks stick. Corn, palm nuts, and rice are used as bird baits; parts of old kills are used for animals, a chicken for the fox, a goat for the leopard. Fairly heavy deadfall traps are constructed, as are complete enclosures with falling doors; in the latter a special type is designed for lions and leopards. Pit traps are dug to a depth of six to ten feet with the bottom furnished with lances fastened point upward and the opening covered with grass; the hunter is responsible for warning the populace of its location. A gun may be set up on two forked sticks with a cord running from the trigger across a game trail to a tree; the gun is aimed at the spot where the cord crosses the path. The ambush is also specially organized for lions and leopards by suspending a piece of meat left from a previous kill in such a position that the animal's head will be close to the muzzle of the gun when the mechanism is tripped. A spear may be fixed in the root of a tree on a game trail; animals are chased down the trail with dogs in the hope they will run into the spear.

A special technique for hunting bush rats is practiced by preschool children and groups of women after the lairs have been exposed by burning the bush. Rats often nest in the center of small, abandoned anthills; the hard outer surface of the hill is chopped away with a short-handled hoe, and a stick is driven into the soft interior. The stick is then withdrawn, leaving a hole into which the hunter breathes heavily; it is thought that this alerts the rat to danger and drives him from his nest.

77

Division of the kill is a complex process which involves considerable knowledge and diplomacy, for the claims of a number of persons must be considered. Certain portions of all kills go to the notables, in theory at least, but which portions and their sizes depend upon the size and type of animal; the same factors, plus a number of political considerations, determine which notables must be considered in which divisions of game. As a simple example, if a medium-sized antelope is taken on a group hunt, one half of the animal and its head go to the one who killed it, one foreleg goes to the beaters, and the remainder is divided among all the other participants. If a large antelope is taken, the chest and one hind leg go to the chief and the notables, one hind quarter and the back to the person who made the kill, one foreleg to the beaters, and the other foreleg to the other hunters. Many disputes occur over the division of game, for the rules are complex, but even simple rules are the subject of much wrangling; for example, if two hunters fire simultaneously and it is truly impossible to determine which one killed the animal, the carcass is in theory divided between the two, right down the middle. In fact, such a situation would be the cause of endless contention which might only be finally resolved through formal litigation.

While hunting is purely a male activity, fishing is practiced both by men and by women, although men predominate. Some men, as with the hunters, are known for their special skill as fishermen, although no term comparable to the hunters' *fundi* exists. Fishing technology includes various applications of hook and line, six kinds of traps and weirs, netting, and poisoning; women are involved in the last two, but men practice all four.

Hook and line fishing is based upon a simple stick, usually about four feet long, a line of varied lengths, and a hook, which may be either of local or Western manufacture. Stone sinkers (*mitumbi*, s. *mutumbi*) are used in some kinds of fishing, and floats (*tupungu*, s. *kapungu*) in others. Fishermen do not view their activity as sport, and as a consequence they do not play the fish which is, instead, jerked from the water at first sign of a bite. Stationary lines are set, some thirty or forty at a time; these are very short lines tied to sticks along the bank. A special implement, the *sokoloni* (s. & pl.), is used to get hook and line into difficult fishing spots, such as places where the bank overhangs the river or where underground pools or channels are known to exist. Night fishing with torches is known but seldom practiced; it is believed that the light is for the use of the fishermen only and, indeed, it drives fish away.

Of the six kinds of fish traps, four involve the use of funnel-shaped structures or mechanisms. Two different principles are operative as the basis of these funnel traps: in the first, the funnel is placed so that the fish is either driven into it or forced to seek it as the only possible outlet (as in the case of a weir, for example), and then held in by the force of the current. In the second, the fish enters the mouth of the funnel and passes on through the small end into another enclosure; the funnel is constructed so that the fish can move through it only in the one direction. Two fish traps involve a closing door; one is a falling door, while the other snaps shut with great speed through a tension mechanism released by the fish pulling at the bait. Baits include insects of various kinds, palm nuts (considered especially good), palm tree grubs, and a dough of palm oil and manioc flour.

Fish poisoning is carried out primarily by women, though in the end it is essentially a cooperative endeavor. The poison, *kabaa* or *kabaa ka lukasu* (s. & pl.), is made by women who crush the leaves and stalks of two bushes, *mantungulu* (s. & pl.) and *tchiya* (s. & pl.). The mixture is placed in a loosely woven basket which is partially filled with dirt; at the riverbank, water is added and the poison drips through the basket as a red liquid. While the poison is not strong enough to kill adult humans, children might be sickened by it, and thus the leaves are not crushed in the regular mortar. The liquid may be distributed as much as five kilometers upstream; men or women then walk along the bank, following the poison by its red color and collecting the dead fish which float to the surface. Women make a special wicker barrier (*eyambo*, pl. *mayambo*) to catch poisoned fish which they cannot take by hand or which escape their surveillance, and men sometimes put traps downstream from the poisoning area to catch fish "which flee from the poison."

Fish nets (*bukoncha*, s. & pl.) are made from raffia fiber. Although the Lupupan fishermen know how to make them, they are often purchased from the nearby village of Lumba Lupata, whose people are considered to be especially adept at the task. A large net can be bought for approximately 200 francs, and smaller nets for prices between 150 and 200 francs. The net used in a

79

particular situation is chosen to be as long as the width of the stream to be fished and as high as the stream is deep. Its top and bottom edges are tied to horizontal sticks, and the fishermen stand on the bottom stick in the water and hold the top stick in their hands. Two people are required to hold the net, and a third enters the water about seventy-five yards upstream and splashes his way toward them. The net is woven so that its meshes are large enough to allow fish to pass through it but small enough to direct them toward the inevitable downstream bulge in its middle. Behind this bulge in the big net is placed a smaller, fine-meshed and sack-shaped net; this is held by rim sticks pushed into the river bottom. When the fish have been moved toward the center of the big net and driven through into the smaller net, the latter is lifted out of the water.

Another net used is a rather large hand net, the mouth of which is shaped into a round opening by a flexible support. Two men hold the net along the river bottom, pushing the mouth down into an oblong shape; when fish enter, the net is lifted out of the water.

Women use three means of catching fish, in addition to poisoning. Small ponds are dammed and bailed, and fish caught in this way are killed with a knife. A special small fishing basket is used to seine fish out of similar ponds; and a longer and larger basket is used to seine in the river.

The villagers divide fish into six major varieties and subdivide one of these groups into six subclasses; the various qualities of each type of fish are well known, and certain types are prized more than others. No fishing is done by hand, and no gorges, harpooning, trained animals, or bow and arrows are used.

When more than one man is involved, such as in net fishing, he who owns the equipment divides and distributes the catch, keeping for himself a larger portion than that he gives to the others. If one borrows a net or hook and line equipment, he is expected to give a small portion of the catch to the owner. The entire course of the river through the lands of Lupupa Ngye is open to all comers. If one has a flighty or venturesome wife, he will not have luck in fishing, and if a male fisherman on his way to fish meets another male fisherman on the path, his luck will be poor. One should not be jealous of another who has better luck, and one should call upon the ancestors and Efile Mukulu for success.

Relatively few foods are gathered in comparison to the variety of cultivated crops, and gathering "expeditions" are rare, occurring only when some special food, such as the mushroom, is in season; in this case, a few women may go out together. Various insects swarm at certain seasons of the year, and these are occasions on which the entire village is involved with considerable ensuing fun and excitement. Women do most of the gathering, on the way to and from the fields, when searching for wood or carrying water, when going to the river to bathe, and on other similar occasions; men gather edible foods in the same kinds of casual situations, but gathering is not their responsibility except in the case of palm tree grubs which are considered a great delicacy and which are usually chopped from felled trees. Women are the specific gatherers of some insects, the leaves of some plants, and fruits of several kinds. Both sexes gather ants, small water animals and insects, rats, termites, mushrooms, and nuts. Children gather wild berries, which they eat on the spot. All in all, gathering does not account for a major portion of the foods which comprise the diet; instead, gathered foods tend to be delicacies and much-welcomed special treats.

A considerable variety of foods is available to the Lupupans, though the formal meals of the day appear to a Westerner to be dull and lacking in variety. Villagers name as food, in addition to those which are gathered, twenty-three kinds of meat, five kinds of fish, seven kinds of ants and termites, seven other kinds of insects, thirty-two vegetables, sixteen fruits (and three fruit juice concoctions), as well as salt (both indigenous and Western) and eggs. These are minimum numbers.

While food tastes vary, of course, the basic item of the diet in almost all households is a maize-manioc porridge (biyashi) referred to by the people as "bread." This dish is made from three cups of water, two cups of sifted maize flour and six cups of sifted manioc flour. The flour is added to boiling water a little at a time, boiled briefly, removed from the fire and muddled, and the thick mixture plopped into a round-bottomed bowl; after sitting for a few moments, the porridge is removed, and may be eaten immediately or later when cold. No salt is used in its preparation; it is considered tastiest when eaten with warmed manioc greens. A piece of the thick porridge is pinched off, held in the right hand, dipped in the greens, and eaten. The taste is flat, and the texture gummy and doughy to the Western palate.

During the month of March, 1960, the food prepared by a sample of six women in the village was recorded. The importance of the maize-manioc porridge is emphasized by the fact that it was eaten at 85 of the 129 meals prepared, a much greater use than that of any other food. The following chart represents the major ingredients of the 129 meals, and the number of times each ingredient was used.

Fig. 8

Food Prepared and Consumed: Lupupa Ngye, March, 1960

Meat, fish, & eggs	Vegetables	Grains	Root Crops	Fungi	Fruits
Fish — 24	manioc	maize (in	manioc (in	mush-	banana
Smoked	leaves	porridge)	porridge)	rooms	— 7
elephant	— 54	— 85	— 85	— 8	pine-
— 12	beans — 21	rice — 21	peanuts — 8		apple
Unknown			manioc — 2		— 2
smoked					
meat — 5					
Chicken					
— 4					
Unknown					
meat — 3					
Goat — 2					
Pork — 1					
Eggs — 1					

Beans and rice tend to be served together, but no other food combinations are especially popular except for the maize-manioc porridge and manioc leaves. Manioc is almost never consumed alone; rather, it is used almost exclusively as an ingredient in the porridge. A strong tendency is evident to eat any scarce commodity on hand until the supply is exhausted; this is particularly noticeable in the case of meat which is always scarce, and mushrooms, for example, which are seasonal. Meals often consist of a single food, such as peanuts or pineapple, and the Western ideal of a varied menu is absent; neither is the diet a balanced one. Some seasonings, such as hot peppers, are used, and it should be emphasized that no account is taken in Figure 8 of possible minor side dishes. Neither does the chart show the consumption of palm oil, a highly valued and frequently used food. Further, diet changes somewhat with the seasons; some families, for example, eat corn on the cob in season, as well as tomatoes and other vegetables, and peanuts provide a substantial portion of the diet for a period after the harvest.

One of the chronic dietary problems for the Lupupans is the lack of meat, and the villagers are very much aware of this. The Belgian agricultural officer estimated the percentages of total animal protein intake for the Secteur de Tshofa as follows:

Pisciculture	0.5%
Fresh fish	1.5%
Dried fish	7.0%
Canned food	1.0%
Domesticated Large animals	0.0%
Domesticated Small animals	16.0%
Fowls	3.0%
Hunting	70.0%
Fresh insects	0.5%
Dried insects	0.5%

It is not known how accurately these estimates apply to the people of Lupupa Ngye, but if hunting is the source of 70 percent of the intake of animal protein, the Lupupans are indeed badly undernourished in this respect. The agricultural officer also estimated that for the year 1959, total consumption of meat in the categories listed above was 70,557 kilograms as against his estimate of the amount needed—96,837 kilograms: the problem of lack of animal protein is a real one.

Food preparation falls exclusively in the woman's domain, though men can cook for themselves in emergencies; since women also take part in planting, cultivation, and harvesting, their usual day is devoted in considerable part to activities concerned with food. Women arise early and leave for the fields at approximately 6:00 A.M.; no meal is prepared or served in the morning, nor do men or women usually eat anything at this time. The first co-wife to return to the house, perhaps between noon and 1:00 P.M., prepares the noon meal if it is not to be taken in the fields. While it is obvious that a lazy woman could avoid this task simply by staying in the fields, the Lupupans are quick to point out that it is the husband's responsibility to regulate such behavior. Although the co-wives do not pool their food reserves, one may borrow from another. Food preparation may take as much as two or three hours, and the "noon" meal may thus be delayed until late afternoon: once it has been prepared and eaten and the kitchen and dishes cleaned, the woman pursues afternoon tasks such as preparation of basic foodstuffs, wood gathering in the forest, and a trip to bring water from the river. Another two hours may be spent in preparing the evening meal, and bedtime is usually about 9:00 P.M. for older women and perhaps an hour later for younger.

Food is served in the cooking pots in which it has been prepared; the woman brings it to her husband's house. Meat is usually cut into pieces before cooking, but if a large piece is prepared intact, the husband cuts it into serving pieces. Custom differs at this point; in some families the husband serves the food to the individual members of the family, beginning with the first wife and finishing with the youngest child; in other households, the husband simply takes his portion, and the remaining food is divided by those who will eat it. The wives take their food and that of their daughters, and retire to their kitchens to eat while male children stay with their father in his house; this traditional custom is clearly changing today. It is considered polite to eat until one is fully satisfied, but he should not finish all the food in a pot, even if he has not eaten for some time and even if he is a husband sitting alone in his house. Women differ in their disposition of leftovers; some say they are kept and served at the next meal, others that they are thrown out into the bush. Since drying and smoking (considered synonymous) are the only real means of food preservation, it is clear that leftovers must be utilized quickly if they are not to be wasted. A number of rules for eating and for food serving are both theorized and observed in connection with visits of various in-laws, immediate family, and strangers.

Probably because famine is so far from their thoughts, the people declare that they would never descend to eating certain foods. Travelers carry peanuts and smoked or dried meat if it is available. No special foods are eaten before especially hard labor, before going to war, or, with some exceptions, when one is ill. Food is never used as a medium of exchange. Cooking was created by Efile Mukulu through the agency of Kalala Lunga (though most women would not know this specifically), and all mothers teach their daughters how to cook. No recipes are kept, and it is supposed that all women cook in the same ways; neither does cooking change. "Since oil, water, and flour are all alike, the only thing that could make one woman's cooked products different from another's is the care of preparation, and some women do take more pains than others, cooking more slowly."

Ritual eating occurs at various points in the life cycle, such as at the appearance of a child's first tooth when the father presents a chicken to the child, the mother cooks it, and all three eat together. Other occasions for ritual eating occur, for example, at gatherings in which men pledge to assist in building a house. Many food prohibitions exist. Neither the husband nor his pregnant wife may eat any animal killed by strangling since this produces a distended stomach which will be repeated in the wife and in the child. Eating sweet potatoes will reduplicate the wrinkled skin of the tuber in the child. Women are enjoined from eating lion, leopard, or python, which are reserved to men "because they are strong, dangerous, angry." Other prohibitions fit both particular occasions and certain societal relationships and responsibilities based upon kinship.

It is evident from the record that in former times cannibalism contributed another source of animal protein. The existence of this practice has been reported over and over again, and from the earliest written records concerning the Basongye (for example, Hinde 1897); the Bala were no exception in this respect. While cannibalism is often practiced as ritual, neither the written record nor the recollections of informants attest to such a reason in this case. Lupupans state unequivocally that human beings were eaten, first, "because the meat is very, very, very good. You like it so much that you don't talk while eating." And second, it was eaten in order to "punish someone who has done something to you," and adultery and warfare are most often mentioned in this connection.

In those cases in which people were deliberately killed, the job was assigned to a special appointee, the *nalupete* (s. & pl.) who was a member of the political hierarchy. The victim was taken to a special house called *Kisongo,* which was located apart from the other houses in the village. There he was killed by the *nalupete* who, theoretically at least, did so by a single blow on the back of the neck with a stick of hard wood. The *nalupete* then cut up, prepared, and distributed the meat; when the killing was formalized and the meat prepared for the notables, it was eaten at the *Kisongo,* but under ordinary circumstances, it could be eaten anywhere.

Human flesh was most often eaten with plantains, but also with maize-manioc porridge; it was considered to be both oily and salty, and much water was taken with it. The flesh was roasted, and all parts of the body were eaten except the hair and nails. Brains were considered especially good, and frequent comparison is made between the eyeballs and boiled eggs. Women never prepared the meat nor did they partake of it. A special song, *kusha bukume* ("dance" "strong"), was sung, but it is no longer known in the village.

Water is sometimes drunk with meals, but most meals are taken without beverages. Two kinds of palm wine are known to the Lupupans, the first obtained by tapping the live tree, and the second by felling the tree, shaping its upper end to a rough point, and allowing the sap to flow into a container. Corn liquor is distilled from a mash made of shelled corn and grated manioc peelings, and a fermented pineapple wine is made. Men are the makers of palm wine, but women are responsible for corn liquor and pineapple wine.

In addition to alcoholic beverages, pineapple, orange, and lemon juice are drunk. The fruit is peeled and pounded in a clean mortar, and the juice is then poured off, brought to a boil for the sake of preservation, and stored in bottles. Salt and red pepper may be added to the juices for flavoring, and lemon juice itself is sometimes used as a flavoring in cooking.

New beverages have been introduced to the villagers, and these include various cola drinks as well as Western beer; both are too expensive, however, to be consumed regularly. Whiskey, gin and other Western hard liquors are known to the Lupupans, but they are never purchased and seldom seen or tasted.

Drunkenness is sometimes a problem in the village, both in individual and group contexts. While drunkenness is tolerated and, indeed, not considered an offense per se, habitual drunkenness, and especially that which disrupts public events, is strongly disapproved. One man in the village would be classified as an alcoholic in Western terms; the Lupupans distinguish sharply between his drinking and that of the casual drunk, saying that "he cannot help it." To sober a drunk, a mixture of peanuts and a small amount of manioc is cooked with oil and fed to the person. "Group" drunkenness occurs in conjunction with the agricultural cycle; in those periods when agricultural work has slacked off, a number of men may be drunk at any given time, and numerous disputes break out, some of which are settled by brief physical combat involving weapons. Women do not often drink to drunkenness, nor do most of the men save at those points in the labor cycle when much more leisure time than usual is available.

Tobacco (*fwanka*, s. & pl.) is grown in small plots either in or very near the lineage land, and in the fields as well. The leaves are prepared by drying them in the sun for two or three days; they are then placed in a pot over the fire and turned and mixed, smashed in a small mortar, and then heated in the pot again. Heating is not employed to dry the tobacco further but to drive out small insects which may be present. At this point, a tobacco stalk and a bush (*byashina*) stalk are burned together and the ash gathered. This is placed with water in a strainer, and the liquid which runs through is added to the tobacco; after the mixture has dried, the tobacco is considered ready for use.

Tobacco is used as snuff, in a pipe, and rolled in a tobacco leaf as a cigar. Snuff is sniffed up the nose by men and by women, though women use it more frequently than men. Snuff is also placed between the lower lip and the teeth and the juice spat out; this is a habit of women and a few men. Men are the prime users of pipes, of which three kinds exist: a bowl made of wood and a stem of a part of the papaya; a straight pipe of wood, shaped rather like a Western cigarette holder; and a calabash water pipe. Cigars are also smoked mostly by men, but neither pipe nor cigar is forbidden to women, and some women do use them. The same is true of Western cigarettes, but their relatively high price in terms of the local economy mostly precludes their use except as a special treat. Smoking is definitely a leisure time activity; almost no one ever smokes while working. Although virtually everyone smokes on occasion, few seem to be dependent on tobacco.

A number of men, particularly older men, cultivate and smoke hemp (*kabangi*). A special water pipe (*mutonga,* pl. *bitonga*) is made for use in smoking, and a small calabash pipe which does not hold water is also used. One hemp smoker described hemp as stronger than tobacco, and stressed that its effect "is like being drunk. Hemp smokers are not normal people when they are smoking; they have hallucinations, get dizzy, and things swim before their eyes." He recognizes hemp smoking as habit forming, and says that an accomplished smoker must have four pipes a day while the usual smoker takes one or two pipes. The smoke is inhaled into the lungs, and a full pipeful, perhaps ten inhalations, is smoked at one time. If a smoker is without hemp "he suffers, tears come from his eyes, and he sweats and trembles." The hemp smoker may differentiate between stimulants and narcotics, using the words *kuchimba,* "something good that one can put aside," and *bukopo,* "something you must have."

Hemp smoking which stays within reason according to local standards is considered normal behavior. Excessive use which interferes with individual or social functioning, is sharply criticized and is considered anormal and improper.

Some of the processes of production, distribution, and consumption are today represented in, or paralleled by, money in the form of the centime and franc introduced by the Belgians. Western currency and what it represents, however, were by no means strange to the people of Lupupa Ngye, for a similar set of values was well established in the traditional economic system.

Chickens, goats, salt, and hoe blades were used as standards of value, but much more specifically monetary were copper crosses (*byombo,* pl. *kiyombo*), which were borrowed from the south. Two types of crosses were recognized, the *mukashi* (pl. *bakashi,* female) and the *mulume* (pl. *balume,* male), of which the former is described as being the larger and more valuable. It seems likely that the crosses were only occasionally seen and used in Bala territory, for they are seldom mentioned today and few can even describe them.

Much more important, and quite probably functioning as true money, was the *ediba* (pl. *madiba*), a piece of locally woven raffia cloth about 24 inches by 48 inches according to some informants, or 25 inches by 27 inches according to others. The *ediba* meets the money criteria of homogeneity, portability, divisibility, and dura-

88

bility, and it also functioned as a means of exchange, a standard of value, and a means of payment. It appears to have been general purpose money, although it is today impossible to be absolutely certain of this. *Madiba* were used to pay fines, to pay for medical services, to purchase a slave, and in matters of loans and interest. They were exchanged for crude iron with the Bekalebwe, used as bounties paid by the chief to those who had killed enemies in warfare, as payments to the *kifwebe* and *kalengula*, masked figures of former times, and as a social welfare payment by the citizens to the chief who, in turn, distributed them to the needy. *Madiba* were also used for the material itself, that is, as clothing, wrapping, matting, the basis for velour work, to make the *kalengula* mask, as a measure of area, and as part of the mark of a hunter who had killed a leopard.

The value of the *ediba* can be compared with other media of exchange. Thus a hoe blade was valued at ten *madiba*, a female copper cross at four *madiba*, a male copper cross at three *madiba*, one half calabash of salt (about a quart) at ten *madiba*, a goat at ten to twelve *madiba*, and a chicken at one *ediba*. While it is clear that actual equivalents in *madiba* are faultily recalled today, and that values undoubtedly changed over time, the following brief table is at least relative to itself and indicates something of the variety of goods which might be purchased.

Commodity	Value in madiba
Hen	1
Goat	10–12
Pusu skin (type of leopard)	2
Male adult slave	200
Male child slave	100
Female adult slave	100
Female child slave	211
Stalk of bananas	2
House	100
Régime of palm nuts	2
Knife	2
Axe	10
Pig (considered rare)	200
Machete	3
Mortar and pestle	3

Matters of loans, interest, and security are somewhat difficult to resolve in looking at the traditional economy, for each of these concepts is surrounded by widely differing opinions today. In a community the size of Lupupa Ngye, lending and borrowing are not likely to be highly formalized, since each individual tends to own all means necessary for production and therefore to own virtually the same things as all other individuals. Thus some informants deny that formal lending ever occurred, saying rather, that when someone borrowed an axe, for example, he was expected to give an unspecified small gift when he returned it; other informants deny that such gift giving was customary. Some speak of interest in fixed terms, some in relative terms, and some deny its formal existence. Security is a concept known to the villagers, but it may be recent only, and again opinions differ, some denying it, some saying that it was used only when lending to someone who was not a friend, and some saying that it was required in every transaction.

Those who hold for formal existence of lending, interest, and security tend to illustrate their contentions with cases involving money, either in terms of francs or *madiba*, with two exceptions. If the loan is small, no interest is charged; if the loan involves use of a tool, a gift should be returned with it, and if it has been used to produce something that makes a profit for the borrower, he should share that profit with the lender, the share being specified only as less than 50 percent. In speaking of larger amounts, informants are likely to use the figure of 100 *madiba*, but to differ widely on the amount of interest to be returned, in this case from 2 to 25 *madiba*. There is concurrence, however, on the term *kutentekyela* for "interest," and the older people (who are the only ones with whom these matters can be discussed) tend to see a sharp distinction between past and present practices, with the former involving a high degree of honor, and with mention of the latter likely to turn into a tirade against the younger generation: "Young people today always have debts and they never repay them, especially those who speak French. All the old people paid cash for their MUB [*Mouvement de l'Unite Basongye*, a political party formed in March, 1960] cards, but none of the young people did."

Those who understand security refer to it as *kyee* (pl. *biyee*), "the representative of money." The holder of security was responsible for it; if he could not return it on payment of the debt, the creditor could demand considerable compensation. The care of security is most important when the object is more valuable than the loan, and villagers are quick to cite the following proverb:

mwana	*akye*	*anyana*	*tashimina*
child	who has no father	he may become thin	he cannot lose (die)

"The child who has no father may become thin, but he doesn't die."

The child is the security; "he who has no father" is something given as security by its owner and is descriptive of the security; "may become thin" refers to the fact that the security may wear slowly; and "he cannot die" indicates that even though the security may wear out or be discarded or lost by him who holds it, the holder remains responsible and must replace it.

If the security and the debt are of equal value, the holder can use the item as he wishes, thus cancelling the debt. An example used is a small box of wooden matches given against one franc; the holder is free to use the matches.

Questions of debt are a source of major concern in the village, not infrequently leading to physical assault. Members of the older generation are wont to blame their children for this state of affairs: "There is not this continual question of debt among the older people. The young people are habituated to taking their father's things; they see that their fathers have something and they just take it. There was not much debt in the old days. People paid for things, and a debt was returned in kind. The Soko affair is the fault of Soko's father who hasn't taught him well." The last statement refers to a question of debt in which Soko, who owed 175 francs to a local store, took his father's gun and gave it to the storekeeper to cover the debt; the gun was valued at 1,800 francs and considerable anger and dispute resulted.

The problem of debt has most likely increased in relatively recent years as a result of Western impact; Western money has become both necessary and desirable, and a new variety of goods is obtainable only by using it. Among the major sources of difficulty are the local stores which extend credit indiscriminately. These shops are owned by Westerners in Tshofa, and are manned by Africans, usually non-Bala. Periodically the owners send out word that they will appear at a certain time to balance the accounts; sometimes they pick up all the goods in the store and take them to Tshofa for a complete accounting. The owner's announcement is a direct threat to the storekeeper who, in turn, puts pressure on his customers to pay off their debts; the following account is typical of what may happen:

> This morning the owner demanded a final accounting, and the storekeeper is trying desperately to collect all debts, aided by his brother. One of the debts was 1,000 frs. owed by Y, who is angry about it because, he says, people are charging things in his name. When the brother went to Y's house to collect, however, Y paid.
>
> The storekeeper's brother then asked Y to help him collect the debt owed by S, but Y refused. (Y could be legitimately asked to do this because he is *kapita* of the village, i.e., the respresentative of the Belgian administration.) According to Y, the brother began to insult him, saying he was an imbecile and that he did not know his work as *kapita*.
>
> Whatever the case, the brother seized a machete and swung it at Y, cutting a chunk out of the middle of his lower lip. At this point L (Y's brother) pinned the brother's arms behind his back and Y hit him. They threw the brother on the floor and Y jumped on his chest three times. Then Y held him while L hit him with the machete, cutting him slightly on the cheek in the melee and receiving a badly swollen eye. The brother was finally dragged off singing what he said later was a song of shame and saying that if he had been in his own village he would have gotten help against these low scoundrels.

Among its population, Lupupa Ngye numbers some habitual debtors who are known to be completely unreliable about paying off their debts, and such people are *eswakaswaka* (pl. *maswakaswaka*); on the other hand, there also seem to be habitual lenders who are known to be "soft touches" and who constantly complain about the amounts owed them. The question of debt is a serious one in the village and a constant source of turmoil.

It is difficult to know whether pawning has ever been practiced in Lupupa Ngye, for no actual instances were observed during the research, and informants are sharply divided. K, for example, says he has never heard of such a thing, and he further says it would be impossible, for when A comes to work for B, B will feed and clothe A, and thus the debt grows larger rather than smaller. On the other hand, older men argue that pawning does exist but that it is a relatively new institution. Such men are careful to draw a sharp distinction between a slave (*mpika*, pl. *bapika*) and a pawnee (*mutumwa*, pl. *mitumwa*), and they base their contention as to the late introduction of pawning by pointing out that in the old days a debtor would have been put into slavery. The creditor fixes the length of time allowed the debtor to pay, and at the end of that time sets conditions; in a case in the village, the creditor gave the debtor three choices in the matter of a debt of 150 francs: pay the debt immediately in cash, pay the debt immediately by turning over his bicycle (a new bicycle is valued at 3,500 francs), or work for the creditor in his fields for two weeks. Others describe this process of working off a debt as "pawning," but of course neither of these instances is pawning in fact. Similarly, informants say that palm, pineapple, and banana trees can be put in pawn in the case of inability to pay a debt, but they separate such instances from those noted above. In sum, pawning as such does not seem to exist in Lupupa Ngye although a very few economic actions suggest it.

In addition to the various processes of distribution and consumption discussed above, gift giving and ritual or formalized payments are prime means of effecting the circulation of goods and services in Lupupa Ngye. Most of these are classified by the villagers as gifts; while "payments" are cash disbursals given directly for goods or services, "gifts" demand no immediate return though some kind of reciprocity is expected eventually.

The term for gift as a general concept is *bwedi* (s. & pl.), but a number of other terms refer to particular situations and types of gifts. *Kwela mukishi* ("to give" "ancestral spirit"), for example, is a libation to the ancestors consisting of the blood of a goat or a chicken dripped on the ground; the libation is made at the start of a considerable number of activities to ask the ancestors for success in the undertaking. It may also be given at the point when work is finished and use is about to begin, such as on the occasion when a xylophone maker has finished construction and is turning the instrument over to the purchaser.

Mukumino (pl. *mikumino*) is a gift of money made to living people; the term is most often used in connection with succession to

93

political office. It is a first acceptance gift, made by the new political dignitary on the occasion of his being named to office, and it is followed one to two years later by *kwaba* ("distribute"), which is a gift by the notable to the other notables. *Mulobo* (pl. *milobo*) is a gift given by someone who has a political title to someone who does not; it accompanies a request for labor. *Kubwikila* (s. & pl.) are gifts given at a funeral, while *ebofu, koonda,* and *kutwela shibo* are all gifts at specific points in the process of courtship and marriage.

The three types of occasions which involve the largest transfer of wealth are, in ascending order, marriage, funeral, and political succession. In the brief discussion of these situations which follows, it should be kept in mind that the average annual income of a horticulturalist in Lupupa Ngye can be estimated to be about 5,000 francs or $100. It is probable that both musicians of the highest rank and the young men who produce raffia basketry have an annual income slightly in excess of this figure. However, when the average is compared to the amounts disbursed on the three major occasions, it becomes clear that they are truly substantial, and it is not surprising that they are sometimes so substantial as to make their payment impossible or, at best, imprudent.

Once a decision to marry has been made by the prospective bride and groom, a preliminary gift (*ebofu*) is made by the father of the groom to the prospective bride who, after accepting it as an indication of her intention to marry, passes it on to her father. In a typical situation, the *ebofu* might consist of one long piece of Western soap (8 frs.), one sack of salt (150 frs.), four packages of cigarettes (Belga rouge, considered an expensive brand at 6 frs. each, for a total of 24 frs.), a demijohn of palm wine (25 frs.), and ten boxes of matches (10 frs.), for a total of 217 francs. *Ebofu* also demands that the father of the prospective groom invite the father of the prospective bride to his house to make further arrangements, and on this occasion the visitor is presented with a chicken which he eats himself, making an additional expense of approximately 50 francs.

At a later date, which varies according to the wishes of those involved, the *koonda,* or bridewealth proper, is passed; *koonda* actually refers specifically to the money which forms part of the bridewealth, while the accompanying goods are referred to as *kifindwa* (pl. *bifindwa*). The transfer of the bridewealth follows a somewhat circuitous route; it is given by the father to his son, the prospective groom, who gives it to his best male friend with whom he has a formal friendship arrangement (*kukuande,* pl. *bakukubande*). His friend then transfers the bridewealth to the institutionalized female friend (*lole,* pl. *balole*) of the prospective bride, who in turn gives it to the bride to be counted in the presence of the four young people. The bride then returns the bridewealth to her best friend who passes it on to the bride's father. In the marriage noted above in connection with *ebofu,* the bridewealth consisted of 1,750 francs cash, one calabash of palm oil (120 frs.), one sack of salt (150 frs.), a carton of cigarettes (100 frs.), two machetes (75 frs.), one piece of cloth (150 frs.), a head kerchief (30 frs.), and two hoe blades (100 frs.), for a total of 2,475 francs.

The third gift is part of *kutwela shibo* which is the formalized announcement of marriage and which is set in motion by the prospective husband who calls his friends together, tells them he is going to marry, and invites them to a dinner to be prepared by his prospective wife; the father of the groom provides sufficient food and drink for this affair. This is the time for further gift giving on the part of various members of the two families, particularly the family of the groom. In the marriage we have been using as our example, the groom's father gave his son three pairs of trousers, three shirts, a pair of shoes, a hat, a machete, two blankets, and a bed; he also gave the bride three lengths of cloth, a pair of tennis shoes, two head kerchiefs, and two skirts. The groom's mother presented him with a gift of 100 francs, and his father's brother gave him 600 francs. From his mother's side of the family, in addition, came 300 francs from his mother's brother and another 300 francs from his mother's sister. Gifts are also given to the bride at *kutwela shibo,* and particularly important is the gift of kitchenware from the mother of the groom; in this particular case, the bride was provided with almost everything she needed, having been allowed to take her pick from among the personal kitchenware owned by her mother-in-law. The bride also received five plates, five pots, and one length of cloth from her mother, and 500 francs from her father. The gifts from mother-in-law to bride are ceremonially transferred through the groom who passes them on to his wife, saying, "Now you are with me." After transfer of the gifts, his wife prepares the meal, and the groom and his friends sit down to eat. It is slightly more difficult to estimate costs in this case, but it is probable that another 4,500 francs is involved here, exclusive of the kitchenware; of this, some 2,630 francs is the cost to the father.

The total value of the basic gifts charged to the father of the groom in this particular marriage, then, amounts to approximately 5,372 francs, or $107.44, which is more than the average annual income of a farmer in Lupupa Ngye. Changing hands in the affair was at least 7,242 francs, or $144.84, and this does not include the cost of the kitchenware or of numerous small incidental expenses.

The second major occasion for transfer and distribution of wealth occurs in connection with funerals, particularly major funerals for a respected adult male of the community. Such a funeral lasts for seven days with the entire village participating actively much of the time. The flow of cash and goods is almost continual, but it takes place most specifically in three contexts. First are the expenditures made by the family of the deceased. Friends and relatives come from other villages and must be housed and fed, musicians must be hired and cared for, and the family must be generous and respond openly to needs and requests of relatives and friends, for at this period the family's and lineage's reputation is on public display as at almost no other time. The family may also be required to make a ceremonial payment to the notables, the adult males, and depending upon circumstances, the women of the village, and this can reach an amount as great as 2,000 francs. Second, after a man has died a period occurs—some say three days and some say for the duration of the funeral—in which it is permissible to take goods from his home and from the homes of his immediate male relatives. Thus the family must be on its guard at all times; if the taker is caught, he simply returns the goods and nothing more is done. This custom is referred to as "taking during a funeral" by the Lupupans, and it is sharply differentiated from stealing which, of course, is punishable. The family is not pleased to lose possessions in this way and attempts to keep close watch on everything; at the same time, the members know the same opportunities will be open to them at the next funeral outside their lineage, and they also know that the value of these goods, and probably considerably more, will be returned to them in the third important economic context of the funeral. This occurs on the last day and involves gifts of cash and cloth, both to individual members of the lineage and to the lineage as a whole, by the families and lineages of relatives and by the institutionalized friends of members of the family. These gifts are indications of friendship, shared grief, and practical understanding of the expenditures being made by the family of the deceased, and they involve as well the prestige of the donors. Each gift is announced publicly by the village herald, and because the announcement is part of a larger ceremony which will reveal answers to a number of questions of particular interest concerning the death, almost all the villagers are in attendance.

The following figures refer to the funeral of a highly respected adult male of one of the most well-to-do lineages in Lupupa Ngye, who fell dead of a probable heart attack late in September, 1959; his was a full-fledged funeral which occupied the full seven days of mourning. During it, the family paid out approximately 2,800 francs, primarily for food, drink, and music; this is more than half the average annual income of a horticulturalist, but it was shared in this case by the three brothers and one of the nephews of the deceased. No payment was required from the family to the notables, and the formal and announced explanation was that since the deceased had died suddenly, no period of illness had occurred and the villagers had not had to stay home to help and to visit the sick; thus no compensation was required for lost time.

Very little was "taken during the funeral," and in fact the custom seems to be in a period of decline though this particular funeral was fully traditional. Taken were four plates valued at 30 francs each, a hat valued at 60 francs, five mats valued at 6 francs each, and a kerosene lamp valued at 50 francs, for a grand total of 260 francs.

At the end of the funeral, the family received a total of 7,000 frs., from twenty-nine different groups and individuals; this sum was later distributed in varying proportions to the three brothers, the nephew, and seven women of the lineage. It must be added that exclusive of the payments made directly by the family to the musicians, the latter earned a total of about 1,500 francs (2,100 francs, including the family's payment), given them by villagers during the course of the funeral. Thus in this particular case a redistribution of wealth occurred in the sum of approximately 11,560 francs, which involved sixteen known individuals (eleven family members, three musicians, and two individual givers at the

97

end-of-funeral distribution) and twenty-seven groups of individuals. The sum involved is a very substantial one for Lupupa Ngye's economy, and it is probable that every adult in the village was affected either as a giver or a receiver of money or goods. While the size of the funeral was greater than usual because of the status of the deceased, and while such a major event occurs relatively infrequently, smaller funerals provide a relatively constant turnover of cash and goods.

The third major source of redistribution of cash and goods occurs in conjunction with succession to political office. In this case the source of funds is the individual who is taking office, although he is, of course, assisted by members of his immediate family and his lineage. Distribution goes to such a considerable number of individuals and, particularly, groups of individuals, that in the end almost every adult in the village is again touched economically. The chieftainship provides the most useful example.

The selection of a new chief (*fumu*, pl. *bafumu*) is the responsibility of the notables, who seek advice from respected elder males of the village and whose decision is always subject to general village approval. The person selected is theoretically first aware of his honor when it is announced to him by the *lukunga* (pl. *balukunga*), the village herald and messenger of the notables; the *lukunga* intones a formula to which the candidate makes appropriate response, either accepting or rejecting this appointment. The day following the visit of the *lukunga,* and assuming the candidate has accepted, the young men come to the new chief's house, take him upon their shoulders, and carry him around the village in triumph. The notables and villagers arrive to pay him homage, and feasting, dancing, and general celebration last throughout the night. To each of those who has carried him on their shoulders the chief gives one piece of Americani cloth; to the singers and dancers at least 200 francs; to the young men as a group, two goats; and to the notables, two more goats. During the celebration, too, the chief's gift of 2,000 francs and one Americani is sent off to the Chef de Secteur; formerly, this went to the chief of the Bala. Three days later, the new chief is expected to give a gift of at least 800 francs to the notables, and one to two years later, a third gift of 6,000 francs to the notables, as well as four goats, four hens, four cocks, and forty casseroles of maize-manioc bread, all of which are consumed at a public feast by the villagers.

In addition to these specific gifts, given as part of his investiture, the chief is expected to continue his generosity throughout his rule. He makes food and shelter available to the passing stranger, he is responsible for the indigent in the village, he must feed the successful war party on its return, and he is expected to originate a constant flow of gifts to the notables, hunters, and the villagers in general. The return to the chief is minimal, and thus his position is one of constant outlay.

The chief of Lupupa Ngye and Lupupa Kampata in 1959 spoke of payments and gifts at his investiture which totaled approximately 14,000 francs, an absolutely staggering sum for a single individual. Even the lowest notable in the hierarchy, the *lukunga*, assumed investiture obligations of 700 francs. The result of these enormous levies is twofold; first, the chief, and most if not all of the other notables, simply never paid the entire amount. Second, it has become increasingly difficult to persuade anyone to accept public office; the chief was deposed in the late summer of 1959, and in the next few months at least three men refused to accept the position. The honor of being chief, or any other political dignitary, is of great consequence to those who do hold office; what prevents them from accepting the nomination is the extraordinary financial obligation it entails.

Marriages, funerals, and political succession are not, of course, the only occasions for redistribution of cash, goods, and services in Lupupa Ngye. Gifts and payments mark the commencement of any special labor such as building a house or making a drum, institutionalized friendships demand a fairly constant flow of gifts and hospitality, and a continuous stream of small transactions takes place. But Lupupa Ngye does not have a market system in which people gather periodically to buy, sell, and barter, nor does it have any strong external trade.

Study of property and budgets indicates that the sums of money moving through the village are small but probably steady. Men spend an average of slightly less than 500 francs per month for such items as matches (a constant purchase), beer, small food items, gifts, tobacco, flashlight batteries, soap, thread, and cloth; their cash income during an average month is about 350 francs, mostly in collection of small debts, as well as gifts, an occasional sale of a commodity in order to obtain cash, or a special skill which results in a sale, such as a tailor who makes and sells a garment. Major cash income, as well as major expenditures other than for emergencies or special occasions, come at the time of harvest and sale of cotton and peanuts, both of which occur in the late spring and early summer.

Women, too, carry on a small flow of exchange, spending an average of some 70 francs per month for matches, medicines, drinks, food, and gifts, and receiving perhaps 40 francs per month from sale of vegetables and various gifts. For women, too, the major income period is at the time of cotton and peanut harvest, particularly the latter when a portion of the crop is theirs to dispose of as they wish.

Savings are a part of the economic situation in Lupupa Ngye, with the lineage head holding monies which belong to the individual members. Despite ardent Belgian campaigns to stimulate savings accounts with financial institutions in the Congo, to the best of my knowledge no Lupupan had such an account. Instead, money was hidden in the house of the lineage head, usually either in a pot buried under the floor or in a strongbox. The maximum amount known to me was 17,000 francs hidden away by the most well-to-do family in the village, and even less wealthy families had 4,000–5,000 francs in reserve.

The fact that we can speak of well-to-do and less well-to-do families in Lupupa Ngye indicates that not only is there an unequal distribution of wealth between men and women but among families, lineages, and individuals as well. One of the wealthiest men has possessions in his house with a total estimated value of approximately 8,500 francs; in addition, he owns five palm trees, two orange trees, and five papaya trees which he values at a total of approximately 2,100 francs though he cannot sell them, a pond which has the standard value of 1,000 francs, 6 goats and 17 chickens with a total value of about 2,650 francs, 5,000 francs savings in a strongbox, and seven fields each about 80 meters square which are impossible to evaluate: his total estate, then, is close to 20,000 francs. On the other hand, the poorest man in the village, a musician, has possessions in his house with a value of approximately 900 francs; he owns no trees, pond, or livestock, and he has no savings and works no fields. Similar differences would be noticeable if lineages as units were the basis for calculation.

But no man is truly poverty-stricken in Lupupa Ngye, nor would it be possible for anyone to perish of neglect. The poorest man in the village has no fields because he does not want to work in horticulture, not because he could not have them. While cooperative labor is not a feature of the economy, and indeed, while it is often difficult to get men to work together on some special project, the villagers close ranks in support of their fellows, both in respect to internal and external problems. The economic system of Lupupa Ngye is essentially a self-sufficient one, and was probably even more so in the past; money or money tokens, goods, and services are interchanged among the villagers with a constant flow of resources from one hand to another. With the coming of the Belgians, however, new factors such as enforced cotton planting intruded upon the system, causing some changes. Essentially, however, Lupupa Ngye's economy remains traditional with some Western features beginning to be integrated into it. The older generation is surely self-sufficient in all things; the younger generation is losing the traditional skills and, with passing time, will become more and more dependent upon Western goods and services.

3. Metaphysical Surroundings I: The Universe and the Nature of Life and Death

Although the people of Lupupa Ngye are deeply concerned with the hard details of wresting a living from the habitat, they see more around them than the conformation of the land and what can be gained from it. Thus the earth and the heavens are viewed, described, and interpreted in ways which conform with the villagers' overall logic of life.

The Lupupans have no distinct conception of a universe in the sense of finite or infinite space in which stars and planets move in relationship to each other, but they do know a number of celestial bodies and encompass them together in a limited "universe." This universe is in a static state; it is neither progressing nor regressing, it does not change for better or worse, and it will probably never end, though any such decision is in the hands of Efile Mukulu. Within this universe lie the earth, sun, moon, and stars, and these various bodies are differently organized and constituted.

The earth (*senga,* s. & pl.) is always considered to be a flat circle, never a ball; the most apt illustration is an overturned round cake tin. The edge of the world is sharp and one could fall from it; around the earth is only water, and the sky, too, is filled with water. Some say that below the surface of the earth is a layer of water, and below this is a layer of rock mixed with a little sand; no one knows what, if anything, lies beyond the water at the edge.

Within the flat circle that is the earth are located four "countries," including the Congo, the United States, Belgium, and Portugal. The reasons for including the Congo and Belgium are obvious; the United States ("America" to the Lupupans) is included because of the presence of the ethnographer; and Portugal finds a consistent place because of the Portuguese traders who live in Tshofa and own some of the stores in Lupupa Ngye. At least one Lupupan says that while he formerly thought the earth was a flat circle, he now knows that it is a flat triangle, for he learned this in school. Whether circle or triangle, however, the strong tendency is to place the Congo in the center of the figure, with the other countries located at the peripheries. Older people tend to locate Lupupa Ngye halfway between the center and rim of the circle, but all are agreed that it is a long, long way to the edge of the world, a terrible journey, and that one would most likely die of exhaustion even were he to complete the voyage.

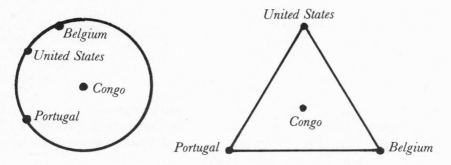

If little is known of the earth as a geologic and geographic body, less is known of other bodies in the universe. The sun (*nguba,* s. & pl.) is almost always acknowledged to be made of fire "which is *really* fire," but some say it is a ball and others simply do not know its shape. The sun is often considered by older people to be bad, "because it kills." One says, *nguba na kantu* ("sun" "with" "every day"), and this refers to the fact that every time the sun comes up, in some village, somewhere, someone is dead. It is said that the sun circulates invisibly during the night to do its killing, and it is agreed that it is the sun, specifically, which kills. On the other hand, the sun is also good, "because when it comes up, you can see clearly and normally," and because "without it, we could not have any crops." The sun's work is to dry things, a task given to it by Efile Mukulu, and it is also masculine and "the chief of all the growing things on earth." In short, some people, particularly the old, believe the sun is bad; some, particularly the young, believe it is good; and others, both young and old, see both good and bad in it.

While some ideas about the moon (*mweshi*, s. & pl.) are equally divergent, a stronger core of common belief can be discerned among the people. Thus the moon is always considered to be good; although some refuse to ascribe sex to the moon or the sun, the majority consider the moon to be female, and no one conceptualizes it as male. Efile Mukulu made the moon, of course, and it is good for a variety of reasons: "It gives us light at night," "It is the mother of all," "It serves us by its light. It is loved by all."

The composition of the moon is a matter of disagreement; some say it is filled with clouds which are what give the light, others that it is a ball of fire, like the sun, and still others that it is made of water. While the light of the moon is cold, it is considered by some to be essential to the crops; as one informant put the matter, "The sun is good; without it we could not have any crops. He is masculine and is the chief of all the growing things on earth. The moon is his wife. The light of the moon is cold, that of the sun is hot. The light of both makes the crops grow. The sun is fire and the moon is water, and both are needed to make crops grow."

The femininity of the moon is emphasized by those who view it as the sun's wife, but some add that the moon, too, has a wife in the big star called *Kwaba;* others say that the moon and *Kwaba* are simply friends. No female-female marital relationship appears in Bala social organization, but those who conceptualize the moon and the star in this way explain it by saying that "Efile Mukulu arranges things as he wishes," and go no further in the matter. The moon is always present though sometimes it cannot be seen in the daytime. The ring around the moon is called *kifunda* (pl. *bifunda*, "circle") by some and *lubeshi* by others, but it is agreed that its appearance is the signal for subsequent serious trouble, even death; since such trouble may occur anywhere in the world, immediate results are not necessarily apparent in Lupupa Ngye. The full moon is called *ubakumbana kifunda* ("fully" "circle"), the half moon, *kukumbana kifunda* ("almost" "circle"), and the new moon, *kubaluka* ("coming out"). No beliefs are associated with the way the crescent moon is tipped; and no anxiety is expressed over the possibility that the moon will not reappear.

The moon has a close association with fertility, as exemplified by the facts that it is female, a wife, essential to the crops, and perhaps associated with water, and this feminine principle is further emphasized by the association of the moon with human fertility. The first day of the new moon is called *mweshi ubabaluka* ("moon" "it rises"; pl. *miyeshi ubabaluka*), and the evening of this day is the occasion for the only regularly recurring ceremonies practiced by the Lupupans. At this time the village protector and fertility figure is brought out, and dancing surrounds it; the figure assures fertility both of women and of crops through its role as intermediary to the ancestors. Further, it is believed that each time the moon rises, a child is started in the body of a woman; again this is not necessarily specific to Lupupa Ngye since it may occur anywhere in the world. Finally, some informants make a connection between the moon and menstrual periods, but this is not widespread nor is the connection the subject of detailed speculation or explanation.

The moon and the stars are special friends, particularly in the case of the moon and *Kwaba,* and some call the stars "the *benebalasha*" (s. & pl.) of the moon; the *benebalasha* are judicial advisors to the chief. A star (*lwenyenyi,* pl. *nyeneni*) is a ball, and its light, like that of the moon for some, comes from the clouds which fill the ball. A shooting star is sometimes called "child" (*mwana,* pl. *bana*) because each one either is or carries, depending on belief, a child from Efile Mukulu. At the instant the star appears, a woman somewhere becomes pregnant, and some believe that she will deliver within two or three months. Every shooting star results in a child, and conversely, for every child born there has been a shooting star.

Certain constellations are recognized by the Lupupans, among them *pibwe na mbwa na nyama* ("hunter" "with" "dog" "with" "animal"), which consists of the three stars in the belt of the constellation recognized by Westerners as Orion. Lupupans visualize the stars as a hunter following his hunting dog which is, in turn, following an animal. *Kimina* is a constellation used as a signal to plant maize, but the two widely divergent descriptions given of it make it difficult to identify. Some say that *Kimina* consists of many stars organized in a circle; it appears directly overhead in the month of November. Others describe the constellation as made up of four stars arranged in a square, which appears only in the months of September and October; in this case, the name of the constellation is often given as *Kiminamebele* (*Kimina* "corn") which signifies "time to plant corn." *Salankinda* is the morning star, and *Kwaba* the evening star; besides its special relationship with the moon, the latter is said to "give light like the moon," to be "bigger than the other stars," to be "close to the moon always," and to be "the first to come out in the night, coming up in the west." Finally among particular stars and constellations is the Milky Way, designated here as *mudiyanyino* (pl. *midiyanyino*), or "dividing line"; the term is most often used in connection with the imaginary dividing line which separates the village into political and legal halves. The Milky Way is called a dividing line because it separates the wet and dry places; in this part of the world, the constellation runs southwest to northeast, and to the north and west of it is the wet side, to the south and east, the dry side. The rain leaves the wet side and travels through the sky to the dry side; on the way home again, it falls to earth. Since almost all the storms in Lupupa Ngye come from the east-southeast, the belief fits perfectly with reality.

Clouds (*makumbi*, s. *ekumbi*) are made of water and contain the rain. The rainbow, *kongolo*, is caused by a snake, Kabuse (occasionally referred to as Katombole); if the rainbow comes before the rain, the rain will not fall, and if the rain has already begun, then *kongolo* cannot appear. It is not Kabuse who stops the rain, but rather, Efile Mukulu (who, of course, created Kabuse); the rainbow is thus a sign that Efile Mukulu has stopped the rain. Many Kabuse exist, all of whom live in the water on the earth, and this accounts for the possibility of having many rainbows on earth at the same time. Both ends of rainbows are in water, and the rainbow itself is the light from Kabuse's eyes. Some hold that the end of the rainbow can be found; Dibwe once came across a spot in the forest where the ground was all red, and he wondered about this until he saw Kabuse and knew that the end of a rainbow had rested at the spot. Some say that Kabuse, who is always at both ends of every rainbow, will eat anyone who finds the end; others say that he does not harm anyone. Finally, some believe that the rainbow is the "father" of diamonds; he created them and in some way is still associated with them.

The wind (*lupunga*, pl. *mpunga*) indicates that rain is on the way; it is created by Efile Mukulu who is blowing through his mouth. The whirlwind is *ngumbu*. Before Western acculturation, only two directions were named, *akutunduka nguba* ("where it rises" "sun") for the east, and *kwatwela nguba* ("where it sets" "sun") for the west. The eclipse is referred to as *bufuku bubayidi kanya* ("night" "has been made" "sunshine"), and is caused by Efile Mukulu, whose motives are unknown. Some believe an eclipse is a punishment from Efile Mukulu, but if so, no one is sure why the punishment is levied or what to do about it. An eclipse is a frightening phenomenon, particularly because of this uncertainty.

Unlike the sky, the interior of the earth is of virtually no concern to the Lupupans; it is not personalized in any way nor is it inhabited by any kind of beings, living or dead. The earth's surface, however, is populated by a number of sentient forms, all of which stand in a particular relationship to man. Among these, of course, are animals, both wild and domesticated.

Wild animals have known habits, and these are the special province of the hunter's knowledge. Wild pigs and antelope, for example, always go where there is food and are thus a constant source of trouble in the fields. Antelope come at any hour of the day, eat, leave, return, and so on, but when wild pigs come to the field, they stay. Antelope are solitary animals, but elephants live in groups. Monkeys are of some special interest because their physical form is like that of humans, and because it is noted that they stay together, living and traveling in groups. However, they do not think like humans nor do they have human-like souls or spirits, and they are killed without hesitation for their meat.

It is felt by many that all animals have their own languages with each one species specific; thus goats talk to goats but they are

107

unable to talk to elephants. No animal can speak like human beings, and thus men and animals cannot and do not communicate linguistically with each other. The calls and cries of some animals are interpreted into Kisongye; for example, the frequently heard dove says *ekuchi mumba ku ku,* which means "father is gone (I don't know where)."

The question of whether animals and other nonhuman objects on earth have spirits is a matter of divided opinion among the Lupupans, but three kinds of phenomena seem to be conceptualized in this connection. Inanimate objects, such as plates or spoons, for example, have an essence which makes it possible for them to travel to Efile Mukulu along with the human spirit at the time of burial; this essence is *kifudi* (pl. *bifudi*), a word which may be defined as "the essence of an inanimate object," and which is explained by Lupupans as "like the photograph of something." Some people say that living things which are not animals, such as plants and trees, have no spirit or essence at all; others suggest that instead, these objects have *mbyo* (s. & pl.), or "seeds." How analogous *kifudi* and *mbyo* are is impossible to ascertain at this point.

Opinion is sharply divided when it comes to animals. Some say flatly that animals have nothing analogous to the human spirit, others argue that "all things have their spirits," but except in humans these are not capable of thought or actions; thus a chair, a mat, clothing, a typewriter ribbon, all have spirits, but not sentience. Still others argue that human-like spirits are found in animals, but not in birds; when this occurs, however, the spirits are no longer human, but are animal. Finally, some argue strongly that human spirits are present in animals, which buttresses the most commonly held beliefs about transmigration.

Quite possibly because animals are not like humans, cannot speak, and do not have human-like spirits (in the belief of most), they are treated with casual cruelty. A baby jackal caught in the bush and brought to the village with a string tied around its neck is stoned, kicked, beaten, and held up by the string and strangled a little, while the spectators laugh. Such behavior is also connected with the fact that despite the nonhumanness of animals, those which do harm to humans or to their property can be punished. Thus a chicken hawk was captured alive one day and brought to the village; when asked what would be done with it, the captor replied, "We'll put it in a pot of boiling water alive, and let it die. It is a bad thing and it will be punished." Similarly, the ears of goats are frequently cropped or cut off entirely, perhaps as punishment for wandering into the fields and eating the crops. Thus while verbal communication with animals is impossible, man and animals understand each other at least well enough so that punishment of animals by man is possible.

Domesticated animals in Lupupa Ngye include chickens, goats, pigeons, and dogs. We have already spoken of the role of dogs in hunting, but except in the rarest circumstances, dogs are not kept or treated as pets in the Western sense. While some claim the animals are fed on a special plate at mealtimes with the same food as that of the master, dogs are extremely thin and show evidence of leading a catch-as-catch-can existence. They are constantly kicked and beaten; the Lupupans often seem to take pleasure in getting in a particularly solid kick, and almost any handy object (stones are virtually absent) is thrown at them on the slightest pretext. Chickens are kept for eggs, meat, and ritual sacrifice; goats are occasionally killed for meat; and pigeons are infrequently kept and only occasionally killed. Goats and pigeons represent a hedge against the future, rather than a constant and specifically bred source of meat, and the former also represent a store of wealth. According to some villagers, "the two most stupid things in the world are chickens and goats, and then come dogs. Pigeons are smarter, for they at least know their wives like humans."

Some dispute exists concerning the origin of domesticated animals, and this is traceable to the well-known journey of a single individual in the village. During the First World War, Senga was called into the army; he walked from the village to Kabalo, and was then taken by truck to Uvira where he saw "a big body of water" (Lake Tanganyika). He walked around the end of it and arrived at Usumbura (now Bujumbura, Burundi), and from there he traveled in the company of some Europeans and other Africans to a town called Mushinga in Nyoro, Ruanda, and there he saw Kidimamungu Hill. "In the side of this hill there is a hole with someone watching its mouth all the time. Out of this hole come cows, and this is where cows come from. They also go into the hole. This is their house; this is where they live; this is where they come from. When they come out, anyone who wants one can have it if he can catch it, but no one knows why. There were many, many cows coming out of that hole. It must still be there, because if they had stopped coming out, the people of Ruanda would have eaten up all the cows that had come out, for the people of Ruanda eat one or two cows per man per day. I saw this with my own eyes, and this is where cows come from."

Basing their knowledge on this tale, some Lupupans argue that all domesticated animals originated from the hole, but others are extremely scornful of this theory. They argue that only cows and horses came out of the hole in the Ruanda hill, while chickens, pigs, sheep, goats, dogs, pigeons, and ducks all originated with Efile Mukulu, who gave them to man "as our meat," and who directed Mulopwe Kamusenge to distribute them at the same time he distributed man.

For the villagers, then, both wild and domesticated animals (as well as insects) are coinhabitors of the surface of the earth; they are clearly sentient beings, but they have nowhere near the capabilities of man. They exist on earth to provide man with meat and other animal products, and are thus indispensable, but they do not figure prominently in the affairs of man in any other way.

Also inhabiting the earth at one time or another have been several other kinds of sentient beings which are neither man nor animal, and all of which have, or have had, a substantial influence on men's lives. These can be grouped on the basis of their human or nonhuman origins, in terms of their presence or absence in contemporary time, according to whether they are malevolent or benevolent, and in other ways, but whatever the system of classification adopted, the simplest facts about them are the following.

Efile Mukulu is a deity, as is his opposite, Kafilefile; neither, however, has spent any time on earth per se, operating instead from an unknown but nonterrestrial base. Kafilefile has now disappeared, though his evil influence lingers, and Efile Mukulu is more or less content to sit back, knowing all and extending his influence, but not participating actively in the mundane affairs of life save in exceptional circumstances. Kalombo Mwipangye and Mulopwe Kamusenge, the former the superhuman trickster and the latter the culture hero and first man, have both disappeared from earth and no longer directly affect it in any way.

110

Of immediate concern to the villagers are five kinds of phenomena which directly affect their lives. These include sorcerers, who are human beings with extranormal powers for good or evil, and persons to be feared and often fought. The only nonhuman beings presently found on earth are the *milungaeulu* (s. *mulungaeulu*), which are enormous, witless beings used by sorcerers and witches for evil purposes. Both *buchi* and witches, by Lupupan definition, are persons of malevolent disposition and intent, and several varieties of the latter exist. Finally, the ancestral spirits, who are in fact considered to be part of the living, are constantly present; some of them are well disposed toward their kinsmen and other humans if properly treated, but some of them are not, and they may do harm to humans under certain circumstances.

These five beings are of special concern, for each plays some particular role in the lives of all humans. While the actions of the five—sorcerers, *milungaeulu, buchi,* witches, and the ancestral spirits —are often interrelated among themselves, their prime focus is on man without whom none of them would exist. In order to understand the nature of man, however, we must first understand the content of the four basic postulates which underlie Lupupan religious philosophy.

The first of these is transmigration of the spirit which inhabits all human bodies, while the second is a belief in a combined predestination and fatalism. The third is the belief that Efile Mukulu is not himself a death-causing agency, and that, in fact, it is men who cause death. The fourth is the belief in the efficacy of magic, witches, and sorcerers, all of which are humanly controlled and which together account for the causes of death. These four postulates underlie the system of belief and are the framework upon which the following discussion is based.

The nature of the human body can only be dealt with if the transmigration of the spirit is also understood. According to the people of Lupupa Ngye the human being is made up of three parts; these are the body itself, *mbidi* (s. and pl.) when alive and *kitanda* (pl. *bitanda*) when dead, the spirit, *kikudi* (pl. *bikudi*), and the shadow, *mweshieshi* (pl. *miyeshieshi*), all three of which are in a close and intimate relationship, sometimes conceptualized along with a fourth factor, conscience (*muchima*).

The human body is nothing by itself; it exists only as a housing for the living spirit; without the spirit, there is nothing. The spirit, however, is reincarnated, and the consensus of belief is that it exists in a body on earth three times; some say that at this point the cycle is finished, while others feel that the *kikudi* returns a fourth and last time in the body of an animal like a lion or a leopard, but never as a goat or a chicken. Since the Lupupans believe in predestination, the length of time that a *kikudi* spends in each body is a factor known both to itself and to Efile Mukulu; if something should intervene in the process, however, and kill the body before the term is finished, the *kikudi* returns to earth in a different body but on the same term. Thus, theoretically, a *kikudi* may be an integral part of an infinite number of bodies but remain on its first term on earth; for the Lupupans, however, this is beyond the realm of belief or even speculation, though one or even two interruptions of a particular term are at least conceivable.

If one is on good terms with the ancestors, one of his familial spirits will return as a child in the family; and since having children is unanimously felt to be the best thing that can happen to a person, the role of the ancestors in creating children makes them of paramount importance to the living. Thus one does everything possible to propitiate the ancestral spirits. "My brother has no children. After I die, supposing he has a child. Then he will think I am a good *kikudi*, because I have intervened with Efile Mukulu to get him a child." It is thought that the spirit of the speaker enters the body of his brother's wife (in this case) and creates the child through the will of Efile Mukulu, who is always cognizant of what is occurring. How the *kikudi* enters—through the vagina, through the stomach wall, through the mouth—is not known. This spirit is the essence of the former living person (though it is not precisely this since the body is changed), and thus all individuals return to "life" in at least three bodies and perhaps in a fourth.

This process can be confirmed in several ways. The identity of the new child may be known through consultation with a sorcerer, or a direct revelation may be made in a dream. If one were admonished in a dream to take good care of some of the property of a deceased, such as his gun, bow and arrows, or something else closely associated with him, he would feel assured that a child with the deceased's *kikudi* was on the way. Most specifically, if the deceased was left-handed (*kibokoswa*) and the new child is also

112

left-handed, the connection is a certainty. The transmigration of the *kikudi* must always skip a generation, since a *kikudi* cannot be shared between two persons (a father and son, for example), but the favorite movement is from grandfather to grandson, followed by other familial relationships. Male children are fairly often given their paternal grandfather's name.

Transmigration may occur in other contexts as well. Thus a traveler who comes across the dead body of another traveler should first make all possible inquiry as to its identity. If the deceased is unknown, the finder should give him a proper burial, and as a result, the dead stranger's *kikudi* may follow the finder and, when he reaches home, enter the body of his wife and become a child. Similarly, while *bikudi* prefer to, and most often do, enter the body of a relative, they are not bound to do so; indeed, they may enter a woman of another household, lineage, subtribe, tribe, or nation (the author, for example, is thought to have a *kikudi* from Lupupa Ngye). Neither must a *kikudi* which has been in symbiosis with a male body continue to return in male bodies; nor must a spirit always occupy a female body.

The concept of transmigration, then, is an excellent explanatory principle for the birth of children of any sex, anywhere, but particularly for explaining family resemblances. While to the outsider the theory seems to provide for a finite number of spirits, and thus an eventual end to humanity, the question does not bother the Lupupans, who dismiss it with their inevitable ultimate explanation—"Efile Mukulu can arrange anything he wishes"—or, in rare instances, say that Efile Mukulu creates a constant new supply of *bikudi*.

In the body-*kikudi* relationship, the body is only something inhabited by the spirit; without the spirit, the body is nothing, and indeed, death can be defined in Lupupan terms as what happens when the *kikudi* leaves the body. The *kikudi* controls the body, and it sometimes gives instructions to the body through dreams; it is the instigator of whatever the body does. When the body is cut or pinched, it is the *kikudi* which tells the body that it hurts and makes it withdraw from the pain-causing agency. The truth of this observation is often clinched by pointing out that a dead body can be cut open without evincing the slightest reaction; the reason, of course, is that the *kikudi* has departed from it. While it is the body which has consciousness of the surrounding world, it is the *kikudi* which regulates this consciousness, allowing the body to see and to know only what it wishes to allow.

The *kikudi* always knows things that the body does not know; it has knowledge of Efile Mukulu, it knows which term it is on in the transmigration cycle, and so forth. On the other hand, the body never knows anything which the *kikudi* does not also know, and thus the *kikudi* has, in effect, "secrets" from the body. All this being so, it appears to the Westerner that the body and the spirit must have separate consciousness, but the matter is not so conceived by the Lupupans. Rather, the body is only a vehicle for the *kikudi* which, having received its instructions from Efile Mukulu, regulates the body's actions, thoughts, and perceptions.

The third part of the human being, the shadow, is considered to be inseparable from the *kikudi* (with one exception to be noted below), and to return with it in subsequent reincarnations. All things have shadows, but since all things do not have *bikudi*, nonhuman shadows are different from human shadows. Some postulate a consciousness for the shadow, but if so, it is not a separate consciousness but one shared identically with the spirit; the shadow and spirit are sometimes visualized as a single entity. The shadow likes places where light is present, but at night or on cloudy days it is still close to the body even though it cannot be seen; it is the body's friend. The shadow and spirit are separated only when the *kikudi* leaves the body through the mouth at death; the shadow stays until the end of the funeral when the last person to leave the graveside rites throws dirt between his legs on the grave and departs without a backward look. At this point, the *mweshieshi* rejoins the *kikudi*, the two to be reincarnated together.

The fourth part of the human being, the conscience, is precisely what the Westerner thinks of as conscience, but not all Lupupans include this in discussing the makeup of the human being. While indications are occasionally made that shadow and conscience are embodied together, all informants deny this in direct conversation: "A tree has a shadow, but it hasn't got a conscience; conscience is a human thing." It is possible, however, that animals also have consciences since one may meet a lion, for example, and go unmolested; but again, this is not a widely held belief.

114

No sure knowledge exists concerning the locus of the *kikudi* in the body. Some say it is in the heart, and add the corollary that when one is ill he is all right until the illness touches the *kikudi*, at which point he dies. Others locate the abode of the *kikudi* somewhere in the stomach region, most specifically, "between the stomach and the intestines." Still others say that the *kikudi* is located in the head (although it exists throughout the body), and add that the head is where the mouth, eyes, ears, and hair are found and thus, obviously, is the center of the being.

Similar ambiguity is present in discussions of the emotions, perceptions, and intelligence. Some say that all human beings have two hearts located physically in the body. One of these represents Efile Mukulu and the other Kafilefile, and the two are in constant struggle. Those who hold this view are likely to state as well that the human being thinks with the heart and perceives with the brain. One of the most complete statements concerning these points was as follows: "We perceive with our eyes which alone tell us what we see. When we are angry, the seat of our emotion is in the heart. We think with our brains. Intelligence, however, is given to us by Efile Mukulu and is seated in the heart. A decision for good or bad action represents a struggle between Efile Mukulu and Kafilefile. In the heart there is a small sack of water, and when one is angry, it is because this water has spread throughout his heart. The sack is called *sumini,* and it can be found in slaughtered animals and dead humans." The last few statements here are difficult of analysis since the Lupupans are apparently confused in at least one aspect of anatomical identification. The "thing in the body that beats" is called the heart (*eshimba,* pl. *mashimba*) but when an animal is slaughtered, the carver often holds up the liver (*eyi,* pl. *mayi*) and describes it as the "heart." Thus it is difficult, if not impossible, to know what the "small sack of water" actually is.

Life begins when the *kikudi* enters the body of a woman; whether the spirit is in fact inside the body during pregnancy is unknown and not discussed. The child, then, has a *kikudi* at least from the instant it is born; if it lives only a few moments, it has still had a *kikudi,* for "spirit" is synonymous here with "life force." A child born dead has no *kikudi;* the spirit has left the body for any one of a number of possible reasons. It will be recalled that the *kikudi* leaves the body through the mouth and that, in fact, its leaving is not only the signal of death but is death itself. After leaving the body, the spirit "goes to Efile Mukulu."

It is my view that the concept of transmigration makes it unnecessary to postulate another kind of life after death, for the afterlife is precisely "life after death," that is, a new existence in a different body. At very least, the idea of three reincarnations after an original existence delays the matter so substantially that ideas of a permanent afterlife do not emerge with clarity; indeed, those which are stated seem clearly to indicate strong influence from, and perhaps an origin in, Christianity. Thus K, for example, says: "We are all like chickens to Efile Mukulu; in the same relationship as chickens on this earth are to their owners. There is a tribunal where dead people go, and Efile Mukulu is the judge. Those adjudged good remain near Efile Mukulu; those adjudged bad are thrust aside. Efile Mukulu's place is probably in the sky." While a few people are optimistic about conditions in an afterlife, most of those who discuss it take a low key and rather gloomy approach. "No, people do not marry after death, for men go to one place and women to another. Good people go to one place and bad people to another, but in both places men and women are separated. People don't do anything; they have no houses, they don't farm, they don't eat, they don't sleep, they just become feeble and exist, thinking about life on earth." In short, they are almost in a state of suspended animation.

It should be reemphasized that accounts such as these do seem to be borrowed (and distorted) from Christianity, for the traditional system requires no afterlife as a part of belief. Those who remain strong traditionalists say that after the fourth term on earth, one goes to be with Efile Mukulu, and let it go at that. Indeed, the joy of the "afterlife" lies precisely in reincarnation, because "everybody wants to come back to be with his children and family."

Reference must be made one last time to the difficulty of understanding Lupupan belief in this matter. Although the body does not have its own consciousness, and although body and *kikudi* are separate entities, one still "wants to come back to be with his children and family." But since individual consciousness must, in Lupupan terms, lie in the *kikudi,* and since the individual lacks knowledge of the term on which its *kikudi* is embarked, then for the

Westerner, one of two logical results must ensue. Either the body *must* have a consciousness, or there is no hope of consciously returning in another incarnation "to be with one's children and family." It must be repeated that this problem for the outsider is not a problem for the Lupupan; even though he has no conscious awareness in life of who his *kikudi* is, his consciousness, which is another way of saying life itself, embraces the totality of existence. "Life" for the Lupupan is not a matter of simple opposite entities labeled "life" and "death," for life encompasses several existences which are lumped into a single consciousness and which extend over such a long period of time as to make an ending too vague to be considered with much care. Thus reincarnation "to be with one's children and family" is not a literal statement, though it may be said literally, but is rather a general statement of the singleness of existence and consciousness. Where the Westerner sees a contrast between life and death and each reincarnation as a separate entity with beginning and end, the Lupupan sees death only as a temporary displacement of his spirit to another vehicle for its continued existence; all his "lives" are one continuing process which ensures the continuity of his experience in a single milieu. Under these conditions it is understandable that an afterlife is hardly conceptualized, and that "to stay with Efile Mukulu" is tantamount to punishment, for both situations indicate an end to a process which is not visualized as having an end, despite the belief in four appearances on earth in different bodies.

After leaving a body, the spirit takes one of two courses—it may follow the general process of reincarnation, in which case it remains a *kikudi*, or it may turn into a vengeful spirit, in which case it becomes a *mukishi* (pl. *mikishi*) until its vengeance has been achieved. We shall discuss *mikishi* in the context of the causes and agencies of death.

Bikudi, then, are separated from the body normally at the time of death; they are also separated abnormally as a result of certain kinds of magic practices. The only other occasion for the separation of body and *kikudi* is in dreams, which are considered to be experiences of the spirit. While the *kikudi* travels during dreams, it cannot be caught out of the body on a sudden awakening, for Efile Mukulu has arranged matters so that the spirit can return instantly to the body from any distance. It is, however, prudent to dream

117

during the night, especially about midnight, when there is minimal chance of a sudden awakening.

The spirit can be trapped by malevolent beings while it wanders in dreams, and if this happens, the dreamer dies. The *kikudi* can also be gone so long a time that his relatives think the dreamer is dead; this happened on one occasion to E. He was ill, and at about five o'clock in the morning, "I traveled to a very big river where there were lots of birds. But they were not really birds; they were people with wings. I didn't have any feathers and I could not fly. I came back to this village, but the village was gone and in its place there was a huge mountain of sand. People chased me, and I tried to get away." When E awoke, he found himself in his mother's arms; everyone thought he was dead, they were mourning for him, and it was ten o'clock in the evening. He later recognized one of the bird-people he had seen as a villager, and he said to him, "I saw you at the big river. You were a bird." The person did not answer, but returned to his house and died. E has never seen the birds or that place again, although he has since been very ill on occasion.

Difficulty with the ancestral spirits can be avoided by proper treatment and, particularly, by being careful not to neglect one's obligations. Neglect or ignorance can have a great number and variety of results as, for example, in the case of the funeral. If the funeral is improperly conducted, the *kikudi* of the deceased, joined by other ancestral spirits which have not yet returned as children, will discomfit the living in general; they will not be allowed to rest well and they will be uneasy and fretful. Neglect of specific aspects of funeral procedure will have contagious results for the child in which the spirit is reincarnated. Thus if the body is not properly washed, the new child will have a very dark skin color and will not allow itself to be bathed except with great difficulty. If the eyes of the body have not been closed, the new child will have huge and staring eyes. All the body joints of the deceased must be moved before burial or the new child will have stiff limbs. If earth from the grave is allowed to touch the body, the new child will have a white patch of skin at that spot. If the head is not placed to the east in burial, the *kikudi* cannot rest properly and will not be reincarnated as a child; in this case, it will become a *mukishi* and seek revenge on the family because it has been badly treated. If proper grave goods

118

are not included, other *bikudi* will not receive the spirit of the dead individual; his *kikudi* will be chased away, and he will take revenge on the family.

On the other hand, the *bikudi* are the source of great comfort and specific assistance to the living; indeed, it is the ancestral spirits which act as intermediaries between man and Efile Mukulu and which, working under the normal patterned arrangements sanctioned by Efile Mukulu, activate many of the processes and procedures of life.

When a person dies and a child in the same family falls ill, it sometimes happens that a sudden and "miraculous" cure occurs; it is the *kikudi* of the recently deceased who arranged the recovery through intercession with Efile Mukulu. If after a death, no one else in the village dies over an unusually extended period of time, such as four or five years, it is again the *kikudi* which has arranged the matter. Dreams are an important way in which the *bikudi* can help the living, since specific requests and instructions can be communicated through them. M, for example, dreamed one night that his father came to him and asked that he sacrifice a chicken for him, but M neglected to do so, and as a consequence his son, C, was "struck by a thunderbolt" and had remained ill ever since. Some time later, M's father appeared in another dream, saying, "If you want your son to be well you must get a chicken, make a little house with four smaller ones around it, and kill the chicken in the middle of the houses. After you have killed it, leave the wings there and prepare the rest of the chicken for C to eat. Afterward, take two eggs and leave them among the houses." M did so, his son's appetite returned almost immediately, and his illness vanished soon thereafter. The four "houses" represented the houses of his father and his four wives, and of course it was his father's *kikudi* which effected the cure with the permission, and thus the power, of Efile Mukulu. This series of events illustrates clearly the relationship of the living to the ancestral spirits: neglect brings retribution, but rectification brings renewed assistance.

Thus the villagers are constantly aware of their relationship to the *bikudi* and are careful to remember them through small sacrifices (*kupa mikishi*, "give to" "ancestral spirits"), irregularly carried out. Feeding the ancestral spirits is accomplished by sacrificing a chicken; the blood of the decapitated fowl is allowed to drip directly on the ground or into a shallow hole dug for the purpose, and in some cases the liver is cut into small pieces and scattered around the house as well. We have already discussed the special land (*elungu*) reserved for the ancestors, and the wild pigs which roam it and act as their representatives. It is also felt that some food should be set aside for the ancestors at each meal; this is accomplished either by leaving food on the plate or through the fact that one always spills something—this food is eaten by insects acting as the agents of the *bikudi*. Finally, some of the older Lupupans suggest that a small portion of first harvest should be left in the fields, but specifically for Efile Mukulu. A piece of each animal killed should be similarly left, and if a number of animals are found in a single trap, one of them should be set free. For the villagers, Efile Mukulu is thought of as "Efile Mukulu and all the things of Efile Mukulu," a concept which includes living animals and the *bikudi*. Thus all things are a part of Efile Mukulu and Efile Mukulu is a part of all things; a firstfruits sacrifice to him is also a sacrifice to the *bikudi* and, in fact, to everything.

In addition to individual circumstances and instances such as these, the ancestral spirits are a general activating force. Sacrifices to them are both assurances that they are not forgotten, and appeals that they use their influence for good. The power and force of the witch and sorcerer are provided by the ancestral spirits, who are also behind the special force, *bwadi*, which is magic associated specifically with masking societies.

The greatest importance of the ancestral spirits, however, lies in the matter of reincarnation and thus of children. We have already seen how this mechanism operates in general, but one means of very specific supplication is open to the villagers. This involves the use of two types of carved representations of the human figure, the first of which is an individually commissioned and owned figurine, the second a much larger figure owned in common by all the people of Lupupa Ngye.

A few Lupupans argue that the small figures should be called *tunkishi* (s. *kankishi*), and the large, *nkishi* (s. & pl.), but while they may be technically correct, they are in a small minority, for in common parlance, both kinds of figures are called *nkishi* (pl. *mankishi*), and we shall follow this usage here. The two kinds of *mankishi* are differentiated by size, accouterments, functions, treatment, and ownership, though they parallel each other closely in all but size. Let us turn to the individually owned figures first.

These figures are ten to twelve inches in height, with the extremes varying from six to approximately twenty-four inches. Each figure is given a personal name, chosen as a matter of taste from among the roster of names given to humans, and each is carved with male or female genitalia, depending upon the sex of the first child desired; a Janus-headed figure produces twins. The specialist carvers are sometimes called *sendwe a michi,* but the term does not seem to be widely or consistently used. Some of the figures are almost literally covered with turret-headed copper nails (*elengyela,* pl. *malengyela*), particularly on the head (excluding most of the face) and shoulders; the significance of these nails is subject to two interpretations. One school holds that each nail represents a consultation with the *nkishi,* while the other, and much larger, holds that the nails are simply decoration; it is probable that both interpretations are correct and that the explanation depends on individual and local practice.

The *mankishi* are said to be used to ensure success in hunting and in fishing, to guard against witches, for small personal magic, to protect houses against accidental destruction by burning, and to obtain children. In fact, the last use dominates the others by far, and there is no mistaking the fact that this is the primary function of the *nkishi.* Indeed, an origin story, which exists in several slight variants, further emphasizes the point.

> Once there was a man who had no children, and so he went to a friend of his who knew many things, and said to him,
>
> "I am your friend, and you know many things. Everyone else has children, but I don't have any. Why not? Can't you find a medicine which will give me a child?"
>
> The friend answered him,
>
> "Make a wooden statue which resembles a child, and make it a male or a female. After that, look for the proper medicines to put into the holes in the stomach and the head. Put in the meat of any animal, a bit of its hair, a bit of its skin, and some charcoal. Then pray to Efile Mukulu. He will help you. Ask to have something like this statue in your family."
>
> The man went away and did as his friend had told him. Then he gave the statue to his wife and explained it all to her, saying,

121

"Each time that you sleep, pray this way to Efile Mukulu."
She did this, and Efile Mukulu accepted her prayers. After nine
months she had a boy. And that is why we have *mankishi*.

A person desiring a child either makes a wooden figure himself
or commissions one from a specialist; the price varies considerably,
depending upon the size of the figure as well as the skill and
cupidity of the carver, with the figures mentioned ranging from 45
to 500 francs (the lower figure seems to be closest to average). Once
the carver has finished his work, the figure is taken to an *nganga* (pl.
banganga), or sorcerer, who combines the four ingredients mentioned
in the origin story cited above, and puts the mixture in holes made
in the figure. These holes are most commonly located at the top of
the head and at the navel, but they are also sometimes found in the
shoulders and in the elbows of the figures. In former times, the most
common receptacle, along with the navel, was the tip of a small
antelope horn which was stuck into the top of the figure's head, but
today, the horn is usually omitted and the mixture put directly in
the head hole. Once the magic mixture has been placed, the figure
is taken home by the supplicant, who then speaks to the *nkishi*,
saying that everything has now been properly carried out. Some
informants state that at this point a chicken must be killed and
some of the blood dripped on the *nkishi* while the supplicant asks for
a child from Efile Mukulu. The chicken is then cooked and
whatever remains of the magic mixture is added to it to be eaten by
husband and wife; the heart of the chicken may at this time be
placed in the head hole. From time to time, peanuts, beans,
bananas, and pineapple may be placed at the feet of the *mankishi* as
a further offering.

While the ultimate object of supplication for children by
means of the *mankishi* is Efile Mukulu, it is in fact the ancestral
spirits which make the effort bear fruit. The Lupupans are
extremely clear and definite when it comes to any question of
sentience in the wooden figure itself: "No, it is only a piece of wood
carved to look like a human." They are equally clear and definite
about the disposition of the food offerings; these are eaten by
children and insects, who in this case act as the agents of the
ancestral spirits. It is the spirits, or more precisely, one particular
spirit, who see the action taken and who then intercede with Efile
Mukulu to send a child to the family.

While to the outsider it may appear somewhat cumbersome to go to the trouble of having a figure made, taking it to the sorcerer, praying over it at home, and remembering to lay food before it from time to time, in these acts lies one of the most important principles activating the behavior of the living toward the ancestral spirits. Certain processes and procedures have been set up by Efile Mukulu, which the people must follow if certain results are to accrue. These processes and procedures are tested and hallowed by time, and most important, the ancestors lay great store by them. The *bikudi* approve of things done in the proper way, they are pleased to be approached, and they enjoy seeing children, particularly, eating the food placed before the figures. In sum, by carrying out these procedures, the people please the ancestral spirits, and when the spirits are pleased they are motivated to assist the supplicant; further, when they are displeased, they are an extremely dangerous force to be reckoned with.

The small, personal *mankishi*, then, are commissioned and used individually, primarily in order to have children; the larger figures serve similar, but extended, purposes, and are owned collectively by the villagers. These village *mankishi* are approximately three feet tall, and they are hung with numerous pieces of magic apparatus from collar and belt, which protect the villagers as a group from various potential sources of harm. The functions of the village *mankishi*, in probable order of importance, are to bring children to the women of the village, to protect the villagers against witchcraft, and to guard the health and welfare of the villagers in general (including, most specifically, protection against all illness, against any persons of ill will, and against thievery). These functions are not markedly different from those connected with the personal *mankishi*, but the village figure is efficacious for all the people while the personal figures protect only the individual owner.

Village protectors are changed when their efficacy is shown to have been lost, and thus some Lupupans can remember back through at least three such figures. The first was named Yankima, and is certainly pre-1950 and may be as early as the 1930's; he (the figures are always male) was taken away by the Belgian administrator, apparently on the complaint of the Chef de Secteur. Shortly afterward, Kabamba was obtained, but his presence also became known to the Belgians, and the chief of Lupupa Ngye disposed of him in 1950 as a response to administration pressures. From 1950 to 1957 the village was without an *nkishi,* but feeling the need once again, the people commissioned the carver Yakyomba of the village Mona to make the figure named Lupika which was still in use in 1960. According to one informant, this was done with the permission of the Belgian administration on the basis that "between European and European there is only friendship, but between Congolese and Congolese there is always trouble and we need protection."

The village *nkishi* is communal property, paid for by assessments made on the individual villagers; it is accompanied by a special drum and special iron gong which are also village property. The holder of the figure, drum, and gong may be anyone in the village, and the property changes hands frequently in response to dreams of any villager in which Lupika asks to have his residence changed. He who holds the property must pay a "deposit" on the drum and gong which is usually double their initial cost; this is because these music instruments may be borrowed by anyone at any time in order to make any kind of music, and it is the holder's responsibility to see that they are returned. The deposit is paid to the notables and is theoretically refunded when the items move to someone else's care; in fact, it is seldom, if ever, returned, but it is considered an honor to be selected to hold the village property and the point is seldom pressed.

Lupika, in one sense, stands for the entire village as its general protector. Individual requests can be addressed to him, but only in the presence of the general public; he is not addressed either in private "audience" or by individuals who pray to him in their own homes. He can be consulted at any time—in group action—but he is always consulted and cared for on the first evening of the new moon. This is a regularly recurring ceremonial and, in fact, is the only such periodic group ceremonial practiced by the people of Lupupa Ngye; even it may be skipped under certain circumstances.

Lupika's public appearances are jealously guarded from the outsider and it was only on a very few occasions that I was permitted to be present. The heavy figure is carried by means of two poles lashed to his base; those who carry and at the same time dance with him may be anyone who wishes to do so. Special songs are sung on the occasion, accompanied by slit wooden gong, drum, double iron gong, and rattle, and general dancing occurs. Lupika is accompanied by special attendants, *bilumbu* (s. *kilumbu*), who are chosen by dream; three or four such persons are usually present, but in 1959–60, only one female occupied the position. The attendants may be male or female, usually the latter, and their duties are to stay close during the dancing and to carry out any assignments which may be given through dreams. Lupika is "fed," primarily with chicken livers, and chicken blood is dripped over his head by him who provides housing for the figure; the occasions for such offerings are signaled in dreams. The figure may lose its power for any of a variety of reasons, but most specifically when its maker dies; it is then taken to another village and brought into confrontation with its counterpart. Crucial in this confrontation are two carved wooden cylinders about $1\frac{1}{4}$ inches long and $\frac{1}{2}$ inch in diameter; these are attached to the figure's belt by means of short strings which pass around the belt and through a hole drilled in one end of each cylinder. These *tukonya* (s. *kakonya*) indicate the comparative strength of the two figures; if both of them on both figures stand straight out from the belt, then the two *mankishi* are of equal and high strength. If the two cylinders of one figure stand straight out and those of the other figure hang down in normal position, the former is the stronger but, more important, the latter has probably lost its power. In this case, a new *nkishi* is commissioned.

The most important function of the village protector figure is its role in assuring fertility to the females of the village in its position as intermediary between man and Efile Mukulu, with the ancestral spirits once again providing the activating force. The ceremonial carried out, the periodic food offerings made to the figure, and the requests addressed to it, are all aimed at obtaining ancestral intervention. Lupika himself is no more than a carved piece of wood, and the food offerings are eaten by insects; but the ancestors are pleased to see all this done properly and thus their good will and intervention in obtaining children can be reasonably well assured.

Thus the first basic postulate in Lupupan belief, that is, transmigration and reincarnation of the spirit, gives us a means of understanding two crucial aspects of Lupupan life. The first is the belief in a total human consciousness in which the individual is part

125

of a far broader conceptualization which involves past and present generations in a continuing cycle of life. The second is the belief in the efficacy of the ancestral spirits who act as intermediaries between man and Efile Mukulu and who, because of this extraordinarily powerful position, must be treated with respect and consideration and must be pleased by the proper performance of various rituals and ceremonies.

The second major postulate in the religious philosophy of the Lupupans is the belief in *kwelampungulu* which is best translated as "fate," though it contains strong elements both of fatalism and predestination. It is believed by the people that when a person is born, Efile Mukulu (who, of course, created *kwelampungulu*) writes his name in a book; the idea of writing is clearly a recent addition to the belief but does not distort the basic idea. At this point disagreement occurs, for some hold that Efile Mukulu adds only the exact length of time the individual is to live, while others believe that all details of that life span are written in the book. Whatever the case, all details of life *are* predestined, and this includes every event of every second of every life. Predestined life, however, is not entirely irrevocable, for men have the power to disrupt it; thus X may be killed by Y quite apart from the designs for X's life set up by Efile Mukulu. In such a case, X's *kikudi* returns immediately to earth as a newborn child and finishes out the term of life on which he was embarked. Instances of this kind are not considered to be particularly rare or exceptional, but of course, Efile Mukulu's decisions are carried through in the vast majority of cases.

The strong fatalistic element present can best be illustrated by examples given by Lupupans. If an individual is faced with a leopard in the bush, he may run until exhausted, at which time he figuratively shrugs his shoulders and says to himself, "If the leopard is going to kill me, it will kill me; if it is not going to kill me, it will not kill me. It is *kwelampungulu*." Very similar is the following. "Supposing I do something bad to you and you chase me out of the house and down the street threatening me with your machete. I run and run with you running behind me, and finally I get tired and know that you are going to catch me. I say to myself, 'Well, if he is going to kill me, he is going to kill me,' and I stop and accept whatever happens." Or again. "Suppose you want a certain woman, but when you ask her to marry you she refuses. You try and try with all the ways you know, but she will not change her mind. Well, sometime you have to say, 'I can't get her. I'll just have to give up. It is *kwelampungulu.*' "

Predestination and fate clearly go hand in hand in Lupupan thought, but they are not counsels of helplessness and despair. Predestination can be avoided, and fatalism is a matter of last resort which comes into play only after one has used all the wiles, skills, and knowledge available to him.

The third postulate is the belief that Efile Mukulu is not an active death-causing agency, and that, instead, it is man who is the chief agent of death. The people of Lupupa Ngye are divided in their belief concerning the origin of death. Some feel that Efile Mukulu taught man how to cause death and then himself took no further part in it. Others believe that Efile Mukulu never intended human beings should know about death; in this version, after Efile Mukulu had created man he turned his back, and Kafilefile took man aside and said to him, "If you want to know how to kill people, I'll show you," and he did. What is most important here is the concept of Efile Mukulu as a superhuman being who does not himself kill, although he has the capacity to do so in those rare instances in which it becomes necessary. Kafilefile does not kill either, although he may have taught man how to kill; in fact, Kafilefile has disappeared from the world of men, though his evil influence continues to be felt. Both Mulopwe Kamusenge and Kalombo have disappeared from earth and play no part in death. The only other superhuman beings, the *milungaeulu,* can cause death but do not do so on their own initiative; rather, they are controlled by malevolent human beings and are thus agents of human rather than of superhuman beings. While the ancestral spirits cause death through vengeful action, this, too, is activated and controlled by men; in any case, the ancestral spirits are part of the human world. Finally, death from sheer old age ("his *kikudi* is tired"), and to a certain extent, from accident, is accepted by the Lupupans, but such events are considered very rare.

This leads us to the fourth basic postulate, the belief in the efficacy of magic, witches, and sorcerers, all of which play an extremely important part in the life of the villagers.

Taken together, the four postulates account clearly for the multiplicity of death-dealing devices found in the belief system of

127

the Lupupans. Given the fact that supernatural beings do not cause death except when impelled by men and, indeed, that Efile Mukulu under all but the most abnormal circumstances eschews any personal part in causing death, and given the fact that a hierarchy of superhuman beings to whom death can be attributed simply does not exist, man has been forced to take the responsibility for death and to create the mechanisms whereby it is carried out. It is not meant, of course, that men have consciously become murderers by direct physical violence, but rather that the total philosophy allows for the vast majority of deaths only through the agency of men acting primarily through magical means. The philosophy contains all the necessary parts to make men's magical actions not only possible, but necessary. Death and the religious philosophy are interacting in that the former depends upon the latter, while the latter validates the means by which the former is believed to take place.

The mechanisms of death, as caused by human beings or by agents manipulated by human beings, are many; we may begin by dealing with the *mikishi*, which involves further discussion of the nature of the spirit. In discussing the *kikudi*, we took little cognizance of anything but the benevolent aspects of the matter; of extreme concern to the Lupupans are the malevolent intentions of some human spirits. The spirit which activates and exists in a living body is called a *kikudi*. Death for the body occurs at the instant the *kikudi* leaves it, but at this point the spirit can take one of two directions; it is Efile Mukulu who decides (or predestines) whether the spirit will remain a *kikudi* or become a *mukishi*.

Two prime distinctions are made between the two kinds of spirits, and a third is sometimes added: *mikishi* are bad, *bikudi* are good; *mikishi* never return as children, *bikudi* always do; and, less often noted, if one "sees" a *mukishi*, he will become ill, but if he sees a *kikudi*, he will not. The origin of *mikishi*, while apparently multiple, are somewhat difficult to ascertain. Some forms are permanent, and thus it is felt by some Lupupans that the spirit becomes a *kikudi* when the individual has led a good life, and a *mukishi* when the individual has led a bad life; it seems probable, however, that this is a recent idea associated with the introduction of Christianity. Others feel that no means exist to enable one to tell in advance; the spirits of some people become *bikudi* and the spirits of others become *mikishi,* and only Efile Mukulu knows why. Another possible source of *mikishi* is from suicides, but again the Lupupans are divided in their belief, some saying that the spirits of all suicides become *mikishi* as a sort of punishment, and others flatly denying the idea. Since some also believe once a *mukishi,* always a *mukishi,* and since by definition, *mikishi* never return as children, it follows that all *mikishi* are unhappy beings; indeed, they are known to cry on the graves where their bodies are buried, and their condition does not make them well disposed toward the living.

The most important source of *mikishi* is a transient state associated with the concept of vengeance. If a person is killed by violence, including magic, his spirit wishes to take vengeance upon those who have done violence to his living body. Some say that the *kikudi* becomes a *mukishi* on the instant it leaves the body; others, perhaps more concerned with formalism, hold that the *kikudi* goes to the presence of Efile Mukulu, as do all *bikudi.* At this time, the *kikudi* explains the violence of the body's death, and asks permission to return as a *mukishi* to take its vengeance; if Efile Mukulu agrees to the justice of the request, it is he who changes the *kikudi* into a *mukishi* and sends it back to earth. Once vengeance is taken, the *mukishi* returns to Efile Mukulu, reports on its actions, is retransformed to the *kikudi* state, and returns to earth as a child in the normal manner.

The existence of the *mikishi* helps to explain the presence of ancestral spirits among the living, and we may now account for this presence in at least four ways. First, *bikudi* are sometimes present for unexplained reasons; second, they are on earth during the time before their reincarnation; third, *mikishi* are present when on missions of personal vengeance; and fourth, some *mikishi* are doomed to remain wandering *mikishi* forever, possibly because they have been suicides, because they have led a bad life, or simply because Efile Mukulu has so decreed. In speaking of these beings among the living, the Lupupans do not always make the distinction between the two types of spirits, and it is often impossible to know which is being described.

Both *bikudi* and *mikishi,* however, are thought to be present among the living at all times, and probably in great numbers; they are found particularly near the cemeteries where their bodies were buried, and in and around their former residences. If one abandons

An African World

a house in which someone has died, the spirit of the deceased, as well as other spirits, will almost surely take it over. If someone in the family returns to it later, he will find living in it virtually impossible, for the spirits will not let him sleep and will cause him numerous other difficulties. It is for this reason that houses in which people have died should be destroyed. While *bikudi* are considered to be well-intentioned toward the living, providing their descendents treat them properly, and while by definition they are not malevolent, one is always slightly uneasy about their presence. *Mikishi,* on the other hand, are considered to be ill-intentioned toward the living and malevolent by definition; one is thus always afraid of their presence. *Bikudi* are essentially harmless, and certainly are so in the daytime, but one is less certain of them at night. *Mikishi* are harmful and to be avoided at all times and costs. Cemeteries in the dark are always places to be avoided.

Since one is constantly in the company of the spirits, it is evident that they are invisible, and we have already noted the feeling that if one sees a *mukishi,* he will become ill, while if he sees a *kikudi,* he will not. In fact, the distinction is this sharp in theory only, for seeing either may cause serious illness or even death, although given a choice, one would rather confront a *kikudi.* Beliefs about seeing spirits, however, are pragmatically held, and some exceptions made to the theoretical consequence; these exceptions occur in magical situations such as when *mikishi* are forced from the body of a person they are killing, when a witch uses a certain kind of magic in order to obtain a victim, and when *bikudi* are captured by a sorcerer or a witch and changed into another form. Ordinary people, however, may see a *kikudi* quite by accident, and some people have done so and survived the experience. Thus a young man, M, while returning to his home in Lupupa Kampata late one night, saw a *kikudi* along the path. At this time, the girl to whom he was engaged was pregnant, "and when your woman is pregnant, you are very prone to accidents of this sort." M was caused a very restless night, and the next day felt generally unwell with a severe headache; it was thought that he had got off very lightly indeed.

Differences of opinion exist over the appearance of *bikudi* and *mikishi,* but this is not surprising in view of the small number of people who have lived to tell the tale. M, for example, says that he recognized the *kikudi* of a specific person who had been dead for

130

about a year, but he was unable to describe the apparition further. K, on the other hand, and not working from personal experience (a fact he gladly acknowledges), says that all *bikudi* are very short, perhaps two feet tall, and with a huge head on which wild hair sticks straight out. While sighting is rare, a person is sometimes aware of the presence of a *mukishi* because he feels terribly cold around his head, then in his fingers, and finally all over his body. If the *mukishi* has come for revenge, his victim is paralyzed; his mouth is shut, his arms are extended in front of him, his body is rigid, and it is emphasized that he cannot eat or drink because of his shut mouth.

Mikishi, then, are malevolent beings; they cause illness, and this kind of illness has a special name, *nakyo* (s. & pl.), as opposed to *naye* (s. & pl.), which is illness caused by Efile Mukulu. *Mikishi* cause innumerable revenge deaths, and the fact that such a death has occurred can be established by a sorcerer. Sorcerers can control *mikishi* in certain ways, and it is the sorcerer who can protect individuals against them. When one suspects that a *mukishi* has come to take his revenge, he goes to the sorcerer and explains the problem. The sorcerer makes magic while the person holds his arms outstretched; it is taken for granted that the person seeking assistance has killed someone, or the *mukishi* would not be pursuing him. Thus part of the magic process is a confession, which cannot be avoided no matter how hard the person tries to suppress it. Once the confession has been made, it is felt that the *mukishi* can possibly be appeased by a rather large gift, often suggested to be in the amount of two pigs. This gift is given by the killer's father to the father of the person killed, and the *mukishi* may then be satisfied. In the ongoing situation of life, however, one treats *mikishi* as he does *bikudi,* that is, with respect, and it is considered that food offerings are for both and that *kwela mukishi* is a preventive as well as positive measure.

In sum, *mikishi* are malevolent spirits, some of which are doomed to a perpetual existence in this form, and some of which are returned to earth on specific errands of vengeance. They are difficult, if not impossible, to control, they are to be avoided in every possible way, and they account for a number of deaths in the village.

4. Metaphysical Surroundings II:
Magic, Witches, and Sorcerers

The spirits of the dead are only one important means of accounting for death; the two other major death-dealing forces are witches and sorcerers, but in order to understand how they operate, it is first necessary to understand the organization of belief concerning magic. Magic is everywhere in the lives of the Lupupans; it is seen in the anormal actions of others or in the discovery of anormal substances, and its presence is validated by misfortune, illness, and death. It is underlain by Efile Mukulu who made it part of man's existence, and the ancestral spirits are the activating force behind it. A person who has bought magic from a practitioner is in a special state of existence called *kukula* (s. & pl.) in which he remains either until the magic has worked or until he throws it away; it is believed that every male in the village, and many females, has been and probably is now in the state of *kukula*. Makers and users of magic must observe specific prohibitions, often in respect to food, and eating habits are one minor way of uncovering suspected workers of magic. The magic of Lupupa Ngye is shared by the Bapupa and by the Bala as a whole, and thus sorcerers from other villages can be consulted and engaged; Congolese magic, however, cannot be applied to Westerners for a variety of reasons which together add up to practicality. Westerners can see and appreciate Congolese magic, however, even if they cannot participate in it.

In considering the magic system of the Lupupans, it is crucial to understand the contrast between the first two classes in the accompanying chart (Fig. 9), for between them they subsume almost all important day-to-day magic, and provide checks and balances which make it possible both to perform magic and to counteract it. Three major distinctions can be made between these two classes. First, *bakidyamuchi* is action-oriented, that is, it involves actions that are initiated and taken by someone against someone else; *bwanga*, on the other hand, is protection-oriented, that is, it consists almost exclusively in countering action-oriented magic. Second, *bakidyamuchi* always involves malevolent intent and action, ranging from malicious mischief to killing, while *bwanga* counters this malignant intent and, where it is action-oriented itself, is a force for good rather than for evil. Third, *bakidyamuchi* almost always involves individual action, that is, it is undertaken by an individual; *bwanga* is often, though not always, performed for the individual, perhaps communally, by a sorcerer or by the chief. In the classification of magic made by the Lupupans, then, forces of good and evil are placed in direct opposition, and since the two forces are constantly in action against each other, the villagers are always alert to the possibilities of magic.

The magic of classes III and IV, consisting of two cult groups and three masked societies respectively, is transient in nature, since the groups appear and disappear. While it might seem logical to assume that the magic of the cults could be classed under *bwanga* since these groups work for good, the Lupupans see the cults as specifically separate. The masked societies in class IV are also

Fig. 9
Classes of Magic

I. *Bakidyamuchi*

A. *Ndoshi*
1. *kukyesa*
2. *mwanyi*
3. *milungaeulu* (?)
B. *Masende*
1. *peshi*
   a. *peshi a kantole*
   b. *peshi a kityfityfi*
   c. *peshi a lupete*
   d. *peshi a kibofu*
2. *shingye ya muninga*
3. *mushila wa mulungu*
4. *kilanda*
5. *kikano kya muninga*
6. *lumoni*
C. *Buchi bw'eshimba*
   (includes *eshimba dibi*)
D. Evil magic of sorcerers
E. Miscellaneous
1. *bandwela*
2. versus hunter

II. *Bwanga*

A. *Bwanga bwa Kwikela*
1. *lukando*
   a. to protect crops
   b. to trap thieves
   c. success in hunting
      1. *milopwe a batwa*
      2. *kwimonena* (?)
      3. Other
2. *kulala kwa mpeshi*
3. *bwanga bwa mpeshi*
4. *kumbakabamba*
5. *bukishi*
6. *emanya*
7. *ngo*
8. *kipaaba*
9. *kutwa*
10. *kabulubulu* (?)
11. Miscellaneous
   a. for soccer
   b. by chief for village
   c. counter magic in general
B. Good magic of sorcerers

III. Cult Magic

A. *Kishatu*
B. *Lupunga*

IV. *Mulawe*

A. *Kifwebe*
B. *Lumachecha*
C. *Kalengula*

considered to be separate, and their magic activities are in any case not prominent. Let us turn at this point to a discussion of the four classes of magic.

The first subgroup under *bakidyamuchi* consists of the magic of the witch, including that which makes a person a witch and that which is used by the witch to perform mischief. The second class, *masende* (s. & pl.), can be defined as "magic used to kill someone," and it is carried out primarily through the actions of sorcerers. The *peshi* subgroup is concerned exclusively with killing by means of lightning, and *peshi a kantole* ("rain" a type of small red-brown bird) is basic to all the other forms, since the mixture made for it is used in all of them. The sorcerer begins by marking four parallel lines on the ground, representing the place where the intended victim is to be found. He then takes a *kantole* bird which he has trapped and killed, and places it together with a *kitufitufi* (a type of beetle), a *kapete* (a special type of knife), an *ebofu* (a rolled ball of *ediba*), and some unspecified garbage; these are mixed, made into a packet, and burned. The resulting ash is either put into a container or made into a packet, and the sorcerer speaks over it, naming the person he wishes to kill (or the house he wishes to burn), and his location. Soon a small black cloud appears in the sky, the sorcerer repeats the information to it, and lightning strikes. The sorcerer then strikes the packet with a knife and if he smells an odor coming from it, he knows he has been successful. *Peshi a kantole* is considered to be fast-acting magic because the *kantole* is a fast-flying bird. *Peshi a kitufitufi* is slow magic which assures that a human victim will be struck; in *peshi a lupete,* the power from the burned mixture is transferred to a knife which the sorcerer holds in his hand, point upward, while twisting his wrist—each time he twists, the lightning strikes. In *peshi a kibofu,* the sorcerer takes the original packet outside his house, lays it on the ground, and strikes it with a stick while repeating the name and location of the person he wishes to kill or the house he wishes to burn. As he strikes, the clouds come out, the rain begins, and the lightning strikes.

In *shingye ya muninga* ("needle" "to" "kill someone"), the sorcerer thrusts a needle into the footprint of his victim, who dies immediately. *Mushila wa mulungu* ("ask" "of" species of tree) involves burning the bark of the *mulungu* tree and sprinkling the resulting ash in front of the doorway of the intended victim. When he steps out of the house and across the line of ash, his immediate death follows. The *kilanda* is also a tree; its bark is burned with a rat, and the mixture is placed before the door of the victim's house; it causes his feet to swell, followed by swelling in the rest of the body, and eventual death. *Kikano kya muninga* ("bracelet" "to" "kill someone") involves a special bracelet owned by the sorcerer; it is put into a bowl of water, and the sorcerer tells it what he wishes to perpetrate upon the victim.

The final subclass under *masende* is *lumoni*, a magic type which illustrates some of the complexities of the classification scheme. The son of a sorcerer is believed to be an especially attractive target for other sorcerers, for they wish to test their powers against his father. In order to forestall these attempts, the father teaches his son *masende* which, of course, gives him the power to kill and thus to protect himself to a certain degree through intimidation. However, the father may decide that, in fact, he does not wish to have his son as a competing sorcerer, and thus rescinds his teaching. At this point the son again becomes vulnerable, and the father replaces *masende* with the power of clairvoyance in matters of *masende;* this is *lumoni.* The son is thus not only protected because he knows when *masende* is being used or about to be used, but he becomes a force for good in the village because he can and does both warn intended victims and threaten those who are making magic with exposure and retaliation. Philosophically, it appears to the outsider that *lumoni* belongs in class II since it is a force for good; the Lupupans, however, group it with *masende* because it concerns *masende* and because the person who has it has invariably had *masende* in the past.

The third major subclass of *bakidyamuchi* is *buchi bw'eshimba* (someone who has eaten "medicine" "of the" "heart"). Known in common parlance as *buchi,* it refers both to a person who has malevolent intentions toward others, and to the magic he uses to carry out these intentions. A person who is *buchi* is spoken of as one who has *eshimba dibi* ("heart" "bad"); he is a wanderer, always on the lookout for some place he can do harm, some advantage he can take of other people, and some way of bringing bad luck and illness. The Lupupans say of him, *koolwa,* "he is against."

Buchi does not include the power to kill, but in order to become *buchi* the individual must go to a sorcerer for a magic transformation. People who are *buchi* share a number of characteristics with witches, and this includes the transformation process which will be discussed below in connection with the latter. Suffice it to say at this point that in opting to be *buchi,* the individual must designate a member of his own family to be killed by the sorcerer; in fact, this person is changed into a new kind of being, a *kiswikiswiki,* which thereafter must do the bidding of its master. When a person who is *buchi* wishes the creature's assistance, he goes to the sorcerer, who binds the *kiswikiswiki* securely into a relatively small object such as a stick or a lance. The carrier goes to a private spot near the intended victim, tells the *kiswikiswiki* what he wants done, and drops the stick which releases the *kiswikiswiki* to perform the action.

Buchi may be performed by a single person, as in the case above, or when an individual leaves a magic potion by someone's door causing him to become ill; or it may be carried out in groups, as when a number of *buchi* go to someone's field, turn themselves into animals, and destroy the crops. Individual *buchi* are commonly suspected of tampering with food by slipping magic potions into it, thus causing illness or bad luck.

Buchi, then, is malignant work, but those who possess it do not have the power to kill. It should be kept in mind, however, that in order to become *buchi* a member of one's family must be given to be killed.

The evil magic of sorcerers (subclass D) has been illustrated repeatedly in previous paragraphs and will not be further discussed here; additional instances of its use will appear frequently in following pages. The miscellaneous category (subclass E) could be expanded almost indefinitely; as examples, two kinds of magic have been included. *Bandwela* is magic levied against an individual's crops by someone who dislikes him or is angry at him for any of a number of possible reasons. *Bandwela* causes the plants to fall ill, and because of the possibility of this magic, the villagers are not pleased to have large numbers of people trooping through their fields. Magic against a hunter is illustrated by the story of the village *fundi* who said one day that he had been hunting the night before, had come to within six or eight feet of an antelope, had raised his gun, and then found it would not fire. After the antelope had run away, he tried the gun again and it worked perfectly. Since this sort of thing had happened to him "five or six times" in the recent past, and since his hunting fortunes had been at a low ebb, he reasoned that someone had been working magic against him. This could have been from any one of the four major types of *bakidyamuchi,* and it would require the services of a sorcerer to discover the true source and to effect countermagic.

The second great class of magic, *bwanga* (s. *manga*), consists only of devices which protect individuals or groups of individuals against the malevolent magic of *bakidyamuchi. Bwanga bwa kwiikela* refers to precisely the same thing; thus *bwanga* has a general sense of "medicine," while *kwiikela,* as it is known in common parlance, refers specifically to self-protection.

Lukando (pl. *nkando*) might be called "economic" magic, since it concerns crops and hunting; at least three varieties are known in connection with protection of crops in the field. The first makes it impossible for a potential thief to move after he has touched produce which he intends to steal; he is thus trapped until the owner arrives. The second makes it possible for the owner to exist simultaneously in the village as himself and in his field as a snake. When a potential thief arrives in the field, the owner-snake appears and is impossible to kill; the thief thus knows he is opposed by magic, and flees. The result of the third type is that when the potential thief touches something he is attempting to steal, he is attacked by invisible insects which torment him until he confesses.

While the protection of crops involves trapping thieves, a distinction is made by the Lupupans between the two, the former considered more specific than the latter. Thus to trap a thief in the general sense, the sorcerer takes leaves of the *kampesese* tree, leaves of the *mpesha* vine, and a piece of the *tatwe* fish, the latter a species said to swell after it has been caught. The three ingredients are mixed, wrapped in leaves, and placed in a special fish trap which is passed around a fire while the specialist says, "If a thief comes here, he cannot steal anything from this place." The apparatus is kept in the sorcerer's house, and if theft occurs in spite of the magic, the mixture is removed from the fish trap and buried in a hole dug in the main route leading to the village; the thief is then unable to leave. This magic can also be used to stop a thief from pillaging crops; the fish trap and its contents are hung in a tree in the field, and the thief is unable to move once he has touched something, until he is released by the owner.

Success in hunting can be achieved in many ways; some of these have been discussed in the previous chapter and will not be repeated here.

Kulala kwa mpeshi ("to sleep" "of the" "rain") is a means of controlling rain, and is thus not specifically protection-oriented but, rather, is of good intent. The specialist takes four leaves of the *mulolo* tree, and places them on top of each other with two tips one way and two tips the other. He then rolls them into a bundle lengthwise, and spits on them. If he wishes to prevent the rain he waves the leaves in his left hand; if he wishes to make the rain fall immediately, he puts the leaves in water; if he wishes to make the rain fall after a short wait, he holds the leaves a while and then throws them away. However, "if it rains all night, stops a while, and then begins raining again in the morning, no magic can stop it," says the same specialist.

Bwanga bwa mpeshi (s. *manga lwa mpeshi*) has two major and, according to a very few, one minor, functions. Most importantly, it protects a house and the family members against the malevolent use of lightning. It also protects against accidental lightning strikes (one of the few instances in which the concept of accident is used), and some say that it protects against witches, though this last interpretation is rare. The magic apparatus is constructed by a sorcerer who digs a hole in the ground, places a magic potion in it, and covers it with an overturned clay pot of local manufacture or a dome of clay shaped like an overturned pot. No one in Lupupa Ngye can make this magic, and thus the material placed in the hole is unknown; further, a specialist from the villages of Mona, Basanga, or Sankia, must be engaged and paid a chicken for his services. When lightning begins striking close, the owner must tip up the pot and pour cold water into the hole and onto the magic mixture; this will calm the storm and prevent lightning from striking his house. The equation of "cool" and "calming" is a frequent one in the minds of the Lupupans. Those who have thought carefully about this magical protection feel strongly that the water should be used only when lightning is coming very close; they say, "there's no use doing it for nothing," meaning that it is a waste of effort to pour the water for a mild storm or for one that is in the distance. This realistic and practical approach to magic is commonplace in Lupupan thought.

Kumbakabamba is a frequently used magic which prevents one from being wounded. The actual mechanism in this case is not widely known, though some say that the practitioner heats a piece of rubber with a piece of iron, and then eats the rubber; this protects against being wounded with a knife, lance, or apparently, any other weapon. With their usual practicality, Lupupans who profess to have such magic will not submit to an empiric test of its efficacy.

Bukishi is carried out by a sorcerer in the public presence and for the public good. A hole is dug in the center of the village, and unknown ingredients are placed in it. Individuals can then make requests at the site, but these must be of a general nature and for the good of the village as a whole, for example, protection against malefactors or against illness in the village.

The use and composition of *emanya* (s. & pl.) remain in doubt, since no one in the village knows how to make it, and since informants differ as to its use. Some say that its form is a woven ball into which a magic mixture is placed for success in war; others indicate that the form is that of a small basket about the size of the palm of the hand, into which a magic mixture is placed and then eaten to prevent the individual's being poisoned. In the first case, the magic would be regarded as a general good, in the second as protective.

Ngo gives us another instance of a classificatory attitude which differs from that in Western thought. "Let us suppose," says the Lupupan, "that someone has killed my child ["by magic means" is inevitably implied here]. *Ngo* is my action of going to the sorcerer to pay him to kill the guilty person. The sorcerer's action is *masende*, but I am not involved in the killing; although it is initiated by me, it is not done by me." The position here is that revenge is good, legitimate, and self-protective, since elimination of the killer means that he cannot strike again. The writer felt that this magic should be placed in *bakidyamuchi* under *masende*, but his notion was strongly rejected by the villagers.

The idea that children are particularly vulnerable to magic is a common one, emphasized, for example, by the previous discussion of *lumoni*. This vulnerability is marked at the ages of five to six years

140

when children are susceptible to a disease called *nyama* ("meat"), in which the afflicted becomes stiff and dies "within ten minutes." In order to prevent this disease from striking or, if it does strike, to prevent it from killing, children are furnished with a magic apparatus called *kipaaba,* which is worn around the neck suspended from a string. This apparatus is in the form of a ball called *kapulu* (pl. *tupulu:* refers to a round object such as a gourd or bell); it is often made of the dried shell of the fruit of the *kuwa* tree, and it contains an unknown magic mixture made by a sorcerer. While the disease is called *nyama,* it is common knowledge that in reality it is caused by the bite of a serpent called *nyoka,* which is sent against the child by a person of ill will. If the child is bitten by the serpent, the *kipaaba* stops the blood from circulating in the body, and thus the venom cannot reach the child's *kikudi.* Once bitten, the child is taken to a sorcerer who effects a cure which requires a period of about two weeks' time. Thus *kipaaba* is preventive magic which falls in *bwanga;* the causation of the bite of the serpent lies with witches or with persons who have *buchi,* and is thus action-oriented and *bakidyamu-chi.*

Kutwa ("to calm") can be employed in several ways, but best known is its use to prevent drunken people from spoiling a particular occasion. The specialist digs a hole in the path leading to the area where the event will take place, and puts in it two leaves of the *mulolo* tree. On the leaves he throws down a palm nut which has been covered with *ntoshi,* a magic white coloring, and on which he has spit. He then takes water, rinses it around his mouth, cleans his teeth with his finger, and spits the water into the hole; this is repeated, and the remaining water poured into the hole. The palm nut is covered with two leaves, face down, of the *eumbuumbu* tree, some unknown words are spoken, and the hole filled and its presence carefully obliterated. The magic is preventive and protective; the principle behind it is that the sorcerer, by rinsing his mouth, has made the effect of alcoholic drink like water; though people drink they will not become drunk, and thus will not be abusive nor engage in any sort of disruptive conduct.

Kabulubulu (pl. *tubulubulu*) is magic made against witches, and it will be discussed in subsequent pages. The miscellaneous categories could be increased almost infinitely, but it should be remarked specifically that the chief is constantly engaged in magic for the well-being of the village. Finally, subclass B concerns good magic of sorcerers, of which several examples have already been discussed.

Bakidyamuchi and *bwanga,* then, are opposed classes of magic which pit malevolent action against preventive and protective counteractions. Together they account for the vast majority of magic actions in the village, actions which are primarily, but not exclusively, individual in nature. It must be understood that the specific kinds of magic listed under these two major headings represent only a small fraction of what might be included were the ethnographer to concentrate specifically upon magic in his investigations. Important to us here are the classes themselves, the principles upon which they are established, and some illustrations of each.

The third major class of magic has been listed as "cult magic" in Figure 9, and confusion is clearly involved in the designation. Some Lupupans refer to this magic as *lupunga,* the name of a cult movement of recent origin, in which the main features are the prevention of storms and lightning strikes in the village; these protective actions have a magic base. While once again, the outsider is tempted to place this magic under the general heading of *bwanga,* the Lupupans do not do so, insisting that it is a different, indeed unique, kind of magic. Other Lupupans say that *all* cults, except those in class IV, are to be grouped under this designation and that the classification thus encompasses the magic of cults, and I have chosen to adopt this view. Its correctness remains in some doubt, however, and is thus subject to revision.

Kishatu (pl. *bishatu*) is a cult of the *lupunga* type; it was introduced to Lupupa Ngye about 1946, and was banned by the Belgian administration perhaps a year and a half later. *Kishatu* is the name of the person who started the cult; according to the Lupupans, he was a Musongye from Sentery. The version known by the villagers was introduced to them either by Kalumbi or Yantambwe, both described as Bala but of no more specific origin. The *kishatu* apparatus and functioning were roughly as follows.

Kalumbi (Yantambwe?) took a clay pot (*elondo,* pl. *malondo,* a large pot used for drinking and cooking water) and placed within it ash, a piece of meat (of any animal), and a piece of the *mutato* (pl. *bitato*), described here as "the loincloth of a witch." Water was added to these items, and the pot covered and buried in the ground.

Over it was built a mound of dirt (any dirt), apparently about three feet high, six feet long, and two feet wide; its long axis was always placed east and west. The mound, in turn, was surrounded by a special house, *shibo ya kishatu* ("house" "of" "kishatu"), about ten by twelve feet in dimension and fitted with doors on the west and east ends. On the ends of the dirt mound were placed single eggs; these were not ordinary eggs, but eggs left after a hen has hatched a brood (*eyi mulekwa*). The eggs were hardboiled and infrequently changed.

The doors of the house were kept closed in the daytime and open at night, and the head of the cult (*kilela*, pl. *bilela*) was charged with this responsibility as well as with building a fire each night outside each door of the house. While the *kilela* was not paid for his work, he was permitted to take possession of chickens brought by the public as offerings to *kishatu*, and he theoretically received a small portion of the hunters' kills. *Kishatu* was by all accounts open to everyone, but differences occur as to the initiation fee, some saying that the cult was free to all, others citing a sliding fee scale which ranged from a minimum of 50 centimes for babies to a maximum of 5 francs for adults.

Kishatu served four functions for the people of Lupupa Ngye. First, and most important, it was considered an extremely potent protection against witches. Eggs of the type used are especially attractive to witches, because they are not normal eggs, "and witches are not normal," and because witches particularly like to eat them. Thus the witch is drawn into the house because of its love for the eggs; once inside, the piece of loincloth begins talking to it and continues to talk until daylight when the witch is discovered by the *kilela*. A second function of *kishatu* is to guard against lightning strikes in the village as a whole. A third use is operative only if antelope horns are added to the mixture in the pot; if done, this ensures good fortune for the hunters. Finally, two pots of water are kept in the house, one at each doorway; they contain special medicine, and women of child-bearing age drink from the pot at the east door in order to continue to bear, while barren women or women past child-bearing age drink from the pot at the west door in order to bear children again.

The demise of *kishatu* in Lupupa Ngye was apparently brought about by the Chef de Secteur, who complained to the Belgian administration; since all chiefs are considered to be witches, the reason for his complaint is plain enough to the villagers. The administrator came to the village and told the people that *kishatu* would have to be destroyed; according to many informants, the villagers refused, saying that if it were to be destroyed, the administrator would have to be the one to do it. He did, burning the house and digging up the *kishatu* pot.

Kishatu was apparently a fairly widespread phenomenon among the Basongye; Kangudie's description (1948) parallels the Lupupan example quite closely, while Toussaint's (1954) for the Kabongo area shows a far more complex version of the cult. Such religious phenomena have clearly been a part of Basongye culture since at least 1931, and very probably before that time; some of them are clearly contra-acculturative, and some, like *kishatu* in Lupupa Ngye, are new solutions to traditional problems (see Coussement 1935; Toussaint 1953; Wauthion 1940).

The fourth great class of magic is *mulawe* (pl. *milawe*) which applies only to three specific cults which had short durations in the history of Lupupa Ngye. These cults differed from those discussed above in two major respects: they revolved around masked figures and, according to the people, they were "just a game." The latter interpretation seems hardly credible, and it is clear that if nothing else, the cults were a mechanism of social control of women and children, as well as a means of redistribution of wealth, but beyond this outsider's interpretation, little can be gleaned as to their function, and nothing shakes the interpretation of the villagers. The three cults were *kifwebe* (pl. *bifwebe*), probably introduced around 1911; *lumachecha* (s. & pl.), introduced about 1920; and *kalengula* (pl. *tulengula*), introduced about 1927. Since these cults are quite clearly not religious per se, their organization will be discussed elsewhere; of prime concern to us here is the fact that they are based upon *mulawe*.

The masks for the three societies were made by specialists; once completed, the *mulawe* magic mixture (unknown contents) was made and, in the presence of the cult members, rubbed on the mask. It is this magic which activates the mask, and the wearer enters into a special state: "when you wear *kifwebe*, you become something else." This state is known as *bwadi*, and the person who enters it by donning the mask is no longer human nor is he a spirit;

he becomes *kifwebe, lumachecha,* or *kalengula.* The magic also "protects" the mask, in that anyone who laughs at it will break out in sores, anyone who insults it will become insane, and anyone who touches it will cut off his own hand by accident. Finally, *mulawe* protects all those who go out with the mask, and brings them good fortune in general. *Mulawe,* then, is an entirely separate class of magic connected specifically and solely with the masked cults.

Having dealt at some length with magic, how it is classified, and how it works, we can turn now to the two most prominent users of magic—witches and sorcerers. Both these are human manifestations; that is, both are living human beings and both can kill, but the similarity ends there, and witches and sorcerers can be sharply contrasted on a number of grounds. Witches (*bandoshi,* s. *ndoshi*) are entirely malevolent human beings whose chief joy in life is to molest others in every possible way including death; sorcerers (*munganga,* s. *nganga*) may be malevolent or benevolent human beings and, most often, both; sorcerers may also be witches. The witch can fly, the sorcerer cannot; the sorcerer has medical as well as magical knowledge, while the witch has only magical knowledge. The sorcerer knows and can perform *bwanga;* the witch does not, cannot, and does not desire to do good. A sorcerer is a more powerful being than a witch with a far greater variety of resources at his command.

Witches are the creation, of course, of Efile Mukulu, but no one knows why they were created. Some say that the force or power of witches is provided by the ancestral spirits, but this is sharply denied by others; if the statement is true, however, it must be remembered that the *bikudi* gain their power from Efile Mukulu, who is always in control of everything but who acts only according to his own, unknown and unknowable, wishes, desires, and judgment. Witches are "real friends" of Kafilefile, and some suggestion is made that their origin may lie in Kafilefile's evil actions. Their clothing is normal in the daytime, but when they go out, which they only do at night save under the most exceptional circumstances, they wear only a loincloth made of woven raffia fiber; wearing Western clothing during their malevolent activities would destroy their power. *Bandoshi* leave their houses through the roof, never through the door, and when they go out they leave their legs behind which, as we shall see, is a fatal error through which their capture and exposure becomes possible.

145

Some Lupupans speak of three types of *bandoshi,* but most divide them into two groups—those which kill and those which do not; different terms are not used for the two types. Those who suggest three types divide the non-killing witches into two groups, those which twist the victim's neck and leave him ill for a considerable period of time, and those which sport themselves in the fields, destroying crops and defecating everywhere.

One becomes an *ndoshi* through one of two means, the first of which is essentially involuntary. In this case, the individual is born into a family in which the mother and father, or sometimes one or the other, are witches, and his parents wish him to be like them. The transformation is made binding by a special medicine, sometimes referred to as *michi* and sometimes as *myanyi.* It is believed that witch-parents slip the medicine into the child's food unbeknownst to him; the child thus becomes an *ndoshi* without his consent or knowledge. One can also seek consciously to become an *ndoshi,* and he may do this for one of two kinds of reasons. First, it may be "because he is unhappy, because he isn't normal. He wants power and he wants people to fear him, and they do." Second, he may become an *ndoshi* in order to carry out revenge. Some association is made by the Lupupans among nonkilling *ndoshi,* involuntary *ndoshi*-ism, and transformation by the parents, particularly the mother, on the one hand; and among killing *ndoshi,* voluntary transformation, and the sorcerer as the means of transformation on the other, but these are not hard and fast rules. Whatever the means, two points are shared in common by all witches and in both kinds of transformation processes. First, once one becomes a witch, no turning back is possible; one becomes "habituated" and cannot stop even in the virtually unthinkable event that he might wish to do so; becoming an *ndoshi* is a permanent transformation. Second, no matter which process is used, at least one human death inevitably results. If the father or mother is the agent, while the transformation cannot be completed without someone's being killed, it is not clear whether a specific victim is designated. If the sorcerer is the agent, he gives the neophyte a magic mixture to drink, but it is also required that the latter name a member of his own family to be killed; at this point the sorcerer instructs the neophyte how to kill, but it is the sorcerer himself who carries out this particular killing.

146

While considerable confusion and difference of opinion exist regarding details, the Lupupans unanimously associate witches and a special kind of light. Some call this *kaloka ndoshi* (pl. *tuloka bandoshi*), or "witch's fire," while others refer to it as *mutato* (pl. *bitato*) and say that it comes from the witch's anus (*kumusushi*, s. & pl.). By far the most commonly used term in this connection, however, is *lukyekye* (pl. *nkyekye*), but according to the Lupupans, *lukyekye* is a word with four applications: the name of a kind of bird, the name of a kind of tree, the light of an *ndoshi*, and the spirit of a deceased *ndoshi*. The first two meanings, of course, have no connection with witches.

Lukyekye as the light of an *ndoshi* may be interpreted to mean the light "as the manifestation" of a witch, and the Lupupans make a fairly regular association between the appearance of the light and the nonkilling witch. Thus one of the best xylophonists in Lupupa Ngye was once staying in a village near Tshofa and was alone in a house at the time; his friends had just left him, and it was midnight. Suddenly he saw a bright light; he could not move or make a sound. The *ndoshi* twisted his neck around "three or four times," struck him on the neck and on the back, and then left him. He was taken severely ill and spent a month in the hospital.

This is a typical telling of such an encounter. *Bandoshi* operate at night; on the appearance of the light, the victim is paralyzed; this type of witch delights in twisting the neck; one is always left ill afterward, for a period ranging from two weeks to a month, and in extreme cases, for as much as a year. In addition to these characteristics of the situation, the light appears only to the victim, and thus others sitting beside him see nothing and understand nothing of what is happening; this is reinforced by the fact that the victim is paralyzed and thus can neither move nor cry out.

Lukyekye as the spirit of a dead *ndoshi* does not always have a connection with the bright, paralyzing light. When one is visited by this manifestation, he is unable to move or speak, and one of the *lukyekye's* characteristic behaviors is to feed its victim "terrible things—leaves, your own hair." A few people speak of the awareness of the victim in terms such as the following: "When you see the witch's light but do not feel your neck being twisted, then you know that the *ndoshi* has come to kill you; if you see the light and feel your neck being twisted, then you know this *ndoshi* is not

147

going to kill you." While most Lupupans associate *lukyekye* as the spirit of a dead *ndoshi* with killing, a few deny this interpretation. One informant, for example, says that such a being might change the skin color of a newborn or very young baby left alone, and that this would result in some malformation of the body—but the *lukyekye* does not kill. Thus some differences of opinion do occur in connection with the details of *lukyekye*, but it is agreed that the word applies to two different manifestations of the *bandoshi;* and that, as a light, it is a characteristic and unmistakable sign.

While some witches are thus simply malevolent without being killers, it is the killing type which is of greatest concern to the Lupupans. Witches can change themselves into dangerous animals such as the elephant, lion, or leopard, and in this guise kill the domesticated animals of the victim or the victim himself; in the latter case, the witch may be out for revenge, or it may be after human meat to eat. Children who see witches or the light of witches are very likely to die, in some cases because they may naïvely approach and say "You're a witch," in which case fear of identification causes retaliation. A witch may slip a potion into the food or drink of a person, causing him suddenly to see the *bikudi* of all his dead relatives following him; this is a recognition signal that he has been bewitched. He is led inexorably to the *ndoshi* and asks what he must do; the *ndoshi* replies, "You must allow me to kill your sister, or I will kill you." The victim replies, "All right. Take her and release me." *Bandoshi* of the killing type control very strong magic; this is sometimes referred to as *boloko* (s. & pl.), but far more frequently as *masende*, discussed previously.

One of the most feared actions of the *bandoshi* involves the capture and subsequent transformation and manipulation of the human spirit; this series of events can be carried out by sorcerers as well as witches, but in the form presented here, it is most often associated with the latter. The *ndoshi* begins by capturing the breath (*muwa*) of his victim; this he seizes, wraps in a piece of cloth, and tucks under his belt so that it cannot be seen. The family assumes that the victim is dead and has the body to prove it, though in reality by seizing the breath the *ndoshi* has captured the person's *kikudi*, or spirit. After the body has been safely buried, the witch creates a violent rainstorm at night to cover his actions, and goes to the cemetery; the rain does not touch him. There he calls the body out of the grave, and puts body and spirit together again. He has now created a new being called a *kiswikiswiki* (pl. *biswikiswiki*) which is normal in physical form but about the size of a baby and invisible to all save the witch. The *kiswikiswiki* is then taken to the *ndoshi's* house where it is put in a calabash suspended from the ceiling, and where it is supplied with bananas for food. The witch warns his family not to touch the calabash, and fastens a cover firmly to it; if someone raises the cover, the *kiswikiswiki* will escape. If the witch's wife is also an *ndoshi*, he may put her in charge of the calabash and of supplying bananas; either witch always knows without looking when the food supply has run out, and replenishes it.

When the funerary rites have been concluded and the loss has been made less sharp by time, the *ndoshi* takes the *kiswikiswiki* (and he may have accumulated several) to the chief who, it is always assumed, must himself be an *ndoshi;* the chief buys it for a price paid in palm oil, salt, and raffia cloths. The *biswikiswiki* are possessed of special insight in relation to the chief, and can know and warn him of people who are contemplating an attack upon him; they can foresee the future, and can give the chief (or another owner, such as a sorcerer) detailed instructions on how to avoid trouble. These actions are considered to be their obligation and their work.

After a *kiswikiswiki* has served its owner faithfully and well, it may obtain its freedom in one of two ways. First, the owner may simply decide to release it through his own volition, and he may do so as follows: (1) The owner may liberate the *kiswikiswiki*, but send it to a far distant land, having first equipped it with the requisite language. Here the *kiswikiswiki* lives like any other person, although it has a tendency to be slightly crazy, and finally dies—it will be recalled that the *kiswikiswiki* has never, in fact, died; rather, its spirit has been captured. (2) If the *kiswikiswiki* has been especially good, the owner may reward it by setting it free in its own village to live out its life; in this case, no memory of its previous state is retained.

The second means of obtaining freedom is through demand; if a *kiswikiswiki* has done its work well, it can demand its release after a certain (unspecified) time on the grounds that it wishes to return to Efile Mukulu in order to avenge itself on the person who has turned it into a *kiswikiswiki*. The owner cannot refuse such a request, and releases it; the *kiswikiswiki* then does return to Efile Mukulu to whom it presents its request; the request is granted since the cause is just, and the *kiswikiswiki* is transformed into a *mukishi*, or vengeful spirit, which returns to earth and kills its tormentor. With this accomplished, the *mukishi* returns to Efile Mukulu, who changes it into a *kikudi* again, and eventually returns it to earth in a new body. If the *kiswikiswiki* refuses to cooperate and to do its proper work, the owner may turn it into a game animal as punishment and sell it as meat to the villagers; the process through *mukishi* and *kikudi* then takes place as noted above.

A *kiswikiswiki* sometimes asks its owner for permission to visit its friends, and the owner may take the occasion to teach a "moral" lesson by granting the request. In doing so, he changes the appearance of the *kiswikiswiki* to that of a snake, but the *kiswikiswiki* does not know it—the ability to make the transformation implies that the owner in this case must be a sorcerer or a sorcerer and witch simultaneously. When the *kiswikiswiki* approaches its former friends, they are frightened and run away because he appears to be a snake. On the *kiswikiswiki's* return, the sorcerer says, "What did I tell you? See, you'd better just stay in your calabash and give up this nonsense of going to see your friends!"

At the instant an owner dies, all his *biswikiswiki* are transformed into *mukishi* and doomed to wander in the bush; they do not return to a human state. When someone with large holdings dies, the *biswikiswiki* can sometimes be heard as they rush forth, moaning and crying. A person who has killed many people during his life and thus has many *biswikiswiki,* finds himself besieged by them when he is himself near death, for they are anxious to hasten his death in revenge. They surround him especially when he is bathing; when one is ill he does not go far to bathe, his wife prepares bath water for him behind the house, and it is here that he is most likely to be besieged. If this happens, he may run back to his house, and when such behavior is observed the people know this must be a person who has killed many and who has many *biswikiswiki.*

There are "some houses in this village where no one is allowed to look up into the rafters," and if the interdiction is disregarded, the person has probably sealed his fate, for the owner must be either a witch or a sorcerer and certainly does not want it known that he has *biswikiswiki* in calabashes; he will kill the indiscreet viewer as quickly as possible. If one should see a *kiswikiswiki*—and they can and do appear to people under certain (unspecified) conditions—he will probably die on the spot, although in some cases he can be saved if he reaches a sorcerer quickly. While *biswikiswiki* do not cause trouble under normal circumstances, they are extremely dangerous as *mikishi* liberated by the death of their owner.

The *biswikiswiki*, then, can be created by the evil machinations of *buchi*, witches, or sorcerers, though it seems probable that the actual transformation can be accomplished only by sorcerers. In the context of our present discussion, the crucial factor about *biswikiswiki* is that they help substantially to account for death, and that the agents who cause, create, and manipulate them are all human; indeed, they are but a more complex variation of the human cycle through body and spirit.

Because of their ability to capture men's spirits, and because of their other malevolent abilities, witches are the subject of much discussion and action in Lupupa Ngye, and means of recognition of them is a frequent topic of conversation. A number of such clues exist, though some of them are more certain than others. It is common knowledge that all chiefs are witches; the association between the two is immediate, constant, and irrevocable, and it is sometimes extended to include all political dignitaries. Some Lupupans feel that anyone who commits suicide must have been a witch, though this belief is not held by all. Those who do not eat, play, or drink with others may well be witches. Albinos (*basaka*, s. *saka*) are automatically considered to be witches, and so are the assistants of sorcerers. Since *bandoshi* cannot eat hen in public, they may be conspicuous by their abstinence. Some people make an association between witches and cannibalism, but this is not strongly believed, and some say with considerable passion that anyone who would have adulterous relations with the wife of his best friend must be a witch. Some *bandoshi* are recognized because they have changed themselves into a dangerous animal and have subsequently been wounded; when they return to human form the wound remains.

A sure sign of the witch occurs when a child's upper teeth erupt before his lowers; such a child is called *lwino*, and when these teeth fall out "at the age of five or six," someone will surely die. The association is so strong that special songs (*kubinga mwafi*) are sung to celebrate the prior eruption of the lower teeth, because the child "has not been trapped by a witch or a sorcerer," and the father kills a chicken which he, his wife, and the child eat together to celebrate the occasion. Nothing can prevent the child's becoming an *ndoshi* if the teeth have already erupted, but the parents can take a first child to a sorcerer when they notice swelling in the upper gums; the sorcerer retards the growth of the uppers until the lowers have erupted. If one has already had a child or two with this difficulty, he does not take subsequent children to the sorcerer since it is evident that the magic is too strong to be thwarted forever. If such a child is given the first of the harvest of corn or beans, everything left in the fields will be spoiled. The mother of the child is afraid of it and does not give it as good care as she would another. People criticize the child, the parents, and sometimes the lineage as a whole, but little if any overt action is taken; the criticism serves, rather, to remind society to be wary of the young witch.

Bandoshi are also recognized on the occasions of their get-togethers, held at night, preferably at midnight. Some say these take place at crossroads, but the overwhelming majority of opinion is that they are held around isolated trees in the bush, preferably around the *etobo* (pl. *matobo*) tree. At these gatherings the witches sing special songs, and they dance together on the tips of the grasses; evidence is supplied by the bent-over grasses in the morning, and some hold that dew is the spit of the *bandoshi*. During the event, the witches may be visible because of their special light, but it will be recalled that they are seen only by specific individuals; since those around them do not see the light, and since those who see it are unable to move or speak in any case, the sight of the light of the *bandoshi* dancing is always an individual and not a shared experience.

A substantial variety of means of protection against witches is undertaken both at individual and group levels. It will be recalled that the village fertility figure gives protection against witches, and that some people feel the small *mankishi* serve the same purpose. The *kishatu* cult is specifically organized to counteract the powers of witches, and other cults have had the same purpose in the past. If one carries a light with him when he goes out at night, he reduces his vulnerability to witches since they do not like light; prudent people, however, do not go out at night at all unless it is absolutely necessary.

Witches can be killed, sometimes accidentally. One of the best-known and most widely circulated stories in Lupupa Ngye concerns the father of one of the best xylophone players in the village. He was an *ndoshi* and was able to turn himself into a lion, but no one knew this until one day someone shot a lion with a poisoned arrow; the lion disappeared and N's father appeared in its place, saying, "Oh, I've hurt myself in the leg." The people saw that it was an arrow in his leg, but he refused to confess he was an *ndoshi,* and so he died; "if he had confessed, the people would have used medicine to save him."

Sorcerers provide magic to be used against witches, and when it takes effect, the tables are turned and it is the *bandoshi* who cannot move and cannot "see the way." The best-known story in this connection concerns a man who had magic in a bottle which he placed at the base of the *mwabi muchi* tree near his house. "One night a woman *ndoshi* arrived at his house, but he was all right because he had the medicine. He grabbed up a long spike and a hammer and he pounded the spike into the *ndoshi's* back, then pulled it out, pounded it into another place, and continued four or five times. After he had driven the nail in in several places, he told the *ndoshi* to go; the *ndoshi* could not go. It died five days later. When he had the *ndoshi* trapped, he called a friend to help him, and they both recognized the woman *ndoshi.*"

In such a situation, using nails in the manner described is the favorite action of some people, while others advocate beating, knifing, and other forms of assault. In all cases, the result is recognition, if not on the spot, at least the next day when someone in the village is found to be wounded or bruised. Some Lupupans recommend that an *ndoshi* not be killed, since it might be a member of one's own family; thus if one has magic and is immune to witches he may content himself with warning the *ndoshi* not to return, but if it persists he may kill it even if it is a member of his family. Recognition is also provided by the fact that when witches go out at night they leave their legs behind; if one has magic which immobilizes witches, he may be in a position to catch one and to rub red pepper on the stumps of its legs. When the witch returns home, it discovers that it cannot put its legs together again because of the pepper, and the next morning, it is recognized.

Finally, the fact that witches have the ability to fly can lead to their undoing, since a magic apparatus exists which can trap them in the air.

On August 25, 1959, there was a man at Shadika who had two wives. The second wife was an *ndoshi,* but the man did not know it, nor did he know how to be an *ndoshi* himself. The first wife had four children, and one night one of her children stayed with the second wife. She gave him medicine and they jumped together and flew through the air all the way to Elisabethville and back. But when they came back, there was a cord strung across the village street; the woman knew how to avoid it, but the boy did not and he was caught. The next morning people saw him and magic was made, because the father said he was not an *ndoshi* and he did not want his son to be one. That night the child stayed with his real mother, and he said to her,

"Let's play and jump and fly through the air."

His mother said, "I don't know how," and so the child took her to the second wife. Thus the first wife found out that the second wife was an *ndoshi,* and she told their husband. He made a complaint against the second wife at the tribunal, and she is now in prison.

The magic apparatus that trapped the boy is called *kabulubulu* (pl. *tubulubulu*), and it consists of a small *nkishi* suspended fifteen to twenty feet above the village street by means of a cord strung between the roof peaks of two houses. The guardian of the apparatus builds a fire directly beneath the *nkishi* each night, at the same time repeating a magic formula. The *nkishi* then traps witches by drawing them to itself through the power of the magic. The cord also draws witches, and it can descend to the ground to trap those who may be walking there. The witches are trapped by their feet, or by the stumps of their legs if they have left their legs behind; the feet or stumps stick to the cord, and the witch hangs with its head over or in the fire until released.

Witches, in sum, are malevolent human beings with special powers. A witch may be a nonkiller or a killer, and in the latter case, its power to kill always involves the sacrifice to the sorcerer of a member of its family who may be killed outright or changed into

154

a *kiswikiswiki*. Witches of the killing type account for many deaths by their actions, and still more deaths are understood through the fact that honest citizens may and do kill witches in self-protection. The belief in witches makes it possible to account for many deaths in Lupupa Ngye, and the villagers constantly use the *bandoshi* as an explanatory principle for death.

We have spoken much of sorcerers in the previous pages; while the origin of witches is attributed only to Efile Mukulu, sorcerers had a much more complex beginning.

Listen. This is how Kafilefile and Efile Mukulu are together. Efile was seated in the house; Kafilefile was seated outside. There was someone who was sick and people said to him,

"Try to go see Efile Mukulu; explain your sickness to him, and see if he will cure you."

Well, when this man came, he didn't know where Efile Mukulu was, and when he came he found Kafilefile seated in the center of the village. He said to him,

"O chief, I have come to say hello and also to find out what is the matter with my body."

Kafilefile did not speak; he just looked at him and said nothing. So the sick man said,

"I am counting on you. I came here just to say hello to you so that you would explain to me what is the matter with my body. I have talked and talked, but you won't say anything to me in return."

But Kafilefile only pointed with his thumb and said nothing. Then he pointed behind him with his thumb, and said,

"Efile Mukulu is down there."

The sick man could not see it. Kafilefile said,

"There, the house down there." Two times he said it, but the sick man didn't understand. Then Kafilefile said,

"I am Kafilefile. Efile Mukulu is in the house. I am not greater than Efile himself. I don't know what goes on in the body of a man. I am here outside. I don't know anything. Efile is in the house. Go to him and he'll explain what goes on inside your body."

So the sick man went to look for Efile's house, but he didn't see it. He was afraid, and he stopped beside it but at some distance from it. He shouted to Kafilefile,

"I can't find the way to Efile's house." Kafilefile said,

"All right, go back to the village. If the day after tomorrow you will come here while all the other people are still asleep, I'll show you the way to Efile's home."

The sick man forgot the time, however; he forgot to get up early, and when he went he found only Kafilefile. He said to him,

"Show me the place where Efile Mukulu is." Kafilefile said,

"No, explain it to me. Efile Mukulu doesn't like people to see him. Explain it to me."

The sick man said,

"I am sick. Look, here I am sick, and here I am sick. My stomach, my head, my chest all hurt. I cannot sit down. I cannot sleep. I am stuck. That is why I came to see Efile Mukulu. But I haven't seen him; I have only seen you, a substitute for Efile Mukulu. I haven't seen the way to Efile Mukulu's. You told me to be here before other people were awake, but I slept until past the hour and the people had already awakened. And now I have forgotten the way to Efile Mukulu's. Well, why don't you speak to me? I accept you as a substitute for Efile Mukulu."

Kafilefile said,

"All right, I'll tell you what to do. Go to the village and ask for the sorcerers. Efile sent them. Watch all that you see there, and don't think it is lies. Efile himself showed them what to do. When you go to the sorcerer, take with you two *madiba* [for payment]. The sorcerer will fool you, but don't think it is all lies. The breath of Efile Mukulu will enter you, and you will be well. You will be able to do your work. Now don't change anything I have said. It is Efile himself who showed the sorcerer what to do. He isn't someone who is like a thief; Efile himself showed him. I am about finished explaining to you, so listen well. At the sorcerer's place, you can't make a lot of noise. When you go, take a piece of *tungulu* [a grass?] and place it above his door in the center of the doorway. Then he will know that you have come correctly. When you enter the house, give him the two *madiba*. The *kankishi* of the sorcerer will tell you right things and wrong things, but you must accept it. And Efile himself will enter into the sorcerer's things and help him."

This sick man went to the sorcerer's, and when he came out he said,

"It is true. The sorcerer is a true man."

And that is how we came to use the sorcerers. We didn't see Efile Mukulu himself; only Kafilefile who showed us the way to the sorcerer's.

The implications of this story are well understood by a Lupupan audience, particularly the notion that two types of sorcerers are to be found, those who cure the body and are thus

156

"good," and those who do magic and are thus "bad." The hints come in those passages in which Kafilefile tells the sick man he will learn some right things and some wrong things, as well as in the repeated theme that the *nganga* will fool him but he will believe anyway. Since Kafilefile was the instrument through which the sorcerer was revealed to the people, both good and bad were created; had Efile Mukulu been the only means of revelation, sorcerers would probably only have been "good," that is, curers of bodily ills. It is further implied that sorcery is as bad as it is good, and that Kafilefile inserted the bad, while Efile Mukulu intended only the good. This division between the good and the bad in sorcery leads some Lupupans to distinguish verbally between the two types: thus *munganga* (s. *nganga*) are said to be sorcerers who work with medical knowledge (which involves good magic as well), while *banganga* (s. also *nganga*) are sorcerers who work with magic knowledge (and thus with evil). However, almost no sorcerers devote themselves entirely to one kind of practice or the other; indeed, a sorcerer who could not do both would be regarded as hardly worth consulting. Since the Lupupans use the term *banganga* far more often than *munganga,* that plural has been adopted here.

It is impossible to know whether all those with medical knowledge must automatically be sorcerers, or whether some are simply laymen who have received knowledge which has trickled to the general populace from sorcerers. Whatever the case, specific remedies are given for at least the following ailments: headache, diarrhea, malaria, sleeping sickness, vomiting, spurting blood, coughing or spitting blood, dizziness and fainting, broken arm or leg, eye trouble, deafness, wax in ears, sore throat, snake bite, sprain, general swelling, sleepy crumbs, toothache of the molar teeth, pimples, falling hair, gonorrhea, general infection, boils, to sober a drunk, to stop menstruation, impotence, chest congestion, colds, coughs, loss of weight, stomach cramps, stomach ache, foot cramps, prevention of miscarriage, general fever in children. Remedies for all these ailments involve the use of particular plants which are often combined in carefully measured quantities and fed to the patient at specific times. The medical use of amputation, anesthesia, and cauterization were probably not known before the advent of Westerners.

Both men and women have special medical as well as magic

157

knowledge; most such knowledge held by women is concentrated in the hands of the *ntasha* (pl. *bantasha*), or midwife, who usually is especially proficient in connection with pregnancy, babies, and general female complaints. Specific remedies are given by almost any *ntasha* for at least the following: nausea with pregnancy, headache of a pregnant woman, stomach ache of a pregnant woman, backache of a pregnant woman, to strengthen a pregnant girl who is really too young to be having a baby, chest ache of a pregnant woman, conception, strengthening a puny newborn baby, stopping excessive crying of a newborn baby, boils in children, *nyama,* diarrhea, malaria, menstrual cramps.

Bantasha are often, but not always, *banganga* as well. Some *bantasha* know only midwifery, some female *banganga* do not know midwifery but do know medical remedies. Some female sorcerers know only magic, some know both magic and medicine, and some women are midwives and sorcerers knowing both medicine and magic. In general, the *ntasha* and the female sorcerer go hand in hand in the mind of the public, and any woman knowledgeable in either is felt to be knowledgeable in both.

It is primarily female *banganga* who use the magic white coloring, *ntoshi,* derived from a white clay which is found in the water and dried and powdered before application. *Ntoshi* is used less in Lupupa Ngye than in some of the neighboring villages, but the villagers do employ it in both magical and medicinal ways. It is used on the face and body, sometimes applied in rudimentary designs, but primarily only to color. It is part of the treatment of certain illness in women, and it is put on the face as a sign of mourning when a chief dies. Female relatives of a dead male must use it throughout the funeral as a sign of respect, or they will break out in sores. *Ntoshi* is carried in a calabash by the mother of twins when her children are publicly shown around the countryside at the time they first walk. When someone gives the customary gift to the twins, she touches the chest of the giver with a brush which has been dipped into the calabash; this both marks the giver publicly and helps make the twins strong. We have previously mentioned the use of *ntoshi* in connection with magic made to calm potential drunks, and it plays a small part in initiation into the *lupunga* cult. A female *nganga* sometimes covers her own face with *ntoshi* as a means of advertising her medical and magic skills to the villagers.

Lupupa Ngye boasts several *bantasha,* at least one of whom is also considered to be a female *nganga* of limited powers and knowledge. It is unanimously agreed that no true male *nganga* is present in the village population, though several men are known to be minor sorcerers. The villagers apply the term *nganga* to them, but when serious problems arise they go outside the village for a true specialist.

The term *wechi* (s. & pl.) is sometimes seen in the literature on the Basongye, but it is not used by the Lupupans, who say it is the Otetela word for "sorcerer." *Lutundulo* ("someone who knows secrets") is a term which can be applied to sorcerers, but it is never substituted for *nganga,* and is a descriptive term only.

The *nganga* is viewed by the Lupupans with a mixture of desire and fear; he is desirable because he can do good magic, prevent the operation of evil magic, and perform medical cures; he is feared because he can perform evil magic, because he must kill at many points in his magic operation and has been the catalyst for killing in order to become an *nganga* himself, and primarily because he is at the seat of all magic practice. "An *nganga,*" say the villagers, "can do all he wishes to do. He can work all the types of magic and he is at the source of all magic." In order for anyone to use any kind of magic, he must consult the *nganga* at some point in the proceedings. A layman cannot himself create magic, but must always buy it from a sorcerer. The sorcerer, then, has enormous powers which he may or may not use impartially.

Since no real *nganga* is to be found in Lupupa Ngye, the villagers are vague on the circumstances and process of becoming a sorcerer as well as the source of power. One minor sorcerer, however, explained the matter in terms of *bukopo* (s. & pl.), and his explanation was confirmed by others.

According to these men, *bukopo* is the force behind magic, a force which exists independently and completely apart from any other force; it is controlled by sorcerers, and not by Efile Mukulu per se, or by ancestral spirits. The sorcerer has at his house a sack containing various objects which have force; the sack is called *mabofu dya bishimba* ("sack" "of" "things which have force"), and the objects are such items as lion teeth, elephant teeth, *nduba* feathers, termites, skin of an animal's heart, and so forth. By themselves, these things have no quality of force, but once "activated" by the *nganga,* they act as a sort of repository of force. The *nganga* receives his *bukopo* from his teacher who may or may not be his father, but *bukopo* can also be obtained from Efile Mukulu through dreams.

An *nganga* can transfer *bukopo* to someone else by showing him exactly how to perform an item of magic, and only by showing, not by telling. At the same time, he must be careful to do this magic himself beforehand; if he forgets to do so, all the *bukopo* goes with it to the new owner and is irretrievably lost. Some of the sorcerer's *bukopo* goes to the initiate in any case, and this is what enables the latter to perform the magic; the *nganga,* however, is not less powerful for having lost this force, for an equal quantity comes automatically from Efile Mukulu to replace what has been transferred to the initiate. A dying *nganga* who transfers all his *bukopo* to his son, however, is left without any power. Thus when an *nganga* transfers part of his power, it is automatically replenished; when he transfers all of it, he has lost it permanently. Some of the minor *banganga* of Lupupa Ngye believe that a fixed quantity of *bukopo* may exist in the world, and it is also suggested occasionally that the individual *nganga* has a fixed quantity of *bukopo,* which apparently can be dissipated; but neither of these beliefs can be conclusively confirmed or denied.

It is of the greatest importance to reiterate that to become a sorcerer one must give up members of his family to be killed. This pattern is the same for all persons who desire to engage in malevolence of any kind; *buchi* costs one member of the family, to become a witch of the nonkilling type costs more, and so on. The best estimate of the number of people who must be killed in order to create an *nganga* is ten, but regardless of whether this is accurate or inaccurate, the principle is consistent throughout the system—the power to do evil costs the deaths of members of the family.

Some Lupupans deny the existence of specialization within the practice of sorcery, and certainly none is found on the level of hunting or fishing magic, for example. Some *banganga,* however, do devote themselves primarily, but not exclusively, to the practice of protection-oriented magic (*bwanga*), while others are most interested in action-oriented magic (*bakidyamuchi*). Specialists in medicinal remedies exist in the same sense, and some Lupupans say that some sorcerers are unabashedly malevolent and are thus "specialists" in causing trouble.

Sorcerers have assistants called *kamashi* (pl. *tumashi*), but they do not seem to be apprentices. Their identity is not secret and, in fact, they may wield secondary power because they are able to control others through their association with the power of the *nganga*. Some Lupupans state categorically that *tumashi* are always witches, but others deny this. The *kamashi's* principal tasks are to run errands for the sorcerer and to gather necessary ingredients for his magic. When a sorcerer decides to promote his abilities through what might be called a sample demonstration, he sends his *kamashi* to a neighboring village with hunting magic which he offers for nothing and which the *kamashi* sets into motion. This, however, is short-term magic, and if the village has good hunting luck, it may send a representative to the sorcerer with payment for what has been done, and also to obtain more of the magic, for which payment is made in full. *Tumashi,* finally, can do some simple visible magic such as holding an adze in the air, letting go, and leaving it hanging there, but it is the *nganga* who makes it possible for him to do this and it is, again, something analogous to the advertisement of the sorcerer's powers.

In the sphere of magic which the people of Lupupa Ngye regard as beneficial, some of the *nganga's* powers are as follows. *Banganga* can exorcise *mikishi*. If trouble has come on the village after a recent death and normal remedies do not work, the *nganga* may exorcise what is obviously the spirit of the dead by digging up the body and burning it. Only a sorcerer can do this, because only he has magic powerful enough to protect himself. Some *banganga* can predict the future, but such persons are very rare, and are known under the special title, *shaynu a bukishi* ("your father" "of" untranslatable); one speaks of the ability of such a sorcerer "to know the future" (*mukubuka*). A similar power is the ability to see evil in others, discussed above as *lumoni*. One of the most famous instances of this kind of power, an instance cited frequently by the Lupupans, occurred in 1948, when eighteen elephants went by the village; the event had been correctly predicted by a sorcerer. It is believed by some, incidentally, that these were not eighteen elephants but eighteen traders who consulted a sorcerer for magic to change them temporarily into elephants, in order to avoid the Belgian administrator who was in the village at the time.

In warfare, the *banganga* make magic for success, but perhaps more importantly, to protect the warriors against pursuit and revenge by the spirits of those they have killed. It is the sorcerer who prevents lightning strikes (*manga lwa mpeshi*), who activates the protection against the dread children's disease, *nyama,* and who is called into consultation in situations inexplicable to those who undergo them. In the last case, for example, at midnight one night, A awoke and felt impelled to look outside his house; sitting there was M, who was not drunk and who would not answer any of A's questions concerning his purpose in being there. A felt that M could only be engaged in magic, and immediately hired a powerful sorcerer from the neighboring village of Basanga to make counter-magic.

It is the sorcerer who puts general beneficial magic into action; this includes the village fertility and magic figure, and the *kishatu* cult. Among his most important functions, the *nganga* searches out the cause of specific deaths in the village; as noted previously, almost no deaths come from what Westerners call natural causes. It is instructive to note the bare outline of procedure in this connection. On the morning of September 28, 1959, K, a young middle-aged man and one of the most respected men in the village, fell dead near the bridge across the Lupupa River as he set out on foot for Tshofa and a meeting with the Chef de Secteur. He had not been ill and the body gave no clues as to the reason for his death. Within hours a sorcerer from the neighboring village of Kalunga had been called in, and he ascertained that the cause of death was magic; he also named two prime suspects, one from Lupupa Ngye and one from Lupupa Kampata. It was then recalled that the former, E, had recently had a dispute with the deceased concerning land; he was said to have appropriated some of K's land, and to have taken some of the crops and tree produce from it. The suspect from Lupupa Kampata, M, was said to have argued recently with K about the chieftainship. By October 3, five days after the death and while the funeral was still underway, this knowledge was fairly general in the village. The day before, M had been very careful to drop by my house to say that he had heard people attributing K's death to magic, but that for his own part he felt it was "an act of God and not the act of a human being." On November 6, it was reported that the sorcerer was still working on the problem, and that he had spent several midnights at K's grave.

162

Eleven days later, it became known that the visiting sorcerer had discovered that the guilty one (still unknown) of the two suspects had either been instructed by, or had given instructions to, the dead man's older brother's wife's mother's brother who lived in the neighboring village of Lumba; the entire family left Lupupa Ngye to go to Lumba to thresh the matter out. On November 20, the suspect in Lumba died suddenly, and this was considered conclusive evidence that he had supplied the magic to the guilty party; it was later rumored that his entire family had died as well. By March 26, 1960, six months after the death, the suspect E had been dropped from consideration, and M had become the sole object of suspicion. On April 19, however, M was named the new chief of Lupupa Kampata and Lupupa Ngye, and the suspicions against him were never mentioned publicly again. It is not likely, however, that the sudden silence was because of the importance of his new position; rather, his ascendency to the chieftainship would be regarded as confirmation of his being a witch and thus an even better suspect. Indeed, it is most likely that this solved the case so far as the people were concerned. However that may be, the investigations of the sorcerer had led clearly to the death of the suspect in Lumba, and possibly to the deaths of his family as well; furthermore, K's death was explained and his *mukishi* had partial revenge at least.

While the *banganga* perform these "good" services for the villagers, they are also at the root of much evil. The person who wishes to do formal evil as a *buchi* or a witch must always consult a sorcerer, and the transformation always involves the death of at least one member of his family. It is the sorcerer who manipulates lightning for the purpose of killing, and it is also he who steals shadows for minor causes. The magic of *kwimonena,* which gives a hunter the power to see game before other hunters do, is controlled by sorcerers, but two classes of *kwimonena* exist, divided on the basis of their comparative strength. In order to obtain the more powerful of the two, the hunter must give up someone in his own family to be killed by the *nganga.* Sorcerers can kill directly by leaving a powder in someone's house, by "cutting" a clay pot filled with water, and by many other means. In a less directly violent sense, the sorcerer can control the physical movements of others, holding a victim blind and helpless, for example, while he takes or does whatever he wishes. An *nganga* can draw a line in the dirt and make magic which prevents his victim from stepping over it; "he can offer you a cigarette but you can never finish it; he can offer you a drink in a skullcap, but you can never finish that either." It is primarily the *nganga* who creates, keeps, and controls the *biswikiswiki,* although witches have this power as well.

Finally, the *banganga* are associated with the *milungaeulu,* which are essentially evil beings sometimes met by accident or by evil design; accounts of such meetings are quite uniform.

> A saw a *mulungaeulu* one night in Sentery. He was working in the post office at the time, and had been writing letters there until about one in the morning. Half an hour later, as he was walking along the road toward home, he suddenly saw the *mulungaeulu;* at that precise moment, he had stopped to light a cigarette. The being was "five or six metres tall" and all white—much whiter than a Caucasian. It had arms and legs like humans, but he never saw its face. He was terribly frightened and ran all the way home.

* * * * * * *

> One day M shot an antelope; the animal fell on the ground and M went up to it to pick it up. He was going to skin it and was looking down at it when he happened to look up and to his right, and there was a *mulungaeulu.* It was terribly, terribly tall, so tall that he could not see its head. It looked like a tree; it was tall and thin. He did not notice what color it was, but it had terribly long and thin arms; he did not see the fingers nor whether it had fingers at all. It had two arms and two legs, and he saw feet. It wore clothing, but he does not know what kind. He could not see whether it had hair on its head because he could not see its head. He had a lamp with him; he turned immediately and fled, then stopped and looked back with his gun poised—it had disappeared. It neither moved nor made any sound when he was looking at it. He thought it might make him sick, kill him, or eat him, but it did not. It was the only one he ever saw.

* * * * * * *

> K saw a *mulungaeulu* once. It was taller than a house, too tall to see the head and face. He was in his house, and he was so frightened that he defecated. He knows nothing about the feet or arms, because when one sees a *mulungaeulu* his stare is fixed on whatever part he first happens to see—K was looking at the chest. However, it wore black clothing, and he says that in overall aspect it was black and white.

In addition to being white (or black and white), and extremely tall and thin, the *milungaeulu* are mute, and move silently and without leaving footprints. While these points are generally agreed upon, sharp division exists when it comes to the source of the *milungaeulu;* two major and one minor views are held.

The first major view is that *milungaeulu* are witches in changed form. In order to achieve this form, the witch must consult a sorcerer from whom it receives magic which enables it to make the transformation at will for the rest of its life; the acquisition involves giving a member of the family to be killed by the sorcerer. *Milungaeulu* are always evil, and they have the power to kill; for those who hold this set of beliefs, a witch who kills is always a *mulungaeulu.* Some say that *milungaeulu* have very tiny arms and huge feet so that they make a great deal of noise in walking, but this appears to be a rather idiosyncratic view. If one sees a *mulungaeulu,* he will suffer no harm if it is not "intended" for him; if it is so intended, he is considered to be as good as dead on the spot, though some people have recovered from such an attack through the fortuitous intervention of a sorcerer. If one believes that the *milungaeulu* are a manifestation of witches, he also believes that they are a human manifestation, since witches are by definition malevolent human beings.

A second major view holds that the *milungaeulu* are beings created by Efile Mukulu but controlled and manipulated by sorcerers for their own purposes; in this case, they are always conceptualized as being evil. If one is intended for a person, he will see it, but otherwise the *milungaeulu* are invisible. The sole purpose of the sorcerer in sending them out—always at night—is to kill. *Milungaeulu* may also be able to capture the breath and thus make it possible for the sorcerer to create *biswikiswiki,* but this is not certain. If one believes that the *milungaeulu* are created by Efile Mukulu, he also believes that they are a nonhuman manifestation.

The third view is a completely idiosyncratic one, but because it accounts logically for some aspects of the matter, it is noted below.

> *Milungaeulu* were all created by Efile Mukulu when Jesus was born. At that time there was at least one in every village; they were everywhere, but they have since disappeared. In those times, they were good and they brought good fortune, but now they are mostly

bad, and if you see one you will not be able to eat and you will slowly die. When I was a child, the people used to get up early in the morning, "at cock crow," to see the *milungaeulu*. I saw them once. In those days, one could look at them without harm; in fact, it was good to see them.

I do not know why, but the *milungaeulu* came to be controlled by the *banganga*. *Banganga* are like traders; when they see something that everyone likes they want to turn it to their own purposes. The number of *milungaeulu* is the same at present as it was when they were first created by Efile Mukulu; none have been created since, and the sorcerers cannot create them, they can only manipulate them. At present the bad *milungaeulu* far outnumber the good, controlled by Efile Mukulu. A good *mulungaeulu* can be seen by everyone, and when one is seen by many people, then it is known to be all right; if only a single person can see it, then it is a bad one controlled by a sorcerer, and the one who sees it is done for. They are invisible—"you can't see the wind, can you?"—and are only visible when they want to be (the good ones) or when a sorcerer sends them (a bad one). The good ones spend their time with Efile Mukulu; the bad ones stay in the sorcerer's magic apparatus where they are trapped.

The influence of Christianity is obvious here, and it seems possible as well that the *milungaeulu* are associated in the speaker's mind with angels, both risen and fallen. Whatever the case, the ideas concerning good and bad *milungaeulu* are not unreasonable and may represent some aspect of traditional belief still held by this older man.

In addition to the many substances used by sorcerers that have been noted, a variety of materials from the body are also employed in magic practice. These materials include pieces of hair, skin, nail clippings, urine, feces, and bath water among the most commonly mentioned. Bath water is never allowed to stand, but is immediately thrown out; once it has soaked into the ground it cannot be used by a sorcerer. Nail and hair clippings are thrown secretly into the bush where they will be destroyed eventually by bush fires. Urine and feces in outdoor toilets cannot be used in magic because they are the mixed excreta of many people, but feces from the bush can be used if the sorcerer can identify their source. In addition to these specific body materials, anything which has been in close and habitual association with a person can be used. Thus a sorcerer can scrape the wall where one rests his head while sitting, and use the material magically; clothing can be used in the same way. If someone spits out a piece of sugar cane after sucking the juice, the residue is potentially powerful and thus the Lupupans are careful about disposing of garbage.

Objects such as these can be used in three ways. Materials from A may be taken by B to a sorcerer in order to effect magic to kill. Materials from one's own body may be taken to a sorcerer to make magic to protect one's self from others. Materials may be taken from the body of the deceased and used to avenge him through magic; a dead person is considered powerful "because he has seen Efile Mukulu." Nail clippings and other such materials are used only in magic made to kill.

Finally, some Lupupans hold the sophisticated view that the power of the *nganga* is a seductive and evil power which progressively affects those who become caught up in it. Thus, says a part-time sorcerer in the village, "a person decides he wants to be *buchi*, and to do that, he must go to a sorcerer, and there is one dead. Then he isn't satisfied with that, so he decides he wants to be a witch who twists necks, and then he decides that he wants *masende* so that he can kill, and there are eight more dead, four for the sorcerer and four for the witch. Then he isn't satisfied with that, but he wants to be an *nganga* himself, and that will cost the deaths of ten." For this man, the sequence is a very distinct possibility, and it illustrates for him the dangers of mixing with *bakidyamuchi*, evil magic.

The religious philosophy of the Lupupans, then, is based upon four basic postulates. The principle of reincarnation provides for a kind of multiple consciousness which accounts for interaction among the living and the dead, while fate and predestination are mechanisms against which these interactions take place. The system hinges, in turn, upon the fact that Efile Mukulu is not the direct agency of death, although he has provided the means by which death is carried out, and retains a day-to-day knowledge of what is happening. Since no other nonhuman spirits exist except the *milungaeulu*, since the latter are not free agents of death, being instead manipulated by human beings, and since accident and sheer old age account for only a minuscule proportion of deaths, the only activating source left is man himself. And if man is the prime agent of death, he must have the means to carry it out; these means he finds in the belief in magic performed primarily by witches and sorcerers. Thus the religious beliefs of the people of Lupupa Ngye are both logical and internally consistent. Taken together they account for life and death and good and evil, pairs of forces which in the end are balanced against each other, thus providing for a never-ending continuity in time until Efile Mukulu decides to change it for reasons which will surely be known only to him. "Efile Mukulu told us it would be this way," and that is the way it is.

5. Human Surroundings I:
Slaves, Kinsmen, and Affines

As the people of Lupupa Ngye live in a physical world and a metaphysical world, so also do they live in a world of human beings with whom they are in constant interaction in a great variety of ways. It is to these human surroundings that we now turn our attention.

If the hypothetical average male Lupupan could somehow stand above his village, and see arranged around him in some kind of structured order all the people and kinds of people he either knew or of whom he had heard, what would he perceive? Farthest away, of least specific concern, and certainly least well-known to him, would be those persons he calls "Europeans," which includes all those with "white" (in Lupupan terms, "red") skins. These people are Belgians, Portuguese, and Americans, and they fill the roles of administrators, traders and storekeepers, and imperfectly understood anthropologists. They come from unknown places for unknown reasons, but in 1959–60, they were firmly ensconced in the seat of power and were persons to be obeyed, deferred to, and "respected" (see Merriam 1961a:173–94).

A slightly stronger bond would be felt by our hypothetical Lupupan for the people called "Congolese," understood to be a large and amorphous mass of "black"-skinned people with whom something is held in common. The nature of this bond is unknown but it is slightly felt; at the same time, *knowledge* of these people is considerably less than knowledge of "Europeans."

Much closer to home and, relatively speaking, much better known, are neighboring tribes, including most specifically the Batetela, very near neighbors to the north, and the Baluba, almost omnipresent in Basongye territory and much disliked for their aggressiveness in economic matters which has ingratiated them with Westerners. Individuals from many other tribes are known, or have been known in the past, and a substantial list of recognized tribal names could be gathered from the Lupupans; knowledge of them as a people, however, is scanty.

Some Lupupans have traveled among one or more of the neighboring tribes and also among the next narrower entity, the Basongye, but familiarity with these groups is not strong. The villagers acknowledge the fact that they are Basongye, and do so with some pride, but this is by no means their primary orientation. Indeed, even in Basongye territory, the traveler is among strangers, and he is not normally at ease until he has returned at least to the Bala, a grouping with all of whose members he claims some kind of relationship.

It is at this point that the Lupupan begins to relax, for he has quite probably traveled fairly extensively, at least within a radius of perhaps fifty kilometers of his home. In this area he knows a number of people personally; they have traveled to his village and he to theirs, and indeed, with a fairly substantial number of them in many different villages, he has established a network of institutionalized friendships. He has traveled along the major routes established by mutual consent among those concerned, and he knows the customary behavior which will assure him of a nonhostile welcome.

These major routes are best known as they extend among the three sister villages—Lupupa Ngye, Lupupa Kampata, and Makola—whose people together constitute the Bapupa. The villager considers himself to be one with these people, though the specific links cannot be traced, and he has kinsmen and affines there who can be counted upon for cordial welcome. Thus, being in Kampata or Makola is almost like being at home, but he is most at ease, of course, in Lupupa Ngye where no one is a stranger except those traveling through to whom he, in his turn, extends his hospitality in the normal course of events.

As our hypothetical villager looks down upon Lupupa Ngye, he sees 276 people, of whom 240 truly "belong there," and the rest are transients. He sees a village divided in half by an imaginary line, and the halves in turn divided in half, making four quarters which are the basic units for legal recourse. He sees certain men filling fifteen major political positions, other men and women who are slaves, and the vast majority of ordinary citizens and their children. Some of these people would be his friends and some his enemies; among the former would be both male and female institutionalized friends, and at least in former times, among the latter would be some groups of institutionalized enemies. Some people would be his kinsmen, members of his immediate family or of his lineage, some would be related to him by marriage, and to some he would not be related at all. Some people would be old, others young; some male, others female, but toward all of them, and shared in groups with many, he would have special social and political relationships and responsibilities.

Thus wherever the Lupupan looks, there are people, some of whom he knows hardly at all, and some of whom he sometimes says he knows all too well; and these people are perceived and ordered in particular ways and in particular groups. The individual Lupupan exists in relationship to, and constant interaction with, these people, and it is these aspects of his humanity to which we now turn.

The population of Lupupa Ngye consists of 276 people, of whom 240 are free men or slaves who have been accepted into the social system, 32 are transients in the village working as the schoolteacher or as storekeepers and roadworkers, and four are slaves who remain outside the formal system. The figures in the accompanying diagram (Fig. 10) indicate the distribution of this population by age groups; included are only those males native to the village and their spouses (many of whom are not) and children, while transient strangers and slaves not absorbed into the social system are excluded.

Fig. 10

Population of Lupupa Ngye: Distribution by Age

Age	Male	Female
81–90	2	3
71–80	1	1
61–70	8	6
51–60	9	13
41–50	14	16
31–40	10	21
21–30	10	17
11–20	23	11
1–10	43	32

The ten-year intervals represented in the diagram would not be a method chosen by the villagers to speak of age groupings; instead, they would divide the people on the basis of criteria which have their analogues in Western terms such as "baby" and "adolescent." As is so often the case in Lupupa Ngye, individuals put different interpretations on the same facts, and the matter of age divisions is no exception. Most villagers, however, class as *bana* (s. *mwana*), all those from the newborn to the thirteen year old; the dividing line is a social age, the time of circumcision. The period from thirteen to thirty-five includes males called *basongwalume* (s. *songwalume*), and females called *basongwakashi* (s. *songwakashi*); their social roles are indicated by the fact that the age grouping is said to include "people who are married, people who are eligible for the army, people who cultivate or who do other work." From the ages of thirty-five to sixty, both men and women are called *bantu bakulu* (s. *muntu mukulu*), but in fact, it is almost exclusively the men who are so designated. The final category includes those from age sixty until death; such persons are called *banunu* (s. *mununu*), and the term is applied, say the people, "when their hair starts to get gray."

We have pointed out that at least four broad social groups are found in the village, including free men and women and their children, slaves, political dignitaries, and transient strangers. Let us discuss each of these categories briefly and in reverse order.

The transient strangers need occupy little of our attention; thirteen of them are roadworkers and their families who live near but not in the village; their houses are across the road or some two or three kilometers south, but they are considered to be centered in Lupupa Ngye. Three of the males and the father of one of them come from the village, but they have cut their ties for the present, at least, and are not considered to be permanent residents. The schoolteacher is a Mushilange who lives with his wife and four children in a house provided at the western edge of the village. One of the storekeepers is also a Mushilange whose wife and child are not with him, and the other storekeeper is a Mutetela with three wives, two of whom are Batetela and one of whom is a Lupupan, and the single child of his second wife; both families live in shacks near their stores.

Finally, an older married couple without children, a younger couple with two children, and a single girl with an infant live within the village in association with particular lineages. They are not, however, Lupupans—the first couple comes from Makola and the origin of the others is not known to me—and they are not considered to be a permanent or structural part of the social system.

By including the holders of the fifteen major political offices as one of the four broad social groups in the village, I do not wish to suggest that they form a class, caste, or aristocracy. They are, however, socially visible as individuals, known for their offices, and extremely proud of having been named to them and thus having received the trust of the villagers. Their titles are not directly inherited, though the rights to them are held by specific lineages. They are today seldom marked by any badges of office or distinctive dress, but of course in a village the size of Lupupa Ngye, their identity is known to all. Political dignitaries, then, make up an informal social group, included here because of its recognizability, because it acts as a unit, and because its members do receive some special attention and some economic benefit because of their "membership" in it.

Slavery is a distinct institutionalized part of Basongye society.

Although the practice has long been banned by the state administration, it persists in a variety of ways; in Lupupa Ngye, however, it is a dying institution.

Slaves (*bapika,* s. *mpika*) in the past could be bought directly, and according to some of the old men of the village, slave merchants traveled through the area, selling people for produce or other exchange. These merchants were in the business of selling slaves, and were not simply casuals passing by; it seems likely that they were Arabs or Arab-inspired, and that the period of time referred to was the late nineteenth and, perhaps, the early twentieth century. The villagers today believe that slaves sold in their village in this way were either Bekalebwe (a Basongye subtribe) or Batetela, and they indicate a general price structure which, of course, may or may not be valid. A child could be bought for four meters of raffia cloth and one chicken; a young to middle-aged man brought 100 raffia cloths; and a woman, because "she will produce children," brought the highest price of 200 raffia cloths.

A second source of slaves was by capture in war, and some men say it was "more important to take slaves than to kill people in a raided village." Men, women, and children were probably taken, though some suggest that men were killed, that only women and children were taken, and that females were a more valuable and sought after prize than males. Sometimes raids were undertaken for the specific purpose of taking slaves, and those who claim to remember seeing the return of the raiders say that a rope was tied around the neck of a slave and then looped around the necks of those who followed him in single file.

A third source of slaves was through debt, in which case the debtor might become a slave to the person owed, or the latter might sell him to someone else. A fourth source was through poverty, for a person driven to desperation might give his oldest child to someone as a slave. In return, the recipient agreed to supply the free members of the family with food, or whatever was needed, and the child could be bought back. While this might appear to be a situation of pawn, the Lupupans regard it as an example of true slavery.

A fifth source for slaves was through punishment for crimes, and it is clear that what is handled through fines and imprisonment today was often formerly handled through slavery. Thus in the case of murder, the injured family could take the culprit and "two or three" other members of his immediate family as slaves. If the rape of a pregnant woman resulted in abortion, the guilty man was made a slave without hope of manumission. An apprehended thief could make restitution of property, or its equivalent, plus a fine, and remain free; if he could not do so, he was taken slave by the injured party, again without hope of manumission.

> My brother, Somwe, was made a slave. He went one day to a field with a friend, and the friend began stealing manioc. He told Somwe to wait for him. When Somwe cautioned him not to steal, his friend said,
> "Don't worry. It's not your affair. You're just waiting for me."
> But while the theft was in progress, the owner arrived, and Somwe and his friend were caught and taken before the notables, who said that Somwe was just as responsible as his friend:

nboinchila	ngifi	we	ngifi.
to attend	a thief	you are	thief

> If you attend a thief, you're a thief.

> Our father did not have enough to pay the fine assessed, and Somwe was sold for seven *madiba* to someone in Kabinda. The notables took the entire payment, and they didn't give any compensation to the owner of the field.

Wastage is also considered a crime in Lupupa Ngye, and the examples are legion and the punishments severe. "A person is grinding manioc flour and someone comes along and provokes a fight. If the flour is spilled during the altercation, the provoker becomes a slave. The reason is that food is very important, and especially in those times there was none too much of it." "Suppose Mandungu is working for APM, and while he is carrying water, someone provokes a fight with him and the calabashes are broken. Mandungu will report this to APM, and the provocateur will become APM's slave." "Suppose I have a field of tobacco, and someone steals some of the crop. I become angry, and in my rage I wantonly destroy what is left. I will be taken before the notables of the village, and if I am judged guilty, I become a slave of the chief as penalty." "Suppose someone becomes angry at someone else or because of something, and he becomes so angry that he burns down

175

his own house. He will be taken before the notables, and if he is judged guilty, he will become a slave of the chief."

Other crimes considered severe enough to bring the penalty of slavery include the wounding of any member of the family of the chief, and irresponsible behavior which leads to injury; an example of the latter is the following: "Suppose I go down to the river to bathe, and I hide in the bushes and then jump out to frighten someone by pretending to be an animal. The person is injured when he tries to get away from me, and I am caught. This is enough to make me become his slave for life and without possibility of manumission."

A sixth source for slaves was apparently through the pressure felt by notables in the political hierarchy to be generous in giving gifts to members of the populace. An example of this kind of generosity is Kadiya, a Mutetela man of perhaps 85 years who has spent his life in Lupupa Ngye as a slave. His story is as follows:

> Kadiya's father was a chief, Chief Otepa of the Batetela village of Nayenge which is somewhere near the present town of Lodja. A man named Mulangwa of the lineage Bena Yankamba of Lupupa Ngye was known to be an excellent sorcerer, and he used to travel around the countryside selling his magic skill. He was once near Lubefu and there he met Chief Otepa for whom he made fertility magic. As payment, Chief Otepa gave Yankamba 50 *madiba*, and Kadiya.
>
> At that time, Chief Otepa had two children only, and he had already sold Kadiya's older brother to the Bekalebwe as a slave. After Kadiya had been "sold," the chief's wives had another son and a daughter, so Mulangwa's magic was considered successful.
>
> It was incumbent upon Kadiya's father to give a child in payment precisely because he was a chief; all notables did this and it applied to payments made for magic or building a house, as well as when the notable had no other ready means of payment.
>
> Kadiya was about seven years old at the time, and he never saw his father, any member of his family, or any person from his village again. "I don't know anything about my father, whether he is dead or alive." Kadiya says that he cried when Mulangwa took him away, but that Mulangwa was very nice to him; he gave him food and clothing, carried him around on his shoulder, and treated him like a member of the family. When he cried for his father, Mulangwa said,
>
> "Oh, don't worry. Your father will come in a while," but Kadiya says,

"He never came and I never saw him again."

I asked him to reflect on his life, and he said,

"I have had luck here. This is the place I know, and my old village would be strange to me. I was lucky that they didn't kill me. I have five children. This is my home now."

The seventh, and final, source for slaves, was the children of slaves. Some hold that children of slaves, their children, and all subsequent lineal issue are slaves as long as their origin is remembered by free people, while others say flatly that the children of slaves are free. Most probable is a middle ground, as explained by the head of the lineage which apparently traditionally held the largest number of slaves. In his view, slaves were involved in marriage with three kinds of partners, and the children of the different unions held different statuses. Children of a union between a male slave and a female slave had a middle status; while not really slaves, neither were they free, and it is significant that the master could sell them. The children of these "half-slaves," however, were considered free, and the master had no control over them, though their origin continued to be known with some resulting stigma attached to them.

When a male slave married a free woman, which was sometimes the case, the woman remained free while the children held the "half-slave" status, with the master having the right to sell them, the right to command, and the right to decide whether he would or would not use them.

Finally, when a master took a slave woman as a wife, she automatically became free, and the children became free members of his family. It is noticeable, however, that in recounting genealogies, the people of Lupupa Ngye recognize and point out the names of a number of women who were freed in this way. While no daily manifestations of this knowledge are made in the course of village life, children of slaves or even children of their children may be reminded of the fact in situations of tension.

All informants agree that one cannot become a slave voluntarily, although he might put himself into pawn; some people make a sharp distinction between the two states and some do not.

Slaves of either sex were owned by men or by women, though ownership by children is never mentioned; the only criterion for ownership is sufficient wherewithal for purchase. Slaves were not marked in any way, although it is possible that some female slaves carried a hole in the right ear; the lack of marking, or of distinctive clothing, is in sharp, and noticeable, contrast to the practice of Ngongo Lutete, whose system of marking we have discussed previously. Slaves were addressed by their personal names, although a slave who rose in the society might be given an acknowledged title and addressed with terms of respect. To his owner, and perhaps to important personages, the slave used the term *"yaya,"* or "father," while to others he responded only with the usual *eyo,* "yes."

Slaves lived within the lineage boundaries of their owners, in houses which they constructed themselves in time made available for the purpose. These houses were located behind those of the owners, and they were occupied only by slaves. Slaves possessing a special skill may have been more highly valued than those who possessed none, and their treatment may have been slightly better. Male slaves worked in the fields, built houses for their owners, acted as carriers, cut palm nuts (considered hazardous work), and were couriers. Female slaves worked in the fields, prepared food, cleaned the house, pressed oil from palm nuts, and acted as carriers. Children were not required to work, and no special occupations were reserved or allotted to slaves. Profit earned by a slave while engaged in work for his owner was the property of the latter, and all the property owned by a slave went to his master upon death. Some informants say that slaves were armed with bows and arrows and knives and used in battle, but others deny this emphatically.

Masters held a number of rights over slaves, but the matter of the right of life and death is in dispute. Some say that this right existed, others that a master could kill a slave but in the event became liable for a fine for wastage, and still others that an owner could not kill a slave under any circumstances. All agree, however, that the owner had the absolute right to sell a slave. Slaves could, and did, fall into debt, and the master was responsible for these debts; he might take care of them by paying himself or by selling the slave. Masters took goods and money from their slaves, but slaves were not held responsible for their masters' debts. Slaves were punished by striking, but not by giving male slaves female work; theft on the part of a slave was punishable by death. Some distinction may have been made in the treatment of, and attitudes toward, slaves who were given as a gift as opposed to those who were purchased.

Slaves also held some rights. Slaves could possess property, even though it was always subject to the right of the master, and some slaves probably became rich, perhaps richer than their owners. Although unlikely, if a master died without heirs, his slaves might inherit his property, and masters could make bequests to slaves. There is some suggestion that slaves could own slaves.

Slaves could escape their lot by several means; one of these, suicide, is mentioned tentatively and without serious conviction. Slaves did run away and, if found, were brought back; one former owner says, however, that they were not punished "because then they would run away again." While some informants deny any thought or possibility of slave revolts, the son of the man who was formerly the biggest slaveholder in the village says that many such cases occurred and that for this reason people were considerate of their slaves and "treated them like children." This man's father told him the following story as a moral warning not to mistreat slaves.

> Once there was someone who was very bad to his slaves. One time he went to the house of a slave and took everything he had. He said,
>
> "You are my slave. You cannot do what you want to do. You must give me everything you have."
>
> The slave did not reply to him, and the master became very angry. He took the slave, tied him up by the feet and wrists, and left him out in the sun for an hour and a half. That night he drank, and then went to sleep. The slave said to himself,
>
> "What right has he got to treat me like that? I am a human being, too," and he crept up on his master and chopped off his head with a knife. Then he ran around the village waking people up, and he told them that he had found his master that way, with his head chopped off, and they believed him.
>
> Then he disappeared.

A master could free a slave at any time for any reason; M's father, for example, once freed a slave because he liked and respected the man, who had been with him for a long time. Slaves could purchase their own freedom, and some insist that this was not a difficult feat to accomplish. Freedom in this manner was possible because the slave was required to work only a certain number of days of the week for the master, with the remainder free for his own use. While it is doubtful that the number of days worked for each was regular or uniform, it is perhaps significant that one knowledgeable informant suggested two days for the master and five for the slave! A slave had to pay double his purchase price to obtain his freedom.

Some informants say that certain slaves, after being released by their masters, were automatically adopted into the lineage, but this seems doubtful. It is clear, however, that some slaves were so adopted, for the lineage genealogies contain the names of such persons and many others have undoubtedly been forgotten.

The present situation in respect to slaves in Lupupa Ngye is more ambivalent than the villagers and the administration would like the outsider to believe. Those concerned say that slavery has been abolished, which it has, and that it has been wiped out of existence, which is not quite true. Among the vestiges of slavery, for example, are a number of people who are now part of specific lineages but who are always recognized either as former slaves or as the children of slaves. While these people are no longer slaves, the children of their former masters say, with some swagger, that they can "command" their children; although they do not in fact do so, they can make life temporarily miserable for the "slave children." Lupupa Ngye also has families who trace their own genealogies through former slaves and could operate as lineages in themselves although they are accepted into, and live within the boundaries of, the lineages of their former masters. The very fact, however, that they remain separate genealogically indicates both that the event of slavery has been recent and that no one has entirely forgotten it.

Finally, one man in the village remained a slave until his death on November 19, 1959, even though he had risen in the village to become the *lukunga*, the lowest-ranked among the notables. Mwembo's father had been a Mutetela slave of Muchipule, and his mother was also a slave; the fact that he was alone in the world, without kinsmen or children except for his wife, meant that he did not enjoy the half-slave status normal to the second slave generation. On one occasion, for example, when the blacksmith, his owner, was showing me the process of making charcoal, it was Mwembo who chopped down the tree, carried it home, chopped it into lengths, laid the fire, went to the house for a live coal, tended the fire, and so forth, all under the direction of his master. Thus slavery in Lupupa Ngye was not dead until the death of Mwembo, whose funeral, incidentally, was fairly elaborate and thoroughly proper.

It is no longer possible to be sure of the quality of the life of a slave in the village, but nothing can override the indisputable fact that men held control over other men. Neither is there anything to suggest that the process of acquiring slaves was anything but bloody, or that slavers, including the Basongye, were anything but contemptuous of human life. Yet it does seem probable that slavery in Lupupa Ngye was softer than that of the Western world, that slaves were less brutalized in slavery, and that some slaves did, indeed, achieve freedom, wealth, power, and standing, as well as effective, if limited, membership in society which is today enjoyed by their children and which, in the future, will be more fully enjoyed by their children's children.

Among free men, and at the basis of the organization of society wherever Lupupans and, indeed, the Bala gather, is a series of social units which place individuals in relationships of various kinds to all other individuals. The smallest such unit is called the *shibo* (pl. *mashibo*), which literally means "house" and which, in terms of social structure, indicates the unit of a man, his wife or wives, and their children. More specifically, however, it is the man and his physical dwelling place which together symbolize the unit; if an otherwise unattached person, such as the man's widowed father, joins the household, the unit remains the *shibo*. The households are recognized by the name of the man who heads them, and are most properly called *shibo* ("house") *ya* ("of") Mulenda (name of the man). Looked at in a slightly different way, a *shibo* is defined as consisting of one or more marriage bonds between one man and one or more women, plus their issue. Each *shibo* also has a physical representation in the house of the male, the house or houses of his wife or wives, and the various outbuildings and crop trees. Since these are for the most part located contiguously in space, they can be, and are, surrounded by an imaginary boundary line (*mudiya- nyino*, pl. *midiyanyino*).

It is clear from the above that the *shibo*, and indeed all the social organization of the Lupupans, is powerfully patrilineal. It is also patrilocal, for marriage always involves a change of residence for the woman from the location of her father's lineage to that of the *shibo* of her husband. Since the men of Lupupa Ngye frequently marry women from other villages, this residence shift can cause severe dislocation and readjustment problems for the woman. A man may occasionally move his residence to that of his wife's lineage in order to fill a vacant spot in the social structure, but this is the exception to the rule. Some marriages today are neolocal, but this arrangement seems to have been very rare in the traditional system; its appearance is due to Western intrusion, occurring when a man moves to a city to work. In these cases, the husband retains his kinship affiliations, and he can return to the social structure of which he is always considered a part.

Overriding the *shibo* and, from the point of view of the overall organization of the village, much more important, is the nontotemic lineage (*kifuko*, pl. *bifuko*). The membership of this social unit may be viewed in two ways, that is, as constituted of a group of males and some females who are related both vertically and horizontally, or as constituted of these males plus their spouses; the former is the kinship basis of the lineage, the latter the group which lives physically within its boundaries. The accompanying chart (Fig. 11) illustrates a portion of a lineage, showing relationships and residence.

Lupupa Ngye contains sixteen lineages within its boundaries, of which two are no longer independent, having been absorbed by others. The fourteen remaining lineages contain 52 *mashibo* and range in size from a minimum of three people to a maximum of 44. Their names and sizes (in 1959) are as follows:

Name	Number of Families	Number of People
Bena Chite Kamamba	7	44
Bena Chite Kadiya (includes Bena Yabakambe)	5	32
Bena Chite Makumbo	4	26
Bena Yankamba (includes Bena Yakitenge)	9	25
Bena Muchipule	5	24
Bena Ngongo Sefu	4	20

Bena Lukale	3	14
Bena Yewusha	4	14
Bena Ekunyi	2	11
Bena Bwende	3	10
Bena Kiyambwe	2	7
Bena Kadiya	2	6
Bena Bakwamwesha	1	4
Bena Mwepu Lombe	1	3

Since the lineages are exogamous, each marriage involves two lineages, and children are considered to have relationships to both, but in matters of descent and inheritance, the system is overwhelmingly patrilineal. At the same time, one never forgets the fact of his dual lineage origin and indeed, in matters of kinship, he considers himself to be related to anyone to whom he can trace any actual relationship whatsoever on either side of his family. This can, and often does, make the choice of marriage partners difficult, since ties between and among the lineages grow more complex through time until a period ensues in which female marriage partners must be

Fig. 11

Lineage Relationships and Residence

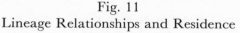

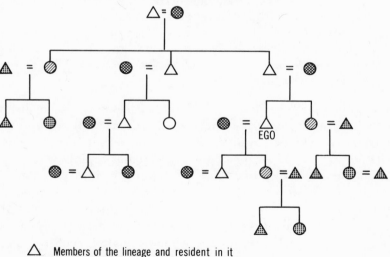

△   Members of the lineage and resident in it
◭   Members of the lineage but non-resident in it
▲   Non-members of the lineage but resident in it
▲   Non-members of the lineage and non-resident in it

sought not only outside one's lineage, but outside Lupupa Ngye as well. We will discuss this matter further in connection with marriage per se, but the bilateral overtones in kinship must be clearly recognized as an important part of the system. These are stressed, for example, in the following note made during a discussion with Efile of the lineage Bena Ekunyi.

> Efile's father's father was in Bena Ekunyi, of course. His father's mother, Kitoto, was from Bena Kilolo Mudimba. His mother's father was Bena Lubi. His mother's mother was Bena Chite Lukomo. Efile acknowledges all four of these *bifuko*, and says that marriage restrictions for him apply to all four. I took it back another generation, and he could name most of the individuals involved; he acknowledges his relationship to all eight, and says marriage restrictions apply for him to all of them. Furthermore, he says, "they apply to my grandchildren as well." In all this, however, he says that Bena Ekunyi is the most important to him and to his line of descent.
>
> Efile is perfectly cognizant of the fact that this could make marriage impossible if carried to its extremes, and he pointed out that it would be impossible for him to trace all the lines in detail, and that thus his children might marry someone from his great-grandfather's *kifuko*, for example. It was for him a matter of logic and the limited possibilities of continuing to trace everyone in every line which had contributed to his present family.
>
> This, in turn, led him to speculate on the possibility that everyone in the village might possibly be related in some distant way. This was quite possible, he thought, but impossible to trace, and "there would be no one who could do it."

In theory, then, the lineages are "closed systems," following the male line but recognizing the female line as well; they involve marriage restrictions, and restrictions on certain other kinds of behavior, on a group of people which expands rapidly whether the genealogies are traced backward or forward in time.

In fact, however, lineages are not quite such closed systems as they appear to be at first glance, for the lines of descent they represent can be altered by the introduction of persons who are not related at all or who are only minimally related; such persons, of course, are absorbed into the ongoing system, though it is some time before their origins are forgotten. The integration of slaves into the lineage system has already been noted, and it is also clear that the adoption of children and adults is by no means a rare event. The villagers cite a number of hypothetical instances in which adoption might occur, two of which are as follows:

> If a friend in another *kifuko* dies and leaves a child, and if there is no one to take care of it, then I will take him into my *kifuko* and he becomes a child of mine. But everyone knows he is of another *kifuko*, and my own children also know it.

* * * * * * *

> Suppose a woman comes to my family with her father, and then she dies and he is alone; perhaps I will take him into my *kifuko*. Then suppose he stays there a long time, perhaps ten years, and then he can become a member of my *kifuko*, but everyone will always know that he is not really a true member and that he is a stranger.

In the hypothetical situation represented by a father whose wife has died and who drinks heavily and beats his child (or is unfit to raise the child for some other reason), the Lupupans feel strongly that another family within the lineage would take the child, care for it, and raise it to adulthood. If such a man were the lone representative of his lineage, which is not outside the realm of possibility, the village notables could intervene and take the child from him. In this case, it is the responsibility of the *yangye* (one of the notables) to see that the child is cared for and, when it is old enough to fend for itself, to return it to the father. The *yangye* is seldom called upon to perform this duty, however, since it is far more likely that a friend of the father would step in and adopt the child.

It is felt by some that only the very young or people who are older than the adopter can be adopted, and this is partially borne out by the terms used in adoption. An older man adopted into the lineage is addressed and referred to as *shaytu* (pl. *bashaytu*, "our father"), an older woman, *nyinaytu* (pl. *banyinyatu*, "our mother"), and a child, *mwanetu* (pl. *bana betu*, "our child"). Informants insist that such a person is last in any line of inheritance of property, and they are equally insistent in saying that people *always* know who has been adopted into a lineage; this seems to be generally true to the distance in either direction that genealogies can be traced.

In addition to these adoptions of the homeless, it frequently occurs that willing males of one lineage are brought into another when the existence of the latter is threatened because no male is left in the direct line. A similar situation occurs, and is frequently evident in lineage genealogies when, because no male was available, the line of descent was figured through a female, impossible according to any but pragmatic rules. Informants are often shocked when such a line of descent in their own genealogy is pointed out to them, but they recover quickly and either give a reason or say that there must have been a reason even if they do not know it, and then drop the matter as being of little, if any, concern.

Fig. 12

A Genealogical Fragment of Bena Chite Kamamba

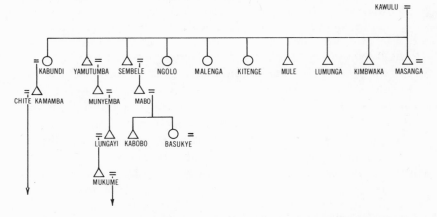

The accompanying diagram (Fig. 12) is a simplified representation of a small portion of the genealogy of Bena Chite Kamamba, but it illustrates a case in which a man who is descended through a woman provides for continuation of a lineage; in this case, the man became the lineage leader and lent his name to it as well. Kawulu, the founder of the lineage, had ten children, six sons and four daughters, but the sons did not leave male progeny behind them, with one or two exceptions. Masanga had only one daughter, while Kimbwaka produced only a son and a daughter, both of whom died of sleeping sickness at the ages of 8 and 5 respectively. Lumunga died of sleeping sickness at the age of 21 without having married, while Mule died of the same disease at 14 years of age. Sembele had a son who in turn had a son and a daughter; while the daughter is still living at the age of 54, married to a Mutetela, the son died of

186

sleeping sickness at the age of 2. This left only Yamutumba, who produced a son and a daughter. The daughter's line has continued to the present, though her descendents, of course, live in other lineages in other villages. The son's line also prospered, and is represented in the village today by Mukume, who is 80 years old and safely descended through males, his four wives, three sons, two grandsons and two granddaughters. It would be reasonable to suppose, were no other information available, that the lineage line passed through Yamutumba to Mukume, but such is not the case.

The last of the ten children of Kawulu to die was Kimbwaka. At this time Yamutumba had already died and his son, Munyemba, was still a child and unable to assume adult responsibilities. Present, however, and available, was Chite Kamamba, the adult son of Kabundi, one of Kawulu's four daughters. At Kimbwaka's funeral, Chite Kamamba was publicly announced to "succeed and replace him," and the lineage in the end took his name.

Fig. 13

Genealogical Fragments of Bena Ekunyi and Bena Yankamba

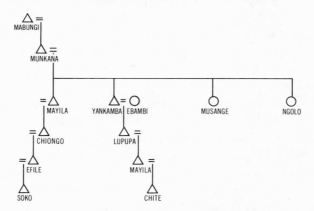

A more complex case is illustrated in Figure 13, which concerns Bena Ekunyi. In this case, the founder, Mabungi, had among other children, a son named Munkana who, in turn, fathered a son and three daughters. Two of the daughters were lost in the Arab slave wars, but the remaining daughter and the son married, and both their lines continue to the present. Since the son had a son, Chiongo, the line should have gone immediately through

187

him. However, at the time of Mayila's death, Chiongo was not old enough to replace him, and the only possible substitute was Lupupa, son of Ebambi, the living daughter of Munkana. Ebambi was married to Yankamba of Bena Yankamba, and thus Lupupa, as well as her other children, were of that lineage. However, Lupupa's son, Mayila, and grandson, Chite, are both living in Bena Yankamba, even though their grandfather took responsibility for Bena Ekunyi.

Again, the explanation is not difficult to discern on the basis of the pragmatic action so often taken by the Lupupans. Simply put, when Efile, the son of Chiongo and the grandson of Mayila, came to the age of responsibility, he took over representation of the lineage as the only male in the direct line; simultaneously, the head of Bena Yankamba called the children of Lupupa back to their original *kifuko*. Thus Lupupa's line appears in two lineages, but those who know the story explain it in terms of the temporary displacement described above.

Further examples could be cited at considerable length, but those indicated have enabled us to elucidate some major points in lineage genealogy. While descent is strictly patrilineal on the surface, circumstances have forced the Lupupans to highly pragmatic stances; the continuity of the lineage is the important point for them, and if that continuity means bending and breaking the rules, so be it.

Men like Chite Kamamba who are brought artificially into the lineage line are not to be regarded as headmen or chiefs of the lineage. While a man of forceful character can and does come to take the lead in influencing the direction of lineage affairs, no formal appointment is ever made. Chite Kamamba and many others in analogous situations are considered specifically to be kinship substitutes, replacing a deceased individual in the lineage system. Theoretically at least, and practically in most cases, announcement of the "replacement" for a dead man is a feature of every funeral. When it is a replacement like that of Chite Kamamba, the announcement is a highly dramatic one, for it means putting a new line into the lineage. In most cases, a son or brother is named, and in all cases, the decision is made by the notables who, of course, know the affairs and personnel of all lineages, and who can be counted upon to make the right decision, but whose decision is final.

Lineage affairs are not the charge of a formal chief or headman, but rather, are attended to by a group of males, and sometimes including females, called *bakulu* (s. *mukulu*), a term which might best be translated as "elders" of the lineage. The word "elders," however, implies the authority of age as a major ingredient of appointment, and such need not necessarily be the case in Lupupa Ngye. Rather, the *bakulu* are chosen for their wisdom, capabilities, maturity, knowledge of the lineage and particularly its history, and qualities of leadership and vigor. Indeed, a young man is fairly often chosen over an older one, and in such a case the latter is sometimes referred to as *mukulu mutwe* (pl. *bakulu mitwe,* "old one" "head"), which indicates that even though he is old he knows little about the lineage. Women can be *bakulu*, and are in a number of lineages, and it is possible that a slave could rise to the position. Persons from other lineages, however, cannot be *bakulu*.

The *bakulu* perform many duties and functions in and for the lineage; in the broadest sense, of course, they make the major decisions concerning it and are responsible for its general welfare. Among specific tasks and problems they confront, Lupupans name the following as representative. It is the *bakulu* who are most responsible for the lineage genealogy. If no relatives of a deceased can be found, it is the *bakulu* who decide on the proper distribution of the inheritance. If a broken marriage is threatened in the lineage, the elders attempt to patch up the rift. Should a young couple marry and then discover that they are distantly related—a possible but not probable situation—the *bakulu* of both families would be called together to thresh the matter out, deciding whether the relationship was distant enough to allow the marriage to continue, and basing their ultimate decision on the wisdom of both families as well as those of the participants in the marriage. The *bakulu* represent the lineage at certain formal village events, and they may sometimes comprise a village council of elders in particularly difficult and noteworthy decisions. On those rare occasions when they act together, they are assembled and led by the *yepa* (pl. *bepa*), one of the two "ward leaders" of the village and a minor political dignitary.

189

Lineages are not represented by any kind of insignia, portable symbols, staffs, clothing, or any other devices, and such representations are in fact not necessary since everyone in the village is well aware of everyone else's affiliations. Members of the lineage, however, hold adjacent land, and the elders hold money in trust for all. The lineage sets aside clothing for funerals and other emergencies, and hoes and salt for use as bridewealth. Each lineage holds cemetery land as common property, and in former times it was guarded by a sentinel who stayed in a house built on the site. In the view of some Lupupans, trees on lineage land are in fact common property; others hold that it is only their products which are available to all, and still others, that individual ownership is practiced. Whatever the case, it is clear that the members of the lineage do profit generally from the products of trees which grow on *kifuko* land.

While lineages do not carry or display visible signs or symbols of their group, they do acquire identities and reputations in the village. Thus one informant characterized the lineages as follows, and his judgments would be echoed by a number of Lupupans. "Mayila and Bena Yankamba are fine people who never get into trouble and who mind their own business; Muchipule people are thieves and defamers; Kyambwe people drink too much and are thus bad, and Mwambongye is the worst; Chite Makumbo people are in the middle. Chite Kadiya people are proud and haughty; Lukale people are terrible because they are always fighting with other people; Ekunyi people are all right except for Soko; Mwepu Lombe people won't take advice; the people of Ngongo Sefu, Bakwamwesha, and Kadiya are good; Bwende people are also good, but Kasambwe is a tough man and no one to tangle with." Such remarks are, of course, almost on the level of gossip, but they do represent a shared core of feeling.

Certain lineages are sometimes said to have especially close relationships with each other, and thus the people of Bena Muchipule, for example, feel a special affinity for the people of Bena Chite Kamamba. They say that the men of each group seek wives reciprocally from the other, and they also point to purported patterns of cooperation. It was suggested by a Bena Muchipule elder that the two lineages quite probably had a common ancestor in the past, although he could not name him.

190

Membership in a lineage, quite apart from the support it gives the individual both internally and, in some cases at least, in respect to other lineages, also carries with it the rights to certain offices in the political hierarchy. The right to become chief, for example, is restricted to otherwise eligible males in specifically named lineages; males in other lineages cannot, in theory and usually in fact, become chief. The other major political offices operate from a like basis; eligibility in the first instance depends upon membership in certain lineages.

It seems probable that the lineages now present in the village are quite stable groups which have persisted as a general body for perhaps as much as fifty or sixty years. It is certain that the Lupupans view them in this way and do not envisage significant change in the present arrangement in their lifetimes. When prodded, the people do, however, suggest ways in which new *bifuko* might be formed, and the outsider can see evidence of lineage loss in the genealogies and in other ways.

It will be recalled that some Lupupans believe Nundu was the founder of the village of Lupupa Ngye itself, and that Nundu had several wives, among them Lubembele, by each of whom he had children. When the children grew up and began to marry, the available partners were of their own family, but the dilemma was solved by Nundu, who decreed that all the children of one mother should build their houses in one location, and all children of the other mothers should follow suit; these units, then, became the first lineages of Lupupa Ngye. Working from this basic premise, informants concede that it is possible this process could be repeated, that is, that a family could become so large it would have to split into units; however, such a thing has never happened so far as the villagers know.

It is often suggested that strangers might come into the village, marry, have children, and thus begin a new lineage, and such a potential founder lives in Lupupa Ngye now. Another suggestion frequently offered is based upon the possibility that an orphaned child might not be officially adopted, but might survive to adulthood, marry, have children, and found his own lineage. To the objection that he could not possibly live without being told what his real lineage was, Lupupans answer that, in such a case, it is a matter of choice on the part of the individual; he may, indeed,

191

choose to reconstitute his father's lineage, but he may also choose to start one of his own.

Still another hypothetical suggestion involves the possibility of an unmarried woman in the village who has intercourse with many men with the result that the father of her child is unknown, even to her. When such a child grows up, marries, and has children of his own, he may create a new *kifuko*. The Lupupans do not visualize such a lineage as being named after the woman or as being "her" lineage in any way, "because a woman cannot found a lineage"; rather, the *kifuko* would be her son's. Says Kingkumba, "Naturally, in order for this to happen, the woman would have to have sons, for daughters get married and go away. If the woman had only daughters, no *kifuko* could be created." This, of course, is a conscious realization of the importance and impact of patrilocal residence, as well as partrilineality, on lineage information.

The processes of lineage disappearance are sometimes straightforward and sometimes quite complex. In the case of Bena Mwepu Lombe, for example (Fig. 14), the simple fact of the case is that the only living male of the lineage has no male children; all other lines from the founder, Mwembo, lead in one way or another through women. Kadiya, the last survivor, has had five wives, of whom one died childless, two are currently with him but are childless, and two left him, one of whom bore his only child, a daughter named Nyongani. His daughter, of course, married a man from outside Bena Mwepu Lombe, in this case one Lukomo from the village of Lumba, and their son and daughter belong to their father's lineage. On Kadiya's death, one of two things may happen; the lineage may simply go out of existence, or someone of another line of issue from Mwembo may be named to replace him. The latter event might occur if a young man were ambitious to form his own lineage, but he would have to be willing, of course, to move to Lupupa Ngye, and he would have to be a person acceptable to the village elders. It does not seem likely that Bena Mwepu Lombe will continue to exist past the death of its only present survivor.

A similar result may eventuate in the case of Bena Bakwamwesha, but with one major difference. The representative of the lineage in Lupupa Ngye is Senga, who lives with his two wives and the daughter of one of them. Senga has a son, 12 years of age, as well as a second daughter, but his son is presently in Elisabethville

Fig. 14
A Genealogical Fragment of Bena Mwepu Lombe

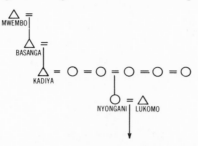

(now Lubumbashi) with Senga's sister; several members of the
lineage have been oriented toward that big city. Thus Bena
Bakwamwesha does have a living representative to carry on after
Senga's death, but it seems unlikely that a city-raised boy will
return to the village, despite the traditional strength of kinship ties.

Two lineages are represented only by fragments which have
been absorbed into other lineages; true to their concepts of kinship,
however, the Lupupans identify the people concerned and their real
affiliations. One of these is Bena Yakitenge, represented only by
Kasendwe and his two sons (his wife, from Lupupa Kampata, is
also with him, but, of course, is not a member of his lineage).
Kasendwe's father came from Kombe, and he has a brother living
there; when his father died, however, no place was available for
him to live, and he came to Lupupa Ngye where his mother's
mother is the living wife of Mayila, one of the leading figures of
Bena Yankamba. He has been formally accepted into the lineage,
but whether he will remain there or return eventually to Kombe
cannot be predicted.

The second fragmentary lineage is Bena Yabakambe, and the
matter is far more complicated, for the lineage fragment is
represented in this case by two descent lines, both of which are
traced through women and both of which involve fictions of
kinship. It is significant that neither of the two principal surviving
males was able to disentangle the threads of his own descent, but
was forced to rely instead upon the *bakulu* of Bena Chite Kadiya,
the adopted lineage.

The founder of Bena Yabakambe had a son, Yambo, who in
turn had a daughter, Mwasamukye (Fig. 15). Mwasamukye

married Sulu, of Bena Chite Kadiya, who had a brother named Bilungu, and the union produced a daughter, Mbu, a second daughter, Mumpasa, and a son, Lwelu. However, when Sulu and Bilungu died, no one was old enough to replace them, and therefore all the children went to their mother's side, that is, Bena Yabakambe. Given this adoption of Lwelu into Bena Yabakambe, his present line to the living Kingkumba and his son, Ngoyi, is perfectly understandable.

Fig. 15

A Genealogical Fragment of Bena Yabakambe

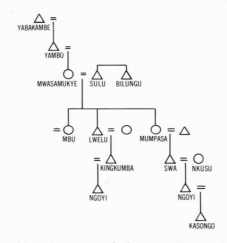

Mumpasa, however, married an unknown man from the village of Kombe, and they had a son, Swa, but Mumpasa subsequently left her husband, and her son went over to his mother's adopted side, Bena Yabakambe. Swa then decided to return to his father's village where he died. His son, Ngoyi, in turn decided to go over to *his* mother's side and to remain in Lupupa Ngye as a member of the lineage, Bena Chite Kamamba, where he still lives with his son, Kasongo. However, since Mulangwa of Bena Chite Kadiya was formally named as the man responsible for the remaining fragments of Bena Yabakambe (and Ngoyi has some relationship, however tenuous, to Bena Chite Kadiya), and since Ngoyi was housed in Bena Chite Kadiya before he decided to take his mother's lineage, he still lives in the Chite Kadiya area. It is probable that both Bena Yakitenge and Bena Yabakambe will

194

disappear from the village scene; indeed, to all intents and purposes they have already done so, being remembered in a formal rather than a functional way.

Fig. 16
Kinsmen: Father's Side

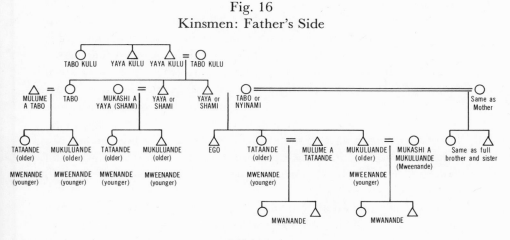

Fig. 17
Kinsmen: Mother's Side

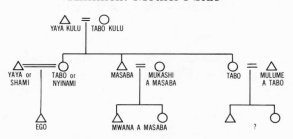

Each person in Lupupa Ngye, then, is a member of an immediate family, but is most strongly oriented to his lineage, of which he is a member by virtue of his father's affiliation, and to his secondary lineage, of which he is a member by virtue of his mother's affiliation. He is thus closely surrounded by patrilineal kinsmen, and is aware, at least, of a much more distant group of matrilineal kinsmen. On both sides of his family, as well, some of his kinsmen are much closer than others, and indeed he differentiates those farthest from him by a special term, *bakwetu* (s. *mukwetu*). These are kinsmen on the fringes of the kinship system, known to be related but traceable only with difficulty. *Bakwetu namu* (s. *mukwetu namu*)

195

are even more distant kinsmen on the extreme fringes of kin knowledge, and quite probably not directly traceable at all. A Lupupan might well use himself and his father's sister as an example, indicating that his fourth generation descendants might possibly marry his father's sister's fifth generation descendants; at this point, he believes, the relationship would be so indistinct that it would surely be *bakwetu namu*—they are related but no one knows how they are related. Some informants use the term in an even more special way, employing it to refer to persons not really in the kinship system at all, but with whom a casual though distinct relationship, usually an affectionate one, has been established. From this point of view, the children of one's longtime friends are *bakwetu namu,* and the usage is similar to the American custom of calling a friend of one's parents "uncle" or "aunt" even though no kin relationship exists.

Kinship terminology is indicated on the accompanying charts (male speaking) (Figs. 16–19) and it will be noted that the greater emphasis is placed upon the relatives in the patrilineal line, and that distinctions are made in terms of age, that is, "younger brother" and "older brother." Many of the terms given are altered in actual usage; thus, for example, *tata ande* ("sister" "my") becomes *tatande* in daily speech. The possessive modifiers are always used by informants in giving kin terms, but with the exception of "father" and "mother," all terms change modifiers as follows:

my child	— *mwana ande*
your child	— *mwana obe*
his (her) child	— *mwana aye*
our child	— *mwana etu*
your child	— *mwana enu*
their child	— *mwana abo*

The possessives for "father" and "mother," however, change both root and modifier.

my father	— *yaya*	my mother	— *tabo*
your father	— *shobe*	your mother	— *nyinobe*
his (her) father	— *shaye*	his (her) mother	— *nyinaye*
our father	— *shaytu*	our mother	— *nyinetu*
their father	— *shabo*	their mother	— *nyinabo*

196

Fig. 18
Kinsmen: Descendants

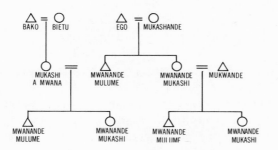

The strength of the patrilineal nature of the lineage is further reinforced by inheritance practices in Lupupa Ngye. The man owns most of the property in each family, and the woman's goods are restricted primarily to clothing, personal adornment, and all cooking utensils. Women's property passes from mother to daughter, but it constitutes only a minor part of the goods which change hands at death.

Fig. 19
Affines

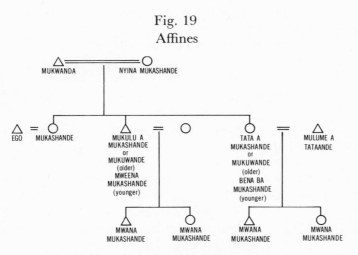

Under normal circumstances, inheritance passes from father to eldest son, then to younger sons in order of their ages from oldest to youngest, then to younger brothers (never to an older brother) again in order of age from oldest to youngest, and finally, and

197

perhaps hypothetically, to the children of oldest sister, providing her husband gives his consent. If none of these persons survive, the question is turned over to the *bakulu,* who would almost always decide in favor of the formalized friends of the deceased. If no one at all survives, and if the deceased man has no friends, then his goods go to the chief, who divides them with the notables.

Confusion exists concerning the question of whether a woman can inherit from a man, with some informants denying the possibility, others saying that it is possible and legal, and still others setting up specific conditions which make it possible. Those who deny such inheritance say that a man cannot leave goods to his wife, and in the hypothetical situation in which a man dies without any heirs and has stated he wishes to leave his possessions to a favorite mistress, that such wishes are disregarded, and the inheritance is divided among his friends. Those who hold that property can go from a man to a woman, but with restrictions, argue that a woman may inherit on behalf of a male child in a situation of legal trust or guardianship until the child reaches majority. More important, however, they state that a woman cannot inherit directly when men are living in the family, although the male inheritors will give her some of the property. If she is the last survivor, she may inherit.

No such arguments occur over male inheritance, which is visualized in clear terms, and so many potential inheritors exist in the male line that it is almost inconceivable that inheritance could reach a female. Finally, inheritance of property implies succeeding or replacing the deceased in the social structure, and it is inconceivable that a woman might replace a man; this alone makes it almost impossible for a woman to inherit directly from a man.

The situation of the married woman, in fact, is a difficult one. Since residence is patrilocal, it is the woman who must leave her family, and often her village, to reside in a strange village with a new set of associates and relatives by marriage. The woman always remains attached primarily to the lineage of her birth, and indeed, she is expected to go to that lineage on any important occasion such as death, marriage, and birth. At the same time, she should not visit home too often, both because she should be a dutiful wife, and because when she visits, her father must give gifts to her, and she should not take advantage of this fact. When a woman dies, she is buried, if possible, in her home village in the cemetery of her lineage. If a woman's father falls ill, she should visit him and then return to her husband, but if he is seriously ill, she should stay with him, take care of him, and at present, make sure he is taken to the hospital if necessary. The same responsibilities are held by a woman toward her mother. In short, a woman should defend and help her parents, for "the lineage of birth is more important to a woman than the lineage of her marriage."

At the same time, a young married woman finds a friend and ally in her husband's mother with whom she may be very close and whom she must treat both with friendship and respect; she has a similar, but more distant relationship with her father-in-law. The Lupupans say: "She takes his parents as hers, and they take her as a child. 'She is our child.' They are very close, and they are very respectful of each other."

Although his affiliation and primary orientation are strongly turned toward his father's lineage, a child almost always has some contact with his mother's family. In this connection, the villagers are wont to quote the following proverb:

bwana	*ku*	*bashobe*	*mukyelengye*	*ku*	*banyinobe*
children	of	your father	European	of	your mother

In loose translation, the proverb means "In your father's house you are a Congolese; in your mother's house, a European." The implication is that in his mother's family, a child can more or less behave as he pleases, while in his father's family, he is told what to do and has much less freedom. The mother's family pampers the child; in his father's house, the child must ask politely, and the chances are that he will be refused as often as he is indulged. The child looks to his mother's father, mother's mother, and mother's brother, in that order, as the source of indulgence, and he has a special relationship, though apparently not a strongly marked one, with his mother's brother. Some indication exists that this is a joking relationship, and men say that as boys they played, joked, wrestled, and exchanged playful insults with their mothers' brothers. If the mother does not have a brother, her father's brother's son may take the same relationship. The mother's brother is charged as well with contributing certain parts of his nephew's education:

199

named in this connection are how to get along in the world; information on women in general and marriage in particular; and what work is, the necessity for it, and how to do it.

Except for his relationship with his mother's brother, a male must be respectful of his wife's relatives, particularly female relatives who are older than she. Respect is also owed one's own sisters, and in fact, informants can run off without hesitation a long list of relatives to whom respect must be shown; one informant, for example, listed father, mother, older brother, older sister, father's brothers, father's sisters, mother's brothers, mother's sisters, mother-in-law, father-in-law, father's father's brother's son (older), and the brothers and sisters of one's mother-in-law and father-in-law. The same informant specifically did not include wife's brothers, wife's sisters, and father's father's brother's son (younger), though no indication is found of a joking relationship with these persons.

Considerable stress is also laid upon respect for persons older than one's self; this has already been indicated in the facts that older persons are named first in genealogies, that inheritance goes from older to younger, and in the respect relationships noted above. Old men are often addressed by the term of respect, *nobeya* (s. & pl.), and old women by *nobeta* (s. & pl.), the two titles translatable roughly as "papa" and "mama" respectively. Similarly, old people, as well as those with power, are greeted with the two hands clapped together, palms parallel, with a slight forward inclination of the head and upper trunk; this may indicate thanks as well as respect.

Both age and marriage contribute to the respect with which a man treats his father-in-law. The two may be in close contact and exchange intimacies on occasion, but this is always at the father-in-law's invitation and discretion. Otherwise, a man treats his father-in-law with deference. Much more important to him is his father's brother, with whom he often has a very close and warmly affectionate relationship. Indeed, the villagers say that father's brother must be treated with respect and affection "because he is also my father," and in a number of families it is evident that the father's brother is closer to his nephew than is the biological father. The boy may spend more time at certain periods of his life in his father's brother's house than in that of his father, and his uncle also has specific responsibilities toward his education. In sum, a child has joint fathers, and the Lupupans say that children have "two fathers and neither one is more important to him than the other."

Two more or less special relationships occur among the villagers, the joking relationship and mother-in-law avoidance. The joking relationship (*kyana*) is a weak social institution in Lupupa Ngye, but it is most strongly expressed in connection with the mother's brother. Other relatives in the same sort of relationship include father's father, father's mother, mother's father, mother's mother, and perhaps father's brother's sons who are older than Ego. Very relaxed relationships are maintained between a man and his grandchildren, and a special term, *mwiikulu*, is used in this connection. In short, the joking relationship exists among the Lupupans, but it is not strongly formed or highly institutionalized.

Mother-in-law avoidance, on the other hand, is felt to be very important, though in practice it is carried out less rigidly than prescribed in theory. One should never confront or speak directly to his mother-in-law. If the two meet on a path, one or both should turn back and seek a new route, or the son-in-law should step off the path, turn his head ("but not your back because you have to see when she has passed"), and wait until his mother-in-law has continued on her way. He should, however, give her a greeting from a distance, but if he is with a friend, the friend should call the greeting for him. In the event of unavoidable direct conversation, both should turn their heads, either to right or to left, and never look at each other. If a woman leaves her husband or is widowed, it is barely conceivable that she might come to live with her married daughter; her son-in-law would put up a partition in the house and would keep up the avoidance patterns as much as possible, though it is acknowledged that this would be an extremely difficult situation. No special words or language are used between the two, and no penalty is prescribed if they do talk together face to face; the latter possibility is almost inconceivable, however, since "all little children learn about this and they know that when they have a mother-in-law, it will be this way." It is felt by the Lupupans that the relationship continues even if a man and his wife are divorced, "because it isn't the mother who has left you," but again this is probably more theoretical than real. Finally, it is clear that the prohibition may be broken in emergency situations such as bodily injury, village catastrophe, and so forth.

When pressed, the villagers give a number of reasons for

mother-in-law avoidance, all of which focus on one overriding idea, that is, that the mother-in-law must be respected. Kingkumba, for example, says that one must avoid his mother-in-law: (1) because Efile Mukulu arranged it that way; (2) because she is the mother of your wife; (3) because she gave you your wife, she is the source of your wife, and you must respect her; (4) a mother-in-law is considered by you to have the status of a chief—you must respect her.

We have discussed the family and lineage units, as well as the various kinsmen and kin and affinal relationships which exist within them. The question of whether actual social groups larger than the lineage exist for the villagers is a difficult one to answer. The groupings which are present and recognized form a hierarchy based upon size, that is, family, lineage, the Bapupa, the Bala, and the Basongye, but two different ways of viewing them present themselves. Thus the *kifuko* may be regarded as a lineage, the Bapupa as a patriclan, the Bala as a subtribe, and the Basongye as a tribe; or the *kifuko* may be regarded as a minimal lineage, the Bapupa as a maximal lineage, the Bala as a patriclan, and the Basongye as a tribe.

The difficulties with either classification lie in the fact that while relationships to these groups are claimed by the Lupupans, they cannot be demonstrated genealogically at any level. Thus, while the three sister-villages of Lupupa Ngye, Lupupa Kampata, and Makola, constitute the Bapupa, no lineages are held in common among them, and while origin discussions always include Lubembele, Nundu, and Mwimbi, no direct relationship from any one of them can be traced to any individual or group in the three villages. Thus we cannot technically regard the Bapupa as a maximal lineage, and it appears at first glance that the grouping must be a patriclan; but the Bapupa are not exogamous as a group. Since no Bala grouping except the village lineage is exogamous, we cannot in any case apply the term "clan," and thus neither of the two possible alternatives noted above fits the case. However, it must be reemphasized that the Lupupans assume they are related by descent to the Bapupa, Bala, and Basongye, even though direct links cannot be traced.

6. Human Surroundings II: The Life Cycle

At this point we turn back to the village and the people within it in order to view the life cycle of the individual, his development as a social being from birth through death.

Women say they first notice pregnancy when, after missing a menstrual period, their skin becomes lighter in color under the eyes and above the eyebrows; others say the woman becomes prettier, and this is a sure sign of pregnancy, noticed by all. Men add that they know a woman is pregnant when she suddenly begins to take special care of her feet and when she is always angry. The physiological connection between menstruation and conception is not known except that the former ceases at the onset of the latter; it is also known that when an older woman stops menstruating, she has passed the age of childbirth. Pregnancy is caused by Efile

Mukulu who creates the child, but it is the semen (*mema*, s. & pl. "water") of the man put into the woman which starts the process; a man must be physically strong to start a child. If a couple fails to have children, it is not necessarily either person's fault, but rather that the blood of the two people is "wrong" and "different"; when a child is born, it is known that the blood of the couple is "right" and "the same." A childless woman can obtain medical assistance to help her conceive; the roots of the *mukuta* and *kambayimbaye* trees (unidentified) are boiled in water which the woman drinks morning and evening for two days, skips two days, drinks two days, and follows the pattern until she misses a menstrual period. Most of the Lupupans deny any knowledge of abortion, and all deny knowledge of medicines for this purpose; one midwife acknowledged that women may carry heavy loads in an attempt to abort themselves, but that this is "never successful." The only conceivable reason a woman might do this would be to spite her husband, but the notion is unreal to the villagers.

Some pregnant women have morning, noon, and evening sickness, and cures for these and other discomforts and illnesses of pregnancy fall into the realm of the *ntasha's* knowledge. Pregnancy is said to last eight to ten months, but some informants insist that the gestation period is "always" seven, nine, or eleven months, and that it is impossible to bear a child in the eighth or tenth month. No foods are considered especially good for a pregnant woman, but food taboos are placed upon her, and we have previously noted that consumption of certain foods will cause malformations in the child. A pregnant woman avoids carrying heavy loads, but she does continue to perform her normal duties "because after all, one must eat." Her husband must not inter a body, carry a dead animal with the help of another (explained as being similar to carrying a corpse to its interment), or eat with strangers; he shares with his wife the food taboos placed upon her.

Intercourse between husband and wife continues until at least the sixth month of pregnancy, but its continuation after this point is a matter of personal discretion and adjustment. Intercourse with the mother of a newborn child is forbidden, but the length of time and the reason for the prohibition vary among the villagers. Some say that "the child will die if the husband has intercourse with his wife while she is still nursing the child." Others say that intercourse should not be resumed until the child is able to walk, usually estimated at two years, on pain of accidents to the child including those which can lead to death; such accidents may possibly be avoided through the use of magic. It is the unanimous view of men that no man could go for this length of time without having sexual relations, and therefore it is reasonable to expect that he will search out other women—no harm will come to mother or child through this. The husband hides such affairs from his wife, but she knows that he is having intercourse with other women. If the family is polygynous, of course, the man does not have to search outside his own family save under exceptional circumstances.

Birth and the care of the new mother are handled by the *ntasha,* who is engaged by the husband. Midwives say they learned their skills from their mothers, and most of them have both medical and magical knowledge; they are paid specialists, but work out of the concerns of friendship as well.

The *ntasha* receives an initial gift of a chicken from the husband of the pregnant woman; it is eaten with her husband and friends after her work has been finished. Formal payment varies from case to case, but a wage in former times of four *madiba* if the child is a boy, and three if it is a girl, is mentioned; added to the *madiba* was a stalk of bananas and a bunch of palm nuts. Payment today is made in francs, and the sums most often suggested range from 20 to 30 francs, with the possible addition of a chicken. The *ntasha* attends the delivery of the child, but performs a number of other duties and services as well. She stays in the house with the mother for approximately two weeks, warms water for her and the baby's bath, bathes the baby, holds and cares for it when the mother is tired, cooks, and does other similar tasks. Her own needs are provided by the family for whom she is working.

Where a choice is possible, a child is born in the sleeping room of the husband's house. The midwife is apparently called when the mother is almost dilated, and on arrival, she prepares a special potion, the content and disposition of which depend on her particular knowledge. The mixture, however, always involves specially selected herbs in water, and the resulting liquid is rubbed gently on the mother's abdomen and is sometimes given her to drink. This measure is believed to speed up the birth: "When the child smells this, he comes out fast!" The woman sits on a mat on the floor and is supported during the birth by her mother and her husband's mother who hold her firmly by the arms. She may cry out, but if she makes too great a fuss, she may be told to cry less and to concentrate more on the business of having a baby.

Children are "normally" born head first, say the *bantasha;* those who come feet first will surely die, either immediately or within a few days. Breech presentation is considered to be very rare and very difficult, though no necessary ill-effects will accrue; midwives recall assisting at few such deliveries. If the birth is difficult, the midwife may press gently from above on the woman's abdomen, but some midwives say that they never treat the patient in this manner. When delivery is normal, the midwife takes the baby firmly by the chin, and then by the shoulders, to help it out; this is considered part of her job, "to hold the child firmly while it is being born." When a boy is born, its head is turned to the right, and as it is born, it turns its head more and more to the right and extends its right arm; a girl carries out the same actions, but to the left, and thus one can tell the sex of the child instantly from the position of the head. If a child is born with six fingers or toes, the extra digit to the outside is cut off immediately, and the child is considered normal (see Hautmann 1949–50:4, for the medical incidence of six-fingeredness among the Basongye). Cauls are not considered to have any evil portent; many children are born with them. If a child fails to put its fingers in its mouth immediately after birth, its normalcy is questioned.

The umbilical cord (*musuku,* pl. *misuku*) is cut at about seven inches, twisted to close it, and intertwined with a long piece of raffia which is wrapped around the child like a belt and tied to the right if a boy and to the left if a girl. This belt remains in place until the umbilical cord drops, estimated by the *bantasha* at between two and ten days. Custom concerning disposition of the umbilicus differs, for some say that it is ceremonially buried at the foot of a palm tree, while others (the majority) say that it is cut into pieces and scattered on the ground for centipedes to eat. A similar difference of opinion concerns disposition of the afterbirth, for some say that it and all blood which has resulted are simply buried in the floor of the room in which the birth took place, while others say that the afterbirth is buried in the roots of a palm tree which the father ceremonially presents to his newborn son or the mother to her newborn daughter. The Lupupans recognize two types of palm, male and female, and the tree given to the child is of corresponding sex.

After the umbilicus has been cut and the belt properly tied, the midwife gently rubs the child over its entire body with earth mixed with a little water. She then washes the child in plain warm water, being especially careful with the hair, including the eyelashes. Washing is designed to rid the newborn of its mucous covering (*lunkufu*) and the accompanying odor; the latter is considered especially distasteful by the villagers. In former times, the infant's hair was left as at birth, but at present it is almost always cut after a few days. After the child is washed, it is wrapped in a cloth or blanket and is clothed as soon as possible; the father buys a ceremonial swatch of cloth and takes it to a tailor to have a Western shirt made. In former times, children were not clothed until they were old enough to walk.

After the child has been attended to, the mother is cleaned and washed, and is then given the baby to nurse. It is considered that the milk comes either immediately or surely within five minutes; no recognition is made of pre-milk fluids. If the mother has no milk, she eats a mixture of the leaves of the *kililampolo* (s. & pl.) tree, beans, and water; this is considered an infallible treatment, and thus questions concerning mothers without milk are unanswerable. Children are said to be nursed four times during the day and four times during the night; if the child refuses to nurse, it is considered abnormal, but no remedies are known. If the mother refuses to nurse her child, this is a sure sign that she is going to die. Difficult births are sometimes assisted by gentle massage of the abdomen, and always by the mixture of leaves and water. If birth continues to be difficult, a stronger mixture may be made, utilizing different and more powerful leaves, and if this does not work, the mother is taken to the hospital; three days of labor is considered "too long" at present.

The *ntasha* is considered to be in command and to be responsible for the final outcome, and thus she must make the decisions concerning life and death. The most important thing in childbirth is to save both the mother and the child, but if a choice must be made, it is more important to save the mother since she can have other children. If a woman dies in labor, an attempt is made

207

to save the unborn by forcing it out of the womb, but it is felt that this is almost never necessary since the child will be born of its own accord; neither is it ever necessary to cut open a woman's body to save a child. If the child is thought to be dead in the womb, it is pulled out in order to save the mother; if a child is born dead, no effort is made to resuscitate it. No child is killed at birth, even those who are terribly deformed; one of the *bantasha* once saw a child born without a mouth, and it was allowed to die naturally. It is not considered serious when a child is born with the umbilicus wrapped around the neck; the midwife simply unwraps it, and no one reports ever having lost a child because of this occurrence. A seven months' baby is considered weak, and is given a standard treatment: a particular root is boiled in water and the water allowed to cool until just warm, after which the child is placed in it, along with the root, and the container covered for a few moments. The steam is felt to be the important element in this treatment, which is carried out six times a day for a week. If the child is not noticeably stronger and bigger by the end of this time, it is felt that the treatment has been a failure, that it is useless to continue, and that the child will probably die.

When a child is born, it cries, and this is the signal for those who have been waiting outside the room to come to see it. They are told, however, to wait until the mother and child have been cleaned, dressed, and moved from the sleeping to the living room, the mother walking there herself. The mother's stomach is tightly wrapped with a cloth (*moshi*) which she may wear as long as she wishes. Once the family and close friends have been admitted, songs for the newborn are sung (*pakutandwa*, s. & pl.). The first food taken by the mother comes in the form of a gift of a chicken from her husband, given "because she was almost like the dead." The chicken is killed and cooked without special ceremony after the mother has first nursed her child, and it is eaten with a few of her special friends. The mother is expected to remain in bed, or at least resting around the house, for five to seven days, during which she should be given much meat and fish; she should also eat manioc leaves cooked in water in order to make her milk flow liberally. The firstborn child is the most important one for the family, and many people come to see it and to bring gifts; as successive children are born, less is made of the event, and the births become physically easier.

The couvade is a part of the process of birth, though it is manifested in slightly different ways in different cases. Some say the husband suffers from specific diseases like malaria or dysentery, but majority opinion indicates he falls ill as soon as the birth pains (*nunda*, s. & pl.) begin, and continues to be ill until the child is born. He suffers primarily from headache and stomach ache, but he loses his appetite as well, and cannot even smoke with any pleasure. It is not surprising when he feels so miserable that he must go to bed. Men know the instant of the birth of their children because at that instant their symptoms disappear. A few men suggest that these symptoms may be due to worry about wife and child, but numerous cases are also cited in which a man is far away from home, falls ill suddenly, recovers just as suddenly, and then learns of his wife's delivery at those very moments.

While no child is killed at birth, the killing of children was practiced in the past, and the practice may well continue today. The term *kishuwashuwa* (pl. *bishuwashuwa*) covers all malformed children, while a midget is *kipinji* (pl. *bipinji*), a Mongoloid child is *kampalamanda*; and a dwarf, or a person suffering from another malformation such as malproportioned arms, is often called *kitesha* (pl. *bitesha*), a term of insult rather than a description of such a person's condition.

In cases of insanity, Mongoloidism, or other highly visible malfunction, the father of the child goes to the notables to explain the situation when he has given up all hope of the child's being normal. The notables visit the child, and then usually counsel the father to wait a while to see whether the condition improves. If no improvement takes place, the father again importunes the notables, who then usually give their permission to have the child killed; the father pays a fee of 500 francs. In matters of this kind, Lupupa Ngye and Lupupa Kampata work together, for killing the child is considered to be the joint responsibility of the *balukunga* of the two villages. The two political dignitaries take the child to Mwipata, a location midway between the villages, where they kill it with a blow to the back of the head delivered by means of a stick. They then lecture the spirit of the child, telling it not to return to the village to cause trouble; since the child's spirit is probably a *mukishi,* it is malevolent, but with the proper words it will be persuaded to cause its inevitable trouble in other villages. The body of the child is then buried in a special cemetery at Mwipata; if it were buried in the family cemetery in the village, general calamity would follow, including many deaths, crop failure, and other catastrophes.

This kind of killing may extend to children of considerable age; an example given by one informant concerned a hypothetical adolescent female of fourteen years who begins to menstruate and does not stop "after seven days." Other manifestations indicate that something is seriously wrong: "the child will not wear clothing, she talks strangely, she eats anything and everything, she plays like a child, she giggles for hours on end, she cries continually, she defecates or urinates in the drinking water." Such a person is not considered to be insane, nor is she possessed; she is simply *kishuwashuwa.* The Lupupans are afraid of her, however, and "the fathers of our fathers taught us to kill them." The result of the general practice of child killing is that almost no malformed persons are found in Lupupa Ngye, except those who have lost fingers or toes through accidents.

In somewhat the same category as the *bishuwashuwa* are albinos (*basaka,* s. *saka*) who, according to Hautmann (1949–50:5), appear among the Basongye in the ratio of one to every 4,000 births. Albinos are created by Efile Mukulu and are human in every respect save for the color of their skin, hair, and eyes. "They are dangerous to other people, and people do not like to look at them. They give you bad luck when you meet them on a path or in the street; they do not kill people, but they are dangerous. If you stay in the same house with one at night and have to go outside, you will find that it is outside, too; when you go back in the house, there it is again. Albinos are always witches. Before the white men came, all albinos were killed by squeezing their chests until their ribs were broken, and then they were left to die. Albinos cannot be the chief or any other notable. Nowadays they are insulted, like mulattos, because they are not white men and not black men, and what are they?"

The opposite attitude is taken toward twins (*mpasa,* pl. *bampasa*) which occur, according to Hautmann (1949–50:5), once in every forty deliveries; triplets (*sweba,* s. & pl.), which are so rare that almost no one has had any experience with them, would also be welcomed, but no one has ever heard of a multiple birth involving larger numbers. Lupupans explain that twins are especially welcome on the simple ground that one always wants to have many children.

While the delivery procedures do not change when twins are born, all is different from this point forward, for "Efile Mukulu has arranged it" so that twins are in mortal danger until the time they are able to walk. The afterbirth is buried at the foot of twin palms, or at the foot of two palms which are very close together. The first day of their lives, twins must be given something other than mother's milk to eat; each must have his own eating plate; twins must be fed eggs or the liver of any animal, and theoretically, they can eat only these foods and milk until they walk. Twins are not shown when the umbilicus drops, and special songs (*lono lwa mpasa*, pl. *ngono ya mpasa*) are sung for them. The firstborn of twins is always named Ngoyi, the second, Mukonkole, and it is unthinkable that they would be otherwise named. Twins must always be given identical things, be treated identically and dressed identically; if given unequal treatment, they will die.

Twins are in special danger if seen by persons outside a very small family group, and thus they are kept isolated in the house until they can walk. Those who can see them are mother, father, and grandparents; if the mother's father comes from another village, however, he cannot see them without paying a small fee. Siblings are never mentioned in this connection, but it is evident that they must be included since it would be impossible to isolate them under the conditions of family life in Lupupa Ngye. Also privileged to see twins before they walk is any mother of twins, though if she has lost a child she, too, will be denied. If the twins are seen accidentally by a stranger, he must pay a small fee to the parents or the twins will die.

When finally the twins can walk, they are carried around the countryside on the shoulders of two young men to show that they have not previously been seen and that they are now out of danger; the parents, however, are careful to treat them identically until they are old enough to leave home for marriage. At this public demonstration, the twins are dressed in their best, and their faces and hands are spotted with white (and sometimes blue) coloring.

The father carries in his right hand a bundle of bush grass (*soni*, s. & pl.) within which is a magic potion to protect the twins and their family from harm at this particular time. In his left hand, he carries a convex fanlike object (*ngabo*, s. & pl. "shield") by means of which he can ward off any magic made against the family. The mother of the twins carries a wooden spoon both as a symbol of the change of status and, equally triumphantly, of the fact that she has successfully brought them through the danger period: "I prepared for the twins with this spoon. Now they are free of it." Another woman in the party carries a small calabash filled with the magic white color in powdered form, and when an onlooker gives a gift to the twins, she dips a brush into the calabash and touches the giver's chest. This marks him as having given, but it also helps make the twins strong. Bystanders are expected to give identical gifts in even numbers, and thus four, eight or sixteen francs is standard, accompanied by two handfuls each of maize flour and manioc flour. The family is accompanied on its expedition by a retinue of musicians and singers-dancers who perform *pakutuka* (s. & pl.), songs sung when a child is first taken out of the house. The head musician also receives the gifts for the family.

A child born physically complete, but dead, is not named; living children are named either at the time the umbilicus drops or one week later. No naming ceremony is held, and the parents simply begin using the single proper name they have chosen. Today a second, Western name is often given as well. The same name is kept throughout life, the one possible exception occurring when a child named after a family member or friend, engages in such outrageous behavior toward that person that his namesake takes his name back and gives the child some other name. In such a situation, the new name cannot be refused. The right to choose names apparently depends on lineage custom, but in most families the father names the first two children (and possibly the first three), and the woman the next. From this point forward, the parents either name the children cooperatively or alternate the right to name individually. Children are often named after family members or close friends; except in the case of twins, no names are prescribed.

As previously noted, a left-handed person (*kibokoswa*) may indicate the return of the spirit of a left-handed ancestor. Other

212

than this distinction, however, no special meaning is attached to left-handedness; a person is made this way by Efile Mukulu and no one knows why. A left-handed person is not considered abnormal; he brings neither bad nor good luck; he is not particularly successful with women—he is simply left-handed.

A new mother stays home with her baby for approximately two months before returning to her customary routine. When she begins to go to the fields again, she nurses her baby just before she leaves, stays in the fields for an hour or slightly longer, and then returns to feed the infant again. As the baby grows older, of course, she stays away for longer periods of time, but she never takes it to the fields until it is able to walk. The infant is left at home in the care of an older child, either a boy or girl, of the age of ten or more. If a mother does not have a child of this age, she makes an arrangement with a friend whose child then comes to help her every day. While such a helper is not paid, she does eat with the family (except for the evening meal), and when the baby no longer needs such intensive care, she is dismissed with thanks and gifts, usually of new clothing. The helper watches over the baby and the younger children, carries them about, entertains them, feeds them, and cleans the house, leaving for the day after the midday meal; she is fully responsible while the mother is away from home. If the helper is a boy, the mother prepares the noonday meal before she leaves, since boys are not expected to cook, but if it is a girl, she is expected to prepare the meal and serve the family if the mother stays late in the fields.

Children sleep with their mothers until they are about two years old. On rising in the morning, the mother or her helper bathes the baby at the house; children are bathed this way until they are about four years of age. Until the baby is four months old, its only food is mother's milk, except in special cases already noted, and cool boiled water; the water is discontinued when the child walks. The first solid food is maize or rice cereal made into mush and served without salt, since it is believed that salt sickens a baby if taken before the age of eight or ten months. The porridge is made rather thin for a young baby, but it is thickened as the child grows older. The infant is the only member of the family who eats breakfast.

Nursing is stopped at about the time the child begins to walk, though some say the event occurs at the time its first words are spoken. Nursing is stopped quite abruptly, and the mother discourages tenacious children by rubbing boiled manioc leaves on her nipples in the hope that the new taste will be attractive to the child. Thumb sucking is considered normal; it starts at birth and is expected to continue until the child is about seven. Mothers say that it is not difficult to break children of the habit and that they simply stop when their parents tell them to; no severe methods, such as spanking, coating the thumb with a bitter substance, or tying down the hand, are acknowledged.

The child's first words are "tabo" and "yaya," and it is encouraged to speak clearly and correctly as soon as possible. Baby talk (*bumama*) is not encouraged and parents do not think it is cute or attractive, for they fear the child may not grow out of it and thus may never talk correctly. While it is recognized as being normal, the parents are glad when it is finished. Toilet training is begun at about the time the child begins to walk, and it is considered to be the task of the mother, although the father helps. The child is shown either where to go in the bush or the location of the outdoor toilet and how to use it; at first his parents take him there whenever they see he needs to eliminate. It is explained to him that "it is shameful to urinate or defecate in the house," and "it makes a bad odor in the house." If the child does not learn quickly enough, he is punished by spanking or by striking with the hand, always avoiding the eyes, mouth, and particularly the nose. Some Lupupans say that a child should never be struck with the hand, but rather with soft switches.

It will be recalled that a child whose upper teeth come in before his lowers is considered to be a witch; thus the appearance of the lowers first is welcomed by a chicken given by the father to the child, prepared by the mother, and eaten by the three together. Eruption of the first tooth is also the occasion of a special song, *kubinga mwafi* (s. & pl.). If all goes well, the first tooth to come in for a boy is the lower right incisor, and for a girl, the lower left incisor. No one has ever heard of a child born with teeth already erupted.

The perfect child for the villagers is obedient, quiet, and manly; a typical description is that "the perfect child always listens to his parents. He would never insult his parents. He never refuses punishment. He carries out all errands given him. He does not cry.

He does not hit back in a dispute. He does not carry tales to his mother, but he does tell her when a brother, for example, is doing something really bad." A perfect child would also be well-mannered in his speech, addressing members of his family by kin terms rather than personal names, and addressing those outside the family with the respect term, "ya," as in "ya Mulenda." Children may, however, shorten the family terms, using "ya" for father, "ta" for mother, "tu" for older brother, "ta" for older sister, and so forth.

Children are expected not to intrude into adult affairs, and as a consequence they are constantly shooed away from scenes of great interest to them, such as a funeral or a technological process like drum making. Indeed, it might be said that they are quite constantly on the move, eluding adults who chase them when they are in the way and who sometimes throw chips of wood or other small objects at them. At the same time, children are allowed to be present at almost any event, providing they keep quiet and relatively still, and on certain occasions, particularly those of tedious adult work, they may take tangential part in the conversation and even become central in the situation by performing tricks or telling amusing stories.

The Lupupans say that the reasons for punishment should be explained to a child, and that he should be scolded before being physically punished. Punishments include pinching the cheek firmly, twisting the ear, switching the bottom, switching the ankles, striking on the upper arms, locking in the house, withholding food, and taking away clothing. The most appalling crime to the villagers is thievery, and when it is done by children, punishment is severe. The child's hands are tied together, palms cupped and facing each other, and the opening between the palms is stuffed with roof thatching which is set on fire. In former times, chronic thievery was punished by removing the fingers at the first joint, and if this were not successful, the child might well be sold into slavery.

Punishment often seems inconsistent to the outsider, and the child's family seldom presents a truly united front; the consequence is that for almost every strong punishment administered by one adult, a compensation is offered by another. For example, Ngefu, who is about five years old, was asked by his father to run an errand; he refused and his father scolded him. Ngefu, in a fit of temper, burned a pair of his new shorts, and his father decreed, as

215

punishment, that he must wear an old and ragged pair of shorts for a week, which embarrassed and humiliated him. At the end of the week, however, his older brother bought him two new pairs of shorts.

In addition to punishment, children are threatened with various forms of the *kibokulu* which can best be translated as "bogeyman." Serving in this capacity are the mask, *kifwebe* (though infrequently today since *kifwebe* is no longer part of the village scene), Westerners, and other phenomena. Parents tell children that they are going to send for a white man to come take them away, referring most specifically to the Westerner who is closest at hand, and this is a highly effective threat. A favorite threat is to invoke *kimungu*, an unidentified animal which is said to live in the ground and to kill goats; "if you don't behave properly, *kimungu* will come get you." Mulenda's father's brother made a model of an animal, and when Mulenda cried excessively as a child, his father's brother took him outside the house, put him down near the model, and said, "If you go on crying, this animal will eat you." Then he went away and made animal noises in the dark. His father's brother on another occasion enlisted the assistance of a friend who got under a floor mat with a blanket thrown over it and made animal noises to frighten Mulenda. Children are also threatened that a *kitesha* (a transvestite) will take them away, or that a fisherman will come along with his fish net, put them in it, and drop them in the river.

Children spend a great deal of time in the care of older children, but by the time they are four or five years of age, they are allowed enough freedom to play with others. Play is often imitative of adult actions, such as slinging a tin can on a cord around the neck in imitation of slit gong players, but a great deal of time is also invested in making "sand castles" in the village street. Children of this age squabble a good deal, and must often be separated by adults. Tantrums are by no means unusual, in private or in public. As they grow older, children change their play, with boys paying more and more attention to imitation of hunting, farming, and other occupations, and girls following female occupations and then being actually involved in them as mother's helpers. In late childhood and early adolescence, children play a rich variety of games and sports, the former often in a musical context.

216

It is in childhood as well that Lupupans learn the important patterns of body care, ornamentation, and clothing. A child should be bathed frequently (though the exact frequency varies), and an adult should bathe at least once a day, usually in the river when on the way home from the fields in late afternoon. In pre-Western contact days, soap was made by a process involving the wood of the papaya tree. After a bath, many Lupupans rub palm oil into the skin, for after using soap, the body "does not feel right," and the oil restores the proper "feeling." Adults wash their hands before eating and, of course, on other occasions, and bathing in general is said to be done in order to eliminate body odors.

The teeth are usually cleaned once a day, in the morning. A small stick is used to dislodge bits of food from between the teeth, and a piece of the *lunyo* vine is chewed and the soft frayed end used for surface cleaning. Finger- and toenails are cut with a knife and the clippings thrown into the bush where they will be burned in bush fires. Care is taken, of course, to dispose of nail clippings privately since they can be used in magic practice. Adults do not color their nails, but children may color their fingernails red simply for fun and pleasure.

Shaving for most men is not a daily necessity, but before the Western razor blade was known, a sharp blade of local manufacture (*epaa*, pl. *mapaa*) was used without water. Some men today wear mustaches, but head hair is always kept very short and the head is often shaved smooth. Older women also often shave the head smooth in the style known as *kapweto*; a shaven head may be a sign of mourning or simply that "one is getting old and doesn't want to take the time with her hair." Younger women, however, are likely to arrange the hair in a pattern such as *mikanda*, which consists of alternate strips of hair and shaved scalp running from back to front of the head, or *shinga*, in which small bunches of hair are tied into bundles with black thread. Other hair styles occur, but with the exception of the shaved head, they do not have special significance.

While the body may be marked in certain ways, no markings are obligatory; it is believed by the Lupupans that they are normal, that they enhance personal attractiveness, and in special cases, that they are necessary for other reasons. In the last instance, for example, the color white is used in connection with the funeral and with some illnesses and cures, and as noted previously the bodies of

217

twins are painted in special patterns when they are first introduced to the world. Tattooing is infrequent, and body staining is unknown.

One of the most frequent body markings is a straight line cut on men from about the center of the forehead to the end of the nose; this pattern may also include cuts over the eyebrows and on the sides of the nose. These marks are made by a man's mistress—never by his wife—and they signify the bond between the two people. Charcoal may be rubbed into the cuts, and this results in a form of tattooing. A few women have roughly similar body markings done not as a matter of love but to enhance personal beauty. Thus Mwipata has the characteristic straight line from tip of nose to the center of her forehead, but in addition has two curving cuts which run parallel to each eyebrow. Under her eyes, her face is lightly marked in the following pattern,

and these marks were all made by her father's wife (not her biological mother), using charcoal which she pricked in with a needle. Mwipata also has a hole in her left nostril burned in with a needle—again the marking was made for the sake of improving her personal appearance and not by a lover. Women's keloid markings are discussed below.

Ear-piercing was apparently not an indigenous pattern, though some women now do so in order to accommodate Western earrings. In the distant past, women may have used nose plugs in the sides of the nostrils, and it is said that men pierced the septum and inserted a piece of chicken bone or human shin bone; both these practices are sometimes said to have been done during Ngongo Lutete's time and are sometimes attributed to the much more distant past.

Many older men have extracted their two upper front teeth, and the practice has been more recently taken up by younger women; young men and old women do not make this body alteration. The teeth are pulled with *lumano* (pl. *mimano*), pliers of local manufacture, and the operation is described as a very painful one. No particular age is specified for it; rather, a wave of pulling hits the village and a fairly wide age group is affected. When the uppers are extracted, the two lower incisors tend to grow into the gap, and the resulting configuration is intensified by filing the lower teeth with an implement of local manufacture (*kakuwo*, pl. *tukuwo*) so that a slope from front to back teeth in the lower jaw is achieved. This, too, is considered a painful operation; it may be performed at any age. The teeth are not purposefully colored.

Body blemishes are regarded in different ways. Cauls (*bitanchilo*, s. *kitanchilo*) are known; some disappear in childhood, and others are permanent. Pimples (*bibungu*, s. *kibungu*) are considered a fact of adolescence which disappear with maturity. Warts (*sundu*, s. & pl.) are thought to be inherited from the father; as one grows older, they, too, disappear. No special treatments are known for these blemishes since cauls are considered incurable and pimples and warts disappear spontaneously.

The use of ornaments to enhance personal attractiveness seems never to have been elaborate; men today occasionally wear one to three metal bracelets on the left arm which are gifts of earlier mistresses, and metal anklets were sometimes worn as medical aids. Ornaments for women in the past cannot be ascertained today. Contemporary ornamentation is Western, the women wearing necklaces, bracelets, and pins, and sometimes using Western cosmetics.

Clothing for men in pre-Western times consisted of a vest (*mutwelo*, pl. *mitwelo*) and skirt (*kikwembe*, pl. *bikwembe*), both made of woven raffia cloth with the vest held together with buttons (*bifungo*, s. *kifungo*). In warfare this more elaborate dress was reduced to a short raffia garment worn around the loins and without a shirt. Women's dress in former times is not recalled by the Lupupans, but women today wear a short blouse, usually gathered below the breasts and hanging barely to the waist (*ebaya*), and a cloth wraparound skirt (*bikwembe*), both made of Western yard goods. Men today wear Western shorts and shirts, sometimes trousers, and young men and boys may wear a single piece of cloth which covers the lower portions of the body and is tied at the neck. Care of the body is an area of general knowledge which must be learned by all Lupupans.

At about the age of seven, children may go to live with a relative on either side of the family. This period is said to range from two to four months for a boy to at least a year, and often much longer, for a girl. The Lupupans are divided as to the desirability of this custom, some saying that a child can "learn a lot of bad things" as well as good ones from his kinsmen, but all are agreed that it "makes a child familiar with another part of his family." The relatives involved are almost always the brothers and sisters of the father or mother, but the male side of the family tends to be stressed, with children of both sexes going to live with their father's sister.

Living with another family contributes heavily to the child's education, and he is, of course, exposed to the culture at large on a daily basis and in special events; an example of the latter is the funeral at which the genealogy of the family may well be recited by an older man. The major formal instrument of education, however, is the father. While no special times are set aside for instruction, it often takes place after the evening meal when the father talks with his child, and most of the villagers remember these occasions as occurring frequently. Rote learning is not practiced at these sessions; rather, the father talks, the child listens, and particular subjects may be stressed and repeated for a week or longer. The Lupupans sometimes say, "our paper was in our hearts," and stress the fact that information given by one's father was remembered well.

The mother may also take part at such sessions, but not jointly with her husband; her discussion occurs on different nights. The father is specifically responsible for educating his son, and the mother for educating her daughter; while cross-sex discussions between the generations can be, and are held, it is felt that a male child, particularly, should not be taught too much by females, and a proverb is cited in this connection.

mwana	*mukuswe*	*na*	*mukashi*
child	he learned the idea	from	woman

"The child [male child implied] learned from a woman."

The concept expressed here is that a male child is a male and should learn from males; if he is taught by women, he will be like women.

220

The father attempts to instill family pride by telling his children stories of famous ancestors; he also teaches special skills, such as swimming, though the child may learn the latter from other adult males. Certain skills, such as playing some music instruments, are acquired in an apprenticeship system. Children also learn from their parents' brothers and sisters, their grandparents, and their own older siblings, but for a boy, one of the most important relatives in respect to education is his mother's brother, who is charged with three areas of special information. These include how to get along in the world, the nature of the world, and what a young man can expect to meet in it; women in general, and marriage in particular; and what work is, especially horticulture, the necessity of doing it, and how to do it.

Patterns of education are changing, of course, with the introduction of Western schooling; Lupupa Ngye has a school with a Mushilange schoolteacher. Instruction goes through the first three grades, and is carried on in Chiluba, which serves as a fairly well-recognized *lingua franca* in the area; instruction in French is begun in the third year. The children attend school from nine to eleven in the morning, and from two to five in the afternoon, save for Wednesday afternoons and Saturday mornings when they go to the river in a group to wash their clothes. Instruction is entirely by rote. Pupils can continue through the next three grades at the Mission Catholique de Tshofa, but acceptance is rather difficult, the school is twenty-five miles away which necessitates living there during the school period; and few children from Lupupa Ngye choose to attend, want to attend, or are urged or forced to attend by their parents. Further education had not entered the village realm of possibility at the time of research, and the best educated Lupupan had managed to finish six grades—he was far ahead of his fellow villagers in this respect.

No bush schools were present in the traditional system, and even the event of male circumcision was neither combined with special education nor was a highly formal or significant ritual. Circumcision today is almost always, if not exclusively, a matter left to the Belgian doctor in the hospital at Tshofa, and it appears this has been the case for the last twenty years or more. Thus some difference of opinion exists regarding details of the practice.

The Lupupans say that circumcision (*kusala*) was carried out

221

with small groups of boys whose ages ranged from approximately seven to twelve years. The reason most often given for the custom is that "Efile Mukulu told us to do it," but it is usually added that if a child is not circumcised, his penis will become swollen. Circumcision was performed in a particular location, though there was nothing special about the spot save that it must be somewhere apart from women, who were forbidden to see the operation; most recently, the site used was behind the cookhouse of the circumciser, who was also a blacksmith, on the edge of the village. The cutting instrument is an *epaa* (pl. *mapaa*), or knife of village manufacture, but this is not a ceremonial circumcision knife, for it is also used for haircutting and other tasks. The last circumciser says that the best time to perform the operation is from six to ten in the morning, "because everybody is cold then," and it is not so painful for the boys.

No special ceremonial form seems to have been followed, and the boys took their turn, watching those who came before them. No premium was placed upon stoic behavior, and it was assumed that most boys would cry; they were enjoined, however, not to struggle to be released.

Some informants say that the novice was required to take a position with his hands and feet behind him and his penis and the front of his body thrust upward. The last circumciser says, however, that the boy sat on the ground with someone supporting him from behind and others holding each knee spread apart. After removal, the foreskin (*munyonga*, pl. *minyonga*) was wrapped in a banana leaf by the boy's father and placed on the hill of a particular termite (*binkotolwa*, s. & pl.); the father remained there until the foreskin had been eaten, and if this was not done, the child would not grow up to take women. The penis was wrapped in *kalama* (pl. *tulama*) leaves, and for the next few days the boy spent most of his time in the rushing water below a small dam built for the purpose. Some informants say that after an initial cleansing of the wound, the boy returned to his father's house where he was instructed to remain for a day and a night, exposing his penis to the smoke of the fire. On the second day, all the boys gathered together at the stream, their activity supervised by one of their fathers. Healing time is said to vary from two weeks to a month, during which time the boy lived in the father's house.

A number of prohibitions were in effect until the wound healed completely, and it was thought that if any of them were broken, the penis would swell and the wound would heal slowly or poorly. A newly circumcised boy must not eat or drink with adults, and his food must be prepared in separate dishes from those used by the rest of the family. He is prohibited from eating peanuts or manioc leaves, and must not use European salt; in the latter case, his wound will hurt when he enters the water. His father must observe the same prohibitions, and in addition must not touch or come near the boy after having intercourse; the boy must not allow anyone who has had intercourse that day to step on a mat on which he is sitting. Some informants say that the father is enjoined from having intercourse with the boy's mother until the wound is healed completely.

All informants deny any type of female circumcision. Some suggestion is made that women's keloids are cut at this time, but even if so, this is clearly not of the same or even parallel significance as male circumcision.

Patterns of courtship in Lupupa Ngye remain mostly unclear. From the standpoint both of men and women, however, it is a strong assumption that the male is, and should be, the aggressor. Most informants say they know of no case in which a woman forced herself on a man; this would be unseemly and even repugnant. But according to men, women have their ways, and these ways are known to men. For example, a woman comes to a man's house and begins insulting him; when he asks why, she answers "Why not?" and "then you know that something is up." When a woman giggles as she passes a man, or when she watches a man very closely when passing, it is an indication that some further action is desired. Despite these signals on the part of women, it is still felt that the real aggressor in any male-female relationship should be the man.

In speaking of ideal physical types, men give some indication that they prefer women with large breasts. A woman should move gracefully when she walks, and should wear her clothes well. Women are said to prefer to be "red" in skin color, which means light, and it is felt that those who are light-skinned find it easier to obtain marriage partners. Overriding these considerations to a considerable extent is the fact that the villagers give a consistent and heavy emphasis to the view that marriage partners should match in physical attributes; that is, a tall man should marry a tall woman, a fat man a fat woman, and so forth. This is a manifestation of a deep-seated value which stresses normalcy as ideal and highly valued behavior.

In addition to these various attributes, a number of women in the village—though not all by any means—are marked with geometrically arranged keloids which begin on the upper chest, extend down between the breasts, and spread out over the stomach at least below the navel and usually to the groin; some decoration may also be present on the lower back (Fig. 20). It is considered extremely shameful to show these markings to anyone other than a lover, husband, or other women of the village, and even saying the word for the markings (*mapaa*) to a man is very embarrassing for a woman. While it is sometimes suggested that the patterns are named, and while it is clear that they are standardized and that certain of them are more popular than others at any given time, no specific names are used in the village.

The cuts are made when a girl is about four or five years old; those who say that this is done "when the breasts begin to develop" are in the minority, and in any case, markings are evident on very young girls. The cuts are made either by the girl's sister or by her mother; male informants tend to say that the mother does the marking, while female informants indicate that the mother marks her first daughter who, in turn, takes responsibility for her younger sisters. The cuts are made with a *wembe,* a Western razor blade, and the operator pinches up the flesh between thumb and forefinger of her left hand and cuts with her right. The operation is performed at one time, not over a period of days, and women say that it is quite painful; it is shameful, but not forbidden, to cry. The design is first traced on the body, with charcoal if the girl is light-skinned or with white latex in the case of a dark-skinned girl. The child is held by the shoulders by one woman while a second performs the operation; these two women have no special titles. Charcoal is rubbed into the cuts, and the people know that this irritates the wound and raises it; if the mark does not show properly after healing, it is later recut. Girls very often take the same designs as those borne by their mothers, but exceptions do occur. No designs are added later and no color other than black charcoal is used in the cuts. The designs do not indicate rank, social position, profession, or any other special

Fig. 20
Women's Keloid Designs

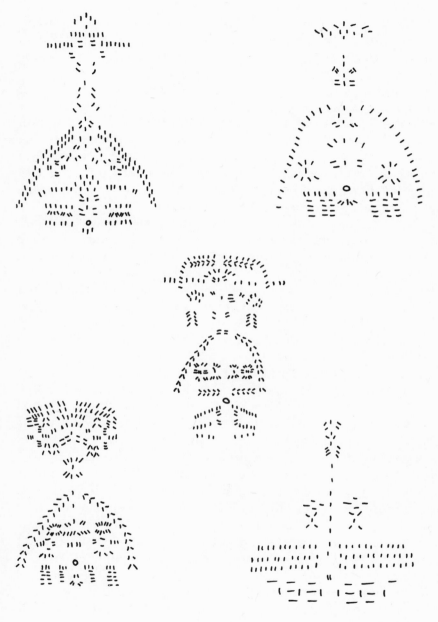

status or role. Girls boast about the excellence of their marks, and two criteria of that excellence are balance in the design, and not too much swelling.

The purpose of women's keloid markings is beautification; girls feel that it makes them more feminine and more attractive to men. Although men do not see the markings except in clandestine ways such as spying upon bathers, or when having sexual relations with women, girls say that men like them very much and think of the markings when thinking of girls. Some girls believe, in fact, that men are so fond of the markings they will not have intercourse with a woman who lacks them. Men are said to run their hands over the keloids as a foreplay to intercourse. Some women do not have markings, "because they do not care to endure the pain and trouble," but most women do; the custom, however, seems to be going out of fashion among the younger girls.

Young men and women engage in heterosexual activities before marriage, and in the case of girls, often before puberty. More or less informal arrangements are made between young unmarried men and women, and these are referred to as "engagements" (*kubangila,* s. & pl.); during this period, intercourse is practiced freely. In fact, the engagement period is regarded as a trial period to see whether the girl can become pregnant. If she does conceive, the marriage takes place after the birth of the child, but if a year or more passes without a child, the couple may decide to call off their liaison. If the couple decides to marry anyway, and still the wife does not become pregnant, the husband will in all probability seek a second wife. In these circumstances, the search will be conducted in secret from the first wife, the man will have intercourse with the second woman, and will marry her only if she produces a child. On making the marriage decision, of course, he notifies his first wife and she is retained even though she remains childless. No similar proofs of capabilities in cooking or housekeeping are required of a prospective bride, though the Lupupan mothers-in-law say they search out this kind of information when their sons first show interest in a girl, and that no girl without domestic skills would progress very far with wedding plans. No formal proofs of virginity are asked at marriage, of course, and indeed, the villagers assume that no individual of either sex is a virgin at marriage.

If a young girl becomes pregnant and, for one reason or

another, does not marry, the child belongs to her father and his lineage, to be raised as his child by him and his wife. When the child's mother does marry and goes to live with her husband, the child remains with his grandparents. At the time of birth, the mother's mother circulates through the village, explaining the situation (in the unlikely event everyone does not already know it), and cautioning the villagers not to call the child's attention to his fatherless state. It is recognized, however, that sooner or later the child will realize that the person he has been calling "father" is really his grandfather, and then his inquiries are answered. No special term is attached to such a child, and most people say that one should be especially kind to him, so that he can never say, "You are forgetting me."

Elopement (*kupengama*, "to hide one's self") on the part of young people who lack parental consent is considered a common occurrence. Theoretically, at least, the parents do not search for their children, for "they will come back and they will be forgiven." Such a couple is expected to stay away for two years, meanwhile keeping in touch with parents either through mutual friends or, today, through letters; on their return they must pass through several of the formal steps leading to marriage, and their reception is greatly enhanced if they have had a child.

The Lupupans say that love (*kwikuminishena*, s. & pl.) is important for the start of a marriage as well as its continuance, but their concept of love is definable more as "mutual respect and affection" than "romantic love." This conception is emphasized by the fact that the father of a boy can, and often does, seek out a wife for him when he is away; in such a case, the boy and girl may not know or even see each other until only a few days before the marriage. As the father may arrange a marriage, so go-betweens may be called upon to help a young man when he has been refused by a woman. Such a go-between is the man's best friend, and it is his task to persuade the woman to change her mind.

In common parlance and feeling, a boy is ready to marry when he searches out women, when he settles down and stops playing and "fooling around" like a youngster, when pimples start breaking out on his forehead ("someone with pimples can't be trusted around women"), and when his underarm hair, pubic hair, and beard (least important) begin to grow. The criteria for girls are

227

far less numerous; indeed, in the minds of many villagers, they boil down to the single indication provided by the development of the breasts. Menstruation is not considered a criterion for marriage, but it is pointed out that girls, like boys, have pimples at this age. Most people say that girls begin to develop about the age of 12, and boys at 12 to 13, with girls ready for marriage earlier "because girls mature faster than boys"; the ages mentioned for marriage range from 13 to 15 for girls and 15 to 17 for boys, though these estimated age ranges are younger than the actual age of marriage at about 16 or 17.

In order to marry, a boy must have the permission of his father and of his father's brother, while a girl must have the permission of her mother and, slightly less important, her father. The father of a boy can prevent his son from marrying, but the mother cannot; neither her mother nor her father can prevent a girl from marrying. In fact, of course, many accommodations are made on both sides.

No omens are known which foretell the proper day for a marriage or whether a marriage will be successful. No particular season, month, week, day, or any time within any one of these, is considered more propitious for marriage than any other.

The Lupupans respond very differently when asked for the qualities of a "perfect wife," though these differences are clearly individualistic and based on the man's view of what marriage is. One man answered that one marries a woman because he has to marry and thus has to have a wife, because he "must" have children, and because he must have someone to cook for him, adding that "a woman should be like a child before her husband to help him in all things." Another man answered quite differently, saying that a man searches for someone who will bear children, someone who will prepare food, someone who is intelligent, and someone who is honest. Still a third Lupupan said, "The perfect wife one knows because when she comes, she walks well. She prepares well for her husband, and she is respectful." Surely the outstanding qualities sought are child-bearing ability and domestic skill, and when asked whether they look for a pretty face and figure, Lupupan males are likely to answer, "One can't eat a pretty face," or "A pretty face may hide a thief." In fact, men do look for physical attributes, and they are not as cold and practical as some of the previous statements might indicate.

228

A woman asked about the "perfect husband," would almost surely include most of the following. The "perfect husband" provides food and clothing, understands and listens to his wife, does not strike her, finds her companionable, does not defame her publicly, does not steal, does not commit adultery, and does not insult other people publicly. A man, then, most directly seeks children and domestic skill from his wife, while a woman seeks economic support, but understanding and a close personal relationship as well.

A number of types of sexual and domestic liaisons between a man and a woman are found in Lupupa Ngye, but these can be reduced to four major categories, including legitimate marriage, marriage to a bought woman, marriage to a self-pawned woman, and liaison with a mistress. For the Lupupans, legitimate marriage (hereinafter referred to as "marriage") is a situation and status sharply differentiated from the other three possibilities, for it is a traditional and proper institution which is ratified publicly on three special occasions.

The first of these occasions occurs when the prospective bride and groom have made the decision to marry. At this point, the father of the groom makes a preliminary gift (*ebofu*) to the prospective bride who, after accepting it as an indication of her intention, passes it on to her father. This gift is not a large one, but it is a necessary part of the movement toward, and legitimization of, proper marriage. As a part of *ebofu,* the father of the prospective groom also invites the father of the prospective bride to his house to make further arrangements; the visitor is presented with a chicken on this occasion, which he eats himself.

The second step comes at a later date, set according to the wishes of all concerned, and it involves the transfer of *koonda,* or bridewealth, from the family of the groom to that of the bride; no dowry is transferred in the opposite direction. While it is at least conceivable that those involved might fail to make *ebofu,* the bridewealth proper is the most crucial part of the marriage arrangements; without it, under normal circumstances, a proper marriage simply cannot take place. Thus a couple who have eloped, had a child, and returned after the customary waiting period must transfer bridewealth if the partners wish to be recognized as truly married. Not only does bridewealth legitimize the union between man and woman, but it legitimizes and thus assigns the kinship of the children of the union. A child belongs both to his father's and to his mother's lineages, but counts his descent and his other truly important relationships on his father's side. If bridewealth is not transferred, children of the union belong to the lineage of the woman's father which, of course, takes them out of the man's family entirely. Thus bridewealth is a crucial factor both in marriage and in assigning kin relationships.

While the term *koonda* is used generally here, and by the Lupupans, it refers in fact to the money which forms a portion of the bridewealth; the accompanying goods are referred to as *kifindwa* (pl. *bifindwa*). It is the future husband and his father who decide the amount of the bridewealth, but the father of the prospective bride decides whether to accept or reject what is proffered. One gives less if the wife's family is "rich," and more if the wife's family is "poor," with "rich" and "poor" referring in this context to the number of marriageable daughters in the family. It is possible to marry without transferring bridewealth if all parties concerned are agreeable, but some say that bridewealth can be skipped entirely in these circumstances and others that it must be paid on a sort of installment plan. In order to do this, arrangements are made with the father of the prospective bride, though no set schedule of payments is laid out. If the wife becomes pregnant, all payment on the bridewealth must be stopped ("Efile Mukulu says so"), but it is resumed after the birth. If the husband dies before he has finished paying the bridewealth, his family is responsible for the debt.

Bridewealth is provided for the prospective groom by his father as a responsibility of fatherhood. If one's father is dead or if he has no money at all, appeal is made to one's older brother, younger brother, and older sister, in that order. If none of these can help, one arranges to marry without the bridewealth under the conditions discussed above. A father looks for any necessary assistance from his father, brother, sister, mother's brother, and friends, in that order. There is some indication that the mother's brother cannot refuse to help in such a situation, and that if he does, the groom's father can seize his property and sell it. The responsibility of the father in the matter of bridewealth extends only to his sons' first marriages; if the sons wish to take a second wife, they must find the wherewithal themselves.

The actual transfer of the bridewealth is a ceremonial process in which goods and money are given by the father to his son, who gives them to his best male friend. The friend, in turn, passes the bridewealth to the best female friend of the prospective bride, who gives it to the bride to be counted in the presence of the four young people. The bride then returns the bridewealth to her best friend who passes it on to the bride's father. What the bride's father does with it is, in general, his own business, though he is expected to make some distribution to members of the family at some point in time. One informant's allocation of bridewealth received is not untypical; on the occasion of the marriage of his first daughter he distributed the bridewealth to the members of the family; with the second daughter, he pocketed the proceeds; at the third daughter's marriage he again distributed the money to the members of the family; and at the fourth marriage, he bought a bicycle for himself.

At the same time, the father of the bride cannot be too profligate with monies received from bridewealth, for he may well be forced to return some or all of them at a future time. Four general principles can be suggested in this connection, all of them arising, of course, from a basic situation in which a man and his wife separate or divorce. (1) If the marriage has been a long one, and if children have resulted, it may well be that the bridewealth is not returned. (2) If no children have resulted from the marriage, and the wife is not a good wife in other ways, the bridwealth must be returned. (3) If the husband is a thief and the woman leaves him because of this, the bridewealth is not returned. (4) If the wife deserts the husband, in fact or in intent, the bridewealth must be returned. These general principles can be altered in special circumstances or by special arrangement, but in general, "right" is distinctly on the side of the husband who makes the decision himself as to whether bridewealth will be returned. Further, the Lupupans say that if a woman makes a public fuss in such a matter, the bridewealth will *certainly* have to be returned, again stressing the male prerogative in the matter. In cases in which bridewealth must be returned, all formal marriage gifts are involved, including *ebofu, koonda,* and *bifindwa,* as well as *kutwela shibo* discussed below.

It must be added here that before the marriage, the prospective groom is expected to perform some specific services for the family of his prospective bride, at the family's place of residence.

231

These tasks may include building a house, clearing a field in the bush, or clearing a field in the forest. Such labor is considered to be a service to the family and not to any specific individual in it. After marriage, the wife's family can always call upon the daughter's husband for labor, so long as they do not abuse the privilege.

The third, and final step in marriage, and the one which visibly seals the compact is *kutwela shibo* ("marriage" "house"), which is set in motion by the prospective husband who calls his friends together, tells them he is going to marry, and invites them to a dinner to be prepared by his prospective wife. The father of the groom provides the victuals, and the mother of the groom gives gifts of kitchen utensils to her son, who in turn gives them to his wife, saying "Now you are with me." The wife then prepares the meal, the friends sit down to eat, and the "marriage ceremony" is completed. The marriage is consummated on the wedding night: "after all, from the night of their engagement they have had sexual relations."

No ritual combat characterizes the marriage night. If a wife fails to have children, no arrangement exists whereby she is sent to another man in the hope that she may have children by him; this is an abhorrent idea to the villagers. No wife lending or wife hospitality is found in Lupupa Ngye, though the people have heard of these practices in other places.

The woman married according to the rules and steps outlined above is *mulangantu*, a properly married woman, and only she can be referred to in this way. While some variations do occur in the process, they affect neither the important outline nor the final result. Thus infant betrothal (*kalonda mwiyafi*, s. & pl., "ring" "little bucket") is occasionally practiced between a boy and girl born on the same day. The parents need not be special friends, and the affiancing is begun by the father of the boy who must obtain the consent and approval of the father of the girl. As noted previously, infants are fed specially boiled water which is kept in a special container; the boy's father obtains a ring (at present usually from the store) which he drops into the infant girl's water bucket. This is left in the bucket as long as the special water is used, and then removed and saved for the girl by her mother; such an engagement is not final until the two grow up and give their own consent to the match. Children may also be affianced at an age as early as eight years, but this is not considered special or different from ordinary betrothal. Under some circumstances, marriage may take place, but the couple may delay living together as man and wife; this occurs when a man does not think his bride is ready for full marriage. The advantage of this arrangement is that since marriage formalities are completed, the man knows that while the girl is maturing she cannot change her mind and marry someone else. Still another variation in customary marriage occurs when an old man and old woman simply begin to live together without any of the formalities; no special term is used for this marriage form. Should a child result from the union, however, bridewealth must theoretically be transferred, though *kutwela shibo* is not carried out.

Marriage is forbidden, of course, between any two persons who can trace any sort of genealogical relationship to each other, but the prohibition for a male also extends to any female with whom he can name even a relationship by marriage. This effectively prevents the operation of sororal polygyny, since when a man marries, his wife's sister becomes his sister and is thus in a prohibited relationship to him. The same prohibition prevents a man from marrying the sister of his deceased wife. On the other hand, the levirate becomes a preferred marriage pattern under certain circumstances. Thus when a man dies, his unmarried brother may be expected to marry his widow; the question, of course, is why the sororate is forbidden and the levirate is a preferred form, since a woman's husband's brother becomes her brother as well at marriage. The answer is that the levirate is practiced only when the surviving brother is officially named by the notables to replace the deceased; in this situation, the brother *is* the deceased, and therefore his relationship to the dead man's wives is "husband." This can be taken to the point at which a son takes his father's wives (except his biological mother) on the latter's death, providing the son has been named to replace the father. In these situations, bridewealth is not transferred, since the union is not regarded as a marriage but as a replacement, although the woman's family may make a demand for a gift of money as high as 300 francs if they are in need. The widow has the right to refuse to marry the brother, but if so, she must repay the bridewealth; an unmarried brother can refuse to marry the widow and demand return of the bridewealth, but in practice, bridewealth is almost never restored under these circumstances. No other forms of preferential marriage occur.

In all the marriage variations noted above, the woman is *mulangantu*; while other types of unions are legal in the society, they never have exactly the same flavor or significance.

A second type of union is known by the term *mukashande a bupika*, which translates roughly as "wife like a slave," and which refers to the fact that a woman in this situation is purchased in a cash transaction. Such a woman is not *mulangantu*, but neither is she a slave; instead, she has an intermediate but definite status. The Lupupans feel that the practice of selling women was begun by Ngongo Lutete, though ultimately it comes from Efile Mukulu, and they say that such women are never Basongye, but rather are Baluba or Batetela; the three women with this status in the village at present are all Batetela. A *mukashande a bupika* is not treated as a wife, and if her family were known, one would not respect her father or avoid her mother; a further contrast with true marriage is that the payment is made all at one time and is not spread out over time as in bridewealth. Such a woman works for the man and is also his sexual partner; children born to her belong to the man and his lineage. If the woman is not a success, she can be resold, although some say reselling can take place only if she has had no children. A woman in this situation has a clearcut but difficult status in society, for she is entirely dependent upon others and lacks the support of a family of her own.

A third kind of union has no precise name, but is associated with security for a debt and is therefore sometimes referred to as *kibambo* or *kye*. In this case, a woman is sold, either by her brother or by her son, in order to pay off the man's debt; the woman offers herself to him as a gesture of assistance. This is regarded as a temporary situation, for when the male relative has accumulated the necessary funds, he buys back the woman; the original purchaser cannot refuse to sell. Any children which have resulted from the new union belong, however, to the father and his lineage. While the relationship is basically a temporary one, the Lupupans point out that it may in some cases lead to permanence.

The fourth and final form of union analogous to marriage is concubinage. Concubines (*makupi*, s. *ekupi*) are frequently kept, but little information concerning them is available. A man may keep a concubine for a lifetime, it is said, and children born of the union belong to the mother's lineage; it is felt, however, that when the children "get older and their father is pointed out to them, they are likely to join his lineage." The woman in the role of concubine is never considered as a wife, and no ceremony marks the union.

Reference has been made in previous pages to the fact that men may have more than one wife. Of the fifty married men in Lupupa Ngye, fourteen, or 28 percent, were polygynists at the time of this research; the total number of marriage unions in the village was 68, of which 32, or just over 47 percent involved polygyny. Examination of the thirty-two polygynous unions indicates some rather clearcut patterns in the marriages; thus only one man under the age of 45 has more than one wife, although twenty-two men under the age of 45 are married. Comparison of the ages of marriage partners indicates that relative ages at marriage are becoming closer; that is, the older men in the village married girls considerably younger than themselves, often as much as fifteen to twenty years, and sometimes as much as twenty-five or more, while the young men marry girls who are about four years younger than themselves.

The men of Lupupa Ngye have married 41 girls from outside the village and only 24 from within it. Of those from outside the village, eighteen come from Lupupa Kampata, nine from Lumba, and the rest are scattered; no woman from Makola is currently married in Lupupa Ngye. The figures also show that it is primarily men who are 45 years of age or older who have married local girls, and this figure has significance for marriage patterns of young men.

Finally, marriages extant in the village represent a reasonably tangled network of relationships. In the following list, the column on the left represents the lineages of local women who have married into local lineages represented by men, on the right.

Female	Male
Bena Ekunyi	Chite Makumbo
	Yewusha
Yewusha	Muchipule 3
	Yankamba

Muchipule	Yankamba 2 Chite Kamamba 3 Bwende
Yankamba	Chite Kadiya Muchipule
Chite Makumbo	Lukale
Chite Kamamba	Kyambwe
Bwende	Muchipule Ngongo Sefu
Chite Kadiya	Muchipule Ngongo Sefu Yankamba
Ngongo Sefu	Chite Kamamba Yabakambe
Yabakambe	Yewusha

In these cases a Bena Ekunyi girl has married a Bena Chite Makumbo man, another Bena Ekunyi girl has married a Bena Yewusha man, and so forth. Thus through the mechanism of a woman going to marry a man of another lineage, ten lineages have established ties with other lineages. On the other hand, males have taken wives from other lineages in the village as follows:

Male	Female
Bena Yewusha	Ekunyi Yabakambe
Yabakambe	Ngongo Sefu
Chite Kamamba	Ngongo Sefu Muchipule
Muchipule	Bwende Yewusha Yankamba

236

Kyambwe	Chite Kamamaba
Lukale	Chite Makumbo
Bwende	Muchipule
Yankamba	Muchipule Yewusha Chite Kadiya
Chite Makumbo	Ekunyi

In this case, a Bena Yewusha boy has married a Bena Ekunyi girl, another Bena Yewusha boy has married a Bena Yabakambe girl, and so on. Through this mechanism of a man marrying a woman of a village lineage, eleven lineages have ties with other lineages. Looking at the marriage networks diagrammatically, first from the standpoint of women married to men, the following results:

Fig. 21
Marriage Networks: Women Married to Men

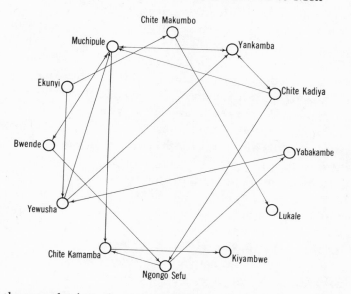

From the standpoint of men married to women of the village, the following results:

237

Fig. 22
Marriage Networks: Men Married to Women

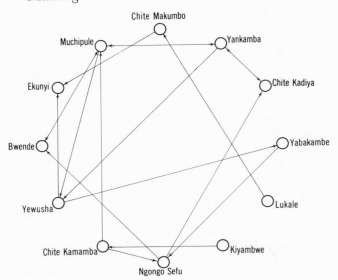

If the two diagrams were combined, the network of relationships would, of course, be doubly complicated, and it must be recalled that whichever way the relationship goes, that is, viewed from the standpoint of males or of females, the children of the unions immediately acquire obligations and kinship to both lineages. It will also be noted that only three lineages in the village have no relationships by marriage with other lineages; these three are Bena Kadiya, Bena Bakwamwesha, and Bena Mwepu Lombe, the three smallest lineages in the village. Thus marriage into any one of these lineages is open to males of all other village lineages, but it is not surprising to find that not a woman of marriageable age is to be found in any one of them. Finally, the two diagrams represent only current marriages and do not picture relationships now not immediately evident because of death or divorce. The full picture of all known relationships among all lineages would be far more complex than what has been illustrated here.

The result of these networks of interrelationships is that an informal and cyclic village exogamy is practiced in Lupupa Ngye. In 1959–60, this cycle had reached a point at which most young men were forced to go outside the village to find marriage partners.

This was due to a number of factors. For one, the old men in the village are, by and large, the polygynists, thus tying up proportionately large numbers of women. Further, the old men had tended to marry women much younger than themselves, thus absorbing eligible marriage partners for younger men. And finally, by marrying local girls, the old men had established the present network of lineage relationships, thus effectively making it impossible for younger men to find girls to whom they do not already have traceable kinship ties. As the older men die, however, the kin relationships they establish with other lineages will be forgotten, and marriage with local girls will become possible again; indeed, the first signs of this situation were probably being seen in 1959–60. Thus so far as the village is concerned, marriage is a continuing cycle of exogamy-endogamy, though of course inside the village, marriage is always lineage-exogamous.

The nature of the polygynous marriage for the woman is essentially one of inequality, and her position depends to some extent upon whether she is the first, second, or succeeding wife. While some women argue that all wives are treated absolutely equally and impartially by the shared husband, pointing out that each wife has her own cookhouse and her own possessions, and that the husband spends two nights with each wife in a strict rotation, inequality begins with the marriage itself, for the bridewealth given for a first wife is always greater than that given for a second. Indeed, it is said by some that the exchange of first gifts, *ebofu*, varies in marriage to a second wife; if the woman was previously unmarried, *ebofu* is given, but if she was previously married, then only *koonda* is transferred. It is also clear that a second wife in most cases comes into a marriage in a poorer bargaining position than a first wife; she has usually been married previously and is now divorced or a widow, and her status is second best. Furthermore, since a man's father gives him the bridewealth for his first marriage, but not for subsequent marriages, it is likely that the sums of goods and money available will diminish in subsequent marriages.

As the amount of bridewealth transferred indicates a differential status, so too do the relationships among the wives, although some women who are second or third wives stoutly deny any differences. The first wife is considered to be the chief wife, and most people feel that she has the right to, and does, order the second wife around. The second wife does not hold money for her husband as does the first, and the husband tends to be less generous with her. The position of the first wife is summed up in the proverb,

lukasu	lwa	kapamba	ndukile	lwa	bwilu
hoe	of the	old	more important than	of the	new

"An old hoe is more important than a new one."

The question, then, is why a woman would agree to become a second or third wife, and the answer is quite simply that one has to make the best match she can, and not all women can be first wives. At the same time, some women do refuse to become second wives.

Several reasons exist for taking a second wife. The first wife often urges it, since she is in the stronger position and thus tends to look at the second wife with some superiority and with an eye toward assistance around the household and with the children. Men also point out the convenience of having more than one wife: "If I have one wife and we come home from the fields together, then I have to wait for my supper." "If one of my wives is ill, then another one can cook and sleep with me." At the same time, men say that it is difficult to handle two wives, and that to do so a man must be a skillful diplomat. It is also more expensive, both at the time of marriage when bridewealth must be accumulated, and in marriage itself when the needs of another woman must be met.

Men deny that having more than one wife confers status on a man: "Look at Mukume. He is our friend. He has four wives, but that doesn't make him any more important than the rest of us." A man with more than one wife, however, is thought of as a relatively rich man who must have more money, bigger or more extensive fields, and more possessions than others. While wealth alone does not confer prestige, it is a part of it, and thus status, wealth, and polygyny are linked in the minds of male Lupupans. Young men who are at present monogamous tend to look toward polygyny as the ideal, but they do not yet have the wealth or experience to achieve it. The greater impact and influence of Christianity, however, has begun to change attitudes, and some young men genuinely wish to remain monogamous.

As we have had occasion to note with some frequency, the desire to have children is extremely high, and is one of the major reasons stated for marriage; indeed, having children is one of the strongest values in Lupupan thought. Thus barrenness in marriage is a severe problem for a woman. It will be recalled that the villagers believe failure to have a child is the result of the "fact" that the blood of the two people is "wrong" and "different." Some tendency exists, however, to blame lack of children in a marriage on the woman, "because it is well known that a man can fail to have children, get a divorce, and then have children with another woman." A childless woman can obtain medical assistance to help her conceive, but the cure is not always effective. Barrenness is considered ample cause for divorce.

Impotence (*muntu mufwe kiseba,* "man dead penis") is caused either by Efile Mukulu, for reasons not understood by humans, or by humanly instigated magic. Impotence is perhaps the worst and most shameful thing that can happen to a man in Lupupa Ngye, and if it becomes generally known, which it most often does, it is the source of great embarrassment and considerable public ridicule. The popular image of such a man is that he can never be calm, but is doomed to be uneasy and unhappy. Most villagers feel that the wife of an impotent man will shortly leave him, or will at least take a lover. It is suggested by some that the husband may urge his wife to seek intercourse with other men in order to conceal his shame through the resulting children which will be considered his. The major medical cure for impotence is to eat four husked palm nuts mixed with four leaves of the *kalama* tree.

Bachelorhood is an abnormal human condition, and it follows almost automatically that a bachelor is a witch or an impotent. Bachelors (*bukupi,* s. & pl.) are also automatically suspected of being adulterers. Very few bachelors are found in Bala society, and almost none are present in Lupupa Ngye.

Incest for the villagers can be defined as "marriage" of any two individuals between whom any degree of relationship can be traced. In practice, it is conceded that slipups may begin to occur at the third generation; that is, while the grandchildren of a male ego are prohibited from marriage with the grandchildren of his sister, the relationship by this time might be so diffuse as to escape notice—as the Lupupans put it; they might get married "if there was no one around who could tell them they were related." If the relationship were discovered later, and if, indeed, it were as distant

241

or more distant than the example used here, the *bakulu* of the two families would come together to discuss the matter. All informants feel that such a marriage would normally be allowed to continue, and some indicate that a token payment might be required from the husband to his mother-in-law. Examples are cited of such cases, and it is clear that when distant relationships are involved, the matter is not considered at all serious.

Such is not the case, however, with close relationships such as between brother and sister or between a man and the children of his father's brother. That sexual relationships or marriage between such relatives might occur is not very real to the villagers, but it can be discussed as a remote possibility. Most believe that if a brother and sister, for example, married unknowingly, they would separate immediately of their own volition upon being informed of their relationship. If their action were deliberate, or if they persisted in their insanity (the Lupupans would consider them literally insane), strong sanctions would be brought to bear upon them. It is suggested that in former times the couple would be killed, but most say that today they would be expelled from their family and lineage. If this were not enough, they would be expelled from the village, and the father of the couple would be forced to pay a substantial fine to the village elders. If the couple repents, further fines would be assessed on their re-entry into the village. If the villagers themselves do not punish the couple properly, Efile Mukulu takes punishment into his own hands by striking the offenders with lightning or sending a snake to wound them fatally, and the villagers, too, will be punished for their laxity by general sickness in the village. Punishment is not visited upon the children of an incestuous couple, nor is it believed they will be malformed in any way; they are not treated in any special manner by others, though they will always be known by their age mates.

In last analysis, the Lupupans fall back upon the sanctions laid down by Efile Mukulu for explanation of reasons for incest prohibitions. Incest is "wrong," it is "shameful," and it is thus "because Efile Mukulu told us." However, it is noteworthy that one informant, in triumphant climax to his argument, said, "If you married your sister, who would be your father-in-law? Your father, and that is impossible!"

The implausibility of close incestuous relationships is emphasized by the fact that the Bala believe in warning signs which can be recognized by an alert suitor. If a male approaches a girl with whom marriage would be incestuous, his heart beats fast and he knows that something is wrong. It would be physically very difficult, if not impossible, to have intercourse with such a girl, while it would be perfectly easy and normal with another girl. Thus means exist for detecting potential incest, and in any case the close track kept of genealogies and the small village situation make incestuous relationships a very rare occurrence.

Adultery is the cause of frequent dispute among the Lupu-pans, and it is always considered that the man is the aggressor, "because the man is always the aggressor in love—a woman couldn't force a man into adultery." Despite what seems to be its considerable frequency (probably a good 10 percent of all cohabitations are adulterous), men tend to regard it as a potentially dangerous proposition, particularly with married women. In view of the fact that death at the hands of the outraged husband was apparently a real possibility in former times, it is little wonder that men are still careful to cover their tracks; punishment today consists of a fine and a jail sentence if the matter is carried to the Congo courts.

If a man has been away from his wife for a year or more, and returns to find her pregnant, the child subsequently born is called *mwana a sanga* ("child of everyone"), but it is considered to be the husband's and is treated by him like any other child, theoretically at least. The men say, incidentally, that if any man were to leave his wife for this period of time, she would surely commit adultery. If a *mwana a sanga* has an accident which leads to its death, some informants say that the woman must tell her husband the name of the father, and this leads to an ordeal. The husband makes a special belt of *elala,* a palm product, and the accused father dons it and straddles the body of the dead child. If he is, indeed, the culprit, all his clothing falls from his body and he stands nude, even though he has been allowed to knot the belt in any way he wishes and to button all buttons. If his clothing remains fast, of course, he is not guilty. On seeing the clothing fall, the husband is free to take his revenge.

Some evidence indicates certain known "rules" to the "game" of adultery. For example, a man who was caught, fined 700 francs, and given a two-weeks jail sentence for adultery with a married woman, was extremely upset and angry. Upon his release he began to threaten to kill the husband or wife, or both, on the grounds that no one had told him the woman was married and that, since he was a stranger to the village, this was not "fair." Lupupa Ngye was upset for one or two nights when it was reported that he was lurking in the neighborhood, but apparently his temper cooled, for nothing further came of the matter.

It is unanimously agreed that adultery is sufficient cause for divorce from the standpoint of the husband, but that a wife cannot sue for divorce on these grounds. When asked to name causes for divorce, a man is likely to mention some or all of the following: "she will not work," "she will not cook," "she will not keep my clothing in proper repair," "she commits adultery," "she is a thief," "she is a troublemaker outside the family." Women usually mention some or all of these reasons for seeking divorce from a man: "he does not give me money," "he does not give me clothes," "he does not give me oil, salt, peanuts," "he does not have intercourse with me," "he commits adultery with the women of my brother," "he commits adultery with my sisters."

The process of divorce is neither complicated nor extensive; when a man wishes to divorce a woman, he speaks to her, gives her the causes of his action, and tells her, "Go home to your family." If she fails to understand the situation ("and women don't understand lots of things"), the husband calls in his best formal friend who explains the situation to the woman. When the woman leaves, she takes her personal property with her, but she must not take any of her husband's property. On the other hand, when a woman wishes to divorce her husband, she simply takes her things and leaves, perhaps saying nothing at all. These, however, are theoretical actions, and in fact a divorce is a difficult business at best, with much arguing, many threats, and interminable disturbance which may drag on for months or even years. Men say, "It is always difficult to divorce a woman. Women are like that; they always make a lot of argument. They are always two-faced; they profit from hanging on to a man."

Indeed, under ordinary circumstances, the woman (whom society places in a strongly dependent relationship) does not wish to rupture marriage ties; for that matter, neither does the man, though it is a simpler matter for him than for his wife. Women often threaten to leave home—men say "in order to try to get their way"—and may carry the threat to the point of packing their belongings and taking to the road; evidence indicates, however, that in most instances women in this situation keep a sharp lookout for men who will argue them into returning before they have gone too far.

Evidence also indicates that perhaps the strongest ties in a marriage are forged by having children. This is not to say that strong bonds of love and affection do not grow up between marriage partners, for they clearly do; rather, children stabilize and fortify a marriage. Thus, for example, if a man divorces his wife and then discovers that she is pregnant, he is almost certain to go to her father and ask to have her back. If the father and his former wife refuse, informants say the man would continue and continue until those concerned gave in; it is significant that all informants feel the woman and her father would find it impossible to refuse a reconciliation forever. In such a situation, it is equally probable that the woman's father would demand a fairly substantial payment, perhaps as much as 500 francs; fathers often take the opportunity of a daughter's first pregnancy to attempt to elicit some further "bridewealth" payment from their sons-in-law.

Finally, an old couple, in particular, may agree by mutual consent to separation. Such was the case with Ngoyi, the wife of Mankonde, who was old and sick and simply wanted to return to her parents to be taken care of as parents will in such a situation. Ngoyi discussed the matter with her husband, received his permission and blessing for the move, and is now considered to be married still but living apart from her husband. Mankonde says he hopes that Ngoyi will return, but he also says, "An old woman around here isn't very necessary." Ngoyi is not strong, she cannot work, and she cannot be of much help to him; he is just as glad she is gone. At the same time he remains responsible for her and sends her a portion of any animal he kills, as well as money from time to time. He says, however, that he gives considerably more to his wives who live with him than he does to Ngoyi "because they work for me. What I give Ngoyi is wasted. I give it to her as a gift because we have children together": again the importance of children to a marriage is stressed. If no children had come of the union, it is likely that Ngoyi would have been divorced, and almost certain that whatever support her husband did give her would be substantially reduced.

Homosexuality is poorly known and understood, and probably not practiced in Lupupa Ngye, although the men believe that the male transvestite (*kitesha*, pl. *bitesha*) is a homosexual—he is not. The *bitesha* will be discussed subsequently as a role in Lupupan society; further information, as well as materials on sexual behavior in general can be found elsewhere (Merriam 1971).

The matter of death was discussed in chapter 3, but it may be noted again that while the primary cause of death is considered to be magic practiced by witches and sorcerers, other causes are admissible under certain circumstances. Thus it is felt that some deaths are natural; people die of old age and it is said of them that they are tired and that their *bikudi* are tired. As a general rule, those who die of old age are only the extremely old, and the attitude toward them is in truth that they are so old and decrepit that no other cause of death is reasonable: "Who would want to kill *him*, and why?" A third cause of death is the wrath of Efile Mukulu who is considered, theoretically at least, to kill in extreme cases of "sin"; in these cases, he kills by striking with a stone, causing a person to fall off his bicycle, or by lightning. This is clearly a relatively new source of death which has arisen through the influence of Christianity; the Lupupans are unsure of it and unable to cite instances of its occurrence. The fourth cause of death is accident, for which the terms *kachiba* and *kibatu* are both used; examples cited are snake bite, bush fire, drowning, war, and personal fights. Again the category is rather unclear to the villagers, but it is a much more definite possibility than being killed by Efile Mukulu for "sin." Thus old age and accident are reasonably clearcut, though infrequent, causes of death; killing by Efile Mukulu for sin is inconsequential, though possible; and death by magic is by far the most probable, accounting for at least 90 percent of all deaths in the village.

One other possible avenue of death is recognized by the Lupupans, and this is suicide. While old people say that they have seen suicides, it is evident that it is a rarely taken alternative and one which in any case is not easily admitted if it has occurred in one's family. The result is that considerable uncertainty about suicide is present among the people.

It is felt that one might commit suicide because of false accusation or because of some kind of frame-up; but as a rare and not very acceptable alternative, suicide does not provide much reason for speculation as to its causes. Neither do the Lupupans see much variety in possible ways for committing suicide, suggesting only hanging and shooting one's self. However, it is a rather commonly held belief that a suicide is in some way evil, and most people consider him to have been a witch.

When a suicide is found, the finder is free to assist him if he is still alive, but if he is dead, the *lukunga* is called to take charge and to handle the body. Some say that the *lukunga* brings the body to the *yangye* for formal verification of the suicide, and others that the notables as a group come to the suicide spot for the same purpose; in any case, once the suicide is officially viewed, the *lukunga* and the *kitapa* (another minor political dignitary) together see that the body is taken a considerable distance away from the village into the bush. Some hold that the two officials take the body themselves, others that they lead the family of the deceased, who do the actual carrying. Once a spot is chosen, those involved build a scaffold, said to be some ten feet off the ground, and the body is placed naked upon it, sometimes covered with a few branches, to dry in the sun and to be eaten by birds and animals. No foods or utensils are put with the body. Many people consider that a suicide must have been insane, and insane people cannot be buried in the earth; an alternative explanation is that a suicide is an affront to Efile Mukulu and that lack of burial is his punishment.

If the suicide himself is "punished," so is his family, which is considered to be disgraced. His father must pay a fine to the *yangye*, because suicide is wrong, because it upsets the normal course of events in the village, and because it takes people away from their work to attend to the various procedures required.

The lack of real knowledge of suicide is further emphasized by the fact that a great variety of beliefs exists concerning what happens to the *kikudi*, or spirit, of a suicide. Some say that such a spirit "leaves the earth and disappears forever," while others hold that it becomes an evil spirit, a *mukishi*, doomed to roam the earth forever. Still others believe that the spirit of a suicide goes to Efile Mukulu to give an account of itself, and that it is punished, beginning with the fact that the body is not buried and continuing to a refusal on the part of Efile Mukulu to return it to earth in a new child. Finally, some hold that the *kikudi* of a suicide follows a completely normal cycle. The wide diversity of belief underscores the rarity of suicide in the village and the area.

In those cases in which death is not sudden, the villagers see what they consider to be unmistakable signs of its approach. The feet, cheeks, and eyes swell, the skin becomes pallid, the teeth take on "the color of manioc leaves" (sometimes also expressed as "black"), and a thick coating appears on the tongue. If possible, people should be in their own houses at the time of death, and the idea of voluntary death (except for the relatively remote idea of suicide) is unknown.

Funerals vary in length and intensity according to the age and status of the individual involved; while the distinctions are not always hard and fast, the usual customs are as follows. A free man receives the most elaborate funeral, which lasts for seven days and involves all formalities including the hiring of professional musicians, grave goods, a coffin, and elaborate distribution and receipt of gifts. The actual extent of the various practices reaches its peak at the funeral of an important man who was wealthy and held political title. The funeral of a free woman is the same as that for a free man, but is less elaborate. The funeral of a slave lasts three days at most, and includes a coffin, but distribution of goods and money may or may not be practiced. An adolescent boy or girl receives a funeral much like that of a slave; a babe in arms is buried on the day of death without ceremony and with one following day of mourning; and a stillborn child is buried immediately, without ceremony and without public mourning.

Special procedures are followed in some cases, as for example when a chief dies, and on at least two kinds of occasions alteration of the dead body must take place. Thus when a pregnant woman dies, the foetus must be removed from her body and buried in her arms, and when anyone, but especially a child, dies of an illness which involves swelling, the body must be cut open so that the sickness escapes, thus allowing the *kikudi* to return normally as a new child. Such cutting is done in the grave.

Burial takes place in cemeteries which are most often located at the back of the land occupied by each lineage. Eleven lineages have cemeteries and they extend burial rights to those lineages which do not have them. In some cemeteries men are buried on the right and women on the left, but this is a matter of lineage preference. Husband and wife are not buried together, and no plot reservation is made by the living; indeed, the latter idea is rather distasteful to the Lupupans. As we have noted previously, cemeteries are places normally to be avoided because of the possibility that *mikishi* may be lurking there. In former times, a special worker, *mashama*, stayed at the cemetery in a house built there; his job was to dig graves, to watch over the cemetery and to keep it clean, and to seal the graves of important people with red earth taken from a termite hill. Such persons are no longer employed and the cemeteries are largely uncared for.

The funeral of a respected adult male is divisible into three major parts from the point of view of the outsider, and while they are not named as such by the villagers, it is reasonably clear that the divisions are felt and perceived by them as well. These parts are the period from death through burial; the period of forgetting; and the exciting climax on the last day of the funeral during which the major problems raised by the death are discussed and resolved insofar as possible.

The corpse of the deceased is taken to his own house and laid out on his own bed where the body orifices are closed or covered and the body washed; in the latter operation, the body is always held by a male friend and washed by a male member of the lineage. The body is then dressed in the deceased's finest clothes, all of which must be spotlessly clean, tied in a sitting position in a chair belonging to the deceased, and placed on the front porch of his house. Male friends then come in a body, and the youngest friend gives and kills a chicken by wringing its neck until the head separates from the body; the symbolic indication is that "if someone killed you, then he will die like this, with force." Blood from the neck is allowed to drip on the shirt of the deceased: "We give you strength to search out whether it was Efile Mukulu or someone here who killed you."

Mourners surround the body, primarily women of the family, who have the greatest cause to mourn, say the villagers, because the deceased supported them. The chief mourners are the women of the lineage (mother, sisters), the brothers and father, and the wife of the deceased. Children of the brothers, the brothers themselves, the sisters, wife, fathers and mothers of the brothers, and the slaves of all the above use white manioc flour on their bodies, whitening their heads and sometimes their backs and shoulders, and drawing designs around their eyes. White is the color of the funeral, partly because it is the traditional pre-Western color of the cloths of indigenous manufacture, and partly because the white color helps the deceased see his way to Efile Mukulu. Mourners also take off their shoes and shirts, and members of the family, both male and female, bare themselves to the waist, all in sign of respect. A cloth is often tied around the chest to protect against illness, "because when one cries a lot, he may get sickness in his chest."

A crush of sound envelops the funeral; those around the body cry, wail, keen, and sing short snatches of melody, none of it coordinated with others who are doing the same thing. The village slit gong player sends out the news of the death in general and also sends specific messages on behalf of the family. His general announcement may be:

anwe	boso	bepa	no	kampanda	bafu.	tatuku
you	everybody	who	are here	someone	dead	we don't know

kibamwipa	anwe	boso	bekino	kipintshi
why he is dead	you	everybody	who are here	place

mwinetu	betufwila.
our friend	he is dead

An example of a personal message of mourning is the following:

mulume	ande	ampanga	bintu	nauno	bafwila.
husband	my	who gave me	things	he comes	to be dead

anwe	bamaunbo	boso	nufwe	nundidise	mulume	ande.
you	everyone of other villages	everyone	come	cry for me	husband	my

Other mourners spread out through the village, though primarily around the house of the deceased, and they also wail, keen, sing, and cry. Close relatives detach themselves from the group around the body and roll in the dirt, or crouch down and throw dirt over their head and shoulders, crying all the while. Soon groups of dancers are formed, tentatively at first, and then in larger numbers. Throughout the funeral, the women dance *kyombela malu* (s. & pl.), a counterclockwise circle dance, and *membe* (s. & pl.), dancing in place around the body; both of these are mourning dances which express the feeling, "He is gone. What shall we do?" A third dance, *kusemba malu* (s. & pl.), is one in which the women form a tight phalanx and sweep up and down the village street, singing; it expresses what the women are saying to themselves: "I cannot stay still. I cannot stay sitting on the mat. My grief is too great. I have to move around." The male friends of the deceased form a phalanx, shooting guns and brandishing spears, and roar through the village searching symbolically both for the dead man and for the person who killed him: "Where is our friend? Where did he go? If we find someone who is keeping him from us, we will kill him!" The mourners speak to the deceased:

sumuntu if it is someone	*bakwipa* who killed	*bakulekyesa* who told you to leave	*bano* all here	*bana.* children
omwipenamu kill him	*atwe* we	*babashala.* who remain	*tushale* we will stay	*bibuwa.* well (be happy)

Thus the opening portion of the funeral is a time of great sound, as grief wells up and out, and the deceased and his possible killer are importuned. The constant arrival of new mourners, friends, and relatives from other villagers adds to the confusion; each must be greeted formally, taken to view the body, and seated ceremoniously. The main female mourners move around the village individually using a stylized walk, peering about, and calling, "Where is he? Have you seen him? Where did he go?" All is motion and sound, and it is directed toward the honor of the dead and toward the suspicion that his death may not have been a natural one.

The rectangular coffin is begun almost immediately after the death, often by a personal friend who has skill in carpentry; it is made out of planking and lined with white Americani cloth, and the maker is paid 100 francs when the funeral is over. If the death has occurred in the morning, it is likely that the coffin will be finished in the afternoon; as soon as it is finished, it is taken to the house and the body is placed in it and left on display for the rest of the day and throughout the night.

Mourning is shared by all who are most closely concerned at the outset of the funeral, and brothers of the deceased may try ritually to commit suicide—they are always prevented by friends and relatives from carrying out the threat. The close male relatives, however, drop slowly out of the circle of the most active mourners, and retire to the porches of nearby houses in the lineage to sit, mourn individually, and to mourn and talk with male friends. Women, however, carry on through the first day and most of the night with undiminished fervor. To say that the mourning patterns are stylized is not to denigrate them, but such stylization becomes more and more apparent as time goes on. At the outset, mourning is earnest, grief is always real and is wildly expressed, and many tears are shed. Those not so closely affected, however, find emotional release in the general scene and in the formal expression of their grief, and to a considerable extent, they enjoy themselves thoroughly. Mourning, then, is genuine, but at the same time, practical; it is traditional and dictated by custom, and much of it is anything but random though the total effect is one of great confusion, especially in these early stages.

The next morning, if the person died the previous morning, and perhaps as much as two days later if he died at night when friends and relatives could not be notified immediately, the casket is carried around the house of the deceased so that he can say goodbye to it, and then carried to the cemetery of his lineage. Both friends and family must be represented among those who carry the coffin. The grave is always dug by the husbands of the sisters of the deceased; it is approximately six feet long, four feet wide, and five and one half feet deep, and it is lined on bottom and sides with new matting. The long axis of the grave is always laid out east and west, and the head of the deceased is placed to the east so that his spirit will "rise like the sun," that is, return as a new child; the grave is so constructed that the head fits into a small enclave cut in the side of the grave in order that "it will be covered in sleep" and that no movement will occur. Before the coffin lid is closed, and before it is lowered into the grave, the father, if he is living, and a brother if not, gives permission to the spirit of the deceased to leave.

oshale	*bibuwa.*	*muntu*	*shimutande*	*atande.*	*oukyie*
we will stay	well	man	who has no children	can have children	one must know

anka	*bakwipa.*	Efile Mukulu	*tatwinaye*	*mwanda.*
it is he	who killed you		if it is (who killed you)	trouble

mbidi	*yetu*	*yishale*	*ankabibuwa.*	*wetutundwile*	*mikishi*
body	our	remains	well (happy, contented)	look for good luck for us with	spirits

ibuwa.	*bikudi*	*bia*	*kutanda*	*kifuko*	*kitame.*
well	spirits	of	put children (of future)	lineage	our

ngiabikita	*banambutwile.*	*bana*	*bobe*	*bashale.*
it is like this that it happens	parents	children	your	will remain

netu	*bibuwa*	*wende*	*biya.*
with us	well	leave well	well

The lid is then nailed on the coffin and it is both lowered into the grave and received by men who have carried it to the cemetery. Placed in the grave with the coffin are a bowl of manioc flour to eat on the journey to Efile Mukulu, the left leg and left breast of a cock, as well as the left hind leg of a goat, considered to represent femininity and thus the fact that the deceased will "generate" a new child, and a plate, knife, and fork to eat with on the journey. The sisters of the deceased speak to him, telling his spirit to go and to return as a new child, and all the women leave. The men then fill the grave, and as he leaves, each man bends down and throws a small last puff of dirt into the grave from between his legs; no one looks back and, on return to the village, dancing commences with renewed vigor.

The second period, that of forgetting, begins with the arrival of an itinerant professional musician shortly after the burial; he is from another village, and is engaged and paid by the family of the deceased. His job is to make people forget, and he sets about his task in three ways. First, he is a jokester who tells funny stories and sings funny songs; he uses the signal gong and drums messages upon it which make people laugh; he insults the villagers in a humorous way. Second, and in a more serious vein, he presents himself as an outlet for the hostile feelings of the relatives and closest friends of the deceased. This is accomplished through *kamwanya* (s. & pl.), a mock battle between a man and his wife with the professional taking one role and the relative the other. The relative rushes suddenly up to the musician, threatens him, and often strikes him with a stick or the butt of a spear; the musician retreats with a frightened air, singing and drumming all the while. He turns back suddenly upon the aggressor and charges him; the two dance briefly, and gradually the confrontation is broken off. Third, the arrival of the musician is the signal for the start of the men's *kikadi* (pl. *bikadi*), which is specifically a "dance of forgetting," and which the men enter in high spirits and with much general amusement.

By the third or fourth day of the funeral, the musician has turned things around and the atmosphere is much less tense. The close male relatives of the deceased have eaten nothing and slept little, the female mourners are beginning to wear out, and thus the visible signs of mourning are becoming muted. People from other villages begin to go home, though many of them will return for the final day, and the villagers who are least closely involved are beginning to return to work. By the end of the sixth day, and through the sixth night, few people are left, the vigil on the mats around the house is kept only by close relatives, and singing and dancing has virtually ceased.

The last day represents the third phase of the funeral, and it is one of large crowds and renewed interest. The family of the deceased prepares food for all and it is eaten communally. In the middle of the afternoon, the notables arrive in a body and are settled on mats around the front of the deceased's house; their spokesman, the *lukunga,* opens the proceedings, and many gifts are given to the family by relatives and friends. This is also the occasion for general announcements of importance to the village, and these are given by the *lukunga* after the last gift has been presented. Now the notables go into serious deliberation, and while they are doing so, singing and dancing begin again. The questions to be answered are whether the family must pay a fine for having disrupted the village through the death, and who will be named to replace the deceased. The decisions are made, the notables return to their places, the crowd holds its breath, and the *lukunga* announces the results.

Now the funeral is over. The people leave, and the family gathers for a traditional bath (with the sexes separated) and the shaving of heads. They will remain visibly saddened for three months, and in mourning until the second funeral, which occurs six or twelve months later and at which the friends of the deceased are called together, given food and drink, thanked for their assistance, and reminded one last time of him who is now dead. The funeral has been a time of noise and confusion: people coming and going, friends talking, drunks causing trouble, the various events of the funeral postponed, the coffin the wrong size, the grave not ready when the coffin arrives. Even the eagerly anticipated announcements of the *lukunga* on the last day are marred by children shouting and people talking behind the house.

But the funeral is achieved, and the dead man is sent off to Efile Mukulu on the strength of all the proper traditions. It is, of course, not an end, but a beginning, for he will return as a new child; his family and friends know this and are comforted by it as they look forward to the same cycle in their own lives.

7. Human Surroundings III: Friends and Leaders

In addition to the relationship groupings of kinsmen, Lupupans are members of groups based on principles other than "blood." Some of these associations are more or less permanent, such as the groups formed by hunters or by raffia basket-makers, while others are of the most temporary sort, such as the constantly shifting group which gathers about a drum-maker. Many of them have been noted in previous pages, but among them are two kinds of non-kin groups of special importance to the Lupupans; these are the formalized friendships established both within and outside the village, and the political hierarchy.

Formalized friendships are established between a man and a man, a woman and a woman, or a man and a woman, but this dyadic relationship may also involve spouses who, in turn, become formal friends. Great store is laid by friendship, and, indeed, it can be said that a basic theme of Lupupan culture is that one needs and wants many friends. While formalizing friendships is not obligatory, the villagers feel that a person who fails to do so is not behaving normally.

The male-male relationship is called *kukuande*, literally "my friend" (pl. *bakukubande;* usually expressed as *kuku*, pl. *bakuku*). When pressed as to the criteria by which a potential friend is weighed, Lupupans answer in terms of the ideal standards of morality common in the village; thus "he must be a man who does not talk too much, who is calm, who does not have sexual relations with the wives of others, and who is not a thief." In fact, standards such as these may or may not play a substantial part in the matter; they probably are increasingly important as the circle of formal friends is extended into other villages, for as one knows his *bakuku* less intimately, the standards by which he chooses them must of necessity be more generalized. In the village itself, one chooses his friends through intimate knowledge of them as people, and his standards tend to be applied less formally and more knowingly. It is usually felt that while a man has many friends, he has only one best friend, and that the best friend is chosen from within his own age group.

In respect to the best friend, it must be assumed that knowledge of each other is so deep that the formalities are sought by mutual consent and the pact formed without hesitation. With others who are less well known, the approach is more tentative and formal, and the outcome not necessarily predictable. Thus when a man wishes to make a new friend of someone not perfectly known to him, he approaches him by means of a gift of a goat, or possibly chickens. This is followed by an invitation to eat together and, if all goes well, the gift is later reciprocated with a gift of slightly greater value. At this point, the two parties have indicated their satisfaction with the potentialities of the new relationship and simply declare themselves *bakuku*—no formal ceremony is necessary for private or public confirmation.

It might be assumed by the outsider that all potential *bakuku* relationships are agreed to in advance, but that this is not the case is evidenced by the fact that a standardized procedure for refusal is known. If a gift has been presented, but the receiver does not wish to make formal friendship, he rejects the overture by returning the gift in person within a week of its receipt. While he may return it directly to the giver, he is more likely to return it to his wife or to a known friend; in any case, he does so as inconspicuously as possible because he does not wish to shame the initiator: "One should always be polite to everyone," say the Lupupans.

It may also be necessary to break friendships, but such a case is considered rare by the villagers, and the provocation would have to be great. Indeed, some say that a friendship of this sort can never be broken, but almost everyone agrees that a friend who trifled with one's wife would no longer be desirable as a friend. "Suppose your friend is trifling with your wife. You would call in another friend, and the two of you would talk with him. 'You have not respected my wife. It is finished between us.' "

Thus one's obligations to his friend include obligations toward his wife: "If you have a friend, his wife is your friend, too, and you must treat her with a great deal of respect." One man said heatedly that anyone who would commit adultery with the wife of his *kuku* must be a witch, one of the strongest statements of condemnation possible in the village.

Men who are friends are expected to assist each other in many ways, but most important is a readiness to help at any time: "Friends help you when you are in trouble." They may be expected to loan money when financial difficulties arise, and to smooth over differences between a man and his father; if the rift is extreme in the latter case, it is the best friend who goes to the father and asks him to forgive his son. We have already remarked on the role of the friend as go-between in matters of the heart, as well as his ceremonial role in the transfer of bridewealth from the family of the groom to that of the bride. Friends can be called upon to help accumulate bridewealth, they stand ready to provide physical protection if necessary, and they assist with work. On some formal occasions, the responsibilities of friendship can become demanding, as in the funeral when a man has special obligations to his friends as a group; in this situation, however, his friends reciprocate formally, and through various informal supportive acts.

Men agree that one should not make friends in a helter-skelter fashion, and particularly not at the same time; to conclude two friendships in one day would be "disrespectful." Some men, however, look upon friendships in very practical terms by seeking to have at least one friend in each lineage of the village; since others say that this is not a particular goal, it is apparently a matter of individual judgment.

The question of practicality is also raised in connection with friendships made outside the village; these are far more extensive in number than those made within Lupupa Ngye, as is shown in Figure 23. Indeed, Mayila, who has relatively few friends, says that he does not have many "because one makes friends when he travels, and I have never traveled much." The process of making such a friend was explained by one man as follows: "For example, a man from Kampata is passing through your village; he is a stranger and he asks you the way. You point out his route to him, and then perhaps you invite him to come in and have a meal with you. Then he visits you again on his way back home and again you invite him to have a meal with you. Then when you go to Kampata, you know you have a friend, and you visit him, and he invites you for a meal, and *kukuande* begins." The extent of the network of friends can be quite extraordinary, as for example, in the case of Efile, who lists friends in such far-flung cities as the former Elisabethville, Léopold-ville, Luluabourg, Albertville, Kasongo, Lubefu, Lusambo, Kabinda, and twenty-six villages and towns within Bala territory. The case for friendships in other villages is made in terms of practicality: it is good to know that one has friends when he is traveling. It may well be that this emphasis upon "outside" friends has its roots in the period of disruption when it was probably absolutely vital to have friends in other villages, both for haven and for assistance in getting safely from one place to another. In any case, the networks are extensive today, and the purpose of the "outside" friends is to have someone who is known to the traveler in as many villages as possible.

Male-male friendship, then, is extremely important to the Lupupans. It was summed up by one informant as follows: "Friends are important. A friend comes to help you when you are in trouble. He is like a kinsman or a substitute for a kinsman. One keeps a friend as long as he can, like a woman. If your friend dies, you take his children if there are no relatives, and they become part of your family."

The female-female friendship is called *lole* (pl. *balole*), and once

Fig. 23
Random Sample of Friendships

| | In Village | | In Other Villages | | |
	Male	Female	Male	Female	Total
Male					
Efile	9	3	34		46
Mayila	4	1	16		21
Kingkumba I	7	4	21		32
Kasambwe	15	1	22		38
Mulenda	8	2	21		31
Kingkumba II	2	3	12	1	18
Female					
Kipa	4	9	5	11	29
Ngoyi	5	6	1	5	17

again ideal criteria are set up by which individuals purportedly judge the advisability of seeking a relationship. One woman, for example, said that a potential friend is one who does not fight with her husband, who does not steal, and who does not tell secrets; another woman's criteria were almost the same in that a friend for her is one who "gets along well with her husband," who does not steal, and who "stays in her house and does not insult people." In citing such criteria, women do not necessarily express reality, for many of them have disputes with their husbands and at the same time have a number of *lole* relationships. Rather, these statements indicate that criteria do exist and that formal friendship is not a matter to be taken lightly. In the end, one makes a friend on the basis of personal factors which are judged both by general village and individual criteria.

Women say that the average number of *lole* relationships held at any given time is "probably forty," but Figure 21 indicates that the number is less than this hypothetical figure. At least one woman stated strongly that proffered friendship could not be refused; if one does not like the person who offers friendship, says this woman, she may say to her, "If you are going to be my friend, you must change this or that about yourself." The strength and importance of friendship is indicated by the same woman when she says that even if a known witch came to her, she would not refuse friendship: "You would pay attention. You would keep a sharp eye on her. You would not give her meat, but only *kalese* (pl. *tulese;* manioc greens), and you would not treat her as well as you would treat a friend who was not a witch. But you would not refuse her."

Men's descriptions of how a female-female friendship is initiated show a pattern identical to that used between two males, but women indicate somewhat less formality. After suitable investigation and thought, a woman simply goes to the house of her prospective *lole* and says (without formulae) something like, "I like you. I want to be your friend." She gives gifts of a stalk of bananas or plantains, two chickens, a basket of manioc, and perhaps even a small amount of cash. Dinner is not taken together, but the gifts are reciprocated if the offer of friendship is accepted.

Balole often eat together and work together, but friendship also means mutual assistance. Thus a woman's friends come to help her when she is ill; they carry water, prepare food, take care of her children, and work in the fields if, for example, a crop must be harvested at that time. In an extreme case, a friend might come to live in a woman's house acting as "your husband's second wife," but extension of sexual favors is not contemplated in this situation. A friend may take a woman's children to be with her for a few days "just to give you a rest," and if, at the birth of a child, no suitable girls are available in the family or lineage to act as helpers, a woman turns to the daughter of her friend. Friends seek each other's advice, and they have a right to criticize each other in ways that nonfriends do not. If a dispute arises between a woman and her husband, the wife may call in a friend to help her settle the matter; the friend, in turn, may call in the husband's *kuku,* and the two together attempt to find a solution.

Where men tend to stress friendships formed with men in other villages, women tend to stress their formal friendships within Lupupa Ngye. This reflects the fact that men travel more than women and thus use their friendship network to practical advantage, and that the role of women in the society is such that frequent small assistance can both be proffered and utilized.

Badumiyanami (s. *dumiyanami*) are female-male friendships, and they are almost always initiated by the woman. In such a case, the woman must always consult her husband "to decide whether it is a good idea," and she must have his formal permission to enter on the relationship. Women say that the kind of man they seek should be

261

someone "who does not strike his wife, who makes people welcome at his house, and who accepts the children of his friends gladly." In addition, he should be someone "who does not argue with his wife, who does not steal, and who can keep secrets." As in the other relationships, these criteria are idealized and simply set the general tone for thought about friendship.

The actual process of initiating a female-male friendship varies according to the individual situation, but usually the woman prepares a meal, goes to the man, and says (without formulae) something like: "We have known each other for a long time. I am happy with you. Let's be friends." If the man accepts the invitation, the woman eats in her kitchen, as is customary, while the proposed friend (sometimes along with another friend of his) eats in her husband's house with her husband. Some say that the only gift given by the woman is a small one of cloth or clothing, and that the man may or may not reciprocate, while others indicate that the woman's husband gives her a goat, a fowl, or some other potential gift, and that the man gives a return gift later. Indeed, most informants see the relationship as involving a slow but steady exchange of gifts over a lifetime of friendship; such gifts are not considered obligatory, but friends simply want to give gifts to each other. Women frequently give mats to men, but men's gifts do not seem to be at all "standardized."

The *dumiyanami* relationship, of course, carries more potential difficulties in its structure than the other two forms, because of the possibility of arousal of jealousy on the part of friends' mates. The Lupupans visualize this as a problem for the husband of the female and not for the wife of the male in the female-male relationship, thus emphasizing once again their assumption of the greater importance of the male. The villagers say unanimously that actual sexual relations do not take place in the *dumiyanami* friendship— after all, "when a man and a woman make friends, she becomes his sister, and it is impossible to have a child with your sister!" If such behavior did occur and was detected, it would lead to extremely grave consequences. Even with such assurances, however, a man may become jealous if he feels his wife is spending too much time with her *dumiyanami,* and in such a case he may successfully demand that the relationship be broken. Informants say, however, that the check upon potential difficulty in this kind of friendship stems from the fact that the woman must obtain her husband's permission before making a male friend.

It is clear that the *dumiyanami* relationship is organized and conceptualized as being of far more practical benefit to the woman than to the man; for him, the benefits are social and human. Thus the woman expects that the man will assist her in her business and social affairs, lending her money if necessary, helping her in case of accident, even assisting her to the extent of traveling to another village on her behest and business. A man in this relationship also gives assistance to his friend and her husband in matters of bridewealth accumulation, and even in arranging marriages; if a woman with children is divorced or widowed, her *dumiyanami* is especially helpful in this respect.

Children are sometimes led into friendship relationships by their parents, and in such cases, the terms for adult friendship are used. It is usually the mothers who agree that their children, who are perhaps seven years of age, should become friends. On a given day, one mother leaves her child at the other's home while she goes off to the fields as usual. If a girl is involved, she is given food and told to prepare it for herself and to eat with her new friend. No formal gift exchange is practiced, "since everything children have belongs to their parents," but the mothers sometimes give their children small items to exchange in imitation of their elders. If the friendship prospers, one child is left with the other mother almost every day; if the children quarrel, the supervising mother intervenes, tells them this is not the way friends behave, and perhaps gives them simple instructions on friendship. It is hoped that friendships thus begun will be prolonged, and indeed, that they will last throughout the lifetimes of the participants.

Teen-aged boys and girls seek and form friendships, but it is not clear how formalized these are. Girls between the ages of thirteen and fifteen are said to seek *badumiyanami* among boys of their own age, and adults accept the notion that one of the purposes of these friendships is sex relations. Girls of the same age may also have a *dumiyanami* who is an older married man, and one of his primary obligations in this role is to instruct the girl in matters pertaining to marriage. Such instruction may be in sexual intercourse as well as in other matters, and sex relations may continue after the girl has married; in either case, the affair is carried on in secret. Similarly, a teen-aged boy may have an older married woman as his *dumiyanami*. Friendships begun among boys and girls of the same age during the period of adolescence may lead to marriage and, as an idealized pattern in the society, such marriages are remembered with special warmth.

Friendship, though made between two people, almost always involves the spouses of those concerned. When a woman has a *dumiyanami*, her husband takes on a relationship analogous to father-in-law to her friend who, in turn, treats the husband with the respect due the new role. *Bakuku* often make *badumiyanami* with each other's wives, and some say that when *balole* are formed, the husbands must become *bakuku*. Whether or not the secondary relationships are formally made primary, friendship in the ordinary sense exists among and between the families of those who have formal relationships.

The Lupupans are constantly involved in a network of friendships. Formal friendships are not made within the lineage, but this is because "you are friends with everyone in your own *kifuko* anyway." Some persons seek to have at least one friend in each lineage, but in any case, friendship with a single individual almost always leads to friendship with his or her wife or husband, and thus relationships with two lineages are formed. A person with the normal ten to fifteen formal friends in Lupupa Ngye probably has ties with almost every lineage in the village, and thus friendship increases the solidarity of the village as a unit. At the same time, outside friendships enable individuals to move with confidence in the wider world and to set up ties between and among villages. Thus friendship provides an extremely important network which contributes to peace and stability through communication both within the village and in inter-village relations.

The second major non-kin group in Lupupa Ngye is made up of political leaders, who are responsible, of course, for the villagers in respect both to internal and external affairs. It is the people who give them the power they wield, and it is also the people who can, and on occasion do, take it away; political leadership is thus an honor in the village, as well as a trust, and it is not a simple role to play.

The political structure of Lupupa in 1959–60 was the product of multiple forces, including the agonies of the period of disruption

(1870–1900), Belgian control, and the tensions of the immediate pre-independence period, and thus only its outline was perceptible. By June, 1960, what was left of the traditional system had been reduced to a shambles, and "governance" was in the hands of minor political dignitaries who were conducting what amounted to a holding operation pending the outcome of independence.

While the focus in this book is upon the village of Lupupa Ngye as it existed in 1959–60, it must be noted that what little—and it is very little—is known of political structure in past times indicates that the Basongye of the Lomami area were never organized into large kingdoms. Indeed, some authorities believe that the village, headed by its chief, was the most viable political unit (Schmitz in Overberg 1908:457), but all point as well to small groupings based on ethnic reality and headed by at least a chief and a *chite*. Such a grouping was apparently the Bala, and Schmitz, who was posted by the *Comité spécial du Katanga* to Dibwe in 1904–05, and to Tshofa in 1906–07, tells us that at that time, the chief of the Bala was Piani-Tschungu (Overberg 1908:475); in 1959–60, the Belgian-appointed Chef de Secteur was his son, also named Piani-Tschungu (Piyani Chiungu), who retained some vestigial authority as the chief of the Bala. These small groupings came under the cumulative authority of grander political leaders such as Lupungu and Ngongo Lutete during the period of disruption, but they have been the traditional reality of the political system in this part of the Basongye area.

Manuscripts in the Belgian archives of the District de Kabinda indicate that from the beginning of firm European control of the area, the Bala were divided into two administrative districts, marked by a north-south line through the villages of Lumba Lupata, Eshadika, Mitombe, and Kipuku. Immediate dispute arose among the people over the powers of the two areas, and thus it was decreed at an early but unknown date, that when, in the succession, the chief of the Bala was selected from one of the halves, the *chite* would be selected from the other. Of immediate significance to Lupupa Ngye, however, is another document from the official archives which indicates that the Bapupa were left out of the selection process and thus never furnished either chief or *chite*. The reason for this state of affairs is not made clear, though it is remarked in passing that the Bapupa had a different "statut" based upon their own "coutumes et institutions."

Bala organization has probably been firmly under Belgian control since the early 1900's, though the extent to which the people continued to look to the traditional structure for direction is unknown. The villagers of Lupupa Ngye, however, and probably the Bapupa as a whole, were apparently never oriented toward the Bala organization. A few villagers can discuss the wider Bala system, but their knowledge is shallow, and it is significant that the only person who was truly interested and at all knowledgeable in the matter was himself a former village chief who had had some personal contact with the Bala dignitaries. Public knowledge does not go much further than the facts that a chief of the Bala (*fumu a Bala*) and a *chite* of the Bala (*chite dya Bala*) exist today; some add a third notable, the messenger of the Bala (*lukunga lwa Bala*). The roles of chief and *chite* are conceived as essentially legal rather than political; Lupupans feel, for example, that flagrant trespassers should be taken to the chief of the Bala. The Bala *chite* is envisaged as handling quite esoteric legal matters; thus people who remained midgets (*bipinji*, s. *kipinji*) "at the time when children born at the same time are beginning to marry" were taken to the Bala *chite* who killed, and probably ate them. Midgets today, on the other hand, are thought by the Lupupans to be under the special protection of the *chite dya Bala*. In the case of suicide, the *chite* is notified, and he may elect to send his messenger to take flesh from the bones of the deceased which he uses in making magic for the protection of all the Bala. Burning one's own house is considered such a flagrant antisocial act that the *chite* is purportedly called to the village to fine the offender publicly.

A very few villagers have some knowledge of the *epata*, or former sacred central place of the Bala near the present location of Mitombe, and they may attempt—without success—to describe some of the sacred restrictions on the political leaders of the Bala. But in truth, Bala political structure has very little meaning to the Lupupans as a whole, and no significant meaning to most of them. It is fair to say that the only real Bala influence today comes through the person of Piani-Tschungu, but even while he may be thought of as chief of the Bala, it is much more important that he is the Chef de Secteur.

Among the Bapupa themselves, that is, the inhabitants of the villages of Lupupa Ngye, Lupupa Kampata, and Makola, a slight indication of political unity is preserved in the fact that the village chief of the moment "rules" over both Lupupas, but Makola is not included, and the office of chief has become so amorphous that it is hardly more than a symbol of power. We are reasonably safe, then, in viewing the political structure of Lupupa Ngye as an isolate which has very remote attachments to the Bala and slightly stronger ones between the two Lupupas.

It will be recalled that the present village of Lupupa Ngye represents only the contemporary, and presumably impermanent, abode of a changing group of people who, beginning at Kadiyala about the turn of this century, shifted their residence from one location to another. While little is known or can be reconstructed about life in one location as compared to life in another, it is fairly probable that at Kadiyala, the people were self-divided into four social-political groups which may have been based upon age. At Mpumba, shortly after 1900, the village plan probably consisted of a central street from which ran four smaller streets, each one the section or quarter of one of the four groups. This physical organization apparently died out shortly thereafter, and by the time the people had moved to Mukikulu, the four subsidiary streets had disappeared. No evidence exists to indicate that this kind of formal organization was ever part of the present Lupupa Ngye, the location of which was probably reached toward the end of the first decade of the present century.

The village today consists of a single broad street, on either side of which are the houses of the adult male residents. Although it is not marked by any tangible boundary, the village is crossed by an imaginary line which divides it into two parts. Dispute as to the terminology applied to this line, and thus to its specificity, is found among the villagers; most refer to it as *mudiyanyino* (pl. *midiyanyino*), which is defined as "limit," "boundary," or "dividing line" in general, and which is also applied to the Milky Way. Others insist that this particular dividing line has a special name, precisely because it does divide the village; two terms are suggested, but claims do not establish either of them as the exclusively proper one: the terms are *kisamba* and *bitumba*. Whatever the terminology, the dividing line separates Lupupa Ngye into two halves, *milondo*, which

267

is the downriver or eastern half, and *mashiba,* the upriver or western half. One informant suggests that the people of the upriver half are grouped together under the term *bangyenundu,* and those of the downriver half as *bamilondo,* but these groupings are only grudgingly acknowledged by others, if they are accepted at all.

Over each of the halves presides a political dignitary, the *yangye* (pl. *bayangye*) for the downriver half, and the *chite* (pl. *bachite;* most often spelled *tshite* in the literature) for the upriver half. Quite certainly representing the organization suspected for Kadiyala and Mpumba, each half is, in turn, divided into halves; the downriver half is inhabited by the *bakipumbu* and *bampumba* groups, while the upriver half houses the *bepa* and *besanga* groups.

This primary organizational device appears to represent the remnants of what was formerly a strongly functioning base for social-political behavior. Informants are vague, confused, and confusing on the matter; the system hardly functions, and the dignitaries that head each quarter are more figureheads than functioning officials; one of the four sections has almost disappeared; and the correlations made between the respective groups and other aspects of organization and behavior are at best ill defined. Thus interpretation of the system may be made in one of three ways, that is, the groups may be viewed as four social-political units which were functioning almost autonomously at the time of Kadiyala, as age-grades, or as a combination of the two.

The argument for the priority of the social-political group rests on two kinds of evidence. First, several informants are able to list what they consider to be the lineages which formed each of the four units at the time of Kadiyala; while they do not agree precisely in the matter, the fact that the lineages can be grouped at all indicates some kind of social unit. Indeed, a few villagers insist that the lineages in the various units are related to each other, thus suggesting either a maximal lineage or a clan system; no actual genealogical relationships, however, can be traced by the Lupupans. Thus while the existence of the groups seems established, the basis for their initial organization remains unclear; we do not know what brought them together, whether they were self-protective groups formed during the period of disruption, or whether their basis was initially social or political.

The second argument for the quarters as original social-political groups is based on knowledge of the feuds and warfare that took place between them, which indicates well-organized political groups from the time of the earliest memories of the village. Such feuds began from incidents of killing, raids on property, or other incitements; they ended either when the village chief intervened to settle the dispute or when one of the groups decided that the affair should be stopped and sent its head to negotiate. In the latter case, A, the head of the group suing for peace, approached B, the head of the opposite group, shouting his intentions loudly, clapping his hands, calling for peace, and carrying a "flag" of truce which traditionally consisted of the skin of a banana hung on the end of a stick. When received, A presented B with two women of his own family, not slaves, who were kept by B for two days and then returned with two hens as a sign of final acceptance of peace. In the period the women were held, B took them in intercourse; if children resulted, they belonged to the family of A unless B requested formal marriage ties.

This intergroup conflict may have been a constant feature of life at Kadiyala; one of the men widely acknowledged to know most about the history of the village tells the following story, recounted here in loose form.

> Kadiyala was on the south bank of the Lupupa River about where Kipumbu River joins it [note that this does not accord with other descriptions of the location, which place Kadiyala far to the north of the present area]. At the time of this battle, the Bampumba lived where we went to cut *mabo a balume* [a type of palm tree cut one day by the raconteur and the author; this places the location about 100 yards west of the present road and 150 yards north of the river]. The Bakipumbu were living where we put a fishtrap in the river with Lubembele [i.e., about a mile and a quarter south along the Kipumbu River].
>
> At this time, my father was the Yampumba and his brother was the Yakipumbu. One day a Bampumba woman went to the river with a calabash to get water, and a Bakipumbu man came along and smashed the calabash for no reason. The Bampumba decided this was a serious offense and that they would make war against the Bakipumbu. So they signaled this on their slit gong, and the Bakipumbu signaled back that it was all right with them and set the date of battle for the next night. On that night they drew up for

battle, and the two brothers faced each other first and said it was really war. So the Yakipumbu threw his spear, and the Yampumba parried it with his shield, recovered it, threw it back, and killed his brother. Then the battle was joined, the Bampumba killed fifteen and lost none, and the Bakipumbu took flight.

Two days later, the Bakipumbu regrouped and challenged the Bampumba to fight again. The Bampumba accepted the challenge and attacked at midnight, burning houses and killing. Some of the Bakipumbu saw how badly things were going and went to the chief of the village and asked him to end the war, saying they would pay damages. But the chief refused, saying that the Bakipumbu had started it and now would have to finish it; that night, the Bakipumbu lost twenty more men and the Bampumba lost none.

But the Bakipumbu tried a third time, and this time the Bampumba, thinking their opponents would be weak again, arrived in battle drunk, and they lost forty-eight men to none for the Bakipumbu. Now the Bampumba had had enough and they delegated one of their number, Yewusha, to pay one woman to the Bakipumbu, but he put it off, and that night the Bakipumbu came again and this time killed twenty-five more Bampumba. The Bampumba said, "Why continue? We paid you," and then they found out that Yewusha hadn't done it. And so today in the village the name exists: *mushiko ya Yewusha* ("someone who forgets his duty" "like" "Yewusha"), and if you call Mwembo *mushiko* he will know what you mean [because he is the descendant of Yewusha and the head of the lineage Bena Yewusha]. Yewusha said it was all his fault, but they refused to excuse him, and ever afterward they called him *mushiko.*

There were lots of people around then, but at Kadiyala there was war, and then a sleeping sickness epidemic, and then a smallpox epidemic, and now we are few.

Whatever the precise accuracy of detail in this recitation, it seems to illustrate the general picture of four volatile groups, doubtless still edgy from thirty years of warfare, and by no means yet bound together into a single peaceful community. This view of the groups, however, tells us nothing about how they happened to form, to come into proximity with each other, and eventually to constitute the basis for the present village.

The age-grade explanation for the formation of the groups can perhaps indicate how they came into being, but informants are no clearer in this case than in the instances cited above. Thus some villagers say that the groups represent children who were born on the same day; other, and more, Lupupans say that the groups are made up of children who were born within the span of two years; still others say that these groups are made up of the children of people who were already grouped together. Neither of the first two explanations seems reasonable simply because of the time involved. "All children born on the same day" would demand a much larger population than the Bapupa ever seem to have had, and by this kind of criterion, strictly interpreted, 365 groups would have formed each year. The same kind of objection prevails when the two-year period is scrutinized; assuming that childbearing begins at about age eighteen, a cycle of nine groups would form, and the absence of the other five groups today would have to be explained—no such explanation is apparent.

Some further evidence may be obtained from the unanimous observation of informants that today all children of a group become members of the group, that is, all *bepa* become *bepa*, all *bakipumbu* become *bakipumbu,* and so forth. However, it is not at all clear in the minds of the villagers whether their own children are members of their parents' *bakipumbu* group, for example, or whether they form a new *bakipumbu* group. Further difficulty is met in the fact that the four groups today are conceptualized as correlating with the common age divisions of the society; thus the *bakipumbu* are correlated with the *basongwalume* (young men of ages approximately 13 to 35); the *bepa* are correlated with the *bantu bakulu* (men from 35 to 60); and the *bampumba* are correlated with the *banunu* (men over the age of 60). In these correlations, the *besanga* do not appear at all, but it is perhaps significant that the only other age classification is *bana,* or children from birth to age thirteen. If this is conceived as a cyclical age-grade system, it is thus possible to say that the new unit has not yet been formed, but a major difficulty with this view is that the *besanga,* while virtually nonexistent as a group, do still have a leader, a man of over 60.

If we attempt to explain these groups in terms of a strict age-grade system, it would appear that the correlations between named group and an age category must change over time, since the children of the *bampumba,* for example, must begin by being *bana* and then *basongwalume.* But the system is clearly not conceptualized

271

in this way; rather, the groups are associated with political power.

The latter state of affairs derives from two further characteristics of the units. The first is that each group has its corresponding political and juridical functionary whose title is taken from the name of his division; thus the *bakipumbu* are headed by the *yakipumbu*, the *bampumba* by the *yampumba*, the *bepa* by the *yepa*, and the *besanga* by the *yesanga*. But even more important, each of these divisions has the right to furnish certain of the political dignitaries in the village hierarchy, and the *bampumba* are clearly most powerful in this respect, since it is from their lineages that are chosen three of the four highest dignitaries and at least twice as many dignitaries as are provided from any other division. This power of the *bampumba* is both recognized by those who are still at all involved in the system, and conceptualized by them as permanent in nature. Thus the idea of a cyclical age-grade system per se becomes less likely and the relative strength of political power as a base for the groups increases. The quarter divisions and their correlates are summarized in Figure 24.

Fig. 24
The Quarter Divisions and Their Correlates

Quarter	Political Leader	Correlated with	Political Officers Provided
bakipumbu	yakipumbu	basongwalume, ages 13–35	shesha
bepa	yepa	bantu bakulu, ages 35–60	chite, kitapa
bampumba	yampumba	banunu, ages 60 and older	fumu, yangye, dipumba, lukunga
besanga	yesanga	—	nyamampe

In the end, it is the disintegrated nature of the quarter divisions that makes resolution of the problem of their origin impossible. At present we can only accept them as political units which may well have sprung from social and age considerations and which remain today as vestiges of a formerly much more important and functional position.

Since the exact nature of the system itself is in doubt, it is not surprising that the role and powers of the four quarter chiefs are equally blurred today. Each chief, of course, must come from the

272

quarter he represents, and he is chosen, theoretically, on the basis of ideal qualities sought in a leader. Thus he is expected to be calm, to avoid fighting, to know the village well; "a person who has done wrong would never be chosen," say the villagers. Who is responsible for making the choice, however, remains unclear, as do the duties of the man in office. The present *yepa,* for example, indicates the following as his primary tasks, but what he names overlaps the duties of other dignitaries, and it is clear that he is not certain of his position. The *yepa,* he says, takes care of strangers in the village when the chief is absent, and serves as a stand-in for the latter—both these roles are shared with other dignitaries. The *yepa* advises people of his quarter, and of the village at large, in time of trouble; when the situation demands it, he convokes the people of his quarter at his house, discusses the situation with them, and then, if necessary, takes the matter on to the *chite* who, it will be recalled, is in charge of the upriver half of the village which includes the *bepa* and *besanga* quarters. The *yepa* is also responsible for organizing the work force for the construction of public buildings, such as the school; again his plans are passed up for the approval of the *chite.* Communal property, such as the village gongs and drums, may be held by the *yepa,* and he also is sometimes the recipient of, and responsible for, sums of money paid for village labor by the central state administration. Ultimately, the *yepa* is responsible for the upkeep of the *gîte d'étape,* or resthouse kept on the edge of the village for Western travelers, and his own house is the meeting place for his quarter and, if need be, for the village at large. It is the latter fact that gives the *yepa* the prerogative of asking for the assistance of his constituents in the construction of a new house when necessary.

The other quarter chiefs indicate similar broad duties, and in addition, in former times each leader constituted a first or lowest court which was responsible for judgment of minor disputes. People today, including the dignitaries in question, disagree on precisely what kinds of disputes are handled at this level, though most agree that they are domestic only. The present *yakipumbu,* for example, says that he still judges cases involving neglect of children, domestic dispute, adultery, and the avoidance of legitimate work. The most recent chief, however, describes the legal duties of the quarter chiefs by saying that they are qualified only to judge domestic cases initiated by women, and that cases initiated by men must go immediately to the higher court made up of the notables; the present *yesanga* denies this.

Cases on this lowest level are personal in nature, and are handled in a personal manner. Thus the *yesanga* says that in the domestic disputes he judges, fines are reckoned in chickens and are payable to him. He, in turn, kills the bird, directs his wife to prepare it, and he, the disputants, and anyone else who has taken part in the case eat it together. According to the same man, such cases must be finally settled on this level; they cannot be carried upward to the notables. Thus if someone disputes the decision and refuses to pay the fine and take part in the consumption of the chicken, the *yesanga* must go to his family and, by some means, work out with them a final and binding decision. The juridical work of the quarter chief, then, is based upon persuasion and moral appeal rather than the naked exercise of power. In return for his efforts, says the present *yakipumbu,* he may receive certain fines or portions of fines, but his is an idiosyncratic view in this respect. The entire matter of distribution of fine monies and other prerogatives of rank, such as portions of large game animals killed by hunters, is now more theoretical than real and extremely difficult to reconstruct.

In addition to their functions in the legal system, some evidence indicates that the quarter chiefs were also war leaders called *miyembo* (s. *mwembo*), and as such were at the forefront of the fighting with specific roles and duties which will be discussed below in connection with warfare.

The description of the four basic social-political units is admittedly fragmentary, and this is so because the system has lost most of its significance. Thus the *besanga* no longer exist as a separable group; the organizational role of the divisions which kept them physically separated, and apparently feuding with each other, has been lost; the chief associations lie more with a village-wide age group than with the quarter group; the responsibilities of the groups are ill defined and the leaders themselves have either abandoned their responsibilities, seen them disappear under the impact of the imposed Belgian legal system, or at best, disagree on what they are. In sum, this organizational basis, while obviously important for what it represented in the past, is now fuzzy and confused in the minds of the people and is no longer a functional principle, save in one respect.

This last important function derives from the vested rights to higher political offices of the *bamwilo* (s. & pl.), or notables proper, which are distributed among the four quarters; the specific rights are noted in Figure 24. These rights are further defined as specific to family-lineage groups; thus in order to be considered as a potential *dipumba,* for example, a man's family must have contained a *dipumba* in the past, as well as belonging to the *bampumba* quarter.

While hereditary right is the prime qualification for the selection of notables, exceptions must and do occur. Thus if no candidate is qualified by hereditary right, or if those qualified by right are unacceptable due to physical, mental, or social defect, the second choice is made from among families in the same quarter who are qualified to produce dignitaries other than that for the particular office at hand. If the village is searching for a *dipumba* and no first-line candidate is available, selection may be made from families which have contributed a *fumu* or *yangye,* and are thus within the same quarter. If the search must go outside the proper quarter, an attempt is made to choose a notable from families which have produced notables; perhaps, as illustration, a *nyamampe* family of the *besanga.* If no acceptable candidates, finally, are to be found in "notable" families, someone from a non-notable family or lineage must be chosen and a new line begun.

It is thus apparent that some distinction is made between notable and non-notable families and lineages, suggesting the possible presence of social stratification based upon political privilege. Certain privileges which are the result of position and not a part of it, do go with the status of notable; thus notables, for example, are not expected to contribute manual labor to village projects, and even their children are theoretically exempt from certain kinds of work. However, these can hardly be called class distinctions; rather, they are symbols or prerogatives of rank. All notables today are expected to till their own fields, and do so, and although they do receive some gifts and payments, they are not supported economically by the rest of the society. Notables are always male: "women are women," say the Lupupans, and the idea of a female notable is simply not to be entertained seriously.

The *bamwilo* are the general council of the village, called upon to settle matters of internal and external dispute, to counsel the villagers, and to make recommendations and policy for the good of the village as a whole. Appointment as a notable is a high honor because it signifies receipt of the trust of the villagers. Notables can only be appointed and installed legally by notables, but in doing so, the latter are acting for, and with the sanction of, the people. The power of the people is extremely strong in this, and other matters, and aside from small prerogatives which over the long run do not balance out against the expenditures demanded of office, the incentive of being a trusted official is of greatest importance. It is significant that deposition from office brings much bitterness to the former notable, but this is not directed so much toward the reasons for deposition as it is toward the loss of faith and trust deposition represents.

At present, the following major dignitaries are found in the political organization of Lupupa Ngye. At the top of the hierarchy is the *fumu* (pl. *bafumu*), or chief, who rules over the entire village and who is considered to fall into a class by himself. Beneath him in importance is the *yangye* (pl. *bayangye*), who is specifically responsible for the downriver half of the village; he is, in addition, something of a second chief, replacing the *fumu* when the latter is absent and also considered to be somewhat apart from the other notables by virtue of his high position. The *chite* (pl. *bachite*), whose office is usually ranked as at least equal to that of the *yangye,* and is considered by some to be higher though not set apart, is probably the most functional officer in the hierarchy; in addition to his responsibility for the upriver half of the village, his job contributes much to the smooth functioning of the entire organization. If the chief is on a slightly rarefied plane, the *chite* is the instrument of his policy and is responsible for activating his orders. Following the *chite* are four lesser officials, in order of importance the *dipumba* (pl. *badipumba*), *nyamampe* (pl. *banyamampe*), *shesha* (pl. *bashesha*), and *lukunga* (pl. *balukunga*), each of whom has specific duties which will be outlined below.

So far as the people of Lupupa Ngye are concerned, the personal requirements of a chief are specific and practical: he must know French, he must have money, he must know how to deal with people, he must be generous, he must not walk alone, and he must always keep an even temper. The most recent chief echoes these requirements, and adds that a chief must never steal, commit adultery, quarrel, or insult another. These, of course, are theoretical requirements; in fact, chiefs do steal and commit adultery, and worse, the very fact that one is chief is an automatic indication that he is also a witch.

The basic requirement for becoming a chief is that the individual come from one of the chiefly families within the proper village quarter. In theory again, the chief is succeeded by his son, but if there is no son or if the son is considered unfit, the successor is chosen from the chief's family; next in line is usually the chief's younger brother. If there is a son but he is too young to rule, an interim appointment may be made until he has reached his majority, or a council of the former chief's friends may be formed as an advisory group. If the chief lacks any heir at all, the appointment moves to another patrilineage, but always within the chiefly families and the *bampumba* quarter, if at all possible.

The selection of a new chief from a new line is the responsibility of the notables, who seek advice from respected elder males of the village and whose decision is always subject to general village approval. The person selected is theoretically first aware of his honor when it is announced to him by the *lukunga*, who acts in his frequent role as emissary of the notables and who intones a formula to which the candidate makes appropriate response, either accepting or rejecting the appointment. In fact, the candidate has friends among the notables who come to him in advance to sound him out and to obtain his prior acceptance. It is at this time that the candidate can refuse the honor, but if the notables are persistent it is considered impossible to refuse more than twice. In this case, again in theory, the candidate can accept provisionally for a period of three months. At the end of this time, he calls the notables together for a feast, gives them a small gift of money, and reminds them of his provisional acceptance. In fact, if one accepts provisionally, he continues in the position; in Lupupa Ngye no one can recall a provisional acceptance which did not turn into a permanent one.

The day following the visit of the *lukunga*, the young men come to the new chief's house, take him upon their shoulders, and carry him around the village in triumph, after which he is returned to his own house where he is seated in state in a chair placed upon a mat. The notables and villagers arrive to pay him honor, and feasting, dancing, and celebration go on throughout the night; in former times, the first music heard by a new chief was xylophone music, but this custom is no longer followed. At this point a series of expenditures begins for the new chief; while these are given as gifts, they are fixed gifts, and they have reached very significant proportions in the economy of Lupupa Ngye. To each of those who carried him on their shoulders, the chief gives one piece of Americani cloth; to the singers and dancers at least 200 francs; to the *basongwalume*, two goats; and to the notables, two more goats. These gifts are accepted publicly during the celebration. At this time, too, the *fumu*'s gift of 2,000 francs and one Americani is sent off to the Chef de Secteur. All these gifts come under the heading of *mukumino*, the first acceptance gift.

Three days later, the new chief is expected to give a gift totaling at least 800 francs to the notables, and one to two years later, a third gift of 6,000 francs to the notables, as well as four goats, four hens, four cocks, and forty casseroles of maize-manioc bread all of which are consumed at a public feast by the villagers.

In addition to these gifts given as a part of his investiture, the chief is expected to continue his generosity throughout his rule. He must make food and shelter available to the passing stranger at his own expense, and while he can command labor, he must reward those who work for him with gifts of food as well as of livestock. In the past he was responsible for feeding a successful war party on its return, and he has many other such obligations.

It is difficult to determine the return that comes to a chief, and certainly it has diminished in recent years. The most recent chief complained bitterly that he received nothing from his people, and that when he objected, they said to him, "If you don't like it, go to the [Belgian-operated] tribunal and make a complaint against us," something he could not do without lowering the dignity of his position. In the past the chief received gifts of manioc and chickens from the *basongwalume*, the people contributed ants to preserve and store against future need, his sources for receiving slaves were numerous, and the villagers cultivated fields for him, although in the last case he was obliged to reward the workers with gifts of food.

None of these behaviors takes place today, although the chief does continue to receive occasional gifts of meat as a prerogative of office. If a large animal such as a bush pig or large antelope is killed, the hunter notifies the notables, who in turn notify the chief through the *lukunga*. The chief then sends a personal friend, whose title is *myandaku* (pl. *bamyandaku*) and whose sole function under his title is to supervise the cutting and distribution of the meat. One hind quarter, the chest, and one foreleg are given to the notables who pass the hind quarter on to the chief via the *lukunga;* the chief is expected to give the *lukunga* 5 francs and both the *lukunga* and *myandaku* a piece of meat. If a stranger kills an animal within the village limits, it must be given to the chief who, in return, must pay the hunter from 200–300 francs and meat at his discretion; what is not used by the chief is given to the notables.

Lion skins are given to the chief, but more importantly, the leopard (*ngye,* s. & pl.) is reserved to him and is his symbol. All leopards killed must be taken to the notables, who notify the chief; the chief must pay the hunter 200–300 francs. The meat is either given to the notables or prepared as a general village feast by the chief's wife; the chief himself cannot eat leopard meat, for the animal is considered as a chief and "you cannot eat your fellow chief or eat yourself." Only the chief can eat the flesh of the chicken hawk (*mumba* s. & pl.); and any attack on his person is considered a very serious crime. As noted above, the chief formerly had some privileges in respect to the labor of his people, but these privileges are sharply restricted today and exercise of them depends almost entirely upon his personal popularity.

The duties of the chief are many. He must know all village affairs and be present when his presence is required; he must act as a controlling force for good, and he is totally responsible for the well-being of his village. He must feed and house strangers, provide workers when required by the Belgian administration, give feasts on specified occasions, accept ultimate responsibility for the upkeep of bridges and paths, distribute cloth and clothing to the needy and slaves to the deserving, make the peace in feud and war, and initiate seasonal activities such as planting. In the past the chief held title to the land, and while this is no longer the case, he is still responsible for settling land disputes. He must care for an orphan and hold property left to it until it comes of age. The chief must not make magic against the villagers, but on the positive side, he is required to make magic for them against snakes, large animals, and lightning, as well as for the protection of the health of the village children and the assurance of good crops. The chief acts as final

arbiter in legal disputes; while relatively minor questions were
solved by the quarter heads, and more important matters by the
notables, all disputes involving theft, adultery, magic, and land
formerly went directly to the chief. In such matters, the chief had a
variable number of special juridical advisers, *benebalasha* (s. & pl.),
who were appointed permanently; these were respected older
friends and they conducted the questioning of accused, accuser, and
witnesses. Fine money in these cases went to the chief, who in turn
distributed it to the *benebalasha* who had conducted the trial. The
chief, finally, made the decisions in matters of declaration of war,
planned the general strategy, and sometimes led the warriors
personally. His house was considered sanctuary in times of war and
peace.

It must be repeated that the chief is the symbol of the virtues
of the community, whether in fact he lives up to these expectations.
A chief must always walk on big paths; to walk on small paths
would be beneath his dignity and thus demeaning to the village. A
chief cannot go out alone at night because loose women might be
about and might accuse him falsely. He is expected to be generous,
honest, and in short, the embodiment of what is correct in Lupupa
Ngye. But at the same time he is a witch and he has power, and
checks are always placed upon him.

These checks are provided by the notables, acting in concert,
and by the people, who keep a watchful eye upon their leader; if
the chief does not live up to the behavior expected of him, he can be
deposed. Between 1900 and 1960, Lupupa Ngye had eight chiefs,
and thus the average tenure of office was seven and one-half years.
The longest reign was that of Yampumba who was in power for
thirty-one years; the shortest was that of Muchipule who was in
power less than a year. Whatever the specific reasons for the end of
the terms of office of the known historic chiefs, they must fall into
one of three general categories: self-deposition, deposition by the
people, or death.

Self-deposition is theoretically the sole responsibility of the
chief; he alone can decide whether he has become too old, tired,
feeble, or incompetent to continue to rule. When such a decision is
made, the chief calls a public meeting of the villagers, announces
his decision, explains his reasons, and asks for public acceptance. If
he has a son, the chief names him as his successor, and the new chief

is installed on the spot with food and drink provided by the son; in this case, the gifts of accepting office are not paid nor is the formality elaborate. If, however, the father never completed his proper gifts, the son is responsible for them, and the son is also responsible for any debts his father accumulated as chief. If no logical successor is present, the chief calls a public meeting, announces his decision to resign and, if it is accepted, turns the selection of a successor over to the notables.

A chief can be deposed only through the action of the notables with the consent of the people. The reasons most commonly given for deposition are adultery, theft, taking other people's goods by force, bearing false accusations, and shirking responsibilities. Deposition may be initiated by an individual or group of individuals in the village who then must proceed through the *chite*, or the *chite* himself may decide that such action is necessary and call the notables together; indeed, he is charged with taking such initiative when he deems it necessary. At the meeting of the notables, the advisability of the move is discussed, and the suggestion for deposition can be overridden. If the decision is to depose, the matter is taken to a public meeting of the villagers, who have the power to reinforce or overturn the notables' decision. After the matter has been thoroughly discussed, and if deposition is agreed upon both by notables and villagers, the chief is called, the charges are placed before him, and he is given a chance to defend himself. After his defense, the chief is dismissed and a final decision is reached; it must be made clear that in such a public meeting the chief can defend himself satisfactorily so that deposition proceedings against him are dropped then and there. If the decision to depose is made, however, he is not officially notified—although he is, of course, perfectly aware of the decision—until a successor has been chosen.

The tenure of a chieftainship may also come to an end through the death of the incumbent. When a chief falls seriously ill, the people of the village are enjoined from playing, shouting, or making other overt demonstration which might be construed as lack of respect. Nothing is done about a search for a successor, theoretically and overtly, however, until the chief actually dies. The fact of death is kept secret, the body is buried in the presence of the family and the *lukunga* only, and the ensuing public interment is carried out with a dummy. Burial for a good chief is in his own house which is thereafter allowed to fall into ruin, sometimes guarded until it does by a sentinel (*mashama*); the house is called *shibo ya mashama*. Burial for a bad chief is popularly supposed to be in the bed of a temporarily diverted creek; after burial the water is turned back into its normal course, and it is believed that this type of burial insures that the chief's *kikudi* will return in its new body purged of evil intent. The secrecy of burial is explained on the ground that the chief is such an immensely powerful figure that if people see the body the children of the village will sicken, crops will not grow, and famine will stalk the land. More pragmatically, perhaps, the death of a chief is the signal for "taking during the funeral," a practice discussed previously in connection with economic redistribution, and a delay in announcement gives the chief's family time to gather its goods together in safe places.

The chief, then, is a powerful figure in the life of Lupupa Ngye; his line may theoretically continue forever, providing he has successors and that he is not deposed. In the figure and behavior of the chief are invested the proper moral and ethical behavior of the villagers, and a chief who continues to win the admiration of the people is a respected figure. At the same time, the continuance of his rule is in the hands of the people, whose power to depose or to allow him to remain in office is absolute.

It is not necessary to elaborate on the roles of the various notables in the detail given to the discussion of the chief, but the office of *chite* can be noted as more or less representative of the notables, and the duties of the remaining offices outlined in brief. All notables are appointed to their positions by those notables who are in office at the time, but abuse of power is limited by the facts that specific notables must be drawn from the proper quarter, lineage, and family, and that all decisions must be submitted to the male villagers who, as a body, can override the selection. All notables must have the same general personal qualifications as those expected of a chief, with specific application to the particular position at hand. Thus the *chite* must know how to deal with people, must be generous, must keep an even temper, must not live apart from other people.

The duties of the *chite* are varied and include the following. He is closely associated with the mechanics of justice, and all major legal complaints are channeled through him, either to the notables as a judiciary body or to the chief. He is largely responsible for the naming and implementation of the nominating procedure for new notables, and he is also responsible for implementing the chief's hospitality to strangers. Although he may delegate the actual duties to lesser notables, it is he who organizes public work; it was he, as well, who saw to it that the villagers planted the crop quotas required by the Belgian government. The *chite* is the instrument through which the deposition of a chief is achieved, and he is responsible for basic law, order, and arrangement for the upriver half of the village.

The incumbent in 1959–60 had been *chite* for thirteen years. His acceptance gift consisted of two cocks, two hens, and 250 francs; his second gift was three goats, three chickens, and 2,800 francs. His income derives from gifts given the notables, from animals killed near the village, and from fines. Like all the other notables, the *chite* says that over the years his outgo has far exceeded his income; but he is proud of his position, proud of having the confidence of the villagers, and willing to keep the post as long as that confidence continues.

The *yangye* is responsible for law and order in the downriver half of the village, and is in the high position of being the replacement for the chief; indeed, he is considered almost as a second chief. He must give hospitality to strangers, arrange for the bridewealth of destitute persons, care for orphans as does the chief, be responsible for general legal matters, give feasts for the villagers, and look out for the general welfare of Lupupa Ngye and its inhabitants. The 1959–60 incumbent of the office had been *yangye* for about eight years, his paternal grandfather was *yangye* before him, and his father was *kapita*. His accession to office was unusual, in that he swears he did not know he had been chosen, but otherwise ordinary in that the villagers arrived one evening before his house led by the *chite*, who said:

	tubakupa	bu	yangye
	we give you	as	yangye
He replied:		nankumina	
		yes (I accept)	
The *chite* said:	kita		mukumino
	make		first acceptance gift
And he replied:	olo	nankumina	
	yes	yes (I accept)	

The first acceptance gift, which he turned over to the *lukunga*, was 400 francs; following this transfer, his wife prepared two cocks, two hens, and a goat which were served to all those who cared to eat. During the dinner, the *chite* announced that an error had occurred: the dishes on which the *yangye's* wife served the food were covered, and since they should have been uncovered, the *chite* levied a fine of 100 francs. Had the dishes been uncovered, the "crime" would have been reversed and the assessment levied in the same way. The second, and major, gift was 5,000 francs and five goats, but the *yangye* never paid these obligations, and probably never will. Income for the *yangye* comes from fine money, from large animals killed by hunters or dead animals found in the bush, from the estate of a person who dies without friend or family (a situation that the present *yangye* notes sadly has never occurred), and from lost objects found and property which is without an owner because it is not wanted—a rare category, again, which is given the special term *kitololwa* (pl. *bitololwa*). Income over the years has fallen far short of outgo, but the *yangye* says, Efile Mukulu willing, he will continue in the job as long as he lives. He is proud of being chosen by the villagers.

Moving another step down the hierarchy, the *dipumba* is, like all other notables, responsible for general order in the village; his role, however, is to carry such matters as he may see or hear about to the notables through the *chite*. He is also responsible for helping those in need, particularly the ill, and he is most specifically active in the quarter of the village in which he lives. The *nyamampe* and the *shesha* are lesser dignitaries whose duties consist primarily in helping the other notables to make decisions and in contributing in whatever ways are possible to the smooth functioning of the village.

The *lukunga* is the lowest dignitary in the hierarchy, and his position is often held up to the outsider as illustrative of a nondesirable status. His two major duties are to act as the town crier, dispensing news and information, and to be the messenger and, in fact, the active arm of the notables as a group. It is the latter role that gives him his low status, for the villagers point with scorn to anyone who "is ordered about," even though in this case it is by other notables to a notable. To the outsider, however, the status does not seem to be commensurate with the position, for without the *lukunga*, most of the actions both by and for the notables would not be carried out. The *lukunga* is everywhere, talking to people, listening to them, defending the prerogatives of the notables, and not above taking what he can get for himself. He is highly visible and of considerable importance in a major funeral where he makes various physical arrangements, acts as intermediary between groups that may be at odds with each other, and announces decisions of the notables which are crucial in settling social and economic problems raised by the death. The *lukunga* leads important visitors through the village, makes a primary assessment of the situation when the notables are called upon to settle a matter, receives news and requests addressed to the notables, and supervises the preparation of food given to them, as well as the distribution of the meat of game animals. When something is lost, the owner reports it to the *lukunga* who goes from house to house describing it and noting any reward which may be forthcoming. The *lukunga* is the bearer of important news to other villages, assists in matters of suicide, and bears the bad news to a deposed notable. In short, the *lukunga* is the channel through whom passes much of the formal business of the village, and he is also in the best position to know what is happening and what may happen, as well as current gossip and confidential information.

One last group forms part of the hierarchy of political power in Lupupa Ngye, and this is the *basalayi* (s. *musalayi*) who, in 1959–60, numbered four men. Qualified for office by virtue of family right and personal capability, these men are ranked above the *lukunga* but below the rest of the notables. In fact, they are not notables per se, but rather, candidates in training and future replacements for the current notables. They act as assistants to the notables, take part in all consultations, but never speak in public; of course their opinions are also the last to be taken in council. This is the training ground for future notables, and those who are *basalayi* are almost certain to become notables themselves.

While considerable dispute can arise over the precise distribution of power in the hierarchy of notables, almost all Lupupans agree that the following diagram represents the situation as well as it can be represented.

fumu

yangye

chite

dipumba

nyamampe

shesha

basalayi

lukunga

yakipumbu   *yampumba*   *yepa*   *yesanga*

the people

A few other political offices are referred to by the Lupupans, but they are either presently unfilled or have only historic reality. Among these are the office of *alangombo* (s. & pl.), a dignitary whose rank was apparently above that of the *chite,* but whose office has receded so far into the past that nothing further is known of it; indeed, some villagers say that it was never a Bala title, but rather, of the Bekalebwe. The *kitapa* (pl. *bitapa*) and the *songye* (pl. *basongye*) are the offices of two very minor dignitaries; some add to them the *kimuni* (pl. *bimuni*), but none of the positions has been filled in the recent past. These personages ranked below the *basalayi,* and it was their duty to assist them and all the other political dignitaries. They were not chosen from notable lineages or families, and the position was considered to be a steppingstone toward possible higher posts; if this did occur, of course, it meant the creation of new notable families. A few Lupupans assess the duties of these minor dignitaries specifically as assistants and messengers to higher ranking dignitaries. These relationships, in descending order, are the *mwepu* to the *fumu,* the *lukunga* to the *chite,* the *kitapa* to the *yangye,* and the *songye* to the *lukunga.* The *mwepu* is a former minor dignitary whose job now has been changed to that of the *kapita,* a title which is outside the political hierarchy; the *kapita* was directly responsible to the Belgian administration to see that the resthouse was kept in proper repair, to assemble required work groups, make sure that agricultural assignments were carried out, and so forth.

Two further officials are present in the village, though neither is placed in the official hierarchy. The first is the *fumu akyata* (pl. *bafumu bakyata*), who is the son of a former chief and whose advice is sought when a new chief is to be named; while the office was filled in 1959–60, it was clearly honorary only, and the holder was frankly bewildered about his responsibilities and privileges.

The *fumu a kashama* is an office now fallen into total disuse, though recalled by a few who dispute about whether it was held locally or only in relation to the chief of the Bala; the job consisted of preparing and preserving leopard skins for the chief.

These minor and half-forgotten positions can be put aside, since they are no longer a part of village organization, and thus the structure that emerges is a power pyramid with the broad base composed of the villagers as a body who have the absolute right to impose and depose any dignitary in the hierarchy. Next are the four quarter chiefs, responsible primarily for keeping peace in their respective areas, settling small domestic disputes, and referring more serious difficulties to the *bamwilo* above them. The *basalayi* form a base for the recruitment and training of new notables, taking part in consultation but having no real power themselves, while the notables are responsible for the day-to-day political and legal functioning of the village. The *chite* and *yangye* are the most important and most responsible officials, while the *fumu* overlooks the entire system, settles some kinds of disputes himself, and is the embodiment of the virtues of the village as, to a lesser extent, are all the officials.

Whenever possible, the officials carry out their duties through discussion and persuasion, particularly on the lower levels of adjudication, and indeed, this principle is given a term in Kisongye: *kwipusena* (s. & pl.). Informants explain its meaning by saying: "Suppose you and I have difficulties with each other, but we decide to sit down together and talk it out. We both listen to each other and we reach an agreement. That is *kwipusena*." More precisely, the term refers to the accord that is reached, not to the process of reaching it.

More formal codification of crimes and punishments is also a part of the system; and thus legal decisions are made, fines levied, and force used when necessary. This formal system, however, had to a considerable extent fallen into disuse by 1959–60, since traditional political and legal power had been appropriated by the Belgian Congo government. The following description of the law is thus perhaps more theoretical than real in its present application, though the traditional legal system had been in operation fairly recently and petty disputes are still settled within the village.

Some evidence indicates that police were available when

needed, though the pressures and cohesion of the small community quite probably made them unnecessary except in extreme cases. Apparently this role was filled by the *mwembo,* who, when functioning as police, were known as *kimankinda* (s. & pl.); they were responsible to the chief and were sent to quiet disturbances and to bring in suspected criminals. When someone in a court case fell ill, a *kimankinda* was sent to take his evidence and to present it before the notables. The *kimankinda* was a public announcer during disputes, and it was he who summed up after court decisions were made and pointed out the morals involved to the assembled people. Both the latter duties are vague in the minds of the Lupupans as, indeed, is the entire concept of the office of *kimankinda.*

It will be recalled that the chief had a variable number of special legal advisers, the *benebalasha,* who were responsible for questioning those involved in a court case, and the formal use of witnesses seems clearly established. The latter (*tumoni,* s. *kamoni*) were never paid, although it is felt that if one appeared for the winning side he was likely to be invited for a meal or for a drink, or to be given a small gift. The concept of perjury is well known and, if caught, a perjured witness was punished.

In domestic cases involving small disputes, the quarter chiefs acted as sole judge. In more complex, but still relatively minor matters such as family quarrels or quarrels between families, the notables acted without the chief. In such cases, some informants say that all notables were required to be present, and others five of the six (without the chief), but no one indicates that more than two could be absent. Serious disputes involving theft, adultery, magic, and land went directly to the chief who served as judge; while the notables were in attendance in such cases, giving advice to the chief along with the *benebalasha,* it was the chief who made the final decision and handed down the judgment. Finally, cases could work their way up the legal ladder from quarter chiefs, to notables, to chief, but the practical mechanism here is today unclear.

While oaths and ordeals played a strong part in the legal system, divination seems never to have been important in the village. With lack of confidence, a few Lupupans speak of certain sorcerers who have the ability "to know the future" (*mukubuka*), but no one understands how this works and it is claimed only for the past.

Two oaths (*kuchipa*, s. & pl.) are apparently the major ones used in Lupupa Ngye; it is believed that if the oath is sworn falsely, Efile Mukulu will send illness or perhaps even death as punishment. Three important situations in which oaths are used are usually cited by the villagers: (1) before the notables when a case is being judged, including a formal swearing in of the principals; (2) the swearing of fidelity by a wife to her husband; and (3) in sealing institutionalized friendship, but only when it is expected that the friendship will be an extremely important one. The two oaths are as follows:

Nya.	*shindesa*	*bande*	*boso*	*babayile.*
No	even if you show me	my (friends)	all	who are gone.

nchimukume.	*ataa*	Efile Mukulu	*angipa.*	*nchimukume.*
It isn't I	or		can kill me	It isn't I

Nya.
No

Loose translation: No. Even if you were to call forth the spirits of my dead friends (before whom I could not lie). It is not I (who is guilty). Or Efile Mukulu can kill me (without changing the honesty of my statement). It is not I. No.

ataa	*mpeshi*	*afwankupila.*	*nchimukume.*
or	rain (lightning implied)	it can come and strike	It isn't I

Loose translation: May lightning strike me (if I am not telling the truth). It isn't I.

Ordeals (*kushingula* s. & pl.) are of five major types, of which the most frequently noted is by poison (*mwafi*, pl. *miyafi*); this ordeal, however, is subject to quite varied descriptions by villagers who claim to have seen it carried out. The *mwafi* itself is a tree, the bark of which is crushed and mixed with cold water. In one version, the innocent drinks the brew without ill effect; if guilty, he lets the cup fall from his hand before he has finished drinking, falls to the ground unconscious, and dies within about three hours. In another version, the suspects are taken to the *mwafi* tree after drinking, and

289

each throws a lance at the trunk; he who is innocent remains well, while he who is guilty becomes violently ill after throwing the lance. In a third version, the stomach of the guilty distends and turns red after drinking and he soon falls dead; the innocent retains his normal stomach and regurgitates the drink.

Two major versions of the ring ordeal (*tukano*, s. *kakano*) are described. In one, it is said that two rings, smaller than finger rings, are treated with magic and placed against the suspect's nose near his eyes; if he is guilty the rings stick to his nose and perhaps work themselves around his eyes—he cannot shake them off. The rings fall immediately to the ground from the nose of the innocent. In the second version, the rings are called "sun" and "moon" and one passes through the other. They are placed on the right eye of the accused and if he is guilty, they enter the eye which swells terribly and remains swollen until guilt is confessed; the rings will not enter the eye of the innocent.

In *mukyobo* (s. & pl.) a stone is placed in a pan of boiling water and the accused must reach in to remove it—he who is burned is guilty, he who is not burned is innocent. Some versions of this ordeal also involve *mwafi*, and in this case two pans are used, one with cold and one with boiling water, both of which also contain *mwafi* bark. To the guilty, the hot water feels cold, and the cold water hot; to the innocent they are as they should be. In *bulama* (s. & pl., "glue"), four suspects are seated on the corners of a mat, and the official conducting the ordeal gives each of them a magic potion and tells them to stand; the innocent do so without untoward event, but when the guilty stands, the mat sticks to him and he cannot shake it off. Finally, a very few persons speak of what may be an oracle (*nakubuka*, s. & pl.), saying that a man in the neighboring village of Sankia has a carved wooden figure which speaks and which can find and name thieves.

It will be noted that in connection with all ordeals, the Lupupans make a dichotomy between the innocent and the guilty, involving both in the actual process and thus emphasizing the contrast between the two. Whether this, in fact, occurred or whether it is simply spoken of in this way is not known. In any case, details of the process cannot be described since ordeals have not been carried out now for a number of years. Old men are the only ones who claim to have been witness to such an event, and the most recent date given is fifteen years before the date of this research.

As it is difficult to reconstruct the event of the ordeal and other details of legal process, so is it difficult to reconstruct the scale of crimes from major to minor, or the punishments meted out for them. Lupupans today, however, speak most often of five different crimes or categories of crime.

It is unanimously agreed that the worst crime is theft—it is "worse than murder, rape, or war." A theft (*kuwiba*, "to steal") in the village is the cause for outrage and immediate magic practice to trap the guilty; people speculate on how *anyone* could commit such a crime against his fellows; and as long as it is possible to do so, the villagers suggest that the thief must have been someone from outside the village. When a non-Lupupan who is a known thief visits Lupupa Ngye, he is carefully watched and, in some cases, is not allowed to stay at all but is escorted to the edge of the village by one of the local officials and told to continue on his journey. In the rather hypothetical reconstructions of fine schedules, theft is always at the top of the list and the fine is usually double that of the next most serious offense listed. In fact, the village has little problem with theft; such thievery as does occur *is* usually committed by a non-Lupupan, and local thieves may well be banished, a severe punishment indeed, but one rarely needed. As in the case of most serious crime, punishment for theft in former times was slavery; as the Belgians took hold, it appears to have changed gradually to fines paid in *madiba*, and then to fines paid in Belgian francs. Most people today say that the fine for theft is 1,000 francs, but this is a hypothetical figure since situations of theft differ so markedly and since almost no such cases are handled locally at present.

A second crime mentioned frequently and with considerable feeling is the willful destruction of one's own property, including burning one's house, destroying clothing, and destroying crops in one's own fields. The Lupupans give a variety of reasons for their feelings about such behavior. Some say, for example, that such destruction is an indication that a person must be crazy, and that he may thus be generally dangerous to the village in other ways. More often stressed, however, are reasons which give some clues into village values. Thus many say that a person must not destroy his property because "he has worked hard for what he has." Others stress that when one dies his property goes to his heirs, and thus destruction deprives his progeny of what is rightfully theirs. Still others point out that if one has so much that he can destroy it, then he should have given the surplus to someone more needy than he. These reactions against willful destruction, as well as those which make theft the most serious crime in Lupupa Ngye, point up the facts that the villagers do work hard for their living, that life in the village is a cooperative affair, and that such actions threaten the existence of the corporate body. In the past, the penalty for destruction of property was slavery; today it is a series of fines, the most serious of which is usually fixed at half that for theft.

A third set of crimes frequently mentioned, and certainly practiced in Lupupa Ngye, are public defamation and false accusation; such cases were taken directly to the *chite,* who called the notables in for final judgment. False accusation of thievery was most serious in this respect, but almost equally serious was defamation of a woman. In former times, defamation and false accusation were punished by slavery; today they are covered by the fine system.

Rape (*tomboshi,* pl. *bantomboshi,* "someone who does by force") is differentiated from adultery (*ekupi,* pl. *makupi,* same as term for "concubine" or "mistress"), and is considered to be a far more serious offense, punishable by slavery in former times and today by a severe fine, equal to that for destruction of property. Murder (*tomboshi,* "by force") is differentiated from homicide (*masaku,* "to defend"); the penalty for the former was slavery for the offender and his family, and for the latter, slavery for the offender and two women and one man of his family. Both offenses are extremely rare in the village today—indeed, no one can remember the last such case—but if either occurred, the offender would go immediately to the state system for trial.

These five categories of crime are the most frequently mentioned and the most important to the villagers; among other offenses noted are trespass, physical injury to a pregnant woman, neglect of children resulting in injury to them, fighting, and avoiding legitimate village work.

As noted previously, it is only the most minor cases which in 1959–60 were still adjudicated within the traditional village system; all important cases went to the state tribunal in Tshofa or were tried before a traveling tribunal which visited Lupupa Ngye once a year. The members of the tribunal were supposedly selected by the Chef de Secteur from among Bala chiefs and notables; while some dignitaries did serve, others were ordinary citizens. In 1959–60 the traveling tribunal judged such cases in Lupupa Ngye as the following: Mwembo borrowed Kasambwe's briefcase four years ago and never returned it; the suitcase was new then, but now, in evidence, it is battered and torn. The decision: "Mwembo, you borrowed the briefcase from Kasambwe and you did not return it. Now it is a debt. You must pay 250 francs to Kasambwe, plus 50 francs fine to the tribunal and 20 francs court costs." At this decision, Mwembo became violently angry and said he would carry the case to Sentery (and paid 20 francs to set the procedure in motion), and if he lost there, to Kabinda, and thence to Lulua-bourg. He did not deny having the briefcase, but was furious because, he said, it was worth not 250 francs but 200. Such petty disputes, often involving failure to pay debts, take up almost the entire time of the traveling tribunal.

While the internal peace has preoccupied most of the time of the notables in recent years, the past was marked by hostilities emanating from outside the village. We have already spoken of the feuding among the quarters which occurred in the Kadiyala days, but equally important were enemies in opposition to Lupupa Ngye and probably to the Bapupa as a whole. Such were the Batetela, the nearest major tribal group to the north, only a few kilometers from the Bapupa; because of Ngongo Lutete's activities, they were bitterly disliked and aggressively fought wherever possible. Among peoples closer to home, the Lupupans describe the Bala located around the present village of Penge as traditional enemies, but particular antagonism was felt in the past toward the nearby village of Sankia. Older informants remember battles with Sankia which took place when they were children, and hypothetical examples of strategy almost always describe Sankia as the protagonist. The Belgians stopped external warfare, but it seems probable that open strife occurred until approximately 1920.

In times of warfare, defense of the village was of paramount importance, and thus locations which offered natural protection were carefully chosen. An early post-Mpumba, pre-Mukikulu site just south of the present setting of Lupupa Ngye, for example, was chosen with defense in mind. Here the terrain slopes to the south and affords a clear view down to the Lupupa River and across it to the hills on the other side. Equally clear is the view to east and west. On the other hand, the view to the north—in the direction of the Batetela—is not good, and there the Lupupans built a palisade (*lupango,* pl. *mpango*) of living trees, now visible on the south side of the new village location. Some Lupupans suggest that other palisades were built of tall poles stuck in the ground and extending all around the village with two entrances which were open in the day and securely barred at night. Seven young men served as sentinels (*samo,* pl. *basamo*), and a ditch outside the palisade completed the defensive arrangements. In addition to these fortifications, manpower was distributed so that the village was never left undefended. Some old warriors say that the fighting force was divided into two parts, the first consisting of many young men and a few old men who went out to fight, and the other consisting of many old men and a few young men who stayed behind to defend the village. While the matter is in dispute, some informants insist that the notables did not take part in battles, but did fight to protect the village if necessary.

Many causes of war (*ngoshi,* s. & pl.) are listed today by the Lupupans, and figuring prominently among them is self-defense. But aggressive warfare was surely not uncommon, and the general tenor of the 1870–1900 period was conducive to the generation of battle. Thus the causes of warfare given today seem trivial unless the explosive state of affairs in the Lomami area is kept in mind.

Theft is often mentioned as a cause of war; "someone from Sankia might steal something from someone in Lupupa Ngye, and the Lupupans would go to war." War might begin because of insult, because a casual visitor to Sankia was held prisoner for no reason, or because a Lupupan was badly treated in another village. Attacks were made because it was felt that the enemy was in a particularly weak position at the moment. Women were a frequent cause of war, "because people were always stealing other people's women," or because "women from Lupupa might be bathing together with women of another village and get into a fight; then they would come back and tell the men, and war would be the result." One old man remembers the time when Yewusha declared war against the village of Imeno expressly to obtain slaves, and succeeded; but other old men say that warfare for the purpose of obtaining slaves was carried out only against the Batetela. War was also made to obtain land, and the southwest corner of present Lupupa territory was won in such a battle with Sankia. Kingkumba was about four years of age (c. 1900) when the following battle occurred; it was a favorite story of his father's.

> I did not see the battle, but I saw the dead afterward, and my father told me all about it. Sankia people did not know where to get the clay to make pots; it was near the Lomami River and the people of Lupupa knew where it was. They would go get the clay, make pots, and sell them to the people of Sankia. So the Sankias began to wonder why they should have to buy pots, and they said to themselves that they ought to get the clay and make pots for themselves.
>
> So one day the people of Sankia came here and demanded to know where the Lupupans got the clay. Lupupa refused to tell. And the Sankia people said,
>
> "If you won't tell us, it is war."
>
> The Lupupans said they didn't want war, and so the Sankias went on through the village and off toward the Lomami to find the clay. The Lupupans prepared themselves quickly for battle, followed the Sankias, and attacked them from the rear near Makola. Twenty-five Sankias were killed, and one Lupupan.

Thus the causes of war were varied and often trivial; even allowing for boasts and exaggerations, it is apparent that the Bapupa were "quick on the trigger" and that warfare was much a part of life.

A declaration of war was a matter of serious discussion among the notables and the people; while the arguments of the *chite* and *yangye* carried extra weight, the chief's was the last word. Some villagers argue that women might force postponement of an attack on the basis of the dreams of one or more women; but others deny that this was possible. Despite the Sankia example cited above, Lupupans insist unanimously that warfare was arranged in advance; while ambush was a known strategy, it was not used unless a prior declaration of war had been made. Indeed, it was considered a sign of weakness to attack without the notification provided by a messenger who crept to within shouting range of the enemy village and cried, "War tomorrow with Sankia, war tomorrow with

Sankia." Upon shouting this, the messenger took to his heels while the villagers poured out in pursuit; it is the Lupupans' view that messengers, having a headstart, were seldom caught.

Lupupans also insist that warfare took place only at night, thus allowing *laissez-passer* for all during daylight hours. Thus traders from traditional enemies such as the Batetela could bring slaves to Lupupa Ngye to exchange for manioc and for raffia cloth squares, *madiba.* In approaching the hostile village, such a trader would come close and shout, "I am here to sell, and not for war. I come in peace." He was then escorted to the chief, who assessed his motives and decided whether to allow him to circulate in Lupupa Ngye. Warfare quite certainly did not stop commerce and other kinds of friendly interaction among the peoples concerned. Actual violence was sporadic and of short duration; while Sankia and Lupupa Ngye were traditional enemies, by far the major portion of their time must have been spent in peaceful, if always wary, interaction.

Bows and arrows, spears, war axes, clubs, shields, lances, bracelets set with sharp points, swords, and special knives were used in fighting. Spears were set in the ground at an angle where the enemy might run into them, and bow and arrow were arranged in ambush situations with trip mechanisms. Natural objects, such as sticks and stones, were not used, nor were there flails, adzes, throwing clubs, launched projectiles, boomerangs, harpoons, darts, throwing knives, bolas, lassos, or traps. Special baskets were made to hold the heads of slain enemies, as were quivers to hold arrows dipped in a special poison, *lengo.*

There is some reason to believe that the knowledge and possession of *lengo* was not shared with surrounding groups, thus giving the Lupupans a psychological, if not physical, advantage in warfare, since it is a powerful poison. *Lengo* is used today by the few hunters who still employ the bow and arrow, and its preparation has been described in this connection.

Some villagers say that everyone fought who could, but major reliance was placed upon young and middle-aged men. Old men ("those who have grandchildren") acted as shock troops, stationed behind the lines but alert to rush to the assistance of beleaguered individuals; they may also have operated as *milopwe* (s. & pl.), that is, warriors who concealed themselves in the grass in order to ambush the unwary on the field of battle. As noted previously, notables apparently did not take part in the fighting, but it is probable that the chief did. Women had no role in battle, but according to some, they entrapped enemy warriors by inviting them in with promises of sexual favors, and then, by a prearranged signal, calling their husbands to spear them. A special group of warriors was made up of the *miyembo* (s. *mwembo*) to whom we have referred previously in connection with their alternative role as *kimankinda*. The *miyembo* were specialist fighters considered to be the strongest, the best, the "professionals." They were consulted by the chief on the eve of battle in matters of strategy, and they led the attack. Some Lupupans argue for the presence of ten to fifteen *miyembo*, while others indicate only four, adding that these were the four heads of the village quarters. Mankonde says that in battle, the four *miyembo* moved out ahead of the others and engaged the four *miyembo* of the opposing forces; beginning about fifty yards apart with bow and arrow, they gradually moved closer together until they were within lance range. As the struggle between the *miyembo* groups progressed, the main forces gradually joined in the battle. It is also Mankonde's idea that behind the *miyembo* the warriors were drawn up in four lines, representing the village quarters, and that the lines entered the battle successively, thus slowly enlarging its scope. The *miyembo* were always at the forefront, giving courage to the others through their actions. And in this same role was cast the village *ntunda* (pl. *bantunda*), or professional slit gong player, who kept up a constant barrage of signaled exhortations, slogans, and war songs.

Rewards to the *miyembo* consisted of feasts given by the chief, payments to especially capable and faithful men, and a liberal policy toward captured women; while most women became the property of the chief, those taken by *miyembo* remained their spoils. Rewards to other warriors were varied. One who killed an enemy had the right to wear an *nduba* feather in his hair; *miyembo* made hats of these feathers. If a man tried to wear feather or hat without having earned the right, it was thought his eyes would go bad and "roll wildly." Those who had killed an enemy also had the right to wear a special belt made of leaves during the celebration of victory. Persons who brought back the heads of the slain were sometimes paid a fixed amount per head by the chief, and the latter was also expected to provide the wherewithal for a victory feast. On the

297

opposite side of the coin, a person wounded in the back was shamed, for it was considered that he must have been running away; he was insulted, especially by the women.

Since war was ordinarily close to home and of short duration, few problems arose in respect to food supplies. Each man supplied himself, though some say that two or three of the *miyembo* were designated to hunt in the field. No special food gives strength to warriors, nor must any designated foods be eaten before battle. Magic to ensure success was carried out by sorcerers who accompanied the warriors.

The general conduct of warfare was apparently usually from afar, with the two sides lined up opposite each other and sending arrows across the intervening space. Some persons deny that individual combat took place, in opposition to Mankonde's descriptions noted previously. All informants endorse the description of tactics given by Torday and Joyce (1922:20):

> The usual method employed in conducting operations is the following: The forces are divided into three groups. A first corps, under the direction of the chief, attacks the enemy's positions, and then retreats, hoping to lure the enemy into pursuit; if the ruse succeeds, the enemies who have followed the first corps are quickly surrounded by the two others which were hidden on each side. [Author's translation]

Ambush (*mushiko,* pl. *mishiko*) was widely used as a part of battle, as were encircling and attacking from the rear. Special emphasis was placed upon silence: "Talking takes your mind off your business. Let your arrows talk for you," but this is specifically contradicted by Torday and Joyce, who say that warriors went into battle shouting insults. A special stratagem was to arrange the time of battle and then attack earlier; this went under the special term, *etombole abedi* (pl. *matombole abedi,* "cock" "first"). Although war is today considered to have been a nocturnal affair, no particular time of night is thought to have been best for attack. Information was sent from one part of the army to another by means of runners, and scouts (*bamposhi,* s. *mposhi*) were sent out from the main body to reconnoiter. No terms seem to exist for "advance," "attack," or "charge," but retreat is signalized by the special term, *bichimu* (s. & pl.).

Given the fact that closely neighboring villages, such as Sankia, were traditional enemies in war, the problem of killing one's own relatives—at least those by marriage—was a potentially serious one. Most informants shrug off the problem, however, by noting that war is a difficult business in which unpleasant situations do occur. Only Mankonde suggests that when a person had numerous relatives in the village under attack, he was placed in the rear ranks, and that if he came face to face with a relative, he could retreat without damage to his honor.

We have already noted that the traditional truce sign was a banana skin carried on a stick, and a palm branch was used both for truce and surrender. Peace was sought by the chief in situations of stalemate or when one side had had enough; he apparently simply stepped forward and called out his intentions. When losers sued for peace they might add, "for the sake of our pride, let us burn down a house in your village; take everything out of it, but just let us burn it."

The chief's house was sanctuary, but it is not known whether this applied in the case of defeat. A conquered village was sacked of everything in it, the houses burned, and the village fertility figure destroyed, although the latter was not a special war objective. In cases in which the village seemed in better repair than that of the victors, the latter might take possession of it permanently. All captured items, including food, livestock, movable possessions, and people, were taken before the chief who retained whatever he wished and gave the rest to the captors. All children were made slaves; male adult captives (*basungi ya mungoshi,* s. *misungi ya ngoshi*) were made slave workers for the chief, and women were made slaves, taken as wives, or both. Chiefs captured in war were held for ransom. According to some informants, the heads of the slain enemy were chopped off and brought back to the village where they were put on sticks, exhibited, and then taken to the chief who paid twenty *madiba* for each. The chief placed the heads on the ground in the center of his living area, the first four placed as the corners of a square, and the remainder in a circle around the square. The heads were not prepared in any way, and old persons of experience indicate that the odor was frightful; the object of the exercise was to indicate the chief's power and to impress subjects and strangers.

Warfare, then, was a reasonably complex activity, though the

299

details of it in Lupupa Ngye will never be known. Old-timers remember it, or tales of it told by their fathers, with pleasure, and they keep a full complement of weapons, but in fact, most confess in private they are glad it no longer occurs.

The political dignitaries of whom we have spoken are men; responsibility for the smooth functioning of the village both internally and externally is in their hands. Close examination, however, reveals a more or less parallel organization of women which works both with and against the visible male organization depending upon the circumstances; thus women are by no means without power in village affairs.

The central figure in this organization is the "chief of the women" (*fumu a bakashi*), who is formally appointed by the women and who is assisted by three *bakapita*, also appointed by the women as a group. The incumbent says that she is the first to occupy the position, and that she has held it since about 1930; she tells of her inauguration as follows:

> One day Piyani-Chiungu came to Lupupa and he gave two sacks of salt to the women when we keened for him. Afterward there was a meeting of the women, and the rest of the women told me to leave. I wondered what was going on, but I left as they said. Later they came to my house and divided the salt. There was half a sack left, and they said, "That is for you. We want you to be our chief." I accepted.

She then assembled food, prepared it herself, and served it to the assembled women. No money or gifts were required of her, but she does receive the largest share of any distribution to the women, and she says that her income exceeds her outgo, in contrast to the unanimous complaints of the male officials. When the notables receive an animal for distribution among themselves, they send a share to her, and when they distribute cash gifts, some is always given to the women and the chief receives the largest share; in matters of this sort, she has the final word. The *bakapita* have no financial obligations upon assuming office, nor are they expected to give a feast; they receive slightly larger shares of income than do other women. Their jobs are to do the bidding of their chief, primarily in notifying the women of meetings or work parties, and to lead in whatever activities are undertaken.

The duties and responsibilities of the *fumu a bakashi* are directed toward both women and men. When the notables are considering matters of direct concern to the women, she is consulted, and matters of general village interest, such as the selection of new notables, are discussed with her. The present chief, however, does not envision the possibility of the women overriding the decisions of the men, for "men are more important than women." Some evidence—though it is admittedly meager—does indicate that in situations of high tension between men and women, the women may, through the organizational powers of their chief, withhold sexual favors from the men as a group. Such a weapon, if it is indeed actually used, would be a powerful one in Lupupa Ngye, and if it is not implemented in fact, the threat of it seems clearly to have been communicated to the men.

In the world of women, the *fumu* acts as something of a judge, though she considers her role to be more that of mediator. If a woman is abused by her husband, the chief may call a meeting of the women and they may decide not to rejoin their husbands until all pay a small fine—again the threat of mass withholding of sexual favors is being used. When controversies between two women come to the chief, she considers it her job to resolve the argument through mediation and sage advice. If she is unsuccessful, the case goes into the male legal channels. The chief has the power to fine women who refuse to participate in work undertaken by the group. If the fine is a chicken, which is often the case, and if the woman refuses to pay, a chicken may be picked up at random with the fined woman becoming responsible to the owner; refusal to accept this responsibility results in the matter being cried publicly by a *kapita,* and the strong factor of public humiliation comes into play. Thus the chief is not without powers—though most of them are subtle—toward both men and women.

In matters of women's work, the chief has three major duties. First, she must organize the women when general work must be done, such as repair of the resthouse. Second, when the men and women are working together, she uses money from the women's reserve to buy food which the women prepare for all to eat. Finally, the repair of paths is a major recurring group activity for the women. While repairing roads and the big paths is the responsibility of men, the paths used most often by women are their responsibility. This includes the paths that lead to water, traveled by women at least once a day, as well as some of those leading to the fields and to neighboring villages. When such paths need repair, the chief instructs the *bakapita* to call the women together, begins the work herself in order to demonstrate what is needed, and then urges the others on to the completion of the job.

Like the male officials, the chief of the women is proud of having been selected, and hopes to continue in the position. She can, however, be deposed by the women if she does not carry out her duties satisfactorily. She feels that she is a more important personage in the village than the *lukunga*, but less important than the other notables. She says she is often called into meetings of the notables and regards herself as a sort of notable. She feels she has the respect of both the men and the women of the village.

The political system is apparently an eminently workable one in which a number of checks and balances are present, in which the power of the people is the ultimate power, and in which even male and female roles are given separate expression. The fact is, however, that toward the end of 1959 and through the first months of 1960, the system disintegrated rapidly and had fallen into a state of almost total confusion by June, 1960. In August, 1959, the chief was deposed as a thief. In October, the *lukunga* and *shesha* resigned their positions in anger, and at the same time three of the *basalayi* resigned as well. On December 19, 1959, the *dipumba* was deposed by the people and a successor named. In January, 1960, both the *yangye* and *chite* were deposed, but successors were never named. Both *lukunga* and *shesha* later reconsidered their resignations, and the *nyamampe* never resigned; in June, 1960, when I left Lupupa Ngye, the traditional government was being run by the *dipumba*, assisted by the *nyamampe*, *shesha* and *lukunga*. The last three, of course, are minor dignitaries, and the incumbents were not particularly forceful or respected men; thus the government was reduced, to all intents and purposes, to the sole discretion of the *dipumba*. This dissolution of tradition can be traced to at least five basic causes.

The first of these is the problem of obtaining competent persons to fill the available positions. Leaving aside the minor dignitaries and the unfilled positions, and considering only the

302

heads of the four quarters, the *bamwilo,* the *basalayi,* and the chief, fifteen positions must be filled. Lupupa Ngye has approximately 120 permanent male residents, but all of them are by no means eligible for office since many are too young, are not from the requisite families, lineages or quarters, or are slaves or the children of slaves. Further, some men are not considered capable of holding office because of social, physical, or personality factors. The upshot is that Lupupa Ngye is hard pressed to find suitable men to fill the offices at hand; the system requires a larger number of officials than the village can provide without resorting to persons whose capabilities for office are marginal. It is possible that the system was established at a time of large population, and not reduced as the size of the village diminished, but we have no way of knowing whether this is, in fact, the case. Whatever its cause, the number of responsible positions to be filled, as opposed to the gross population size, is a major political problem.

A second, and equally serious problem, is the expense of public office. It will be recalled that the cost of accession to the chieftaincy was approximately 14,000 francs, almost three times the average annual income for a male Lupupan. The *yangye* paid about 9,000 francs, the *shesha* about 2,000 francs. Even though the payments are spread out over a period of two or three years, they are large sums, indeed, and people are reluctant to undertake these debts despite the personal pride derived from public office. Those who are dignitaries and who have paid the required sums comment bitterly that they were given office only so the notables, to whom much of the payment goes, might line their own pockets, and at least three men refused to accept the position of chief during the period in question squarely on the basis of exorbitant financial obligation. The payment of such substantial amounts of money is apparently an innovation of the late 1940's; with each succession the sums have increased, until many people in the village feel that some notables are appointed and deposed rapidly in order that the more secure notables can profit financially. Whatever the truth of this accusation, it is evident that the required payments have risen too high to be supportable in Lupupa Ngye. Political office in 1960 was headed either toward those who were rich without consideration of merit or, as in the case of the chief, to a dead end because no one would accept.

A third problem, and one which can beset any political organization, is special grievance against political officers. The chief of Lupupa was accused and convicted by public opinion of being a thief. The *yangye* was the chief suspect in the magical slaying of one of the most respected men of the village who died suddenly and of no visible cause in September, 1959. The *chite* seemed to bear malice toward all and was accused of using his office for personal gain and of working magic upon the people. The *dipumba* was accused of neglect of office, of using the office for personal gain, and of defamation of the young men of the village. Charges such as these caused enormous disruption in Lupupa Ngye; they hark back to the problem of obtaining good officials and they look forward, as well, to a further problem.

This fourth question involves the struggle of younger men against the old, a common occurrence in human social behavior, but one which was especially marked in Lupupa Ngye in the time period under discussion. The primary reason was simply the struggle between generations as the younger people attempted to assert power, but the movement of some of the young men into the wider world and their return, as well as the growing rush toward independence in the Congo which, in Lupupa Ngye at least, was carried on almost exclusively by the younger men, made for added restlessness. The young men, less closely bound to traditional village organization and excited by the possibilities they sensed in the future, were cast loose and formed a less stable group than did their elders. The incidence of drinking was high among them, and they were sharply criticized for this by the older men who, almost unanimously, also bemoaned the lack of respect which had developed among the young men toward the notables. On the other hand, the young men saw their elders as entrenched in power and unwilling to share it with them. The manifestations of this state of affairs appeared in real village strife, in accusation and counteraccusation, in the defilement by the young men of the village magic controlled by the old men, and in the real power moves of the young men which unseated the *dipumba*, the *chite*, and the *yangye*. The situation in Lupupa Ngye was more than the ordinary struggle of the young to assert themselves; it amounted to a small revolution which augured permanent changes in traditional life.

Underlying all these problems were the changes imposed upon

Lupupa Ngye by the Belgian government, changes which reduced to rubble the power and standing of the traditional form of government. This appeared most visibly in the tribunal system which made it possible not only for a complainant to take his case to a higher court if he was not satisfied with local justice, but also to bypass the traditional authorities completely. Further, the tribunal system brought traveling courts to the village itself, and in these courts, theoretically at least completely impersonal to Lupupa Ngye and its problems, the notables themselves could be defeated. In a case in the spring of 1960, the *chite* unwisely brought complaint against one of the young men, and lost; this single case quite probably did more to widen the rift between young and old and to damage the prestige of the notables than any single event in recent history. The notables were not above the law in traditional days, but their punishment for transgression was handled by other notables, thus making evident to the people the checks and balances which existed *within the government*. In 1959 and 1960, however, this function had been taken out of the hands of the traditional government and made embarrassingly public instead; in the process the political system lost its dignity and authority. Thus a theoretically good traditional system was undermined by usurpation of power from outside; the result was a village in political chaos.

8. The Quality of Life

The people of Lupupa Ngye, like people everywhere, perceive the physical world in specific ways which shape their attitudes and behavior toward it and which allow them to exploit its resources effectively. Similarly, they order the metaphysical world in terms of their own beliefs, and receive from this ordering a sense of their secure place in the broad scheme of life and death. And these facets of experience are joined inevitably by the human factor, for all human beings are surrounded by others with whom they are in constant interaction. The particular quality of life for any given group of people results from the interplay and interrelationships among all three of these aspects of experience.

Understanding that quality of life, however, is an extraordinarily complex and difficult matter, for values and attitudes require a subtlety of comprehension virtually inaccessible to the outsider. What the Lupupan thinks and feels about his own life style may be very different from what the outsider thinks he senses, and the problem cannot be resolved by technical means. Indeed, a sense of the quality of life is probably possible only in comparative terms: the Westerner who views Lupupa Ngye sees that culture against the background of his own, and as the two contrast and coincide. For the Lupupan, however, the standard of comparison is not with the West, but rather, with other Bala groups, the people of Lupupa Kampata, the Makolas, the Sankias. If the basis for establishing the quality of life is essentially comparative, the Westerner and the Lupupan begin from different bases. Thus the quality of life, and understanding it, is a relative proposition; while the outsider can describe infant mortality rates, morbidity, caloric intake, and so forth, and by this means arrive at a mechanical "quality" which relates to survival, a much more delicate understanding is required to sense inner feelings, and attitudes toward others. The outsider's perceptions are always, indeed, those of an outsider, and his understandings are much more easily descriptive and analytic than they are shared as an inner sense and awareness of what it means to be a Lupupan.

One of the most basic facts about Lupupa Ngye is that it consists of a small group of people who live together as a homogeneous unit. The population of the village is 276 people, of whom 240 "truly belong"; of the 240, in turn, seventy-five are children no older than ten, and five are very old people whose contribution to the village is minimal, leaving a hard core of some 160 adults actively responsible for the functioning and well-being of the village and its inhabitants. This means not only that the people are inevitably thrown together, but also that they are constantly in situations which compel them to make mutually agreeable decisions.

This situation is intensified by the fact that Lupupa Ngye is virtually a self-sufficient entity which neither requires outside goods and services nor shares a system of traditional political governance with others. It is true that some economic items come from outside the village: thus slit gongs are purchased from the Batetela and double iron gongs from the Balutobo or the Bekalebwe, but knowledge of how to make these objects is present in Lupupa Ngye and could be put to use in an emergency. The village, too, is self-sufficient in terms of food supply, material for clothing (raffia) and knowledge of how to weave and cut the cloth to pattern, medical and religious knowledge, the making of music, and so forth. It is also true that networks of friends are established in villages throughout the area and that people visit back and forth; goods and services are traded and purchased, and a small but constant stream of strangers comes by the village. The point, however, is that Lupupa Ngye is not dependent upon others to sustain itself; if it were cut off entirely from outside human contact, it would not perish technically, "esthetically," or in any other known sense.

Save for its ties with its sister village, Lupupa Kampata, Lupupa Ngye is also a self-sustaining entity in respect to political governance. Knowledge of the Congo as a state is virtually nonexistent; the "Basongye" entity does not touch the village in traditional political terms. The Bala group has some influence, but in 1959–60 only through the powerful support of the Belgian administration; it is reasonably clear that the Bala never controlled the Lupupans politically. Among the Bapupa, political ties are not strong; while Ngye and Kampata share a chief, the office has fallen upon hard times, though it clearly had greater importance in the past. Thus to all intents and purposes, Lupupa Ngye is an independent political entity and has been since its formation early in this century; while it so existed under the general aegis of the Belgian colonial administration to which it was broadly responsible for its actions, it did not depend upon that administration for its day-to-day existence. Lupupa Ngye can easily and meaningfully be regarded as a self-sufficient and individual entity.

Within that entity, life is carried on according to a number of principles; among these principles, in turn, the outside observer can distinguish patterns, themes, or sanctions which seem to be especially meaningful, and which serve as particularly strong guides to behavior.

One of these, which is almost as basic as the facts of Lupupa Ngye's small size and relative isolation, is the belief, both of males and females, in male dominance. This principle is accepted as a flat fact of human existence, and thus the Lupupans make sharp differentiations both between the roles and the personality characteristics of men and women. Such tasks as war, hunting, fishing, palm nut cutting, and the like are reserved to men, while the women are occupied with gathering firewood, bringing water, cooking, and so forth. These roles should not normally be reversed, say the villagers, for it is considered shameful for a person of one sex to assume the tasks and roles of the other. Thus one Lupupan noted that "women's work is shameful for a man to do. If a man did women's work before he was married, he would probably get accustomed to it and then he could not change his habits and would never be able to get married. Also, the women would think he was a woman, and no one would marry him." Once married, however, a man and a woman enter into a special relationship which allows a certain amount of private shading of these attitudes, though publicly the situation remains the same. The same informant continued: "If there are special heavy jobs, such as preparing a large amount of palm oil from palm nuts, the husband may help his wife bring the necessary water and may work with her on the nuts. A man can help his wife collect wood or bring water if he does so in secret in the forest. When they get near the village, however, she should take the load and carry it in. Many men do this."

Other conditions may further mitigate the theoretically hard and fast role lines. A man may carry water for an important outsider, because this is a job paid for in cash wages. If a woman were in charge of one of the small Western-owned stores in Lupupa Ngye, a man could take work with her because such a position falls outside the traditional pattern. But if a woman in the traditional structure had wealth, she could not pay her husband or other men to carry water to the house; the husband would refuse since "it is the wife who obeys the husband, not the husband who obeys the wife," and other men would refuse on what are essentially identical grounds, that is, "it is the woman who obeys the man, not the man who obeys the woman." These differentiations are drawn between traditional male-female relationships on the one hand and the outside, Western-oriented job situation on the other.

The role of the woman is considered subordinate to that of the man, and not only is it the woman who obeys her husband and who finds various occupations closed to her, but she is enjoined from certain activities unless accompanied by her husband. While a woman may bring a complaint before the legal authorities against a man who is not her husband, she must always be accompanied by

309

her husband in doing so. A woman cannot travel without her husband, nor can she "own" fields for agricultural or other purposes. While men and women do share a number of tasks, what is important is that, for the Lupupans, it is always the man who leads, who is to be obeyed, and who takes precedence.

Male dominance and predominance is evident also in the judgments made by Lupupans on the general personality characteristics of men and women. One man says: "Women are quick to insult everybody; they are always in arguments and fights; and they gossip. Men are more important and stronger. Women cry more. Men are quicker. Women get angry faster." Women say much the same things: "Women get angry too much. Women are not strong and need men. Men are proud and haughty. Men are strong; they are more important. Women cry more. Men are quicker." Others echo these generalizing statements. From a man:

> Women are not strong. Women cannot have a lot of money. Women fool around a lot. Women get angry faster than men. Women cry more than men. Men are quicker in physical actions. Women lie more than men. Women fight among themselves more than men. Men are more intelligent than women—a man has to keep peace among his wives.

Another man says much the same things:

> Women are not strong. Women are garrulous. Women look for trouble, and then they cry when they get it. Women get angry more than men. Men are quicker. Men are more intelligent.

And a woman added (to a woman):

> Women have more patience than men—they must have, to put up with husbands who drink!

Thus Lupupan belief about men and women, taken as groups, stresses differences in roles and in personality characteristics. Men are considered to be dominant, physically stronger and quicker, and more intelligent than women, and they are not to mix into feminine roles and tasks. Women, on the other hand, are thought to be physically weaker than men, emotional, rather petty in personal relationships, less intelligent than men, and in a position of

310

subordination. This framework of belief is modified somewhat under the conditions of marriage in which the sharpness of the distinctions begins to blur slightly, by the introduction of nontraditional situations into village life, and by the women themselves who are not powerless in their relationships with their husbands and with other men. Male dominance, however, is a fact of life in Lupupa Ngye, and both men and women know it (Merriam 1971:74–76).

While population size and relative isolation are immutable physical facts of existence, and male dominance is an equally immutable belief, it is another, unstated principle which shapes almost all aspects of village life. This is the attitude that behavior must be normal, and that anormal or abnormal behavior is to be viewed with the greatest suspicion. The principle of normalcy runs through the culture of Lupupa Ngye with great regularity; it is found in mundane matters more or less shared with most cultures of the world, in observable forms specific to this particular culture, and in deep attitudes and beliefs which put strong pressure upon the individual to make his behavior accord generally with that of others.

Among the mundane matters are all those customs, beliefs, attitudes, and behaviors which urge the individual to be like others simply through inculcation of a way of life. Such, for example, is the care of the human body; children are taught what is proper in this respect as a part of their general knowledge of how a Lupupan behaves. Inevitably, knowledge of this kind places pressure on the individual to conform, but it must be pointed out that considerable room is left for individual variation; that is, while women have keloid markings, by no means do all women have them, and while men may sport the forehead-to-nose-tip markings made by their mistresses, by no means do all men have them. All societies allow for variation of this sort within specified limits; the question is whether those limits in Lupupa Ngye are narrower than in societies with larger populations and with more effective outside contacts.

As proper care of the body is important to the Lupupans, so, too, are politeness and formalism. An important person entering the village is greeted by the women who surround and move with him, singing and ululating. He is given gifts, and various political dignitaries are responsible for housing and feeding him, and making

311

him welcome and at home. Singing, dancing, feasting, and drinking are all features of the greeting given to a villager who has been gone a long time. Among the twelve different forms of greetings between individuals are several which denote respect, such as *nemunaya*, which means "greetings" but is reserved exclusively to the chief. Titles of respect and politeness are also frequent, such as *nobeya* ("papa") used in speaking to a male older than the speaker, or the prefix *ya* attached to the given name and used by a younger to an older person, as in *ya*Mulenda. Canons of politeness in everyday behavior are, of course, almost endless. One does not interrupt his conversation with a friend to speak to someone else. A woman does not welcome company in her kitchen; only old friends may be greeted there. Thanks and respect must be indicated by clapping the hands together, palms parallel, with a slight forward inclination of the head and upper trunk.

Formalism is found in the oaths used in the culture, in the speech formulae employed, for example, in naming persons to political office, and in the fact that almost every important event in the culture is visualized as being organized around a highly specified structure. These structures may be omitted by common consent, but usually they are carried out even though the ultimate result is previously known by the entire village. No chief is named unless his prior acceptance has been received by the notables, yet at the proper time, the *lukunga* is sent to the nominee and the two engage in a formal dialogue, the parts of which are known to both and the result of which is acceptance by the nominee of an office which he has already consented to accept. A similar formality marks almost all other important ritual. Such formalism is present in all cultures, but the Lupupans, while less formal than many other African societies, use formality widely and as an important part of their culture.

These mundane examples have indicated areas of culture in which the Lupupans' behavior is much alike within a range of variation: it is important that the body be cared for and decorated in certain ways, and it is also important that individuals be polite and respectful of seniority and power, and that they know and understand the formal ways of carrying certain matters through. Aspects of culture such as these are taught to the young by the various agents of education in the society who use a variety of techniques; among them is the inculcation of shameful, which appears with relative frequency in the culture. It is considered shameful for a man to do women's work save under certain prescribed circumstances, and it is in the relationships between the sexes, as well as with almost all aspects of bodily functions, that shame sanctions are found.

Nakedness in mixed company is considered very shameful, but it is less shameful when in company of the same sex. Under ordinary circumstances, a woman would never expose her body before men, and even when bathing in the company of women the water provides some desired covering. It is not shameful, however, to expose one's body in sex play or simply in the presence of one's wife or husband. Neither is it considered shameful for a woman to expose her breast when nursing a child in public, or to bare herself to the waist at a funeral as a sign of mourning and respect for the deceased.

Similar attitudes are taken toward elimination of body wastes. One does not relieve himself in mixed company, and individual outhouses, screened for privacy, are located at the edge of the bush behind the houses of the lineage. It is considered extremely shameful for an adult to eliminate in the house, for he is "acting like a child." However, it is not shameful for very old people, simply because "they are like children." Habitual bedwetters are known in the village, and this, too, brings much shame.

Thus, shame sanctions are strong in the culture of Lupupa Ngye, applying most specifically to relations between sexes and to the functions of the human body (Merriam 1971:76–78).

Every society shapes the individuals who comprise it, training them to observe norms and standards which make it possible to predict behavior and thus for people to live successfully with one another. In the case of the people of Lupupa Ngye, the emphasis laid upon body care, politeness, respect, and formalism, and upon the shame sanctions represents one technique of teaching in respect to general and more or less mundane patterns of behavior like these. The Lupupans, however, lay a very special emphasis upon being like other people, upon a pattern of normalcy that reaches beyond usual societal emphases on learning to do things properly. This pattern runs throughout the organization of society and culture and is manifested in scores of ways, some of which are subtle and indirect, and others which are primal and sharply objectified.

Thus, for example, when speaking of the ideal male body, men constantly stress normalcy. Kadiya says: "A man should not be too tall or too short. He should have a normal body; he should not be different from others. The proportions of his body should be good; if he is small, he should not have big feet, or if he is big or tall, he should not have a small head." Totally independently Mayila says that a man's body should be "normal." While he likes a dark skin color, he adds hastily that it should not be too dark; for him, a man should not be too short or too tall, too thin or too fat. This attitude about normalcy in the physical body is repeated over and over by Lupupans, who also carry it to a preference for matching in the physical characteristics of marriage partners. The villagers say that people who are married should be "matched," that is, a short man should marry a short woman, a tall man a tall woman, a thin man a thin woman. A fat man and a thin woman do not make a good match, nor do a tall man and a short woman, a tall woman and a short man, and so forth. Thus physical ideals emphasize normalcy, and it will be recalled that in former times, children with physical deformities were killed. This is not to suggest that Lupupans objectified the matter by indicating that such children were killed simply because their bodies were not normal, but only that their lack of normalcy made them particularly vulnerable in this society.

Many instances of the stress on normalcy have been discussed in previous pages. For the Lupupan, doing things alone is abnormal and leaves one open to suspicions of being a witch; thus people do not usually eat alone or walk alone or farm alone or sit quietly alone. Strangers are "different" people, and while hospitality to them is important, one must always be wary of them. No Lupupan would eat alone with a stranger, because such a person may well be *eshimba dibi*, one with a "bad heart," who would slip magic potions into the food.

Bachelorhood is a strange and suspicious state; a person who remains a bachelor is almost always suspected of being a witch. So is the chief, whose social-political role sets him sharply apart from others. People who do not have institutionalized friends are considered peculiar—it is "normal" and it is important to have friends. People whose actions are outside the normal are criticized and, where it is thought necessary and possible, are quickly brought into line. Thus when Mwembongye, interpreting the coming independence of the Congo in personal terms, decided one evening to build the fence along his property line out to the middle of the main street, cutting off all foot traffic in front of his house, the action was the cause of scandalized, and amused, talk in the village. The notables took action the next morning and the fence was removed.

All these instances of behavior in the village—and many others which might be noted—indicate the stress placed by Lupupans on the desirability of being normal, of doing things essentially as others do them, of being a well-integrated part of the group. This extremely strong sanction functions as a means both of keeping the group together and assuring its perpetuation. Since Lupupa Ngye is a small and virtually self-contained community, cooperation among its people is vital. If the village were rent by discord and dissension, if substantial numbers of villagers insisted upon extreme individualism, Lupupa Ngye simply could not continue to exist. Thus its culture is organized to stress the group but at the same time to allow enough variation so that special necessary skills are present. Almost every male Lupupan has some such skill which sets him off from others: some men are carpenters, others are woodcarvers, masons, makers of fish traps, blacksmiths, fishermen, palm nut cutters, weavers, hunters, and so forth. These special skills, however, are sanctioned as proper within the culture, and thus having them and working at them is a positive value; their true value, of course, lies in the contribution they make to the well-being of the society as a whole.

When the matter of normalcy is put this way, it enables us to view some of the patterns of Lupupan behavior in a new and clearer light. Thus, for example, the crime of the destruction of one's own property makes better sense. Lupupans say one should not destroy his own property because he has worked hard for what he has, because the action deprives his progeny of what is rightfully theirs, and because if he has so much that he can destroy it, he should give the surplus to someone more needy than he. What is being said here by the villagers is precisely what we have said immediately above: destruction of one's own property is an act against the corporate group which needlessly destroys resources that someone can use. Similarly, in cases of incest, it is the father of the male partner who must pay a substantial fine to the community. This indicates that in Lupupa Ngye one is responsible not only for his own conduct but for the conduct of others, most specifically members of his family. The same pattern applies to the family of a suicide, and both kinds of cases stress the fact that all persons are responsible for the society as a whole and strengthen it by helping to regulate the behavior of individuals.

A further expression of this atmosphere is found in the abstract values professed by the villagers. In speaking of the best thing that one could imagine happening to him, Lupupans unanimously emphasize the desirability of having children. Every male says that the best thing in life is "to have a wife, because then I can have children," or to be married, or simply "to have children." Similarly, the worst thing that can happen is the death of one's wife or of one's children; again these two possibilities are *always* placed at the top of the list. Lupupans do not speak easily of the general purpose of life; when pressed they usually respond that this is a matter best left to Efile Mukulu and that human beings are not in a position to know. However, those who do express a more definite idea say that Efile Mukulu created man to have children: "We are here for Efile Mukulu, to work for him, to make children for him." Not only, then, is it of cardinal importance to contribute to the living group at any given point in time by stressing cooperation and solidarity, but it is equally important to assure its continuity and future.

Again similar are men's assessment of what makes a good or bad reputation, and most frequently a good reputation is based upon normalcy. Kasambwe says, for example, that he would like to be known as a man who is "rich, normal, honest, and strong," while Kadiya says that he wants to be known as "normal, like others, and not as an adulterer." A bad reputation comes when one "doesn't eat with others, when he is greedy, when he is proud," and other poorly regarded characteristics are lying, adultery, thievery, and jealousy. The good reputation rests, then, on the normalcy of the man it represents.

Thus in terms of manners, values, and behaviors, the Lupupans constantly stress the importance of the group and of its stability and continuity; the way to accomplish this in a small and essentially independent society, they believe, is to be normal, to avoid deviation, and to act in ways which will help the group to persist, not to hinder it.

The stress on normalcy is reinforced by Lupupan practicality, a theme which seems to run through both thought and behavior. The villagers have a strong tendency to meet their problems head on and to argue from cause to effect within the network of their own beliefs. Theirs is not a life marked by many frills; religious ceremonial is kept to a minimum, symbolic interpretation is rare, esthetic speculation is virtually absent. Instead, pragmatic values come to the fore, and life is visualized in clearcut terms involving direct relationships among people and between man and his habitat.

It would seem that life in Lupupa Ngye could be described as even and regular, with disruptive actions and events avoided insofar as possible. Since the people make a good living from the land and its products, life in the village can also be described as comfortable. The question then arises as to whether we can also describe it as "monotonous," and the answer is that we might, indeed, save that the villagers themselves keep it from being so. While living in a small, self-sufficient, and more or less isolated community may be safe, comfortable, and regular, it is not always a bed of roses, nor can it work perfectly. Thus it cannot be supposed that everyone in Lupupa Ngye is identical, that continued cooperation within a group of people is bought cheaply, or that sharp differences of opinion do not exist.

Even in Lupupa Ngye not all individuals agree or wish to conform. This means either that such persons must be expelled from the society, as is the case, for example, with thieves or with unrepentant incestuous couples; or room must be made for them in roles which, however deviant, are still useful; or they must simply be tolerated on the edges of society, even though they perform few useful tasks. In a society the size of Lupupa Ngye, we could predict comfortably that few persons in any of these categories would be present or dealt with, and the prediction would be correct. No villager has been expelled for theft or incest within real living memory, and expulsion is thus theoretical rather than real; other than the very old, only one adult in the village lives at its social fringes, and he "supports" himself as a slave; and only four men are cast in useful but deviant social roles. It is important to emphasize, however, that even in a small society such as this which stresses normalcy so strongly, provision *is* made for those who cannot or do not wish to follow the main thrust of local life.

The "deviant but useful" role in village life is that of musician. Being a musician is the only sanctioned way to escape the dominant male role in Lupupa Ngye and still be tolerated as a "useful" member of the society. Where the Lupupan male horticulturalist is hard-working, the musician is a loafer; where the former is frugal, the latter is spendthrift; where the one is expected to be a family man, the other is expected to be a chaser after women who neglects his own wife and family. And so it goes, for whatever the "mainstream man" of Lupupa Ngye is, the musician is not. The role with its escape from normal responsibilities, however, is not bought cheaply, for the status of musicians in society is low; they are stereotyped as lazy, heavy drinkers, debtors, impotents, hemp smokers, physical weaklings, adulterers, poor marriage risks, and so forth. People do not want their children to become musicians because musicians are ordered about by others, and thus to be a musician, one must accept the role and its correspondingly low status. At the same time, rewards are not lacking, for music is a vital necessity in Lupupa Ngye, and thus musicians are at a premium. The compromise made in this ambivalent situation is that the musician is allowed to indulge in deviant behavior which the society tolerates in order to have his music; this means, too, that the musician is allowed to escape normal male responsibilities.

All this is not to say that musicians are complete ne'er-do-wells, for they do participate in normal village life, contribute to the network of social relations, take part in political deliberations, and so on. At the same time, not one major musician is a steady farmer, and all are considered to be lazy, heavy drinkers, and poor marriage risks. One was the outstanding debtor of the village and at the same time the single known impotent; another was the constant butt of jokes about his physical weakness; at least one, and probably two of the musicians were considered to be heavier than normal hemp smokers, and at least two were known adulterers. The behavior of the musicians, then, tends to fit the stereotype of behavior in that role; musicians do, indeed, escape normal male tasks and responsibilities, but it must be kept firmly in mind that they also contribute to normalcy and stability of the village through the product of their special labor.

While the musician is in a deviant but useful role, the *kitesha* (pl. *bitesha*) or transvestite, struggles along on the fringes of society, supporting himself in any way he can, though seldom, if ever, as a full-time horticulturalist. The role of the male *kitesha* is seen rather differently from the outside and the inside. Those who are not *bitesha* speak of those who are as "men who act like women," and are at no loss to characterize their behavior in some detail. One man says, for example, of the *kitesha*: "He doesn't want to work; he doesn't want to be with other men; he doesn't even have a concubine; he eats everywhere except at his own house; he doesn't do the things that other men do; he never keeps a job; he has good luck; he acts like a woman, rushing about hither and yon, acting like a woman and wiggling his hips when he walks." The same male Lupupan adds that *bitesha* wear women's clothing, and that "a true *kitesha* plays the *kisaghshi* [a music instrument] all the time; he never stops." And "he plays and dances all the time in his own particular manner." Among male *bitesha*, "male" and "female" types pair off and have homosexual relations, according to the same man. "Male *bitesha* do women's work; they carry water, prepare food, and do other female tasks, for their families or perhaps for other people."

To this villager's view of the *kitesha*, Mankonde added other observations: "*Bitesha* like to expose their genitals in public, but they do not have homosexual relationships. They are not interested in women . . . but in a desperate situation, a *kitesha* may have public intercourse with a female *kitesha*. This is terribly shameful; no one would even look at such a thing on purpose, but people cannot help seeing. Then they know he is a *kitesha* and they leave him alone; he does not have to work in the fields."

In 1959–60, one male *kitesha* lived in Lupupa Ngye, with his female *kitesha* wife. He was often cited clandestinely (because of Belgian law) as the only real slave in the village, bound to one of the leading patrilineages. He saw himself in rather different terms from those applied to him by others: "Yes, I am a *kitesha*. I don't like to do anything. I only like to eat. I don't like to work in the fields. I just like to eat. I don't like to wear a shirt or trousers. I like to stay with women. I like to steal." Mulenda says that he likes his

319

An African World

wife and likes to have intercourse with her. He is keenly aware of the fact that he is the only *kitesha* in the village, but he knows two others in neighboring villages; when they come to Lupupa Ngye they stay with him, and when he goes to their villages, he stays with them. "*Bitesha* always stay with *bitesha*, because all *bitesha* are friends." When they are together, they talk about things which concern themselves and their role, tell stories about *bitesha*, and especially talk about women. "I like women; I don't want to be without them." Mulenda says that he has had sexual intercourse with but two women in his life, both *bitesha*, and the second, his wife. He has had limited experience because women "don't like a *kitesha* because he goes around with his chest bare, and because he doesn't give them anything since he does not work."

Mulenda says that he was a *kitesha* from the moment he was born, but cites no reason for this, not even the customary "Efile Mukulu made us that way." He is very much aware of the fact that other men do not respect him, and says that they insult him continually. He adds that he cannot cook and that no *kitesha*, male or female, likes to prepare food. He does, however, like to gather wood, and to take care of children, both female tasks. He emphasizes that all *bitesha* like children. He does not like to carry water or to dig manioc in the fields. Physically he says he is as strong as other men (which is true), and sexually he feels he is like any other man. He does play the *kisaghshi* and he likes very much to dance. He denies male and female types of male *bitesha* and homosexual acts of any sort. He says that he would have intercourse with a female *kitesha*, or another woman, in public; he "just doesn't know" why *bitesha* like to do this, though to the outsider it is clearly a means of establishing public notice of the role.

The role of the male *kitesha* in Lupupa Ngye is firmly patterned and there are numerous expectations of the individual, recognized both by himself and by others, though the two views do not always coincide. More important, his position enables the *kitesha* to avoid the normal male role, even though he does so at considerable social cost to himself and to society. As an individual he is scorned and lives on the fringes of society; his contribution to that society is minimal at best (Merriam 1971:94–97).

Both the musician and the *kitesha* play roles which allow them to behave in ways not tolerated from an ordinary citizen; their roles

320

allow them to escape what is normal in the society and to gain lifelong release from the major pressures to conform. We have spoken here, however, only of men; what of women in the society? The answer can be undertaken with much less certainty, simply because of the nature of the research pattern, but on the surface, at least, it appears that women have much less outlet than men for expressing their nonconformity. While female music specialists are recognized, the role allows only for slight deviance from the normal; recognized female musicians are thought to exhibit difficult and perhaps slightly deviant personalities, but they do not escape normal female responsibilities by this means. Female *bitesha* are also found among the Bala, and the male *kitesha's* view of them (the only "inside" view available) is that they do not like men, prefer the company of women, but most of all wish to be with male *bitesha*. They like to have sexual relations with men, particularly male *bitesha*, and they do not like to wear men's clothing. They do not like to cook or to do other female tasks save to gather wood "because that is the easiest work."

We can complete our discussion of deviant roles in Lupupa Ngye by recalling the practice of special skills, such as blacksmith or hunter. While these skills do not constitute a role as such, they do allow their practitioners some respite from the general conformity emphasized in the society. Moreover, taken as a whole, they provide a degree of individualism in the village; since everyone is skilled in some way, however, this individualism is not great enough to provoke suspicion. Thus skills are encouraged because they contribute to the smooth operation of the village, just as does the skill of musicianship but in a much less marked way.

It is clear that some individuals choose rather drastic ways of avoiding normal responsibilities and the normal ways of life, and that everyone has some ways of breaking what would otherwise be a monotonous constraint. Given these safety valves, it might be supposed that life is otherwise calm; after all, comfort and support are provided by the kind of life the Lupupans lead, with its close and intimate association with kinsmen, neighbors, and friends in a small society. It is evident, however, that the very closeness of the social relationships leads to tensions and strains which result in aggressive attitudes and behavior.

Such behavior is particularly noticeable at the slack times in

321

the agricultural cycle, when rather suddenly there is little to do in the fields, and the people find themselves together in the village with a large portion of their time released. These periods occur sometime at the end of October, when planting has ended and weeding not yet begun; in February, after the cotton has been planted and other crops harvested, but weeding the cotton not yet begun; at some point in May, depending on the amount of rainfall and other factors that affect the crop; and most particularly, from approximately mid-July until the end of August, or from major harvest to the start of clearing fields again. During these slack periods, and especially during the short ones when there is not time to undertake major projects such as building a house, male Lupupans drink heavily. Their manner changes from a rather peaceful, though never placid, demeanor to one of fierce aggression. Fights break out, during which a few sharp blows with the fists are exchanged, though bystanders never allow them to progress further; on some occasions tempers flare so strongly that very short encounters are fought with machetes. The causes of these outbursts are often obscure; most of them go back to insults, imagined insults, defamations, bad debts, and similar rather minor problems which, under other circumstances, would not loom so large. During these periods, the entire village seems tense, its atmosphere charged, and its usual relaxed peacefulness changed to tight awareness and even apprehension.

It is not only in the slack agricultural season, however, that the stresses and strains of life are manifested. As a whole, the Lupupans have short tempers. Small arguments flare up constantly, sharp words are exchanged, and the incident is then gone almost as quickly as it began, but is not nearly so easily forgotten. Accusations and counteraccusations float constantly through the village, often over what seem to the outsider to be trivial matters, but which are important enough to the villagers to cause almost continual strife. Marriages, while stable in terms of their degree of permanence, are often filled with small strife and bickering, though this is not always the case. Women frequently threaten to leave their husbands and return to their fathers' lineage; sometimes they hastily pack some of their belongings and actually begin the journey out of Lupupa Ngye, knowing, however, that some friend or relative will surely stop them since a stable marriage is a positive value. Thus their action is more strategic than real, but it contributes to the somewhat restless atmosphere. In sum, someone in the village is always angry with someone else, perhaps threatening to do him violence, though seldom carrying out the threat, throwing ugly words in his direction or to someone who will carry them for him. And when this particular flare-up dies down, others which have been simmering take the stage. Thus an undercurrent of unrest marks the human relationships in the village, though the surface is calm and peaceful, the people joking and laughing with one another, and the atmosphere apparently relaxed.

This unrest is sharply emphasized by the presence of witches and sorcerers, whose activities contribute a never-ending counterpoint to the outward flow of village life. Witches are malevolent human beings whose delight it is to cause misery for their normal fellows, while sorcerers are the agents in the continuing struggle between good and evil. Both witches and sorcerers use magic in their machinations, and the Lupupans are always on the lookout for signs of magic being worked against them. Many persons may be suspected of being witches by such signs, as well as by visible actions, and thus the villager is always alert for significant clues; persons who may be witches include the chief, other political dignitaries, those who do not eat, play, or drink with others, albinos, sorcerers' assistants, people who do not eat hen in public, those who have adulterous relations with the wife of their best friend, children whose upper teeth erupt before their lowers, bachelors, and so on. One may see signs of the witch in almost any one of his fellows, and witchcraft is a constant topic of conversation and speculation in the village.

Witches, however, can only attain their power to kill through the assistance of sorcerers, and each transformation involves the death of at least one member of the witch's family. Sorcerers can also manipulate lightning for the purpose of killing, and a hunter must give up a member of his family to the sorcerer when he obtains the powerful hunting magic. In the process of becoming a sorcerer several family members must be turned over to the instructor, and of course, sorcerers cause other deaths as well as less drastic evil actions. It is not surprising, then, that almost no deaths are considered by the Lupupans to be the result of what Westerners call "natural causes," or that every individual takes constant means to protect himself from the actions of witches and sorcerers.

The underlying tensions of village life appear in a number of less drastic ways as well, and one of these is in jealousy of the skills of others, expressed as a denigration of the difficulty of those skills. Thus, for example, a carpenter with no previous experience of drum-making watches the process for a few moments and then announces, "It's easy. I could make one myself." This kind of comment is commonplace, no matter what the task or skill involved. In fact, of course, the carpenter *could* learn to make a drum, and quite probably with relative ease; it is the necessity of his announcing it that is of interest to us.

Another manifestation of the kinds of tensions that lie beneath the surface is found in the degree of cooperative group activity in the village. Under the circumstances of the drive toward normalcy we would be justified in supposing that the Lupupans would be a highly cooperative society in the sense that relatively large groups of people would pool their labor. In fact, this is not the case. While certain aspects of a major funeral, such as dancing, involve coordinated physical activity, and while the political town-meeting requires intellectual coordination, these are relatively rare examples. Instead, a hunter who wishes to organize and coordinate a cooperative hunting-party with beaters, netholders, spearmen, and so forth, finds his task virtually impossible. Members of the group are invariably two or three hours late and usually must be routed out individually; they do not listen to the leader's instructions, and thus once in the field they do not know what to do and, in any case, are careless about doing it. The result is that virtually no hunting is carried on cooperatively. Similarly, orders from the notables are seldom obeyed without trouble and dissent, and those who lag behind simply say they do not feel like doing whatever the order requires, even though it might clearly and admittedly be to their advantage. Some instances of apparent cooperation occur, such as termite-gathering, but closer examination reveals that while large numbers of people are engaged in the activity, they are working individually or in pairs or family groups of three or four. A similar situation can be described in conjunction with dancing for the village fertility figure; while the crowd may be large, both the dancing and the responses to the situation tend to be individual.

Thus it is once again apparent that rigid conformity has not been established in Lupupa Ngye despite the pressures toward normalcy. The difficulty of organizing coordinated cooperative labor is clear further evidence of individual independence as well as a certain intragroup hostility and competitiveness which mark the covert culture.

We have been arguing here that the single most important theme running through the culture of Lupupa Ngye is the principle of normalcy, and that this theme is an outgrowth of the situation of a small, self-contained society which cannot afford to lose the skills and essential cooperation of its members. At the same time, the very closeness of living raises a strong need for individual outlets, and these are found through the exercise of certain roles and behaviors. Despite these outlets, tension remains and is expressed in a number of ways.

On a still deeper level, it seems probable that the closeness of human contact and the constant awareness of the needs of others as well as the unremitting surveillance under which one lives, must lead to unease and to longing for another way of life. That this may well be the case is indicated by the concepts of "beauty" held by the Lupupans. Three terms in the Kisongye of the village might be translated as being concerned directly with beauty, but on close examination one of them turns out to express the inherent quality of goodness in a nonhuman thing (*bibuwa*), and the second the inherent quality of goodness in a human thing (*biya*). The third term is *kutaala*, which is a relatively rare word in the vocabulary of the Lupupans; its close association is with "water," but not with all kinds of water, such as water standing in a pan. Most specifically *kutaala* is associated with water in the river and, by extension, with the river itself. As it flows past the village, the Lupupa River is deep and calm, and a further association is made by the people between *kutaala* on the one hand and coolness and calmness on the other, the latter ideas expressed by a further term, *kwikyela*. *Kwikyela,* in turn, is apparently an expression of the emotional ideal that individuals would like to be calm, cool, and even self-contained. Thus it appears that what is "beautiful" for the Lupupans is what is calm, cool, and collected, and that the pressures of social life lead to a desire for withdrawal from the never-ending contact which is the lot of all villagers. While the society demands constant contact with others and behavior which is normal, that is, that which leads to perpetuation of the society, individuals seem to be straining internally in an opposite direction, toward individualism and toward freedom from the constraints imposed by a small society. And this straining appears in the two major roles available to the dissenter, in the small skills available to all, in the outbreaks of violence, and the refusal to give total coordinated cooperation, all of which apparently make it possible to continue to live in the situation imposed by Lupupa Ngye.

On the surface the village is peaceful, human relations are reasonable, life is not a terrible struggle for physical survival, and in fact, from the outsider's point of view, the people are content with their lot. Yet a word such as "content" is relative to the people who use it, and we have seen that all is not quite so peaceable as it seems. Indeed, at times the internal stresses and strains, coupled with the novel external pressures generated by national independence early in 1960, appeared to be more, perhaps, than the villagers could handle. Despite this, life could be good in Lupupa Ngye and, I suspect, *was* good for most of its inhabitants, but change is inevitable, and the Lupupa Ngye examined in these pages is not the Lupupa Ngye which exists today. Its contribution to the outside world, however, is to help us see, and hopefully, to understand, another way of life chosen by man.

Bibliography

Alpers, Edward A.

1967 The East African slave trade. Nairobi: East African Publishing House, Historical Association of Tanzania Paper No. 3.

1968 The nineteenth century: prelude to colonialism. In B. A. Ogot and J. A. Kieran, Zamani: a survey of East African history. Nairobi: East African Publishing House and Longmans, Green, pp. 238–54.

Anciaux, Léon

1949 Le problème musulman dans l'afrique belge. Bruxelles: Institut Royal Colonial Belge, Section des Sciences Morales et Politiques, Mémoires, Collection in-8°, Tome XVIII, fasc. 2.

Ankermann, Bernhard

1906 Über den gegenwärtigen Stand der Ethnographie der Südhälfte Afrikas. Archiv für Anthropologie 4:241–86.

Anonymous

1882 Work of the German African Association in western equatorial Africa. Proceedings of the Royal Geographical Society 4:678–85.

1883 Lieutenant Wissmann's journey across Africa. Proceedings of the Royal Geographical Society 5:163–65.

1885 Wissmann's Kasai-Fahrt. Globus 48:301–02.

1886a M. le Dr. Ludwig Wolf sur le Kassai et le Sankourou. Le Mouvement Géographique 3:75–76.

1886b Le Sankourou. Découverte d'une route fluviale directe entre Léopoldville et Nyangoué. Dix-huit cents kilomètres de voies navigables de Kwamouth à Kassongo. Le Mouvement Géographique 3:49–50.

1887a Observations de M. le Dr. Louis Wolf sur le cours de Sankourou. Bulletin de la Société de Géographie de Lille 7:477–78.

1887b Retour de l'expédition Lenz. Bulletin de la Société de Géographie de Lille 8:165–66.

1887c Voyage de M. Gleerup à travers l'Afrique. Bulletin de la Société de Géographie de Lille 7:78–79.

1888 De Nyangoué à Loulouabourg. Le Mouvement Géographique 5:30–31.

1890 La station de Lousambo. Le Mouvement Géographique 7:31.

1891a Les arabes sur le haut Congo. Le Mouvement Géographique 8:83–84.

1891b L'expédition Le Marinel. De Lousambo à Bena Kamba. Le Mouvement Géographique 8:39–40.

1891c Les nouvelles venues de camp de Lousambo. Le Mouvement Géographique 8:88.

1892a Les arabes du haut Congo. Le Congo Illustré 1:130–31.

1892b Arthur Hodister. Le Congo Illustré 1:129.

Bibliography

1892c L'expédition Bia au Katanga. De Lousambo à Bunkeia. Exploration du haut Sankuru et de la région lacustre du haut Lualaba. Le Mouvement Géographique 9:125–26.

1892d Le Major Hermann von Wissmann. Le Congo Illustré 1:145.

1892e Tribu des Zappo-Zap. Le Mouvement Géographique 9:34.

1893a L'architecture negre. Le Congo Illustré 2:2–3.

1893b Le Capitaine Chaltin. Le Congo Illustré 2:113.

1893c La musique chez les noirs. Le Congo Illustré 2:48, 66–67.

1893d Les peuplades du Kassai. Le Congo Illustré 2:90–91, 98–99.

1893e Les tambours. Le Congo Illustré 2:152.

1894a Les chefs arabes du haut Congo. Le Congo Illustré 3:17–20, 30–32, 38–39, 46–47, 50–51.

1894b Les taureaux de selle. Le Congo Illustré 3:12–14.

1897a Le cannibalisme au Congo. Congo Belge 2:99–101, 221–22.

1897b Participation de l'État Indépendant du Congo à l'Exposition internationale de Bruxelles. Bulletin de la Société Royale Belge de Géographie 21:478–516.

1897c Les tatouages: district du Lualaba-Kassai. La Belgique Coloniale 3:377–78.

1901a La compagnie du Kasai. Le Mouvement Géographique 18:607–15.

1901b L'organisation des territoires administrés par le 'Comité Spécial du Katanga'. Le Mouvement Géographique 18:563–66.

1903 L'habitation au Congo. Le Belgique Coloniale 9:595–96, 630–32.

1904 Une inspection sanitaire au Katanga. La Belgique Coloniale 10:92–94.

1907a Chaltin, Louis-Napoléon. In Société Royale de Géographie d'Anvers, Manifestation en l'honneur des explorateurs belges au Congo. Anvers: J. van Hille-de Backer, pp. 307–46.

1907b Dhanis, Francis Ernest Joseph Marie (Baron). In Société Royale de Géographie d'Anvers, Manifestation en l'honneur des explorateurs belges au Congo. Anvers: J. van Hille-de Backer, pp. 155–260.

1907c Jacques, Alphonse-Jules-Marie. In Société Royale de Géographie d'Anvers, Manifestation en l'honneur des explorateurs belges au Congo. Anvers: J. van Hille-de Backer, pp. 261–92.

1907d Le Marinel, Paul-Amédée. In Société Royale de Géographie d'Anvers, Manifestation en l'honneur des explorateurs belges au Congo. Anvers: J. van Hille-de Backer, pp. 145–54.

1928 Rapport sur la situation économique du district du Lomami. Congo 2:313–22.

1933 Coutumes indigènes. Questionnaire. Bulletin des Juridictions Indigènes et du Droit Coutumier Congolais 1:23–28.

1956 Jurisprudence. Tribunal de Territoire de Kongolo, Jugement N° 6 du 12–3–1949. Bulletin des Juridictions Indigènes et du Droit Coutumier Congolais 24:267–68.

1957 Jurisprudence. Ordre public. 4.—Cession de puissance paternelle. Bulletin des Juridictions Indigènes et du Droit Coutumier Congolais 25:28–31.

n. d. Vocabulaire. Français—Kituba—Tshiluba—Tshisonge—Tshikuba—Tshitetela. Lusambo: École Professionnelle.

Ascenso, Michele

1903 Nel Congo indipendente. Dal Sancuru al Lago Moero. Bolletino Societa Geographica Italiana, ser. 4, 4:110–17.

Barthel, Karl

1893 Völkerbewegungen auf der Südhälfte des afrikanischen Kontinents. Mitteilungen des Vereins für Erdkunde zu Leipzig 1–87.

Beak, Vice-Consul

1908 Report by Acting Vice-Consul Beak on his recent tour of the Katanga portion of the Congo Free State. In Great Britain, Parliament, House of Commons. Further correspondence respecting the Independent State of the Congo. British Sessional Papers, LXXI, Command Paper 3880, Africa, No. 1, pp. 16–35.

Bennett, Norman R.

1968 The Arab impact. In B. A. Ogot and J. A. Kieran, Zamani: a survey of East African history. Nairobi: East African Publishing House and Longmans, Green, pp. 216–37.

1969 Introduction to the second edition. In Alfred J. Swann, Fighting the slave-hunters in central Africa. London: Frank Cass, second edition, pp. vii–xlvii.

Boone, Olga

1961 Carte ethnique du Congo. Quart sud-est. Tervuren: Musée Royal de l'Afrique Centrale, Annales, Série in 8°, Sciences Humaines, n° 37.

Borms, Commandant

1901 Le pays des Batetela. La Belgique Coloniale 7:289–91, 303–05.

Boulger, Demetrius C.

1898 The Congo state or the growth of civilization in central Africa. London: W. Thacker.

Bours, L.

1936 La propriété foncière chez les Bekalebwe. Bulletin des Juridictions Indigènes et du Droit Coutumier Congolais 4:195–203.

Brady, Cyrus Townsend, Jr.

1950 Commerce and conquest in East Africa with particular reference to the Salem trade with Zanzibar. Salem: The Essex Institute.

Briart, Paul

1891 Sur le Lomami. Expédition Delcommune.—Lettre de M. Briart. Le Mouvement Géographique 8:124–25.

1898 Sur le Lomami.—Observations faites par le Dr. Paul Briart.—1890. Le Mouvement Géographique 15:7–9, 70–72, 82–84.

Brode, Heinrich

1907 Tippoo Tib: the story of his career in central Africa. London: Edward Arnold.

Bulck, G. van

1948 Les recherches linguistiques au Congo Belge. Bruxelles: Institut Royal Colonial Belge, Section des Sciences Morales et Politiques, Mémoires, Collection in 8°, Tome XVI.

Burdo, Alphonse

1885 Les arabes dans l'Afrique centrale. Paris: E. Dentu.

Bibliography

Burton, W. F. P.

1927 The country of the Baluba in central Katanga. Geographical Journal 70:321–42.

Cameron, Verney Lovett

1877 Across Africa. New York: Harper & Bros.

Campbell, Dugald

1929 Wanderings in central Africa. London: Seeley, Service.

Cauteren, W. Van

1904 Vers le Katanga. De Banana à Pweto. Bulletin de la Société Belge d'Études Coloniales 11:565–75.

Ceulemans, P.

1959 La question arabe et le Congo (1883–1892). Bruxelles: Académie Royale des Sciences Coloniales, Classe des Sciences Morales et Politiques, Mémoires in-8°, Nouvelle Série, Tome XXII, fasc. 1.

1966 Introduction de l'influence de l'Islam au Congo. In I. M. Lewis (ed.), Islam in tropical Africa. London: Oxford University Press for the International African Institute, pp. 174–92.

Chaltin, [Louis-Napoléon]

1894 La question arabe au Congo. Bulletin de la Société Belge d'Études Coloniales 1:163–96.

1930 Phases de la campagne arabe au Congo. La Renaissance d'Occident 32(Jan.):24–44.

Chapaux, Albert

1894 Le Congo. Bruxelles: Charles Rozez.

Clendenen, Clarence, Robert Collins, and Peter Duignan

1966 Americans in Africa 1865–1900. Palo Alto: The Hoover Institution on War, Revolution, and Peace, Hoover Institution Studies: 17.

[Coart, E., and A. de Haulleville]

1902 Notes analytiques sur les collections ethnographiques du Musée du Congo, Tome I, Fasc. 1, Les arts. Bruxelles: Annales du Musée du Congo. Ethnographie et Anthropologie, Série III.

1907 Notes analytiques sur les collections ethnographiques du Musée du Congo, Tome II, Fasc. 1, La ceramique. Bruxelles: Annales du Musée du Congo. Ethnographie et Anthropologie, Série III.

Comeliau, Marie-Louise

1943 Dhanis. Bruxelles: Éditions Libris.

Cordella, Ernesto

1906 Appunti sulla zona del Maniema (riva sinistra del Lualaba). Bolletino Societa Geographica Italiana, Roma, S. 4, 7:963–78.

Cornet, Joseph

1971 Art of Africa: treasures from the Congo. London: Phaidon.

Cornet, M.

1954 Tribunal de chefferie des Bena Niembo (Territoire de Kongolo). Jugement n° 6 du 7-3-1951. Bulletin des Juridictions Indigènes et du Droit Coutumier Congolais 22:227–28.

Cornet, René J.

1944 Katanga. Le Katanga avant les Belges et l'expédition Bia-Francqui-Cornet. Bruxelles: Éditions L. Cuypers.

1952 Maniema: le pays des mangeurs d'hommes. Bruxelles: Éditions L. Cuypers.

Coussement, Grégoire

1935 Crimes et superstitions indigènes. La secte du Punga et du Mama Okanga. Bulletin des Juridictions Indigènes et du Droit Coutumier Congolais 3:64–67.

Cram, W. G.

1936 With the M. E. C. M. in Congo. Congo Mission News 96 (Oct.):16–18.

Croene, A.

1955 Énoncés de la coutume Basonge. Bulletin des Juridictions Indigènes et du Droit Coutumier Congolais 23:103–04.

Danckelman, A. von

1885 Beiträg zur Kenntniss der meteorologischen Verhältniss des aequatorialen Afrika. Mittheilungen der Afrikanischen Gesellschaft in Deutschland 4:265–74.

De Deken, Constant

1897a Comment un esclave devient chef. Le Mouvement Géographique 14:93.

1897b Un harem indigène. Le Mouvement Géographique 14:95–96.

1897c Un village indigène. Le Mouvement Géographique 14:94.

1902 Deux ans au Congo. Anvers: Clément Thibaut.

De Gryse, Jean

1892 Lettre adressée à des amis. Missions en Chine et au Congo 45:139–41.

De Jonghe, E.

1937 Les arbres-à-esprits au Kasai. Bulletin des Séances, Institut Royal Colonial Belge 8:378–92.

De Jonghe, M. E.

1935 La mission d'études du R. P. Van Bulck (janvier 1932–août 1933). Bulletin des Séances, Institut Royal Colonial Belge 6:108–15.

De Meuse, F.

1894 De la condition de la femme. Le Congo Illustré 3:33–35.

Delcommune, Alexandre

1922 Vingt années de vie africaine. Récits de voyages, d'aventures et d'exploration au Congo Belge, 1874–1893. Bruxelles: Ferdinand Larcier. 2 vols.

Deremiens, L.

1953 Quelques considérations sur la coutume des Bena Ebombo. Bulletin des Juridictions Indigènes et du Droit Coutumier Congolais 21:60–66.

Deuxième Section de l'État-Major de la Force Publique

1952 La Force Publique de sa naissance à 1914. Bruxelles: Institut Royal Colonial Belge, Section des Sciences Morales et Politiques, Mémoires, Collection in 8°, Tome XXVII.

Dhanis, Francis

1895 La campagne arabe du Manyema. Le Congo Illustré 4:25–27, 33–35, 41–43, 53–55, 60–63, 68–70, 77–79.

1907 La campagne arabe. In Société Royale de Géographie d'Anvers, Manifestation en l'honneur des explorateurs belges au Congo. Anvers: J. van Hille-de Backer, pp. 58–64.

Dillen, K.

1951 Tweelingen bij de Bena Ngungi (Basonge). Kongo-Overzee 17:97–110.

Droogmans, Hubert

1894a Le Congo. Quatre conférences publiques. Bruxelles: Van Campenhout.

1894b Notice sur l'État Indépendant du Congo. In Antwerp, Exposition Universelle, 1894. Le Congo à l'Exposition universelle d'Anvers, 1894; catalogue de la section de l'État Indépendant du Congo. Bruxelles: O. de Rycker, pp. 3–46.

Fourche, J.-A. Tiarko, et H. Morlighem

1941 Les communications des indigènes du Kasai avec les âmes des morts. Bruxelles: Institut Royal Colonial Belge, Section des Sciences Morales et Politiques. Mémoires in-8°, Tome IX, No. 2.

François, Albert

1949 Trois chapitres de l'épopée congolaise. Bruxelles: Office de Publicité, Collection Nationale, 9me Série, N° 100.

Frobenius, Leo V.

1893 Die Fensterthüren im Congo–Becken. Globus 64:326–28.

1894 Die Ba Tshonga. Eine Rassenreihe im östlichen Congo-Becken. Globus 65:206–10.

1906 Bericht über die völkerkundlichen Forschungen vom 30. Mai bis 2. Dezember 1905. Zeitschrift für Ethnologie 38:736–41.

1907 Im Schatten des Kongostaates. Berlin: Georg Reimer.

1928 Atlantis: Volksmarchen und Volksdichtungen Afrikas. Vol. 12: Dichtkunst der Kassaiden. Jena: Eugen Diederichs.

Gann, Lewis

1954 The end of the slave trade in British central Africa: 1889–1912. The Rhodes-Livingstone Journal 16:27–51.

Gilain, Commandant

1897 Les tribus de Kassaï. La Belgique Coloniale 3:91–92.

Great Britain Naval Staff, Naval Intelligence Division

c1920 A manual of Belgian Congo. London: H. M. Stationery Office.

Grootaert, J. E. A.

1946 Pensées autour d'un tam-tam 'Lokombe' (Mutetela). Brousse 3–4:20–22.

Guébels, Léon

1928a Polygamie à Lupangu. Revue Juridique du Congo Belge 4:312–18.

1928b Une société indigène au Lomami en 1916: la chefferie de Lumpungu à Kabinda. Revue Juridique du Congo Belge 4:62–67.

Guthrie, Malcolm

1948 The classification of the Bantu languages. London: Oxford University Press for the International African Institute.

Hamme, P. E. Van

1952 Enquête sur le droit coutumier des Bakwa Lubo. Bulletin des Juridictions Indigènes et du Droit Coutumier Congolais 20:317–24, 337–51.

Hasssenstein, B.

1891 Major v. Wissmann's zweite Reise quer durch Zentral-afrika, 1886 und 1887. Petermanns Geographische Mitteilungen 37:57–60.

Hautmann, Friedrich

1949–50 Anthropologische Beobachtungen im Kivu und im Kasai (Belgisch-Kongo). Bulletin der Schweizerischen Gesellschaft für Anthropologie und Ethnologie 26:4–5.

Heenen, G.

1923 Notes sur le district du Lomami. Bulletin de la Société Belge d'Études Coloniales 30:5–21.

Henry, Lieutenant

1897 Souvenirs de la campagne contre les arabes. De Kiroundou au Tanganyika. Le Congo Belge 2:18–20, 29–30.

Hiernaux, Jean

1964 Note sur l'anthropométrie des Songye (Congo). Boletim Sociedade Geografia de Lisboa 82a:337–41.

Hilton-Simpson, M. W.

1911 Land and peoples of the Kasai. London: Constable and Co.

Hinde, Sidney Langford

1895 Three years' travel in the Congo Free State. Geographical Journal 5:426–46.

1897 The fall of the Congo Arabs. London: Methuen & Co.

Hodister, A.

1892 Trois lettres de M. Hodister. Le Mouvement Géographique 9:81–82.

Iliffe, John

1968 Tanzania under German and British rule. In B. A. Ogot and J. A. Kieran, Zamani: a survey of East African history. Nairobi: East African Publishing House and Longmans, Green, pp. 290–311.

Institut National pour l'Étude Agronomique du Congo, Bureau Climatologique

1954 Bulletin climatologique annuel du Congo et du Ruanda-Urundi, année 1953. Bruxelles: Communication N° 13.

1960 Bulletin climatologique annuel du Congo et du Ruanda-Urundi, année 1959. Bruxelles: Communication N° 19.

Jacques, Alphonse

1907a Expéditions de la Société antiesclavagiste de Belgique. In Société Royale de Géographie d'Anvers, Manifestation en l'honneur des explorateurs belges au Congo. Anvers: J. van Hille-de Backer, pp. 79–92.

1907b Expéditions envoyées au Tanganyika par l'Association Internationale Africaine. In Société Royale de Géographie d'Anvers, Manifestation en l'honneur des explorateurs belges au Congo. Anvers: J. van Hille-de Backer, pp. 65–78.

Jacques, V.

1891–92 Conférence de M. le capitaine F. Vandevelde sur les collections ethnographiques rapportées de son dernier voyage au Congo. Bulletin de la Société d'Anthropologie de Bruxelles 10:59–67.

1894–95 Les Congolais de l'exposition universelle d'Anvers. Bulletin de la Société d'Anthropologie de Bruxelles 13:284–332.

1897 Les Congolais de l'exposition universelle de Bruxelles–Tervueren. Bulletin de la Société d'Anthropologie de Bruxelles 16:183–243.

Kamer, Henri et Hélène

n. d. Arts du Congo. Paris: Galerie Kamer.

Bibliography

Kangudie, Pierre
1948 Le kishatu. La Voix du Congolais 4:112–13.
Keay, R. W. J.
1959 Vegetation map of Africa south of the Sahara/carte de la vegetation de l'Afrique au sud du Tropique du Cancer. London: Oxford University Press.
Kerken, Georges van der
c1919 Les sociétés Bantoues du Congo Belge et les problèmes de la politique indigène. Bruxelles: Émile Bruylant.
Kitenge, Gabriel
1951 Le marriage. Bulletin du Centre d'Études des Problèmes Sociaux Indigènes 17:108–21.
Kochnitzky, Leon
1949 Negro art in Belgian Congo. New York: Belgian Government Information Center, 2nd edition.
Laloy, L.
1895 V. Jacques—Les Congolais des l'exposition universelle d'Anvers. Anthropologie 6:710–11.
Lassaux, H.
1926 Les événements de Luluaburg en 1895. La révolte des Batetela. Congo 1:567–83.
Laurent, Émile
1896a Le café au Congo. Le Mouvement Géographique 13:349–52.
1896b Rapport sur un voyage agronomique autour du Congo. Bulletin Officiel de l'État Indépendant du Congo 12:169–220.
1896–97 Lettres congolaises. Revue de l'Université Libre de Bruxelles 2:33–45, 135–46, 307–16, 363–85.
1897 Lettres congolaises. Le Congo Belge 2:40–41, 66–67, 79–80, 89–93, 103–04.
Lavigerie, Charles Martial Allemand, Cardinal
1888 L'esclavage africain. Conférence sur l'esclavage dans le haut Congo faite à Sainte-Gudule de Bruxelles. Bruxelles: Société anti-esclavagiste.
Le Marinel, Paul
1888 De Nyangoué à Loulouabourg. Le Mouvement Géographique 5:55.
1907 Notes sur les découvertes et l'occupation des régions du Kassai, du Luba et du Katanga. In Société Royale de Géographie d'Anvers, Manifestation en l'honneur des explorateurs belges au Congo. Anvers: J. van Hille-de Backer, pp. 41–52.
Lebrun, A. G.
1956 De la tenure de la terre chez les populations indigènes du Territoire de Kabalo. Bulletin des Juridictions Indigènes et du Droit Coutumier Congolais 24:181–222.
Lemaire, Charles
1895 Au Congo: comment les noirs travaillent. Bruxelles: Ch. Bulens.
Lenz, Oscar
1886 Une lettre de M. le Dr. Oscar Lenz. Le Mouvement Géographique 3:70–71.

Livingstone, David

1874 The last journals of David Livingstone, in Central Africa, from 1865 to his death. London: John Murray. 2 vols.

Louillet, P.

1939 Quelques couplets de la danse Ngwaya. Annales des Pères du Saint-Esprit 55:121–23.

Lumeka, P. R.

1967 Proverbes des Songye. In Africana Linguistica III. Tervuren: Musée Royal de l'Afrique Centrale, Annales, Série in 8°, Sciences Humaines, n° 61, pp. 39–49.

Macar, Ghislain de

1895 Chez les Bakubas. Le Congo Illustré 4:172–74.

Maes, J.

1924 Aniota-kifwebe. Les masques des populations du Congo Belge et le matériel des rites de circoncision. Anvers: Éditions "De Sikkel".

1932 Le muganga médecin-féticheur des Basonge. Pro Medico 9:84–87.

1935 Fetischen of Tooverbeelden uit Kongo. Tervuren: Annales du Musée du Congo Belge, Ethnographie, Série VI, Catalogues illustrés des Collections ethnographiques du Musée du Congo Belge, Tome II, Fasc. 1.

Maes, J., et Olga Boone

1935 Les peuplades du Congo Belge: nom et situation géographique. Tervuren: Musée du Congo Belge, Publications du Bureau de Documentation Ethnographique, Série 2. Monographies idéologiques, Vol. I.

Maesen, A.

1950? Traditional sculpture in Belgian Congo. In The arts in Belgian Congo and Ruanda-Urundi. Brussels: Information and Documentation Center of Belgian Congo and Ruanda-Urundi, pp. 9–34.

1951a Une acquisition du Musée du Congo Belge. Brousse 1–2:5–6.

1951b La sculpture décorative. Les arts plastiques 5me série, 1:16–30.

1958 Masques du Congo. Belgique d'Outre-mer 13:101–04.

n. d. Commentaires des planches. In Umbangu: art du Congo au Musée Royal du Congo Belge. Tervuren: Musée Royal du Congo Belge, L'art en Belgique III.

Mangat, J. S.

1969 A history of the Asians in East Africa c. 1886 to 1945. London: Oxford at the Clarendon Press.

Martelli, George

1962 Leopold to Lumumba: a history of the Belgian Congo 1877–1960. London: Chapman & Hall.

Masui, Th.

1897 Guide de la section de l'État Indépendant du Congo à l'exposition de Bruxelles-Tervueren en 1897. Bruxelles: Imprimerie Veuve Monnom.

Mercenier, P.

1942 Bij de Basonge, opper-Kasayi. Aequatoria 5:87.

Merriam, Alan P.

1961a Congo: background of conflict. Evanston: Northwestern University Press.

1961b Death and the religious philosophy of the Basongye. The Antioch Review 21:293–304.

Bibliography

1962a Contemporary sculpture of the Basongye. Yellow Springs: Antioch College. Mimeo.

1962b The epudi—a Basongye ocarina. Ethnomusicology 6:175–80.

1962c A prologue to the study of the African arts. Yellow Springs: Antioch Press, Founders Day Lectures No. 7.

1964 The anthropology of music. Evanston: Northwestern University Press.

1965 Music and the dance. In Robert A. Lystad (ed.), The African world: a survey of social research. New York: Frederick A. Praeger, pp. 452–68.

1966 [Field material on perception]. In Marshall H. Segall, Donald T. Campbell, and Melville J. Herskovits, The influence of culture on perception. Indianapolis: Bobbs-Merrill.

1968 Art and economics in Basongye raffia basketry. African Arts/Arts d'Afrique 2:14–17, 73.

1969 The ethnographic experience: drum-making among the Bala (Basongye). Ethnomusicology 13:74–100.

1971 Aspects of sexual behavior among the Bala (Basongye). In Donald S. Marshall and Robert C. Suggs (eds.), Human sexual behavior: variations in the ethnographic spectrum. New York: Basic Books, pp. 71–102.

1973a The Bala musician. In Warren L. d'Azevedo (ed.), The traditional artist in African societies. Bloomington: Indiana University Press, pp. 250–81.

1973b Politics and change in a Zaïrian village. Unpublished MS.

1974a Change in religion and the arts in a Zaïrian village. African Arts 7:46–53, 95.

1974b Culture history of the Basongye. Bloomington: African Studies Program, Indiana University. Forthcoming.

1974c Social and cultural change in a rural Zaïrian village. Forthcoming in African Studies Review.

Michaux, Oscar
1913 Au Congo. Carnet de campagne. Épisodes & impressions de 1889 à 1897. Namur: Dupagne-Counet.

Moeller, A.
1936 Les grandes lignes des migrations de Bantous de la Province Orientale du Congo Belge. Bruxelles: Marcel Hayez.

Mohun, R. Dorsey
1894–95 The death of Emin Pasha. Century Magazine 49:591–98.

Norden, Hermann
1924 Fresh tracks in the Belgian Congo. Boston: Small, Maynard.

Northern, Tamara
1966 The Clark and Frances Stillman collection of Congolese sculpture. New York: Museum of Primitive Art.

Olbrechts, Frans M.
1959 Les arts plastiques du Congo Belge. Bruxelles: Éditions Erasme.

Overbergh, Cyr. van
1908 Les Basonge. Bruxelles: Albert de Wit, Collection de monographies ethnographiques III.

Pogge, Paul

1883–85 Bericht über die Station Mukenge bis Oktober 1883. Mittheilungen der Afrikanischen Gesellschaft in Deutschland 4:179–205.

Polidori, G.

1908 Annexe C (Letter to the President of the Comité Spécial du Katanga). Bulletin Officiel de l'État Indépendant du Congo 108–18.

Rouck, René de

c1935 Atlas géographique et historique du Congo Belge et des territoires sous mandat du Ruanda-Urundi. 4th edition. Bruxelles: Éditions R. de Rouck.

J. E. S.

1950 Jurisprudence. Tribunal de Centre de Kipushi. Jugement n° 3338 du 3–2–1949. Bulletin des Juridictions Indigènes et du Droit Coutumier Congolais 12:372–73.

1952 Jurisprudence. Tribunal du Secteur de Pania-Mutombo. Jugement n° 120 rendu le 16/4/48. Bulletin des Juridictions Indigènes et du Droit Coutumier Congolais 20:268.

Samain, A.

1913–14 Basonge's en Baluba's. Onze Kongo 4:297–306.

1923? La langue Kisonge: Grammaire—vocabulaire—proverbes. Bruxelles: Goemaere, Bibliothèque-Congo XIV.

1928 Vertelling van twee slimme mannen: de man van de houwen en de man van de gelt. Congo (Bruxelles) 1:520.

Schrader, Ferd.

1883 Wissmann & Pogge au travers de l'Afrique. Revue Géographique Internationale 8:81–84.

1883–84 Traversée de l'Afrique. De l'ouest à l'est, depuis San Paolo de Loanda jusqu'à Zanzibar, par le lieutenant Wissmann et le Dr. Pogge, en 1881 et 1882. Bulletin de la Société Géographique Commerciale de Bordeaux 6:281–93.

Siroto, Leon

1969 Foreword. In Henri A. Kamer and Leon Siroto, Congo. New York: Galerie Kamer.

Société Royale de Géographie d'Anvers

1907 Manifestation en l'honneur des explorateurs belges au Congo. Anvers: J. van Hille-de Backer.

Sohier, A.

1934 L'évolution des coutumes. Bulletin des Juridictions Indigènes et du Droit Coutumier Congolais 2:122–24.

Sohier, Jean

1962 Note sur l'évolution du régime matrimonial en droit coutumier Katangais. Publications Université de l'Etat, Elisabethville 4:45–52.

1963–64 Institutes coutumières Katangaises (les personnes et les biens). Problèmes Sociaux Congolaises 62:3–83; 63:1–79; 64:3–90; 65:3–82.

Soors, M.

1950 A propos des découvertes préhistoriques en Haut-Ituri. Zaïre 4:59.

Stanley, Henry M.

1899 Through the dark continent. London: George Newnes. 2 vols.

Bibliography

Stappers, Leo

1950a Nsompo, het aqua lustralis bij de Baamilembwe. Kongo-Overzee 16:299–300.

1950b Tussen Luba en Songye. Zaïre 4:271–76.

1951a Godsverering bij de BaaMilembwe. Aequatoria 14:121–24.

1951b De kasongo-Fetisj bij de Baamilembwe. Kongo-Overzee 17:373–78.

1951c De kisheeta-fetisj bij de Baamilembwe. Kongo-Overzee 17:379–93.

1951d De mpunga fetisj. Zaïre 5:351–69.

1951e Uit het verleden der Baamilembwe. Kongo-Overzee 17:1–8.

1952 Prayer of a Milembwe woman after a child's birth. Kongo-Overzee 18:6–7.

1953a In hoeverre verschilt het Kisongye van het Tshiluba? Aequatoria 16:1–7.

1953b Miadi. Rouwplechtigheden. Builande-tekst in het dialekt van Kiambwe, gewest Kabinda. Kongo-Overzee 19:10–19.

1953c Tonparallelisme als mnemotechnisch middel in spreekworden. Aequatoria 16:99–100.

1953d Zuid-kisongye bloemlezing. Milembwe-teksten. Tervuren: Annales du Musée Royale du Congo Belge, Série in 8°, Sciences de l'Homme, Linguistique, vol. 6.

1955 Schets van het Budya. Kongo-Overzee 21:97–143.

1964 Morfologie van het Songye. Tervuren: Musée Royale de l'Afrique Centrale, Annales, Série in 8°, Sciences Humaines, n° 51.

Steinmann, Alfred

1943 Afrikanische Masken zur Behandlung von Krankheiten. Ciba-Zeitschrift 8:3120–24.

Studstill, John D.

1969 Trois heros luba. Unpublished MS.

Swann, Alfred J.

1910 & 1969 Fighting the slave-hunters in central Africa. Philadelphia: J. B. Lippincott, 1910. Second edition. London: Frank Cass, 1969.

Timmermans, P.

1962 Les Sapo Sapo près de Luluabourg. Africa-Tervuren 8:29–53.

Torday, E.

1910 Land and peoples of the Kasai basin. Geographical Journal 36:26–57.

Torday, E., and T. A. Joyce

1922 Les Basonge. In Notes ethnographiques sur des populations habitant les bassins du Kasai et du Kwango oriental. Bruxelles: Annales du Musée du Congo Belge, Ethnographie, Anthropologie—Série III: Documents ethnographiques concernant les populations du Congo Belge, Tome II—Fascicule 2, pp. 13–41.

Toussaint, R. E.

1953 Notes sur la secte 'Toni-Toni' en Territoire de Kabongo. Bulletin des Juridictions Indigènes et du Droit Coutumier Congolais 21:99–104.

1954 Le kishatu en territoire de Kabongo. Bulletin des Juridictions Indigènes et du Droit Coutumier Congolais 22:270–80.

Trivier, E.

1891 Mon voyage au continent noir. Paris: Fermin-Didot.

Vandenbulcke, le R. P.

1935 Comment traiter les chefs noirs? Museum Lessianum Louvain 13:150–71.

Vansina, Jan

1966 Kingdoms of the savanna. Madison: University of Wisconsin Press.

n. d. Introduction a l'ethnographie du Congo. Bruxelles: Éditions Universitaires du Congo.

Verbeken, A.

1933 Accession au pouvoir chez certaines tribus du Congo par système electif. Congo 14(2):653–57.

1959 A Luluabourg en 1895: la révolte des soldats Batetela. Revue Congolaise Illustrée 31:31–32.

Verhulpen, Edmond

1936 Baluba et Balubaïsés du Katanga. Anvers: L'avenir belge.

Vermeesch, A.

1924 Monographie agricole du district du Lomami (Katanga). Bulletin Agricole du Congo Belge 15:3–34.

Verstraelen, Frans

1964 La conscience morale des Baluba et de quelques autres peuplades dans le sud-est du Congo. Anthropos 59:361–99.

Wack, Henry Wellington

1905 The story of the Congo Free State. New York: G. P. Putnam's Sons.

Walker Art Center

1967 Art of the Congo. Minneapolis: Walker Art Center.

Wangermee, E.

1908 Annexe B (Letter to the President of the Comité Spécial du Katanga). Bulletin Officiel de l'État Indépendant du Congo 97–107.

Ward, Herbert

1890 Five years with the Congo cannibals. New York: Robert Bonner's Sons.

Wauters, A.-J.

1886a L'exploration du Sankourou. Nouveaux détails. Le Mouvement Géographique 3:70.

1886b La huitième traversée de l'afrique centrale. De Banana à Zanzibar par le Lieutenant Gleerup. Le Mouvement Géographique 3:73–75.

1891a Le pays entre Loulouabourg et le Loualaba. Le Mouvement Géographique 8:32.

1891b Le pays entre Loulouabourg et le Loualaba mis au courant des derniers itinéraires de Wissmann, Delcommune, P. Le Marinel & Hodister. Le Mouvement Géographique 8:supplement to the issue of 5 Avril. Map.

1894 La conquête du Manyema par le Commandant Dhanis. Le Congo Illustré 3:151–60.

1898 La densité et la répartition de la population au Congo. Le Mouvement Géographique 15:103–06.

1901 Carte des territoires de la compagnie du Kasai. Le Mouvement Géographique 18:supplement to the issue of 1 Decembre. Map.

Wauters, G.

1949 L'ésotérie des noirs dévoilée. Bruxelles: Éditions Européennes.

Bibliography

Wauthion, R.
1933 Le droit coutumier des Bena Bayashi. Bulletin des Juridictions Indigènes et du Droit Coutumier Congolais 1:28–30.
1940 Quelques notes sur des sociétés indigènes (Région de Kongolo). Bulletin des Juridictions Indigènes et du Droit Coutumier Congolais 8:310–14.

Whitely, W. H.
1966 Maisha ya Hamed bin Muhammed el Murjebi yaani Tippu Tip kwa maneno yake mwenyewe. Nairobi: East African Literature Bureau.

Wichmann, H.
1883 Neuere Forschungen in Congo-Gebiet. Petermanns Geographische Mitteilungen 29:177–86, 220–29.

Wildeman, É. de
1905–07 Mission Émile Laurent (1903–1904). Bruxelles: F. Vanbuggenhoudt, État Indépendant du Congo. 2 vols.

Wingert, Paul S.
1973 African masks: structure, expression, style. African Arts 6(2):56–64.

Wissmann, Hermann von
1881–83 Bericht von Lieutenant Wissmann. Mittheilungen der Afrikanischen Gesellschaft in Deutschland 3:249–54.
1883 Bericht von Lieutenant Wissmann. Mittheilungen der Afrikanischen Gesellschaft in Deutschland 4:37–56.
1888 On the influence of Arab traders in west central Africa. Proceedings of the Royal Geographical Society 10:525–31.
1891 My second journey through equatorial Africa from the Congo to the Zambesi in the years 1886 and 1887. London: Chatto & Windus.
1902 Unter deutscher Flagge quer durch Afrika von West nach Ost. Berlin: Globus Verlag, ninth edition.

Wissmann, Hermann von, Ludwig Wolf, Curt von François, and Hans Mueller
1891 Im innern Afrikas: die Erforschung des Kassai während der Jahre 1883, 1884 und 1885. Leipzig: F. U. Brockhaus.

Wolf, Louis
1888 Explorations sur le Kassai superieur et le Sankuru. Bulletin de la Société Belge de Géographie 12:26–43.

Wolf, Ludwig
1888a Die Erforschung des Sankuru. Petermanns Geographische Mitteilungen 34:193–98.
1888b Exploration du Sankourou et de ses affluents. Le Mouvement Géographique 5:53–54.

Young, Crawford
1969 The Congo. In James Kritzeck and William H. Lewis (eds.), Islam in Africa. New York: Van Nostrand-Reinhold, pp. 250–69.

Zandijcke, A. van
[1953] Pages d'histoire du Kasayi. Namur: Grands Lacs, Collection Lavigerie.
[Zandycke, A. van]
1950 La révolte de Luluabourg (4 juillet 1895). Zaïre 4:931–63, 1063–82.

Index

Index

Index

Index

111–12, 118–20, 126; transmigration of, 111–16, 125–26; human, 111–20
spouses, 264
Stanley, Henry Morton, 9
stars, 105–6
strains of village life, 321–25
street, main village, 50–51
suicide, 246–48, 266
sun, 103–4

taxation: of Bala by Congo Free State, 25–26; cotton and peanut crops to pay for, 68–69
teeth: ceremonies on eruption of child's, 214; extraction of, 218–19
temperatures of Lupupa Ngye, 48
tensions of village life, 321–25
terminology: concerning land, 58–59; concerning kinship, 196; concerning beauty, 325
terrain surrounding Lupupa Ngye, 50–51
theft, 291
time, how reckoned, 40
time schedules, 62–63
Tippu Tip, 8–11, 13–15, 24
tobacco, 87
Torday, E., xvi–xvii, 298
Toussaint, R. E., 144
trade routes, Arab, 8
transients in village, 173
transmigration, 111–16, 125–26
transvestite, 60, 319–21
travelers, 259
tribunal system, 293, 305
tsetse fly, 41
Tshofa, 48, 50, 68–70, 83, 221
twins, 210–12

universe, Lupupans' concept of, 102–7

Vansina, Jan, 4–7, 14
Verhulpen, Edmond, xi, xvi, 3–7
village council, 275–76
village protective figures, 123–25

warfare, 293–300
wastage, as a crime, 175
Wauters, A.-J., 12, 16
wealth distribution, 100–1
wealth transfer, 93–100
wind, 107
Wissmann, Hermann von, 15–16, 21–23
witches, 111, 135, 141–68, 323
wives, 226–46, 256
Wolff, Dr., xv, 16
women: lineages of, 198–99; organization of, 300–2; male dominance over, 308–11; deviant roles of, 321
wounds, magic to prevent, 140

xylophone music, for chief, 278
xylophonist, and magic, 147

Yakalala, 27, 30–31, 38, 40, 44–46
Yakyomba, 124
Yampumba, 280
Yamukoshi, 39
yangye, 276, 283–84
Yankamba, 39, 40, 44
Yankima, 123
Yantambwe, 142
yearly cycle, 62–64
younger vs. older men, 304

Zaïre, xi, xviii, 47
Zandijcke, A. van, 13
Zappo Zap, 13–15, 18, 22